MARITIME CROSS-BORDER INSOLVENCY UNDER THE UNCITRAL MODEL LAW REGIME

This book covers the pressing issues of cross-border cases involving admiralty and bankruptcy law. For example, what should happen when a shipowner files an insolvency proceeding in one country, while at the same time facing an in rem action against its vessel in another country? Should the in rem action arising in one country be stayed or dismissed because of the existence of insolvency proceedings in another country?

The book discusses the relevant issues regarding the treatment of maritime creditors throughout insolvency proceedings, the determination of the 'centre of main interest' of an offshore shipping company, and the scope of a debtor's assets. The author uses a comparative law analysis, selecting four leading shipping countries – Australia, the UK, the US, and Singapore – and examining their approaches to the above three problems when applying the UNCITRAL Model Law regime.

The book also proposes a solution to help eliminate the ambiguity arising from maritime cross-border insolvency cases under the UNCITRAL Model law regime, with a view to enhancing the development of the shipping industry.

Maritime Cross-Border Insolvency under the UNCITRAL Model Law Regime

Commonwealth and US Perspectives

Jingchen Xu

•HART•

OXFORD • LONDON • NEW YORK • NEW DELHI • SYDNEY

HART PUBLISHING

Bloomsbury Publishing Plc

Kemp House, Chawley Park, Cumnor Hill, Oxford, OX2 9PH, UK

1385 Broadway, New York, NY 10018, USA

HART PUBLISHING, the Hart/Stag logo, BLOOMSBURY and the Diana logo are trademarks of Bloomsbury Publishing Plc

First published in Great Britain 2020

A catalogue record for this book is available from the British Library.

Library of Congress Cataloging-in-Publication data

Names: Xu, Jingcheng (Writer of Maritime insolvency), author.

Title: Maritime cross-border insolvency under the UNCITRAL model law regime : Commonwealth and US perspectives / Jingchen Xu.

Description: Oxford, UK ; New York, NY : Hart Publishing, an imprint of Bloomsbury Publishing, 2020. | Includes bibliographical references and index.

Identifiers: LCCN 2020033916 (print) | LCCN 2020033917 (ebook) | ISBN 9781509935994 (hardback) | ISBN 9781509935987 (ePDF) | ISBN 9781509936007 (Epub)

Subjects: LCSH: Conflict of laws—Bankruptcy—Commonwealth countries. | Conflict of laws—Bankruptcy—United States. | Conflict of laws—Maritime law—Commonwealth countries. | Conflict of laws—Maritime law—United States. | United Nations Commission on International Trade Law. | Bankruptcy. | Maritime law.

Classification: LCC K7510 .X8 2020 (print) | LCC K7510 (ebook) | DDC 346.07/8—dc23

LC record available at https://lccn.loc.gov/2020033916

LC ebook record available at https://lccn.loc.gov/2020033917

ISBN: HB: 978-1-50993-599-4
ePDF: 978-1-50993-598-7
ePub: 978-1-50993-600-7

Typeset by Compuscript Ltd, Shannon

To find out more about our authors and books visit www.hartpublishing.co.uk. Here you will find extracts, author information, details of forthcoming events and the option to sign up for our newsletters.

PREFACE

Due to the unique mobility of ships and the special operational structures of shipping companies, it is difficult to harmonise the international cross-border insolvency regime with the admiralty regime governing ships. This book explores the fundamental tensions that arise between the cross-border insolvency regime and maritime law when a shipowner files an insolvency proceeding in one country, but has simultaneously to deal with admiralty arrests of its vessels in other countries. The problem of maritime cross-border insolvency has risen to prominence in recent years with the global financial crisis and the current declining shipping market. The tensions and inconsistencies in the way in which maritime cross-border insolvency scenarios have been dealt with by the courts of different countries have given rise to significant debates and need to be addressed urgently.

This book is based on my doctoral dissertation. I am very grateful to Professor Martin Davies for his kind supervision and instruction during my doctoral studies (SJD). In addition, I would like to thank Professor Robert Force and Professor Adam Feibelman for their generous advice as my doctoral committee members.

I would also like to thank my supervisors in the Centre for Maritime Law at the Faculty of Law of National University of Singapore for their assistance and support in securing the book contract and revising the manuscript. In particular, I would like to thank Associate Professor Paul Myburgh for his valuable and insightful comments and suggestions throughout, and Professor Stephen Girvin for his consistent support in organising the book workshop that significantly improved the calibre of the final product. I would also like to acknowledge the generous funding support of Centre for Maritime Law that made this book possible.

Finally, many thanks to my parents and friends for their moral support, and to Dr Roberta Bassi and the Hart Publishing team for their professional and efficient overview.

Jingchen Xu
Singapore
22 May 2020

TABLE OF CONTENTS

Preface v
Table of Cases xiii
Table of Statutes xxiii

1. Introduction 1

2. Bankruptcy Law: Fundamental Aims and Relevant Prominent Principles 9
I. Fundamental Aims of the Law of Insolvency 9
A. Fresh Start 9
B. Maximisation of Asset Value for All Creditors 10
C. Equal Treatment of Equivalent Creditors 11
II. Liquidation and Reorganisation 12
III. Stay of Proceedings 13
IV. Secured Creditors and Unsecured Creditors 14

3. Cross-Border Insolvency: Theoretical Divergence and Its Status Quo 16
I. The Problem with Cross-Border Insolvency 16
II. Theoretical Divergence 17
A. Traditional Exposition: Territorialism and Universalism 17
i. Territorialism: The 'Grab Rule' 18
ii. Universalism 20
B. New Pragmatism 21
i. Co-operative Territorialism 22
ii. Modified Universalism 23
III. The Evolution of Theories and the Status Quo 24

4. The UNCITRAL Model Law 27
I. Access 28
II. Recognition 30
A. Foreign Proceedings 31
B. Foreign Main Proceeding and Foreign Non-Main Proceeding 33
C. Public Policy Exception 34
III. Relief 36
A. Article 19: Interim Relief 36

B. Article 20: Automatic Relief for Foreign Main Proceeding 37
C. Article 21: Additional Appropriate Relief 38
IV. Co-operation and Co-ordination 38

5. Maritime Claims: Characteristics, Secured Status and Enforcement Methods 40
I. Maritime Liens 41
A. Legal Characteristics of Maritime Liens 42
B. Underlying Nature of Maritime Liens 43
C. Policy Rationale of Maritime Liens and the Doctrine of Personification 45
D. Secured Status of Maritime Liens 47
II. Statutory Rights of Action in Rem 48
A. Legal Characteristics and Nature of Statutory Rights of Action in Rem 48
B. Secured Status of Statutory Rights of Action in Rem 49
i. Majority Position 49
ii. Minority Position 50
III. Ship Mortgages 51
IV. Conflict of Laws 53
V. Enforcement of Maritime Claims 55
A. Action in Personam 55
B. Action in Rem 55
i. Action in Rem under the Personification Doctrine 55
ii. Action in Rem under the Procedural Theory 56

6. Key Conflicts between the UNCITRAL Model Law and Maritime Practice 58
I. Treatment of Maritime Creditors under the UNCITRAL Model Law Regime 59
A. Relief from the Automatic Stay 60
B. In Rem Claims and the Personification Doctrine 61
II. Determination of the Centre of Main Interest 62
III. Scope of Debtor's Assets 64

7. Australia 66
I. Overview 66
II. The Regime of Insolvency and the Secured Status of Maritime Claims in Australia 66
A. Overview of the Regime of Insolvency 66
i. Winding-Up Proceedings 67
ii. Administration 68
iii. Schemes of Arrangement 69

B. Stay Provisions under the Corporations Act ... 70
C. Secured Status of Maritime Claims ... 71
i. Maritime Liens ... 71
ii. Statutory Rights of Action in Rem ... 72
III. Cross-Border Insolvency in Australia ... 73
A. Overview of Australian Implementation of the Model Law ... 73
B. Article 20 of the CBIA and the Staying of Proceedings ... 74
C. Application of Article 20 in the Maritime Context ... 76
i. Yu v STX Pan Ocean ... 77
ii. Tai-Soo Suk v Hanjin Shipping Co Ltd ... 79
IV. Attitudes of the Courts Toward in Rem Actions and the Personification Doctrine in Australia ... 81
V. Status of Chartered Vessels in Cross-Border Insolvency ... 82
VI. Summary ... 83

8. United Kingdom ... 84
I. Overview ... 84
II. The Insolvency Act 1986 and the Secured Status of Maritime Claims in the UK ... 84
A. Overview of the Insolvency Act 1986 ... 84
i. Winding Up ... 84
ii. Administration ... 85
iii. Company Arrangements ... 85
B. Stay Provisions under the Insolvency Act 1986 ... 86
C. Secured Status of Maritime Claims ... 88
i. Maritime Liens ... 88
ii. Statutory Rights of Action in Rem ... 89
iii. Secured Status ... 90
III. Cross-Border Insolvency in the UK ... 91
A. Overview of the Cross-Border Insolvency Regulations 2006 ... 91
B. Article 20 of Schedule 1 to the CBIR 2006 ... 92
C. Application of Article 20 in the Maritime Context ... 93
i. Harms Offshore Aht 'Taurus' GmbH & Co Kg & Another v Bloom & Others ... 94
ii. The Bank of Tokyo-Mitsubishi UFJ Ltd v The M/V Sanko Mineral and Glencore Ltd ... 96
iii. Ronelp Marine Ltd & Others v STX Offshore & Shipbuilding Co Ltd & Another ... 98
iv. In the Matter of Hanjin Shipping Co Ltd ... 100
IV. Courts' Attitudes Toward in Rem Actions and the Personification Doctrine in the UK ... 101

V. Status of Chartered Vessels in Cross-Border Insolvency 102
VI. Summary 103

9. United States 104
I. Overview 104
II. The Bankruptcy Code of the United States 104
A. Overview of the Bankruptcy Code 104
B. Automatic Stay of Proceedings 105
C. Relief from the Automatic Stay 106
i. Lack of Equity in Property that is not Necessary for Reorganisation (section 362(d)(2)) 107
ii. Lack of Adequate Protection (section 362(d)(1)) 107
III. Cross-Border Insolvency in the United States 109
A. Chapter 15 Overview and Article 20 109
B. Application of Chapter 15 in the Maritime Context 110
i. Evridiki Navigation Inc v Sanko SS Co 111
ii. In re Hanjin Shipping Co 112
IV. US Attitude Towards in Rem Actions and the Personification Doctrine 115
V. Status of Chartered Vessels in Cross-Border Insolvency 116
VI. Summary 119

10. Singapore 120
I. Overview 120
II. The Regime of Insolvency and Secured Status of Maritime Claims in Singapore 121
A. Overview of the Regime of Insolvency 121
i. Winding Up 121
ii. Judicial Management 122
iii. Scheme of Arrangement 122
B. Moratorium under the Companies Act 123
C. Secured Status of Maritime Claims 125
i. Maritime Liens 126
ii. Statutory Rights of Action in Rem 127
III. Cross-Border Insolvency in Singapore 129
A. Overview of Singapore's Implementation of the Model Law and Its Article 20 129
B. Application of Article 20 in the Maritime Context 131
i. Re Taisoo Suk 133
IV. Courts' Attitudes Towards in Rem Actions and the Personification Doctrine in Singapore 135
V. Status of Chartered Vessels in Cross-Border Insolvency 137
VI. Summary 138

11. Policy Reflections on the Treatment of Maritime Creditors under the UNCITRAL Model Law Regime 139
I. Maritime Liens 142
A. Secured Claims 142
B. Relief from the Automatic Stay 144
C. In Rem Claims and the Personification Doctrine 149
II. Statutory Rights of Action in Rem 152
A. Secured Status 152
B. Time Point 152
C. Factors Needing to be Considered 153
D. Rationale 154
III. Ship Mortgages 156
IV. Conflict of Laws 158
A. Conflict of Laws in the Arresting Countries 158
B. Conflict of Laws in the Foreign Main Proceeding 160
i. The Availability of Lien Status 160
ii. Priorities 163
V. Summary 164

12. Policy Reflections on the Determination of the Centre of Main Interest and the Scope of Debtor's Assets 165
I. Determination of the Centre of Main Interest of Shipping Companies 165
A. The Recast EU Regulation 167
B. The Model Law 169
i. The Interpretation of the COMI 169
ii. Relevant Date for the Determination of the COMI 176
II. Scope of Debtor's Assets 179
A. Chartered Vessel: Debtor's Assets? 179
i. Time or Voyage Chartered Vessels 180
ii. Demise Chartered Vessels 180
B. Security to Release from Ship Arrest 186
i. Security Provided by Debtors 187
ii. Security Provided by Third Parties 187
III. Summary 189

Bibliography *191*
Index *197*

TABLE OF CASES

Australia

Ackers v Saad Investments Co Ltd [2010] FCA 1221 .... 33, 172
Advance Healthcare Group Ltd [2008] FCA 1604 69
Aichhorn and Co KG v The Ship MV Talabot [1974] HCA 21 81–83
Akers v Deputy Commissioner of Taxation [2014] FCAFC 57 .... 34–35, 75
Australian Securities and Investments Commission v Plymin (2013) 21 ACLC 700 68
Caltex Oil (Australia) Pty Ltd v The Dredge Willemstad [1976] HCA 65 81–83
Comandate Marine Corp v Pan Australia Shipping Pty Ltd [2006] FCAFC 192 .... 50, 57, 71, 81, 151, 155
Danny Morris & Another v The Ship Kiama [1998] FCA 256 .... 50, 73, 76, 152
Hur v Samsun Logix Corp [2009] FCA 372 75
In re Legend International Holdings Inc [2016] VSC 308 32
Kapila in the Matter of Edelsten [2014] FCA 1112 178
Kim v Daebo International Shipping Co Ltd [2015] FCA 684 .... 72–73, 75, 77, 152–53
King in the Matter of Zetta Jet Pte Ltd [2018] FCA 1932 178
Legend International Holdings Inc (as debtor in possession of the assets of Legend International Holdings Inc) v Legend International Holdings Inc [2016] VSC 308 [96] 172
Lehman Bros Holdings Inc v City of Swan (2010) 240 CLR 509 70
Moore v Australian Equity Investors [2012] FCA 1002 .... 172, 178
Morlines Maritime Agency Ltd & Others v The Skulptor Vuchetich [1997] FCA 432 .... 54, 158
Quick v Stoland Pty Ltd (1998) 29 ACSR 130 68
Re Kyra Nominees Pty Ltd (1980) 5 ACLR 60 67
Suk v Hanjin Shipping Co Ltd [2017] FCA 404 .... 31, 80
Tai-Soo Suk v Hanjin Shipping Co Ltd [2016] FCA 1404 .... 59, 75–77, 79–80, 82–83, 102, 140, 180
The Ship Sam Hawk v Reiter Petroleum Inc [2016] FCAFC 26 .... 54, 72, 81–82, 143
Tucker, in the matter of Aero Inventory (UK) Ltd v Aero Inventory (UK) Ltd (No 2) [2009] FCA 1481 74
Wild (Foreign Representative) v Coin Co International plc (Administrators Appointed) [2015] FCA 354 172
Wood v Astra Resources Ltd (UK Company No 07620218) [2016] FCA 1192 178
Yakushiji v Daiichi Chuo Kisen Kaisha [2015] FCA 1170 .... 50, 73

Yakushiji v Kaisha (No 2) [2016] FCA 1277 80
Yu v STX Pan Ocean Co [2013] FCA 680 ....59–61, 72, 75–80, 82–83, 140, 144, 151

Canada

Holt Cargo Systems Inc v ABC Containerline NV (Trustee of) [2001] SCC 90 ....2, 40
Re Nortel Networks Corporation [2015] ONSC 2987 39
The Ioannis Daskalelis [1974] SCR 1248.... 54, 163
The Miss Donna [1978] 1 FC 379.... 50, 152

China

Mobil Sales and Supply Corp v The Owners of the Ship Pacific Bear [1979] HKLR 125 .... 54, 159
In re Qinzhou Guiqin Shipping Group Co [2014] Yong Ningbo Maritime Ct First No 63; [2015] Zhe Higher Ct Maritime Final No 169; [2015] Zhe Higher Court Execution No 45 146

Cyprus

Hassanein v The Hellenic Island [1989] 1 CLR 406....159

EU

Case C-341/04 In re Eurofood IFSC Ltd [2006] ECR I-3854 ....167–68, 172

Malaysia

Ocean Grain Shipping Pte Ltd v The Dong Nai [1996] 4 MLJ 454.... 54, 159
The Ocean Jade [1991] 2 MLJ 386.... 54, 159

New Zealand

ABC Shipbrokers v The Ship Offi Gloria [1993] 3 NZLR 576.... 54, 158
Fournier v Ship Margaret Z [1999] 3 NZLR 111.... 54, 158
Kim and Yu v STX Pan Ocean Co Ltd [2014] NZHC 845.... 180, 185

Raukuna Moana Fisheries Ltd v The Ship Irina Zharkikh [2001] 2 NZLR 801 155
Ship Betty Ott v General Bills Ltd [1992] 1 NZLR 655 ..... 54, 143, 158
Williams v Simpson [2011] 2 NZLR 380 33

Singapore

Beluga Chartering GmbH (in liquidation) v Beluga Projects (Singapore) Ptd Ltd (in liquidation) [2014] SGCA 14 ..... 129, 133, 153
Electro Magnetic (S) Ltd v Development Bank of Singapore [1994] 1 SLR 734 124–25
Hickley Singapore Trading Pte Ltd v Sogo Department Stores (S) Pte Ltd [2001] 4 SLR 154 123–25
Korea Asset Management v Daewoo Singapore Pte Ltd [2004] 1 SLR 671 123
Kuo Fen Ching and Another v Dauphin Offshore Engineering & Trading Pte Ltd [1999] SGCA 95 ..... 50, 57, 60–61, 128, 135–38, 151–52, 155, 188
Lim Bock Lai v Selco (Singapore) Pte Ltd [1987] SGHC 35 ..... 127–29, 133, 135, 138
Precious Shipping Public Co Ltd v OW Bunker Far East (Singapore) Ptd Ltd [2015] SGHC 187 ..... 54, 60–61, 126, 136–37, 151, 158
QCD(M) Sdn Bhd v Wah Nam Plastic Industry Pte Ltd [1997] 2 SLR 544 123
Re Opti-Medix Ltd (in liquidation) [2016] SGHC 108 129
Re Taisoo Suk[2016] SGHC 195 ..... 59, 127, 129, 133–35, 137–38, 144, 154, 180
Re Zetta Jet Pte Ltd [2019] SGHC 53 ..... 173, 175, 177, 179
The Andres Bonifacio [1993] SGCA 70 ..... 54, 158
The Capricorn [1998] SGHC 366 135
The Fierbinti [1994] SGCA 74 ..... 135, 137
The Halcyon Isle [1980] SGPC 3 126
The Hull 308 [1991] SGCA 34 127–29
The Kusu Island [1989] SGCA 11 ..... 135, 137
The Ocean Jade [1991] SGHC 33 ..... 126, 143
The Oriental Baltic [2011] SGHC 75 128
The Posidon [2017] SGHC 138 147
The Vinalines Pioneer [2015] SGHC 278 126

South Africa

Seaspan Holdco 1 Ltd v MS Mare Traveller Schiffahrts GmbH (MV Seaspan Grouse) [2019] ZASCA 02 50
Transol Bunker BV v Motor Vessel Andrico Unity [1989] 4 SA 325 ..... 54, 158

UK

Belmont Park Investment Pty Ltd v BNY Corporate Trustee Services Ltd [2011] UKSC 38 189
Burnard v Aaron and Sharpley (1862) 31 LJCP 334 .... 64, 181
Citibank NA v Hobbs Savill & Co Ltd (The Panglobal Friendship) [1978] 1 Lloyd's Rep 368 51
Cosco Bulk Carrier Co v Armada Shipping SA&Another [2011] EWHC 216 (Ch) 92–94, 131
Ensign Tankers (Leasing) Ltd v Stokes (Inspector of Taxes) [1992] 1 AC 665 184
Fenton v City of Dublin Steam Packet Co (1838) 8 Ad & E 835 .... 64, 181
FMS Wertmanagement AÖR v Vietnam Shipbuilding Industry Group & Others [2013] EWHC 1146 (Comm) 88
Fraser v Marsh (1811) 13 East 238 .... 64, 181
FSL-9 Pte Ltd v Norwegian Hull Club (The FSL New York) [2016] EWHC 1091 (Comm) 186
General Share & Trust Co v Wetley Brick & Pottery Co (1882) ChD 260 184
Harms Offshore AHT 'Taurus' GmbH& Co KG v Bloom [2009] EWCA Civ 632 .... 59, 94–95, 140
In re Aro Co Ltd [1980] Ch 196 .... 48, 50, 89–90, 127, 142
In re Atlantic Computer Systems [1992] Ch 505 124
In re Australian Direct Steam Navigation Company (1875) LR 20 Eq 325 94
In re HIH Insurance Ltd [2008] 1 WLR 852 .... 91, 103
In re Stanford International Bank Ltd [2010] EWCA Civ 137 .... 33, 170, 172
In re Toisa Ltd (an unreported case of English High Court (Commercial Division), held by Judge Burton orally) 177
In re Videology Ltd [2018] EWHC 2186 (Ch) 171–72, 177
In re 19 Entertainment Ltd [2016] EWHC 1545 (Ch) 32
In the Matter of Hanjin Shipping Co Ltd No CR-2016-005448 (High Court of Justice, Chancery Division, Companies Court (6 September 2016)) 100, 102–03
Lazari GP Ltd v Jervis [2012] EWHC 1466 (Ch) 148
Luke v Lyde (1759) 2 Burr 882 2
Moor v Anglo-Italian Bank (1879) 10 ChD 681 87
Perpetual Trustee Company Ltd v Lehman Bros Special Financing Inc [2009] EWHC 2953 (Ch) 39
Port Line v Ben Line Steamers [1958] 2 QB 146 .... 64, 119, 180–81
Re Allied Domecq Plc [2000] BCC 582 86
Re Anglo-Continental Supply Co Ltd [1992] 2 Ch 723 86
Re Blue Jeans Sales Ltd [1979] 1 All ER 641 184
Re David Lloyd & Co (1877) LR 6 Ch D 339 .... 87, 123
Re HIH Casualty and General Insurance [2008] UKHL 21 .... 35, 129
Re Hopkins (1881) 18 ChD 370 87

Re Northsea Base Investment Ltd & Others [2015] EWHC 121 (Ch) 166, 168–69, 176
Re Pan Ocean Co Ltd [2014] EWHC 2124 (Ch) 189
Re RAC Motoring Services Ltd [2000] 1 BCLC 307 86
Re Rio Grande do Sol Steamship Co (1877) 5 ChD 282 .... 14, 87
Re Savoy Hotel Ltd [1981] Ch 351 123
Republic of India v India Steamship Co Ltd (The Indian Grace (No 2)) [1998] AC 878 .... 44–45, 57, 62, 71, 81, 89, 101–03, 136–37, 142, 150–51, 155
Ronelp Marine Ltd & Others v STX Offshore & Shipbuilding Co Ltd & Another[2016] EWHC 2228 (Ch) 98–100, 103
Rubin &Another v Eurofinance SA & Others [2012] UKSC 46 .... 91, 93
Sandeman v Scurr (1866) LR 2 QB 86 .... 64, 180–81
Singularis Holdings Ltd v PricewaterhouseCoopers [2014] UKPC 36 129
Stena Bulk AB v Copley [2015] 1 Lloyd's Rep 280 102
The Aline (1839) 166 ER 514 42
The Andrea Ursula [1973] 1 QB 265 .... 64, 180–81
The August 8 [1983] 2 AC 450 (PC) 101
The Banco [1971] P 137 101
The Bank of Tokyo-Mitsubishi UFJ Ltd v The M/V Sanko Mineral and Glencore Ltd [2014] EWHC 3927 (Admlty) 96–98, 111, 140, 144, 154
The Beldis [1936] P 51 101
The Berge Tasta [1975] 1 Lloyd's Rep 422 180
The Bold Buccleugh (1851) 7 Moo PC 267 .... 41–45, 47, 71–72, 88, 126, 141–43, 148, 150–51
The Bolivia [1995] BCC 666 90
The Cella (1888) 13 PD 82 .... 43, 49–50
The Colorado [1923] P 102 42
The Constellation [1965] 2 Lloyd's Rep 538 .... 14, 87, 94
The Dictator (1892) P 304 .... 44, 56–58, 62, 81, 101, 142, 150, 155
The Dundee (1824) 66 ER39 42
The Fesco Angara [2010] EWCA Civ 1050 126
The Gemma [1899] P 285 56
The Great Eastern (1868) LR 2 Ad & EC 88 .... 64, 181
The Halcyon Isle [1981] AC 221 .... 44–45, 48, 54, 62, 72, 81–82, 89, 126, 142, 155, 158–59
The Heinrich Bjorn (1885) 10 PD 44 .... 47, 89, 142–43
The Hill Harmony [2011] 1 Lloyd's Rep 147 180
The Lyrma No 2 [1978] 2 Lloyd's Rep 30 147
The Monica S [1968] P 741 48–50
The Mons [1932] P 109 147
The Moschanty [1971] 1 Lloyd's Rep 37 186
The Neptune (1824) 166 ER 81 146

The Nied Elwin (1811) 1 Dods 50 .... 65, 188
The Pacific (1864) 167 ER 356 50
The Ruta [2000] 1 WLR 2068 147
The Sanko Mineral [2014] EWHC 3927 (Admlty) 59
The Selina (1842) 2 NC 18 147
The Sertao [2018] EWHC 1013 (Admlty) 156
The Stream Fisher [1927] P 73 147
The Sydney Cove (1815) 165 ER 1399 146
The Tasmania (1888) 13 PD 110 .... 64, 180–81
The Tervaete [1922] P 259 101
The Tolten [1946] P 135 .... 41, 43, 88
The Tribels [1985] 1 Lloyd's Rep 128 186
The Two Ellens (1872) LR 4 PC 161 .... 43, 50, 71
The Zafiro [1960] P 1 .... 49–50, 73, 94
Transag Haulage Ltd v Leyland DAF Finance Ltd [1994] BCC 356 184
Welsh Development Agency v The Export Finance Co Ltd [1992] BCC 270 184

US

Bank One Louisiana NA v Mr Dean MV 293 F 3d 830 (5th Cir 2002) 44, 143
Bogart v The Steamboat John Jay 58 US 399 (1854) 52
Bominflot Inc v The M/V Henrich S 465 F 3d 144 (4th Cir 2006) 54
Burns Bros v Central RR 202 F 2d 910 (2d Cir 1953) 55, 116
Central Hudson Gas and Electric Corp v Empresa Naviera Santa SA 845 F Supp 150 (SD New York 1994) 55
Coastal Marine Management LLC v Additional Return LLC CV-No 16-11616-NMG (District of Massachusetts 2018) 145
Continental Grain Co v Barge FBL-585 364 US 19 (1960) 55, 116
Detroit Trust Co v The Thomas Barlum 293 US 21 (1934) 52
Evridiki Navigation Inc v Sanko SS Co 880 F Supp 2d 666 (D Maryland 2012) 59, 111–12, 114, 119, 140–41, 144
Hapag-Lloyd Aktiengesellschaft v US Oil Trading LLC 814 F 3d 146 (2d Cir 2016) 116, 150
Hertz v Friend 559 US 77 (2009) 172
IFG Leasing v Captains Courageous Inc 21 BR 134 (Bankr ND California 1982) 53
In re ABC Learning Centres Ltd 728 F 3d 301 (3d Cir 2013) 113
In re Adams 27 BR 582 (District Delaware 1983) 108
In re Atlas Shipping A/S 404 BR 726 (Bankr SD New York 2009) 112
In re Bear Stearns High-Grade Structured Credit Strategies Master Fund Ltd 374 BR 122 (SD New York 2007) 173

In re Bear Stearns High-Grade Structured Credit Strategies Master Fund Ltd 389 BR 325 (SD New York 2008) 33, 173
In re Betcorp Ltd (in liquidation) 400 BR 266 (Bankr District of Nevada 2009) 74
In re Cambridge Properties Inc 82 BR 35 (ED Louisiana 1988) 108
In re Daebo International Shipping Co Ltd 543 BR 47 (SD New York 2015) 116–17, 183, 185
In re Ernst & Young Inc 383 BR 773 (Bankr District of Colorado 2008) 35, 174
In re Ephedra Products Liability Litigation 349 BR 333 (SD New York 2006)......35
In re Fairfield Sentry Ltd 440 BR 60 (SD New York 2010).......... 172, 177, 179
In re Fairfield Sentry Ltd 714 F 3d 127 (2nd Cir 2013) 35
In re Gold & Honey Ltd 410 BR 357 (Bankr ED New York 2009).......... 33, 35
In re Government Securities Corp 972 F 2d 328 (11th Cir 1992) 189
In re Hanjin Shipping Co Ltd 2016 WL 6681169, [2016] AMC 2113 (District of New Jersey 16 September 2016) 59, 113
In re Hanjin Shipping Co Ltd 2016 WL 6679487, [2016] AMC 2126 (Bankr District of New Jersey 20 September 2016).......... 112–14, 116–19, 140, 180, 185
In re H&S Transport Co 42 BR 164 (Bankr MD Tennessee 1984) 47, 143
In re Korea Line Corp No 11-10789 (Bankr SD New York 20 April 2011) 118
In re Lehman Bros Holdings Inc 422 BR 407 (Bankr SD New York 2010)..... 39, 189
In re Louisiana Ship Management Inc 761 F 2d 1025, 1985 AMC 2667 (5th Cir 1985) 105
In re Lykes Bros SS Co Inc 196 BR 574 (MD Florida 1996) 181–83, 186
In re Mellor 734 F 2d 1396 (9th Cir 1984) 107
In re Mclean Industries Inc 74 BR 589 (Bankr SD New York 1987).......... 106
In re Mclean Industries Inc 76 BR 328 (Bankr SD New York 1987).......... 105
In re Millennium Global Emerging Credit 458 BR 63 (SD New York 2011) 171, 178–79
In re Millenium Seacarriers Inc 419 F 3d 83 (2d Cir 2005).......... 148
In re Modern Boats Inc 775 F 2d 619, 1987 AMC 509 (5th Cir 1985).......... 105
In re Moreggia & Sons Inc 852 F 2d 1179 (9th Cir 1988) 117, 183
In re New Era Company 125 BR 725 (SD New York 1991) 107
In re Nortel Networks Inc 532 BR 494 (Bankr Delaware 2015) 39
In re North Atlantic & Gulf Steamship Co 204 F Supp 899 (SD New York 1962) 47, 143
In re Ocean Rig UDW Inc 585 BR 31 (SD New York 2018) 176–77
In re Orlando Coals Inc 6 BR 721 (Bankr SD West Virginia 1980).......... 108
In re PCH Associates 804 F 2d 193 (2d Cir 1986) 117, 182–83
In re Pillowtex Inc 349 F 3d 711 (3d Cir 2003) 181
In re Pittman 7 BR 760 (Bankr SD New York 1980).......... 108–09
In re Probulk Inc 407 BR 56 (SD New York 2009).......... 189
In re Qimonda AG Bankruptcy Litigation 433 BR 547 (ED Virginia 2010) 35
In re Ran 607 F 3d 1017 (5th Cir 2010).......... 177

In re Ritz-Carlton of DC Inc 98 BR 170 (SD New York 1989) 107
In re Rogers Development Corp 2 BR 679 (Bankr ED Virginia 1980) 108
In re SPhinX Ltd 371 BR 10 (SD New York 2007) 33
In re STX Pan Ocean Co Ltd No 13-12046 (Bankr SD New York 1 July 2013) 118
In re Suntech Power Holdings Co Ltd 520 BR 399 (SD New York 2014)....... 177, 179
In re Toft 453 BR 186 (Bankr SD New York 2011)..35
In re Topgallant Lines Inc 208 BR 589, 1997 AMC 1491 (SD Georgia 1996) 105
In re Tri-Continental Exchange 349 BR 627(ED California 2006)................ 172–73
In re Wasserman 122 BR 839 (Bankr District Massachusetts 1991) 108
In re Waterman Steamship Co 63 BR 435 (SD New York 1986)..........................105
In re Westchase I Associates LP 126 BR 692 (WD North Carolina 1991)...........108
In re WorldCom Inc 339 BR 56 (SD New York 2006) 182
Insurance Co of N America v S/S American Argosy 732 F 2d 299
(2d Cir 1984)... 55, 116
Leary v United States 81 US (14 Wall) 607 (1872) 64
Liona Corp v PCH Associates 949 F 2d 585 (2d Cir 1991).......................... 117, 183
Liverpool & London Steamship Protection & Indemnity Association v
Queen of Leman MV 480 F 2d 1024 (2d Cir 1973)..163
Local Loan Co v Hunt 292 US 234 (1934) 10
Mackensworth v SS American Merchant 28 F 3d 246 (2d Cir 1994)............ 65, 188
Matter of Buchman 600 F 2d 160 (8th Cir 1979) 105
Matthews v CTI Container Transport International Inc 871 F 2d 270
(2d Cir 1989)... 182–83
National Equipment Rental Ltd v Priority Electronics Corp 435 F Supp 236
(ED New York 1977)..182
Northern Pipeline Construction Co v Marathon Pipe Line Co 458
US 50 (1982) 105
Ocean Ship Supply Ltd v M/V Leah 729 F 2d 971 (4th Cir 1984) 54
Orix Credit Alliance Inc v Pappas 946 F 2d 1258 (7th Cir 1991) 182
Petroleos Mexicanos Refinacion v M/T King A 554 F 3d 99 (3d Cir 2009).......65, 188
Royal School Laboratories Inc v Town of Watertown 358 F 2d 813
(2d Cir 1966)..55
SEL Maduro (Florida) Inc v M/V Antonio de Gastaneta 833 F 2d 1477
(11th Cir 1987) 55
The China 74 US 53 (1986)..44, 55, 115, 142, 150
The Eastern Shore 24 F 2d 443 (D Maryland 1928)..55
The Eclipse 135 US 599 (1890) 52
The JE Rumbell 148 US 1 (1893) 52
Trinidad Foundry & Fabricating Ltd v M/V KAS Camilla 966 F 2d 613
(11th Cir 1992) 54
Tucker v Alexandroff 183 US 424 (1902) 44, 62, 115, 142, 150
United Airlines Inc v HSBC Bank USA NA 416 F 3d 609 (7th Cir 2005) 117, 183
United Savings Association of Texas v Timbers of Inwood Forest Associates Ltd
484 US 365 (1988)..107

United States v Shea 152 US 178 (1894) 64, 180
United States Lines Inc v GAC Marine Fuels Ltd 68 BR 690 (Bankr SD New York 1986) 106
Winter Storm Shipping Ltd v TPI 310 F 3d 263 (2d Cir 2002), overruled by Shipping Corp of India v Jaldhi Overseas PTE Ltd 585 F 3d 58 (2d Cir 2009) 56
World Fuel Services Inc v M/V Hanjin Montevideo No 2–16–CV–06584 (CD California 2016) 113–14, 141

TABLE OF STATUTES

Australia

Admiralty Act 1988 (Cth), s 4(3) 72
Admiralty Act 1988 (Cth), s 15(2) 71
Admiralty Act 1988 (Cth), s 17 .... 42, 53, 72
Admiralty Act 1988 (Cth), s 19 .... 42, 53
Corporations Act 2001 (Cth), pt 5.1 .... 66, 69
Corporations Act 2001 (Cth), pt 5.3A 66, 68, 73, 79–80
Corporations Act 2001 (Cth), pt 5.4 66–67
Corporations Act 2001 (Cth), pt 5.4B 66–67, 79
Corporations Act 2001 (Cth), pt 5.5 .... 66–67, 74
Corporations Act 2001 (Cth), pt 5.6 66
Corporations Act 2001 (Cth), s 95(A) 68
Corporations Act 2001 (Cth), s 249L 67
Corporations Act 2001 (Cth), s 411(16) 71, 76
Corporations Act 2001 (Cth), s 435A 69
Corporations Act 2001 (Cth), s 435C 69
Corporations Act 2001 (Cth), s 436A 69
Corporations Act 2001 (Cth), s 436B 69
Corporations Act 2001 (Cth), s 436C 69
Corporations Act 2001 (Cth), s 437A 69
Corporations Act 2001 (Cth), s 438A 69
Corporations Act 2001(Cth), s 439C 67, 69
Corporations Act 2001 (Cth), s 440D 70, 72, 76–77, 79, 82, 144
Corporations Act 2001 (Cth), s 440F 70, 79, 144
Corporations Act 2001 (Cth), s 440G 70, 76, 79, 144
Corporations Act 2001 (Cth), s 444A 69
Corporations Act 2001 (Cth), s 444C 69
Corporations Act 2001 (Cth), s 444D 69
Corporations Act 2001 (Cth), s 444D(1) 71
Corporations Act 2001 (Cth), s 444D(2) 71
Corporations Act 2001 (Cth), s 444F 71
Corporations Act 2001 (Cth), s 445D 69
Corporations Act 2001 (Cth), s 459A 68
Corporations Act 2001 (Cth), s 459P 68
Corporations Act 2001 (Cth), s 471B 13, 15, 68, 70, 72, 79, 144, 157
Corporations Act 2001 (Cth), s 471C 13, 15, 70, 72–73, 75–79, 144, 157

Corporations Act 2001 (Cth), s 472 68
Corporations Act 2001 (Cth), s 490 67
Corporations Act 2001 (Cth), s 491 67
Corporations Act 2001 (Cth), s 494 67
Corporations Act 2001 (Cth), s 494(1) 67
Corporations Act 2001 (Cth), s 495 67
Corporations Act 2001 (Cth), s 497 67
Corporations Act 2001 (Cth), s 499 67
Corporations Act 2001 (Cth), s 500 67
Corporations Act 2001 (Cth), s 500(1) 70
Corporations Act 2001 (Cth), s 500(2) 70
Corporations Act 2001 (Cth), s 600A 69
Cross-Border Insolvency Act 2008 (Cth), s 8 74
Cross-Border Insolvency Act 2008 (Cth), s 10 74
Cross-Border Insolvency Act 2008 (Cth), s 16 ....75–79, 144, 157
Cross-Border Insolvency Act 2008 (Cth), s 21 74
Cross-Border Insolvency Act 2008 (Cth), s 22 74
Cross-Border Insolvency Act 2008 (Cth), sch 1, art 17 83
Cross-Border Insolvency Act 2008 (Cth), sch 1, art 20(1) 75
Cross-Border Insolvency Act 2008 (Cth), sch1, art 20(2) 82, 140, 144
Cross-border Insolvency Act 2008 (Cth), sch1, art 20(3) 156

Canada

Bankruptcy and Insolvency Act, art 2 ....15, 157
Federal Court Act RSC 1985, c F–7, s 43(8) 57
Marine Liability Act 2001, s 139 ....42, 153

China

Maritime Code of the People's Republic of China, art 272 159

EU

Council Regulation (EC) No 1346/2000 of 29 May 2000 on Insolvency Proceedings, art 3(1) 167
Council Regulation (EC) No 1346/2000 of 29 May 2000 on Insolvency Proceedings, recital 13 167
Regulation (EU) 2015/848 of the European Parliament and of the Council of 20 May 2015 on Insolvency Proceedings Recast, art 3 ....167, 169

Regulation (EU) 2015/848 of the European Parliament and of the Council of 20 May 2015 on Insolvency Proceedings Recast, art 20 169

International

UNCITRAL Model Law on Cross-Border Insolvency (UNCITRAL Model Law), preamble 28, 61, 140
UNCITRAL Model Law, art 1 32
UNCITRAL Model Law, art 2(a) 30–31
UNCITRAL Model Law, art 2(b) 33, 62
UNCITRAL Model Law, art 2(c) 34
UNCITRAL Model Law, art 2(d) 30
UNCITRAL Model Law, art 2(f) 34
UNCITRAL Model Law, art 4 31
UNCITRAL Model Law, art 5 29
UNCITRAL Model Law, art 6 .... 27, 34–35
UNCITRAL Model Law, art 9 29
UNICTRAL Model Law, art 10 29
UNICTRAL Model Law, art 11 29
UNICTRAL Model Law, art 12 29
UNICTRAL Model Law, art 13(1) 29
UNICTRAL Model Law, art 13(2) 29
UNICTRAL Model Law, art 15 30
UNICTRAL Model Law, art 15(2) 30
UNCITRAL Model Law, art 16 .... 30, 173
UNICTRAL Model Law, art 16(3) 33, 63, 170, 173
UNCITRAL Model Law, art 17 .... 30–31, 34, 37, 77, 165
UNCITRAL Model Law, art 17(1)(a) 30
UNCITRAL Model Law, art 17(1)(b) 30
UNCITRAL Model Law, art 17(1)(c) 30
UNCITRAL Model Law, art 17(1)(d) 31
UNCITRAL Model Law, art 17(2) 178
UNCITRAL Model Law, art 17(3) 18
UNCITRAL Model Law, art 17(4) 18
UNCITRAL Model Law, art 18 .... 31, 80
UNCITRAL Model Law, art 19 .... 36–37, 153
UNCITRAL Model Law, art 20 .... 2, 31, 33–34, 36–37, 64, 78, 81, 97, 129–31, 137–38, 139–40, 153, 179–80, 185–86
UNCITRAL Model Law, art 20(1) 37, 59–60, 75, 81–82, 131
UNCITRAL Model Law, art 20(1)(a) 76, 94, 110, 165, 180, 185
UNCITRAL Model Law, art 20(1)(b) 76, 110
UNCITRAL Model Law, art 20(2) 37, 59–61, 75, 77–79, 131, 139, 144

UNCITRAL Model Law, art 20(3) 38, 60, 156
UNCITRAL Model Law, art 20(4) 37, 60
UNCITRAL Model Law, art 21 .... 31, 33–34, 36–38, 153
UNCITRAL Model Law, art 21(1) 38, 78
UNCITRAL Model Law, art 22(1) 38
UNCITRAL Model Law, art 25 39
UNCITRAL Model Law, art 26 39
UNCITRAL Model Law, art 32 61–62

New Zealand

Companies Act 1993, s 246 32

Republic of the Marshall Islands

Marshall Island Maritime Act, s 302 (A)(4) 183

Singapore

Companies Act, s 4 121
Companies Act, s 210 122
Companies Act, s 210 (3AA) 123
Companies Act, s 210(10) 127
Companies Act, s 211 122
Companies Act, s 211B 125, 129
Companies Act, s 211C 125
Companies Act, s 211H 123
Companies Act, s 227B(a) 122
Companies Act, s 227B(b) 122
Companies Act, s 227C 124, 127, 133
Companies Act, s 227D 124, 127, 129, 133, 144
Companies Act, s 247 121
Companies Act, s 253 122
Companies Act, s 254 122
Companies Act, s 258 123
Companies Act, s 262(3) 15, 123, 126, 128–29, 132–33, 144, 157
Companies Act, s 272(1) 122
Companies Act, s 291 122
Companies Act, s 292(1) 122
Companies Act, s 293 122
Companies Act, s 299(2) 15, 123, 128, 144

Companies Act, s 377(14) 130
Companies Act, sch 10, art 20 130
Companies Act, sch 10, art 20(1) 130
Companies Act, sch 10, art 20(2) 130, 132–33, 138, 140, 144, 157
Companies Act, sch 10, art 20(3) 131, 157
Companies Act, sch 10, art 20(4) 156
High Court (Admiralty Jurisdiction) Act, s 3 .... 42, 53

South Africa

Cross-Border Insolvency Act 2000, s 20(2) 145

UK

Companies Act 2006, s 895 86
Companies Act 2006, s 896 86
Cross-Border Insolvency Regulations 2006, art 2 91
Cross-Border Insolvency Regulations 2006, sch 1, art 4 91
Cross-Border Insolvency Regulations 2006, sch 1, art 15 93
Cross-Border Insolvency Regulations 2006, sch 1, art 20(1) 92, 94, 130
Cross-Border Insolvency Regulations 2006, sch 1, art 20(2) 92, 97, 140, 144
Cross-Border Insolvency Regulations 2006, sch 1, art 20(2)(a) 92, 157
Cross-Border Insolvency Regulations 2006, sch 1, art 20(4) 93, 156
Cross-Border Insolvency Regulations 2006, sch 1, art 20(5) 93
Cross-Border Insolvency Regulations 2006, sch 1, art 20(6) 93
Insolvency Act 1986, pt I 84, 86
Insolvency Act 1986, pt II 84
Insolvency Act 1986, pt IV 14, 84, 94
Insolvency Act 1986, s 1A(1) 87
Insolvency Act 1986, s 4(3) 86
Insolvency Act 1986, s 4A(2) 86
Insolvency Act 1986, s 4A(3) 86
Insolvency Act 1986, s 4A(4) 86
Insolvency Act 1986, s 4A(5) 86
Insolvency Act 1986, s 84 85
Insolvency Act 1986, s 89 85
Insolvency Act 1986, s 90 85
Insolvency Act 1986, s 112(1) 14, 86
Insolvency Act 1986, s 112(2) 14, 86
Insolvency Act 1986, s 122 85
Insolvency Act 1986, s 123 85
Insolvency Act 1986, s 124 85

Insolvency Act 1986, s 127 .... 14, 87
Insolvency Act 1986, s 128(1) 14, 87
Insolvency Act 1986, s 130 14
Insolvency Act 1986, s 130(2) 14, 87, 90, 93
Insolvency Act 1986, s 183(1) 14–15, 86–87, 97, 144, 157
Insolvency Act 1986, s 183(2)(a) 14, 86–87, 144
Insolvency Act 1986, s 183(3)(a) 15, 87, 94, 97, 157
Insolvency Act 1986, s 248(a) 15, 51, 157
Insolvency Act 1986, s 248(b)(i) 51–52, 157
Insolvency Act 1986, s 251I 10
Insolvency Act 1986, s 285(4) 90
Insolvency Act 1986, s 426 91
Insolvency Act 1986, sch A1 86–87
Insolvency Act 1986, sch B1 .... 85, 94, 144
Insolvency Act 1986, sch B1, para 3 85
Insolvency Act 1986, sch B1, para 43 .... 87, 90, 97–98, 100
Insolvency Act 1986, sch B1, para 44 87
Merchant Shipping Act 1995, sch 1, s 7 52
Senior Courts Act 1981, s 20(2) 42, 53
Senior Courts Act 1981, s 21(4)(b)(ii) 57

US

Fed R Civ P Supp, r B 56
Fed R Civ P Supp, r B(1) 56
11 USC § 362 .... 14–15, 104, 110, 144, 157
11 USC § 362(a) 14, 105–06
11 USC § 362(a)(5) 106, 110
11 USC § 362(d) 107, 110
11 USC § 362(d)(2) 145
11 USC §365 183
11 USC § 522 10
11 USC § 524 10
11 USC § 541(c)(1)(B) 189
11 USC § 544 53
11 USC § 544(a) 183
11 USC § 1501 104
11 USC § 1506 .... 109, 119
11 USC § 1515(a) 109
11 USC § 1516(3) 173
11 USC § 1520 .... 104, 110, 157
11 USC §1520(a)(1) 110, 140, 144
11 USC § 1520(b) 156

28 USC §1334 105
28 USC §157(b)(2) 105
28 USC § 157(b)(2)(B) 105
28 USC §157(b)(2)(K) 105
46 USC § 31301 42
46 USC § 31341 .... 42, 53, 141
46 USC § 31342 .... 42, 53, 113, 141
46 USC §§ 31343 .... 42, 53, 141
Uniform Commercial Code (UCC) § 1–203(b) 181–82
Uniform Commercial Code (UCC) § 9–102(73) 15, 157

1

Introduction

Both admiralty and insolvency law have their roots in antiquity, but they have never been compatible.[1] An early codification of insolvency (or bankruptcy) law can be found in Table III of the Twelve Tables (around 450 BC), which provided that 'if a debt for which a judgment was given remain unpaid for thirty days, the debtor could be taken captive by his creditors'.[2] It was not until the nineteenth century that the law of insolvency gradually abandoned its criminal characteristics and became related only to merchants.[3] However, insolvency law has been developing in line with national social and economic policies, which lie fundamentally in the distribution of assets and relate to the interest of sovereignty.[4] Therefore, the law of insolvency varies dramatically from nation to nation. Nevertheless, insolvency practice is usually land-based and focuses on land-based issues.[5] The basic principle of insolvency law is to treat equivalent creditors equally for the purpose of distribution and rehabilitation and to stay all other proceedings once the insolvency proceeding begins. This basic principle was further strengthened by the trend towards universalism in the area of cross-border insolvency at the end of the twentieth century, when the United Nations Commission on International Trade Law (UNCITRAL) Model Law on Cross-Border Insolvency (the Model Law) was enacted.[6] The concept of universalism calls for all courts to co-operate with each other and to ensure that all of the debtor's assets are distributed to its creditors under a single and orderly system of distribution in the debtor's home insolvency proceeding.[7]

[1] JM Landers, 'The Shipowner Becomes a Bankruptcy' (1972) 39 *University of Chicago Law Review* 490; DR Thomas, *Maritime Liens* (Stevens & Sons, 1980) para 99.

[2] B Wessels et al, *International Cooperation in Bankruptcy and Insolvency Matters* (Oxford University Press, 2009) 3: '*Aeris confessi rebusque iure iudicatis XXX dies iusti sunto. Post deinde manus iniectio esto*'.

[3] ibid 8.

[4] G McCormack, 'COMI and Comity in UK and US Insolvency Law' [2012] *LQR* 140, 158.

[5] M Alwang, 'Steering The Most Appropriate Course Between Admiralty and Insolvency: Why An International Insolvency Treaty Should Recognise the Primacy of Admiralty Law Over Maritime Assets' (1996) 64 *Fordham Law Review* 2613, 2618.

[6] UNCITRAL Secretariat, *UNCITRAL Cross-Border Insolvency Law with Guide to Enactment and Interpretation* (United Nations Office at Vienna, 2014) 19.

[7] See JL Westbrook, 'A Global Solution to Multinational Default' (2000) 98 *Michigan Law Review* 2276.

On the contrary, admiralty law developed centuries earlier than the bankruptcy regime. It is an ancient and well-established body of law that focuses on the special nature of the international shipping industry and on the enforcement of maritime claims against maritime assets.[8] The origin of maritime law can be traced back to 800 BC to a maritime code that was purportedly administered on the island of Rhodes; the first mention of this code is found in Justinian's Digest in the sixth century AD.[9] In addition, early codification of maritime rules in the Middle Ages can be found in the Rôles of Oléron, which consisted of both stated principles and judgments relating to the sea, ships, seamen and merchants.[10] For centuries, maritime law has developed a 'sophisticated and generally harmonious' system of dealing with the bankruptcy of shipowners, which provides sufficient and special protection for maritime creditors, especially for maritime lien holders.[11] As Lord Mansfield elaborated, 'the maritime law is not the law of a particular country, but the general law of nations'.[12] In particular, maritime creditors are allowed to arrest vessels in rem wherever they are found and to realise their claims from the proceeds of the vessels' judicial sale, regardless of, and independent from, the shipowner's foreign insolvency proceeding.[13] Creditors and claims without a sufficiently direct connection to the ship and its operation are excluded from this admiralty process. It may, therefore, be argued that admiralty law is based on maritime exceptionalism, justified by maritime heritage and customs and the particular policy considerations that arise in the context of the international shipping industry.

Since shipping companies, by their very nature, are involved in cross-border transactions, the international scope of these companies and worldwide dispersal of their assets might give rise to insolvency proceedings in multiple jurisdictions. 'A res may concurrently be the subject of an arrest in the admiralty court and an asset capable of liquidation in insolvency proceedings'.[14] However, due to the unique mobility of ships and the special operational structures of shipping companies, it is difficult to harmonise the international cross-border insolvency regime with the admiralty regime governing ships. Furthermore, the Model Law has been developed with little regard to the admiralty in rem proceeding, in the sense that it provides a regime of automatic stay order upon the recognition of a foreign main proceeding, freezing all claims in the local forum from commencing or continuing any action against the insolvent debtor.[15]

[8] *Holt Cargo Systems Inc v ABC Containerline NV (Trustee of)* [2001] SCC 90 [25].

[9] W Tetley, *Maritime Liens and Claims*, 2nd edn (Editions Yvon Blais, 1998) 7–8; Digest of Justinian, Book XIV, Title 2, Art 9.

[10] Tetley (n 9) 171.

[11] S Rares, 'Consistency and Conflict – Cross-Border Insolvency' [2015] *Federal Judicial Scholarship* 14, available at www.austlii.edu.au/au/journals/FedJSchol/2015/14.html, accessed 5 June 2020.

[12] *Luke v Lyde* (1759) 2 Burr 882, 887.

[13] M Davies, 'Cross-Border Insolvency and Admiralty: A Middle Path of Reciprocal Comity' (2018) 66 *American Journal of Comparative Law* 101, 101.

[14] Thomas (n 1) para 99.

[15] UNCITRAL Model Law on Cross-Border Insolvency (The Model Law), Art 20.

Therefore, this book will explore the fundamental tensions that arise between the cross-border insolvency regime and maritime law when a shipowner files an insolvency proceeding in one country, but has simultaneously to deal with admiralty arrests of its vessels in other countries. In other words: should an in rem action that arises in one country be stayed or dismissed because of the existence of an insolvency proceeding in another country? Suppose that a shipping company suffers from financial distress and subsequently initiates an insolvency proceeding or raises a risk of insolvency. The primary assets of the shipping company are vessels, travelling internationally. Maritime creditors may arrest the companies' ships around the world at any port where the vessels are calling, either before or when the insolvency of the shipping company is initiated. Under such circumstances, it is important for a maritime claimant to be able to ascertain which jurisdiction or legal process is available to him to recover the claim, admiralty or bankruptcy? Also, how should the *forum arresti* deal with the assets that have been arrested by creditors in its jurisdiction? Should *the forum arresti* transfer its authority over the assets to the forum in which the bankruptcy proceeding has been brought by the debtor? Alternatively, should it retain the arrested assets and proceed to satisfy the claims of domestic creditors against the insolvent debtor? If *the forum arresti* adopts the Model Law, does the Model Law provide any solution to this issue? Should the Model Law be allowed to hurt or shake the regime of maritime lien, which is the most fundamental regime and the underlying basis of credit of the generally harmonised admiralty system?

The problem of maritime cross-border insolvency has risen to prominence in recent years with the global financial crisis and the current declining shipping market. The impact of 'the Great Recession' (2008–2011) on the shipping industry has been extremely severe. Due to the worldwide economic crisis, the demand for export and import is sharply declining. The declining trade and surplus shipping capacity lead to low freight rates and tight credit, resulting in negative cash flow and increased financial pressures. In order to raise funds, shipping companies may be forced to sell their vessels at a distress price far below their book values. Such a vicious circle leads to a stagnation of the shipping market, and finally distress as market pressures overwhelm inertia.[16] The whole shipping market has been impacted by the Great Recession, from the liner shipping market and the dry bulk shipping market to the tanker market.[17] Accordingly, cross-border insolvencies have become increasingly commonplace for many international shipping companies in recent years. Many shipping companies have been forced to seek reorganisation or other insolvency proceedings, trying to extricate themselves

[16] M Stopford, *Maritime Economics*, 3rd edn (Routledge, 2009) 98.

[17] See eg B Meenaksi, 'The Impacts of the Global Crisis 2008–2009 on Shipping Markets' (2009) World Maritime University Dissertations 212, available at commons.wmu.se/cgi/viewcontent.cgi?article=1211&context=all_dissertations, accessed 5 June 2020.

from financial difficulties. Prominent examples include Korea Line Corporation,[18] Sanko Steamship,[19] STX Pan Ocean,[20] and recently Hanjin Shipping.[21] As a result of all these issues, maritime cross-border insolvency has become a vitally important problem that urgently needs to be resolved.

The current declining shipping market shows the pressing need to address these issues at both the theoretical and practical levels. In theory, it is important for each country to balance the interests between an admiralty proceeding and an insolvency proceeding, and the interests between the insolvent shipping company and its creditors. Due to the sharply divergent policy objectives of bankruptcy law and admiralty law, these two legal branches choose different approaches to deal with insolvent shipowners and their creditors when shipowners encounter financial difficulties. In practice, the tensions and inconsistencies in the way in which maritime cross-border insolvency scenarios have been dealt with by the courts of different countries have given rise to significant debates and need to be addressed urgently. In order to promote international trade and the shipping market, both debtors and maritime (and indeed non-maritime) creditors need certainty and predictability. The conflicts arising from maritime cross-border insolvency cases, especially from the recent bankruptcy of Hanjin Shipping, illustrate the need for greater clarity and certainty for all involved parties.

The aim of this book is to examine three major problems arising when the application of the UNCITRAL Model Law regime involves maritime creditors and maritime assets at both a theoretical and practical level. In addition, the book endeavours to provide policy reflections on each problem in order to eliminate the ambiguity of the characteristics of maritime claims in cross-border insolvency cases, with an eye to enhancing the development of the shipping industry.

[18] Korea Line Corporation filed for a receivership in the Korean bankruptcy court in 2011. Korea Line used to be the second largest dry bulk shipping company in Korea. When Korea Line filed for bankruptcy, it operated about 140 vessels. See 'Updated 1-Korea Line says in court receivership' (Reuters, 15 February 2011), available at www.reuters.com/article/korealine-court/update-1-korea-line-says-in-court-receivership-idUSTOE71E03I20110215, accessed 5 June 2020.

[19] Sanko Steamship filed for bankruptcy in Japan in 2012. Sanko Steamship was one of the oldest shipping firms in Japan. Before it filed for bankruptcy, it managed a fleet of 185 ships, which included 46 tankers and 27 dry bulk carriers. See 'Japan's Sanko Steamship Declares Bankruptcy' (Maritime Executive, 18 December 2012), available at www.maritime-executive.com/article/japan-s-sanko-steamship-declares-bankruptcy#gs.7a9l8NY, accessed 5 June 2020.

[20] STX Pan Ocean filed for bankruptcy in Korea in 2013. STX Pan Ocean was the largest bulk shipping group in Korea and also the largest bulk shipping company in the world. When STX Pan Ocean filed for bankruptcy, it had more than 340 vessels, including 270 bulk carriers. See 'Valemax Operator STX Pan Ocean Applies for Court Receivership' (Maritime Executive, 7 June 2013), available at www.maritime-executive.com/article/Valemax-Operator-STX-Pan-Ocean-Applies-For-Court-Receivership-2013-06-07#gs.B=jiTjk, accessed 5 June 2020.

[21] Hanjin Shipping filed for rehabilitation proceeding in Korea in 2016, but the rehabilitation proceeding was later terminated. Hanjin then declared bankruptcy in February 2017. Hanjin was the largest container line in Korea and the seventh largest container shipping company in the world. It formerly operated 60 liners, approximately 140 vessels. See In-Soo Nam, 'Hanjin Shipping is Declared Bankruptcy', (Wall Street Journal, 16 February 2017), available at www.wsj.com/articles/hanjin-shipping-is-declared-bankrupt-1487296151, accessed 5 June 2020.

The first problem is the treatment of maritime creditors in insolvency proceedings. Under the regime of the Model Law, it is envisaged that all claims against the debtor and its assets – including maritime claims – should be suspended by an automatic stay, upon the recognition of a foreign main proceeding in the arresting country. This book will analyse the question whether maritime creditors can be exempted from the automatic stay mechanism granted by the Model Law; if not, should the Model Law provide an exception for maritime claims to proceed regardless of a foreign insolvency proceeding?

The second problem is how to determine the centre of main interest (COMI) of the debtor. COMI is a critically important new concept introduced by the Model Law, but the Model Law itself does not define it. The Model Law only provides a presumption that, absent proof to the contrary, the debtor's COMI is the state where the debtor's registered office or habitual residence is located. This book will analyse whether this presumption is consistent with the realities of maritime commercial practice and the shipping industry; and if not, to what extent the presumption can be rebutted.

The third problem is the scope of the debtor's assets. In order to reduce maintenance costs and meet the commercial need for fleet flexibility, it is common for shipping companies to charter vessels (demise, time or voyage charter) from third parties. This book will analyse whether chartered vessels should be regarded as the debtor's assets and therefore should be included into the asset pool and subjected to the automatic stay order under the Model Law regime. In addition, this book will also answer the question of whether the surety bond or security provided by a debtor or a third party for the release of vessel arrest is regarded as the property of the debtor.

This book begins by examining the most significant concepts of the cross-border insolvency regime (including the UNCITRAL Model Law regime) and the maritime law regime. This analysis explores the different policies underpinning these two regimes and demonstrate how the three problems mentioned above arise.

This chapter has introduced the historical development of the conflicts and tensions between bankruptcy law and maritime law, such as the conflicts of legislative purpose, the conflicts of underlying policies, the conflicts of jurisdictions and the conflicts of enforcement of security interests, etc. It has further explored the practical problems arising from these conflicts, and how these problems become more complex when a third factor, ie cross-border insolvency is involved. The chapter has also explained the urgency and necessity of solving these problems, and outlined the basic structure and methodology of this book.

Chapter 2 gives a brief policy review of the domestic bankruptcy proceeding. It illustrates the fundamental aims of bankruptcy or insolvency law – fresh start of the debtor, maximisation of the debtor's assets and equal treatment of creditors. In addition, the chapter differentiates the liquidation and reorganisation proceeding, which are the two most common bankruptcy proceedings. The scope and effect of the stay order for different insolvency proceedings are examined.

Finally, Chapter 2 highlights the distinction between secured creditors and unsecured creditors. Secured claims usually receive greater protection and higher priority in bankruptcy proceedings because of their interest in the security, as compared with unsecured claims. This difference leads to different analyses of the treatment of maritime creditors in later chapters.

Chapter 3 begins with a brief overview of the conflicting issues arising in the area of cross-border insolvencies. The chapter then discusses the different theories underpinning international insolvency law, including territorialism, universalism, co-operative territorialism, and modified universalism, and argues that the overarching key question remains the proper balance of the competing interests of local protection versus international co-operation. Finally, Chapter 3 concludes that the current trend is towards a collective and co-operative approach to addressing international insolvency. Although universalism is the future of international bankruptcy, this ultimate goal may take time to achieve. Thus, as an interim or transitional solution, modified universalism has currently emerged as the dominant theory.

Since the Model Law represents an attempt to impose a modified universalism approach, Chapter 4 provides an overview of the purpose and structure of the Model Law. The four principles of the Model Law are discussed in detail, namely: (1) access, which provides the foreign representatives with an easier access to the court in the enacting state where the recognition and relief are sought; (2) recognition, which simplifies the procedures for recognition of a foreign insolvency proceeding by a court in enacting state and brings certainty to the recognition process; (3) relief, which creates a stay mechanism upon the recognition of a foreign insolvency proceeding; and (4) co-operation and co-ordination, which place the burden on both courts and representatives in different jurisdictions to communicate and co-operate with their best efforts.

Chapter 5 begins with a policy review of maritime law, including the rationale of maritime liens and the uniformity of maritime rules. In addition, the chapter classifies maritime claims into three basic categories: maritime liens; statutory rights of action in rem; and ship mortgages. Chapter 5 then explores the secured status of each respective category. It is crucial to determine whether a maritime claim is a secured claim – when there is an interplay with bankruptcy, secured claims generally have a better chance of being exempted from the stay order granted by bankruptcy courts. The different approaches adopted by countries to address the issue of conflict of laws regarding the recognition of foreign maritime liens are examined. Because the scope and ranking of maritime liens differ from country to country, one issue that always arises for courts is whether to recognise a foreign maritime lien claim, and what the ranking of this foreign maritime lien claim should be compared with other domestic insolvency claims. Finally, Chapter 5 provides a brief introduction to the in rem action and personification doctrine. The in rem action is a special enforcement tool developed by admiralty law, where a person may bring an action in rem directly against the ship to enforce his maritime claim. This helps readers to understand the different enforcement procedures between maritime law and insolvency law. This is also an important argument for maritime creditors to relief from the automatic stay mechanism under the UNCITRAL Model Law regime.

Chapter 6 outlines the three major issues that may arise when the Model Law regime is applied to maritime creditors and maritime assets as mentioned above. The chapter also lists the major arguments that are brought forward by parties on each issue. It is pointed out that different countries may have different approaches to each issue, and accordingly links are made to the chapters that follow, which discuss in detail each selected country's position on these issues.

The next part of the book adopts a comparative approach, selecting four leading shipping countries that have adopted the UNCITRAL Model Law regime – namely, Australia, the United Kingdom (UK), the United States (US), and Singapore – and provides an in-depth analysis of how the four countries have respectively approached and attempted to resolve the above three problems when applying the UNCITRAL Model Law regime. The comparative studies show that decisions made by courts across the world are inconsistent due to the different bankruptcy procedures and admiralty regimes in different countries, and that there is currently no harmonised and feasible solution available to the problems generated by maritime cross-border insolvencies.

Chapter 7 analyses the Australian approach to the maritime cross-border insolvency practice under the Model Law regime, especially the three problems identified in Chapter 6. Australia adopts the Model Law in its entirety and is willing to promote harmonisation and co-operation on cross-border insolvency area. Recent decisions illustrate that the Australian courts will take the unique nature of admiralty into account and, in certain circumstances, are willing to narrow down the cross-border insolvency for a particular admiralty claimant to proceed with its claim despite the automatic stay protection provided by the Model Law. Chapter 7 concludes that, if the foreign proceeding is more like a winding-up proceeding, relief to proceed with in rem arrest is more likely to be granted than for an administration proceeding. The chapter also points out the uncertainties that remain in the Australian practice.

As a leading shipping jurisdiction and a typical common law jurisdiction, the legal position in the UK is of significant interest. Chapter 8 takes a close look at the application of the Model Law regime to admiralty claimants in the UK. In a winding-up proceeding, courts in the UK are willing to narrow down the cross-border insolvency for secured admiralty claims. However, in an administration proceeding, courts still prefer to grant a broad order to stay all the proceedings upon the recognition. The chapter analyses the possible position held by the UK courts regarding the three problems identified in Chapter 6. Finally, the chapter points out the uncertainties that remain in the UK's practice.

Chapter 9 provides a comprehensive analysis of the US approach to how maritime claims are harmonised with the UNCITRAL Model Law regime. The US adopted the Model Law as Chapter 15 of the US Bankruptcy Code. The US is a major shipping jurisdiction, and is in favour of the universalist approach. It encourages the protection of debtors' global rehabilitation and champions the interests of creditors as a whole. Although in some cases the courts do consider the interest of maritime lienholders, US courts are more inclined to interpret Chapter 15 of the Bankruptcy Code in a universalist way to avoid the piecemeal seizure and distribution of assets by individual nations. Chapter 9 analyses whether the personification argument is upheld by the US courts in cross-border insolvency cases, and how to determine the scope of debtor's asset under the Model Law regime.

Chapter 10 reviews Singapore's application of maritime practice in cross-border insolvency to afford shipowners and creditors with more predictability within the Asia Pacific region. Singapore adopted the UNCITRAL Model Law into its Companies Act in 2017 to achieve the goal of becoming an international hub for debt restructuring. Chapter 10 examines the considerations taken into account by Singapore's Ministry of Law when adopting the Model Law, and analyses the influence of Singapore's approach to maritime cross-border insolvency practice after the Model Law was adopted.

Finally, based on the previous analysis, this book provides detailed policy reflections on the three problems. Chapter 11 begins by comparing the current status of treatment of maritime creditors in cross-border insolvency cases. Due to the different bankruptcy procedures and admiralty regimes adopted in different countries, decisions made by courts across the world are inconsistent. It illustrates that there is currently no clear and settled solution to the problem. Chapter 11, therefore, proposes policy reflections on the treatment of maritime creditors under the Model Law regime. Chapter 11 argues that a maritime lien holder should be allowed to proceed with its enforcement action regardless of any pending or subsequent insolvency proceeding, whereas a statutory right of action in rem, or a ship mortgage, should not always prevail over an insolvency proceeding but be analysed on a case-by-case basis. Moreover, with regard to the conflict-of-laws issue that may occur in the forum in which the foreign main proceeding has been brought under the Model Law (FMP court), Chapter 11 suggests that the *lex fori* rule is a more appropriate and pragmatic rule for the purpose of the FMP court's recognition of lien status and distribution.

Chapter 12 discusses the current status of the determination of the COMI and suggests that the registered office or habitual residence may not always be the appropriate location of the COMI of the debtors. Especially for offshore shipping companies, courts should pay more attention to the factors that are ascertainable to third parties. In addition, the chapter reviews the current status of the determination of the debtor's asset scope and suggests that courts should look into the economic substance of the bareboat charterparty to decide whether to recharacterise a lease into a security interest, while time or voyage chartered vessels are clearly not assets of the insolvent debtor. Finally, Chapter 12 also suggests that bank guarantees or LOUs are not regarded as assets of debtors and can satisfy specific claims that are undertaken by bank guarantees or LOUs outside bankruptcy proceedings.

2

Bankruptcy Law: Fundamental Aims and Relevant Prominent Principles

Bankruptcy law is essential to support a modern, competition-based economic model. A business lacking in efficiency must make structural changes, restructure its debts or exit the market in an orderly fashion.[1] 'A transparent and solid insolvency system gives both local and foreign investors confidence in the rules governing economic development, including those that generally safeguard investments'.[2]

Due to each country's unique domestic social values and economic policies regarding financial matters, bankruptcy law varies widely in different countries. Countries need to consider various factors when enacting their bankruptcy laws, such as political and economic systems, social policy, legal culture and historical tradition, etc.[3] Therefore, the bankruptcy law of each country differs significantly not only in terms of abstract notions – such as legislative intention or value orientation – but also in the specific provisions of insolvency proceedings, such as the order of distribution, the rule of priority, and the treatment of secured creditors.[4] Nevertheless, notwithstanding the aforementioned differences, most Anglo-common law countries share similar fundamental principles of the law of insolvency. The following sections will introduce the fundamental aims and relevant prominent principles of the regime of insolvency.

I. Fundamental Aims of the Law of Insolvency

A. Fresh Start

In the realm of consumer bankruptcy, the most basic and fundamental underlying theory of bankruptcy law is to provide an 'honest but unfortunate' debtor with a

[1] B Wessels et al, *International Cooperation in Bankruptcy and Insolvency Matters* (Oxford University Press, 2009) 1.

[2] ibid.

[3] See eg J Pottow, 'Greed and Pride in International Bankruptcy: The Problems of and Proposed Solutions to Local Interests' (2006) 104 *Michigan Law Review* 1899, 1910; N Martin, 'The Role of History and Culture in Developing Bankruptcy and Insolvency Systems: The Perils of Legal Transplantation' (2005) 28 *Boston College International and Comparative Law Review* 1, 4; E Warren, 'Bankruptcy Policymaking in an Imperfect World' (1993) 92 *Michigan Law Review* 336.

[4] See generally J Silkenat and C Schmerler, *The Law of International Insolvencies and Debt Restructurings* (Oceana TM, 2006).

financial 'fresh start'.[5] Bankruptcy law allows an 'honest but unfortunate' debtor to be released from their accumulated debts after their existing non-exempt assets are distributed or a portion of their future earnings has been surrendered, even if their debts have not been fully paid.[6] Creditors are prohibited from collecting the debts that have already been discharged.[7]

In economic terms, the non-waivable right of discharge of individual debtors can be justified by contractual notions of risk allocation and cost minimisation, in the sense that 'discharge shifts the costs of overextending credit from debtors to creditors, who are in a better position to minimise those costs'.[8] In addition, the non-waivable right of discharge and the accompanying effects on the flow of credit can be justified by the presence of a wide array of other social insurance programmes, such as unemployment insurance, health insurance, and social security.[9] From the perspective of morality, the justification behind the policy of a fresh start is to forgive an insolvent debtor and release it from its past obligations without it being punished for outstanding debts. Consequently, the debtor may regain the motivation to engage in economically productive activities, knowing that it will be able to retain the fruits of its efforts, and may have a second chance of financial success.[10] As a result, the concept of the 'fresh start' has been embodied in the law of bankruptcy and is essential to modern bankruptcy law.[11]

B. Maximisation of Asset Value for All Creditors

In the realm of corporate bankruptcy, the major aim of the law of bankruptcy is to maximise the value of the assets of the debtor. An insolvent debtor may have limited assets that are only able to fully satisfy part of its creditors' claims. Therefore, the

[5] *Local Loan Co v Hunt* 292 US 234 (1934); see eg C Hallinan, 'The Fresh Start Policy in Consumer Bankruptcy: A Historical Inventory and an Interpretative Theory' (1986) 21 *University of Richmond Law Review* 49; J King, 'Moving Beyond the Hard–Easy Tug of War: A Historical, Empirical and Theoretical Assessment of Bankruptcy Discharge' (2004) 28 *Melbourne University Law Review* 654; B Adler et al, 'Regulating Consumer Bankruptcy: A Theoretical Inquiry' (2000) 29 *Journal of Legal Studies* 585.

[6] T Sullivan et al, *As We Forgive Our Debtors: Bankruptcy and Consumer Credit in America* (Oxford University Press, 1989) Ch 18; T Jackson, *The Logic and Limits of Bankruptcy Law* (Harvard University Press, 1986) Ch 10. Non-exempt assets include any property of debtors that can be sold by trustees or bankruptcy courts in order to pay off the claims of creditors. Exempt assets, however, can be kept by debtors and are exempted from bankruptcy estates. Exempt assets usually include pensions, household appliances, damages awarded for personal injury etc. See eg 11 USC § 522.

[7] See eg 11 USC § 524; Insolvency Act 1986, s 251I.

[8] T Jackson, 'The Fresh-Start Policy in Bankruptcy Law' (1985) 98 *Harvard Law Review* 1393, 1398; see also Jackson, *The Logic and Limits of Bankruptcy Law* (n 6) 228–29; T Eisenberg, 'Bankruptcy Law in Perspective' (1981) 28 *UCLA Law Review* 953, 976–91.

[9] Jackson, 'The Fresh-Start Policy in Bankruptcy Law' (n 8) 1398–99.

[10] E Warren et al, *The Law of Debtors and Creditors* (Wolters Kluwer, 2014) 306; see also H Hurd, 'The Virtue of Consumer Bankruptcy' in R Brubaker et al (eds), *A Debtor's World: Interdisciplinary Perspectives on Debt* (Oxford University Press, 2012) 221–22; K Gross, *Failure and Forgiveness: Rebalancing the Bankruptcy System* (Yale University Press, 1999) 91.

[11] See eg Hallinan (n 5).

law of insolvency seeks to provide an orderly procedure to collect and maximise the value of the assets of the debtor. Following this procedure ensures that creditors achieve the maximum benefit in the distribution of the assets of the debtor.[12]

When an insolvent debtor holds valuable assets its creditors may race to the courthouse to collect its remaining assets, resulting in piecemeal individualistic actions. It has been argued that a collective proceeding to distribute assets in an orderly manner ensures more value-preservation than a chaotic process of seizure and sale by a large number of competing creditors.[13] A collective bankruptcy proceeding tends to reduce the strategic costs that would otherwise be associated with a race to the courthouse; it also increases the aggregate pool of assets that are available to all creditors.[14] In addition, a collective proceeding can preserve the 'going concern' value of a company and increase the efficiency of the administration procedures. Therefore, the law of insolvency has long established a strategy: all for one and one for all.[15] Specifically, the law of insolvency provides the mechanism of a 'common pool' of debtor's assets, from which creditors can expect to obtain the maximum return on their claims both collectively and cooperatively. Accordingly, in order to avoid diminishing or destroying the value of a debtor's 'common pool', bankruptcy usually takes into account the overall interests of all creditors and is reluctant to allow individual creditors to take foreclosure action outside the bankruptcy proceeding.[16]

C. Equal Treatment of Equivalent Creditors

The third aim of bankruptcy law is to treat creditors in similar situations equally. Bankruptcy law ensures 'equal treatment of creditors of the same claims', for the purpose of predictability and fairness.[17] In the case of liquidation proceedings, all creditors in the same class should receive the same proportionate distribution of the value that is available to that class; this means that the distribution among creditors is based on the objective characteristics of the claim rather than on personal favouritism or some other subjective criteria.[18] In the case of rehabilitation proceedings, creditors in the same class will receive equal treatment under a reorganisation plan.[19] In addition, in order to fulfil the aim of 'equal treatment', the law of insolvency empowers a single court to adjudicate all claims against the

[12] Warren et al (n 10) 7.
[13] T Jackson, 'Bankruptcy, Nonbankruptcy Entitlements, and the Creditors' Bargain' (1982) 91 *Yale Law Journal* 857, 862.
[14] ibid.
[15] Wessels et al (n 1) 14.
[16] ibid.
[17] See E Warren, 'A Principled Approach to Consumer Bankruptcy' (1997) 71 *American Bankruptcy Law Journal* 483, 483.
[18] ibid.
[19] See generally Silkenat and Schmerler (n 4).

debtor and the assets of the debtor. In other words, upon the commencement of an insolvency proceeding in a bankruptcy court, the court generally shall have jurisdiction over all claims by creditors against the debtor and the debtor's assets.[20] Nevertheless, due to their social concerns and economic policies, different jurisdictions have granted different rules of priority in the treatment of claims. It has been argued that the difference in the ranking of claims is probably the 'most fundamental difference in "prominent principles of domestic law"'.[21]

II. Liquidation and Reorganisation

Generally, despite the variety of social and economic policies embodied in the law of insolvency of various countries, the regime of insolvency in most Anglo-common law countries resolves the relationship between debtors and creditors through two processes: US-Chapter 7-like liquidation and US-Chapter 11-like reorganisation proceedings.[22] Generally, liquidation provides an orderly and efficient approach to terminating an unsuccessful business, whereas reorganisation encourages the development of the business, securing a socially desirable outcome for both debtors and creditors, and offering the hope of saving employment. (Hereinafter the proceedings of the same nature as US-Chapter 7 and Chapter-11 proceedings will be collectively referred to as liquidation or reorganisation respectively.)

A liquidation proceeding is a process by which a company is ultimately terminated. Upon the commencement of a liquidation proceeding, the company ceases to carry on its business and its assets are collected and realised for the purpose of distribution among creditors.[23] After the distribution, the company discharges its liabilities and ceases to exist. A reorganisation proceeding, however, unlike a liquidation proceeding where the debtor's business ceases immediately upon the commencement of the proceeding and the debtor's assets are sold piecemeal to realise the claims of creditors, allows the debtor to keep its assets and continue in operation while paying creditors over an extended period of time, and reducing the total amount of debt to be paid.[24] A reorganisation proceeding provides a financially distressed corporation with time to rehabilitate its business and gives it the possibility of surviving as a going concern. Upon the commencement of a

[20] Warren et al (n 10) 862–63; J Westbrook et al, *A Global View of Business Insolvency Systems* (Martinus Nijhoff, 2010) 7.

[21] Wessels et al (n 1) 17.

[22] Different countries provide different names for the proceedings of the same nature. For example, a US-Chapter 7-like liquidation proceeding is called a winding-up proceeding in the UK, Australia and Singapore. A US-Chapter 11-like reorganisation proceeding is called an administration proceeding in UK and Australia, a judicial management proceeding in Singapore or a rehabilitation proceeding in Korea.

[23] Westbrook et al (n 20) 75–76.

[24] ibid 76–77.

reorganisation proceeding, following a stay order that suspends all the actions of any creditors, the administrator of the debtor will negotiate with its major creditors and propose a plan of reorganisation, in which it will promise to pay creditors a certain percentage of their claims over a stated period of time. The plan of reorganisation will then be subject to the approval of the various classes of creditors as well as the confirmation of the court. Upon the confirmation of the plan of reorganisation, the debtor will be discharged from all its pre-petition debts, except as provided in the plan, in the sense that the business debtor obtains a 'fresh start' through the reorganisation.[25]

III. Stay of Proceedings

A stay order on the actions of creditors (also known as a moratorium) can be found in most insolvency systems across the world and is essential in order for there to be an orderly liquidation and successful rehabilitation.[26]

An efficient insolvency proceeding mandates that creditors must be suspended from enforcing their claims against the debtor and its property during the insolvency proceeding unless they obtain the consent of the debtor or the approval of the court.[27] Nevertheless, as discussed below, some jurisdictions allow secured creditors and certain parties to proceed with their claims regardless of the stay order.[28] The regime of the stay order is designed for the purpose of achieving the underlying aims of bankruptcy law, namely a 'fresh start', maximisation of the debtor's assets, and the equal treatment of creditors. This regime is said to be for the benefit of both the debtor and its creditors.[29]

The virtue of a 'fresh start' would be impossible to achieve if actions against the debtor based on pre-existing debt were allowed to proceed during or after his insolvency case. The stay essentially serves as an injunction, freezing the status quo of the claims of creditors, and enables the insolvency court to have sufficient time to ascertain the situation of the debtor and adjudicate a resolution for the insolvent debtor and all creditors.[30] In addition, especially in a reorganisation proceeding, the stay provides the insolvent debtor with 'breathing space' in order to formulate and implement a recovery or restructuring plan to rehabilitate itself as a going concern.

In addition, the stay order preserves the maximum value of the assets of the debtor and ensures the availability of equal distribution to creditors. The stay

[25] Warren et al (n 10) 336.

[26] J Westbrook, 'Developments in Transnational Bankruptcy' (1995) 39 *St Louis University Law Journal* 745, 746.

[27] Westbrook et al (n 20) 69.

[28] See eg Corporations Act 2001 (Cth), ss 471B, 471C.

[29] Jackson, *The Logic and Limits of Bankruptcy Law* (n 6) 10–13.

[30] Westbrook et al (n 20) 69.

order prevents aggressive creditors from diminishing the asset pool with individual enforcement action before, or even after, the commencement of insolvency proceedings.[31] Furthermore, instead of a chaotic race to the courthouse, staying the individual enforcement actions of creditors ensures an orderly and efficient proceeding of liquidation or reorganisation; in the meantime the stay order protects the creditors from one another.[32]

The extent, scope, duration and even severity of the regime of stay orders differ between jurisdictions. Some countries grant a broad and strong stay order. For example, in the US, the stay order arises automatically upon the filing of an insolvency proceeding, whether the debtor has petitioned for liquidation or reorganisation.[33] This automatic stay applies to a wide array of litigation including: the commencement or continuation of proceedings; the enforcement of pre-petition judgments; acts to obtain possession or exercise control over property of the estate or of the debtor; the creation, perfecting or enforcement of a lien; the recovery of claims etc.[34] A US stay order is broad in the sense that it freezes any enforcement action by either secured or unsecured creditors.

Conversely, some countries have relatively narrow stay orders. The stay order is not automatic and may only come into effect by the application of the parties or at the discretion of the court.[35] In addition, the stay order may only extend to unsecured creditors, and secured creditors will not be affected by it.[36] In the UK, for example, an automatic stay will be imposed against creditors in the case of a compulsory winding-up proceeding,[37] but there is no automatic stay on proceedings against the debtor upon the commencement of a voluntary winding-up proceeding.[38] In addition, a UK compulsory winding-up stay order only has an effect on unsecured creditors, whilst secured creditors – generally – are not subject to the stay.[39]

IV. Secured Creditors and Unsecured Creditors

Generally, the law of insolvency categorises creditors into one of two classes – secured and unsecured creditors. A secured creditor is one who has a security interest or lien in the property of a debtor, in the sense that the creditor can recover

[31] Wessels et al (n 1) 31.
[32] Jackson, *The Logic and Limits of Bankruptcy Law* (n 6).
[33] 11 USC § 362.
[34] 11 USC § 362(a).
[35] See eg Insolvency Act 1986, Pt IV, Ch 5; ss 112(1), (2), 183(1), (2)(a).
[36] See Silkenat and Schmerler (n 4) 228, 259, 370, 397.
[37] See eg Insolvency Act 1986, ss 127, 128(1), 130.
[38] Insolvency Act 1986, Pt IV, Ch 5; ss 112(1), (2), 183(1), (2)(a).
[39] Insolvency Act 1986, s 130(2); *The Constellation* [1965] 2 Lloyd's Rep 538; *Re Rio Grande do Sol Steamship Co* (1877) 5 Ch D 282; *Re Aro Co Ltd* [1980] 1 All ER 1067.

the repayment of its claim against the collateral if the debtor is in default.[40] A security interest or a lien can be created either by contract or by the operation of law. An unsecured creditor, however, is a creditor who does not have such an interest in the property of a debtor in order to secure repayment of its claim.

Under the law of insolvency, a secured claim usually receives greater protection and higher priority than an unsecured claim, due to its security interest in the collateral.[41] The court will generally satisfy a secured claim before an unsecured claim.[42] Nevertheless, each jurisdiction has somewhat different standards to determine what constitutes a security interest and how a creditor can properly obtain a security interest. Moreover, the treatment of secured creditors in an insolvency proceeding varies between different jurisdictions. In some jurisdictions, such as the UK, Australia and Singapore, secured creditors are unaffected by the subsequent liquidation proceedings. They are allowed to foreclose on their collateral as they see fit, outside of the bankruptcy proceeding, and to also recover their debts from the proceeds.[43] However, in other jurisdictions, such as the US, secured creditors are stayed from taking action against the debtor or its property.[44]

[40] See eg Insolvency Act 1986, s 248(a), which defines 'secured creditor', in relation to a company, as 'a creditor of the company who holds in respect of his debt a security over property of the company'; Art 2 of Bankruptcy and Insolvency Act of Canada, which defines 'secured creditor' as 'a person holding a mortgage, hypotec, pledge, charge, lien or privilege on or against the property of the debtor …'; Art 9–102(73) of the Uniform Commercial Code of the United States (UCC), which defines 'secured party' as 'a person in whose favo[u]r a security interest is created or provided for under a security agreement, whether or not any obligation to be secured is outstanding'.

[41] See eg A Schwartz, 'A Theory of Loan Priorities' (1989) 18 *Journal of Legal Studies* 209; L Bebchuk and J Fried, 'The Uneasy Case for the Priority of Secured Claims in Bankruptcy' (1996) 105 *Yale Law Journal* 857; R Mann, 'Explaining the Pattern of Secured Credit' (1997) 110 *Harvard Law Review* 625.

[42] Westbrook et al (n 20) 71.

[43] See Insolvency Act 1986, ss 183(1), (3)(a); Corporations Act 2001 (Cth) ss 471B, 471C; Companies Act (Singapore), ss 262(3), 299(2).

[44] See 11 USC § 362.

3

Cross-Border Insolvency: Theoretical Divergence and Its Status Quo

I. The Problem with Cross-Border Insolvency

As companies become more multinational in their capital structures and operations, the system of insolvency also faces the challenging issue of cross-border insolvency. A case involving the issue of cross-border insolvency can generally be described as an insolvency proceeding in which the debtor has either assets or creditors (or both) in more than one country.[1] As discussed in Chapter 2, each country has framed its insolvency law in response to its particular economic environment, social policy and legal culture, reflecting the balance between creditor and debtor protection.[2] Notwithstanding that the insolvency laws of various countries share similar prominent principles as discussed in Chapter 2, the specific procedures and rules that have been implemented according to those principles are quite different. Therefore, the treatment of certain types of creditors or particular claims may be diverse due to the dissimilar insolvency procedures and rules of different countries.[3] When a multinational company files for an insolvency proceeding it gives rise to a problem of cross-border insolvency with regard to how to resolve the conflicting claims of the creditors from different countries, as well as the interaction of the conflicting laws of insolvency in different jurisdictions. The threshold problems for the bankruptcy court in each country are: (1) which country's court has jurisdiction over the administration of an international insolvency proceeding? (2) which country's substantive insolvency law applies to the international insolvency proceeding? and (3) whether the country should recognise an insolvency-related judgment if rendered by a foreign court and, if so, to what

[1] S Story, 'Cross-Border Insolvency: A Comparative Analysis' (2015) 32 *Arizona Journal of International & Comparative Law* 431, 432–33; see also UNCITRAL Secretariat, *UNCITRAL Cross-Border Insolvency Law with Guide to Enactment and Interpretation* (United Nations Office at Vienna, 2014) 19.

[2] S Gopalan and M Guihot, 'Recognition and Enforcement in Cross-Border Insolvency Law: A Proposal for Judicial Gap-Filling' (2015) 48 *Vanderbilt Journal of Transnational Law* 1225, 1227; M Dean, 'International Insolvencies: The Difficulties, The Traditional Solution and The Ideal' (2001) 9 *Insolvency Law Journal* 88, 88.

[3] B Wessels et al, *International Cooperation in Bankruptcy and Insolvency Matters* (Oxford University Press, 2009) 17.

extent the effects of this foreign insolvency proceeding should be extended to the assets located in the jurisdiction that recognises the foreign insolvency judgment.[4]

In addition to the problems of the appropriate choice of law, choice of forum and recognition of foreign insolvency proceedings, additional concerns in an international insolvency proceeding include: (1) whether different courts will treat the same type of creditors fairly and equally; (2) whether the distribution of the assets of the debtor will be delayed due to its characteristic of being scattered worldwide; and (3) whether the sovereignty of a country and a diverse array of national public policies would be infringed by a single international insolvency proceeding, etc.[5]

Two traditional theories have emerged regarding the implementation of a cross-border insolvency case: territorialism and universalism, which then generated their modified versions, co-operative territorialism and modified universalism respectively.[6] In the absence of a framework of substantive international insolvency law, the focus of international bankruptcy jurisprudence has long been on the issues regarding choice of law, choice of forum and the recognition of a foreign insolvency proceeding. Nevertheless, 'the overarching key question consistently boils down to the proper balance of the competing interests of local protection versus international co-operation'.[7] This chapter examines the different theories underpinning international insolvency law and argues that the overarching key question remains the proper balance that can be obtained with regard to the competing interests of local protection versus international co-operation.

II. Theoretical Divergence

A. Traditional Exposition: Territorialism and Universalism

Traditionally, most countries adopted a 'grab rule' approach: collecting the assets that were physically or constructively located within its territory and distributing them to local claimants according to the local rules of insolvency, with little or no

[4] J Westbrook, 'Theory and Pragmatism in Global Insolvencies: Choice of Law and Choice of Forum' (1991) 65 *American Bankruptcy Law Journal* 457, 459; H Buxbaum, 'Rethinking International Insolvency: The Neglected Role of Choice of Law Rules and Theory' (2000) 36 *Stanford Journal of International Law* 23, 30; S Franken, 'Cross-Border Insolvency Law: A Comparative Institutional Analysis' (2013) *Oxford Journal of Legal Studies* 97, 102.

[5] Gopalan and Guihot (n 2) 1227–28.

[6] E Adams and J Fincke, 'Co-ordinating Cross-Border Bankruptcy: How Territorialism Saves Universalism' (2009) 15 *Columbia Journal of European Law* 43, 47. A third alternative approach has been advocated – corporate-charter contractualism, which proposes a system that allows the debtor to specify in its corporate charter the country or countries that would administer its bankruptcy. This theory is not as influential as the other two theories, so it will not be discussed in detail in this book. See R Rasmussen, 'A New Approach to Transactional Insolvencies' (1997) 19 *Michigan Journal of International Law* 1.

[7] Wessels et al (n 3) 40.

regard for the insolvency of a multinational company as a whole.[8] This is because the law of insolvency has been one of the 'most parochial and nationalistic areas of the law' since it is seen as the last chance to recover value from a financially failed business.[9] However, given the inherently collective, compromising and value-maximising nature of the law of insolvency, in the late twentieth century the trend gradually moved towards a universalist approach in order to address international insolvency cases on a worldwide basis.[10]

i. *Territorialism: The 'Grab Rule'*

Territorialism envisages that each country has jurisdiction over the administration of all assets that are located within its territory for the benefit of its local creditors, and distributes these assets according to its local rules of priority.[11] In other words, each country will open an insolvency proceeding and apply its own substantive insolvency law to the administration of the debtor's assets located in its jurisdiction. The local insolvency proceeding has no extraterritorial effect. Creditors must file their claims in each country in which an insolvency proceeding is open. As a result, the insolvency law of each country governs the substantive and procedural rules with regard to the administration and distribution among local creditors.[12]

The approach of territorialism is based upon the concerns of national sovereignty and local public policy.[13] The theoretical underpinning for the approach of territorialism is derived from the notion of sovereignty, by definition of which a country has the ability to exercise its power to dominate a territory, including the assets of an insolvent debtor, located in its territory.[14] Territoriality allows the local country to effectuate its rules of priority and economic policies to the maximum extent of its sovereignty.[15] In addition, territorialism can be justified by the legitimate expectations of local creditors in the sense that any financial crisis should be

[8] E Warren et al, *The Law of Debtors and Creditors: Text, Cases, and Problems*, 7th edn (Wolters Kluwer, 2014) 885; Wessels et al (n 3) 40.

[9] Warren et al (n 8) 885.

[10] See eg Warren et al (n 8) 885; L Clark and K Goldstein, 'Sacred Cows: How to Care for Secured Creditors' Rights in Cross-Border Bankruptcies' (2011) 46 *Texas International Law Journal* 513; American Law Institute, *Transactional Insolvency: Co-operation Among the NAFTA Countries, Principles of Cooperation Among the NAFTA Countries* (Juris Publishing, 2003) 18; A Walters, 'Modified Universalisms and the Role of Local Legal Culture in the Making of Cross-Border Insolvency Law' (2019) 93 *American Bankruptcy Law Journal* 47.

[11] L LoPucki, 'Co-operation in International Bankruptcy: A Post-Universalist Perspective' (1999) 84 *Cornell Law Review* 696; L LoPucki, 'Universalism Unravels' (2005) 79 *American Bankruptcy Law Journal* 143; Adams and Fincke (n 6) 47; T Kraft and A Aranson, 'Transnational Bankruptcies: Section 304 and Beyond' (1993) *Columbia Business Law Review* 329.

[12] Adams and Fincke (n 6) 55.

[13] See eg Adams and Fincke (n 6) 55; Buxbaum (n 4).

[14] LoPucki, 'Co-operation in International Bankruptcy' (n 11) 760; Wessels et al (n 3) 43.

[15] LoPucki, 'Co-operation in International Bankruptcy' (n 11) 760.

resolved by the application of local policies and priorities, for example the expectation of an employee to have its claim realised before other unsecured and secured claims. It has been argued that these legitimate expectations that give rise to vested local rights should be respected and protected.[16] Furthermore, the approach of territorialism can provide predictability on the ground that the distribution of a debtor's assets will depend upon the insolvency law of the country in which its assets are located at the time that the insolvency proceeding is filed. Thus, it is easy for local creditors to predict the way in which they will be treated in a local insolvency proceeding.[17] Finally, the approach of territorialism offers transactional simplicity on the ground that no choice-of-law rule in favour of foreign insolvency laws is contained in the country's cross-border insolvency rules; this ensures that the domestic insolvency law will apply to assets located in the jurisdiction of that country.[18]

Nevertheless, the 'grab rule' has its weaknesses. First, the approach of territorialism will lead to a piecemeal disposition of the assets of the debtor and an unco-ordinated territory-based distribution of value to local creditors; this may give rise to concerns regarding inefficiency.[19] An international debtor may need to file for bankruptcy relief in each country where it has assets or creditors, incurring duplicative administrative expenses. Second, piecemeal territorial asset disposition may diminish the overall value of the assets of a debtor, which may reduce the possibility of a successful reorganisation of a multinational business.[20] The purpose of each unco-ordinated local proceeding is to maximise the return of value for local creditors; therefore local administrators are reluctant to hand over local assets for ongoing international operations, instead being inclined to collect local assets and distribute the assets according to their local procedures and priorities.[21] Third, the territorial treatment of creditors' claims will raise concerns regarding fairness, as similarly situated creditors should be treated equally, regardless of their location.[22] Thus, the approach of territorialism has been criticised for its national chauvinism and overt discrimination against foreign creditors.[23]

[16] LoPucki, 'Co-operation in International Bankruptcy' (n 11) 709–13; F Tung, 'Is International Bankruptcy Possible?' (2001) 23 *Michigan Journal of International Law* 31; I Fletcher, *Insolvency in Private International Law*, 2nd edn (Oxford University Press, 2007) 12.

[17] LoPucki, 'Co-operation in International Bankruptcy' (n 11) 751; Buxbaum (n 4) 26.

[18] LoPucki, 'Co-operation in International Bankruptcy' (n 11) 751–52; Franken (n 4) 103.

[19] Tung (n 16) 34; E Biery et al, 'A Look at Transnational Insolvencies and Chapter 15 of the Bankruptcy Abuse Prevention and Consumer Protection Act of 2005' (2005) 47 *Boston College Law Review* 23, 26.

[20] JL Westbrook, 'Multinational Enterprises in General Default: Chapter 15, the ALI Principles, and the EU Insolvency Regulation' (2002) 76 *American Bankruptcy Law Journal* 1, 8.

[21] ibid.

[22] Biery et al (n 19) 26.

[23] G McCormack, 'Universalism in Insolvency Proceedings and the Common Law' (2012) 32 *Oxford Journal of Legal Studies* 325, 328.

ii. Universalism

In contrast to territorialism, universalism advocates that all the assets of a debtor and claims against the debtor should be administrated in a single forum – the 'main' insolvency proceeding, where the appropriate court has full jurisdiction over all the assets of the debtor wherever located and can make distributions to creditors under the law of that forum.[24]

This system promotes a co-operative and centralised administration of the debtor's assets in one single insolvency proceeding. Under the approach of universalism, the insolvency proceeding is required to be commenced in the debtor's 'home country', arguably the location of the debtor's registered office or principal place of business.[25] The fundamental principle of universalism is 'one law, one court'.[26] Ideally, all assets of the debtor and claims against it, wherever located or initiated, would be transferred to the main insolvency proceeding, and would be administered or adjudicated under a single insolvency framework.[27] It has been envisaged that the main insolvency proceeding should have extraterritorial effect, in the sense that it can reach all of the debtor's assets and claimants worldwide, displacing the local insolvency law of other countries to the extent necessary to achieve the aim of a 'unified' administration of an international insolvency proceeding.[28]

The claimed advantage of universalism is that it promotes the efficiency of a cross-border insolvency proceeding. By avoiding piecemeal dispositions and requiring a single proceeding it will increase the selling price of a multinational company and avoid the costs of multiple concurrent proceedings, thus maximising the value of the assets of the debtor and ensuring the maximum return to creditors.[29] In addition, by controlling and administering the assets of the debtor in a single court, it increases the possibility of a successful reorganisation proceeding and preserves the going concern value of the debtor.[30] Further, it ensures a fair distribution among creditors that are in a similar situation, wherever located, by subjecting them to the same insolvency regime and according to the same rules of distribution.[31] Finally, the approach of universalism also claims that it can provide predictability ex ante to creditors, in the sense that home-country law is the one

[24] Buxbaum (n 4) 26; Adams and Fincke (n 6) 48; S Bufford, 'Global Venue Controls Are Coming: A Reply to Professor Lopucki' (2005) 79 *American Bankruptcy Law Journal* 105, 108; A Guzman, 'International Bankruptcy: In Defense of Universalism' (2000) 98 *Michigan Law Review* 2177, 2179; see also eg Westbrook, 'Theory and Pragmatism in Global Insolvencies' (n 4) 461.

[25] See Adams and Fincke (n 6) 48; JL Westbrook, 'A Global Solution to Multinational Default' (2000) 98 *Michigan Law Review* 2276, 2316.

[26] Tung (n 16) 40.

[27] Biery et al (n 19) 29.

[28] Westbrook, 'Theory and Pragmatism in Global Insolvencies' (n 4) 468; Guzman (n 24) 2184.

[29] Adams and Fincke (n 6) 49.

[30] Westbrook, 'A Global Solution to Multinational Default' (n 25) 2285.

[31] Buxbaum (n 4); U Drobnig, 'Secured Credit in International Insolvency Proceedings' (1998) 22 *Texas International Law Journal* 53, 66.

law that can be 'most reliably predicted in advance', lowering the costs of credit and facilitating economic activities.[32]

However, the approach of universalism has been criticised due to the indeterminacy of the standard of the 'home country'; this is due to multinational companies not having home countries in any meaningful sense, especially in the case of corporate groups.[33] In addition, the 'home country' standard is vulnerable to strategic manipulation and will promote eve-of-bankruptcy forum shopping as well as jurisdictional competition.[34] Furthermore, in order for universalism to work effectively, it requires that the ancillary forum transfer their authority over the asset that is located within their jurisdiction, or the enforcement of claims of creditors rendered, to the forum where the main insolvency proceeding is initiated.[35] As a result, it would seem that the ultimate goal of universalism appears difficult to achieve; this is due to countries being unwilling to relinquish their preferred distributional implication of their own insolvency law.[36]

B. New Pragmatism

As stated above, neither pure territorialism nor pure universalism can handle the complicated situation of cross-border insolvency in practice. In fact, 'in practice, no country applies either the universality principle or the territoriality principle without any deviation. Every domestic insolvency law is a mixture of those two principles'.[37] Therefore, in aiming to find a flexible and practical method, territorialism and universalism began to modify and amend their own theories, forming two new theories known as 'new pragmatism': co-operative territorialism and modified universalism. Treating universalism and territorialism as two ends of a spectrum, co-operative territorialism begins with the idea of pure territorialism and then moves towards the centre of the spectrum by incorporating certain aspects of universalism. Conversely, modified universalism starts from the other end of the spectrum with the idea of pure universalism, and thereafter incorporates certain territorialism tendencies, albeit in a purely discretionary manner.[38]

[32] Westbrook, 'Theory and Pragmatism in Global Insolvencies' (n 4) 469; Guzman (n 24) 2198; see also L Bebchuk and A Guzman, 'An Economic Analysis of Transactional Bankruptcy' (1999) 42 *The Journal of Law & Economics* 775.

[33] LoPucki, 'Co-operation in International Bankruptcy' (n 11) 713–17.

[34] LoPucki, 'Universalism Unravels' (n 11) 193; Biery et al (n 19) 29.

[35] Tung (n 16) 51.

[36] See LoPucki, 'Universalism Unravels' (n 11); Tung (n 16) 45; Franken (n 4) 109.

[37] A Berends, 'The UNCITRAL Model Law on Cross-Border Insolvency: A Comprehensive Overview' (1998) 6 *Tulane Journal of International and Comparative Law* 309, 314.

[38] Clark and Goldstein (n 10) 518–19.

i. Co-operative Territorialism

The approach of co-operative territorialism begins with the structure of territorialism but concedes that international co-operation shall be provided when necessary.[39] Under the approach of co-operative territorialism, a multinational debtor initiates insolvency proceedings in each country where the debtor has substantial assets. Each country is then expected to administer the assets of the debtor located within its jurisdiction as a separate estate and according to its local law.[40] In other words, each of the proceedings is parallel with none of the proceedings being main, secondary or ancillary. Whether to agree to co-operate with other courts in an international insolvency proceeding is subject to the discretion of local courts.[41] When international co-operation is needed in a cross-border insolvency case, each court will appoint an administrator; the administrators of various estates would thereafter negotiate co-operative asset disposition on a case-by-case basis, entering into a specific agreement that provides the terms for co-operation in a particular case.[42] By entering into such an agreement, the issue of cross-border insolvency can be resolved through mutually beneficial procedures or substantive resolutions without imposing an entirely new regime on recalcitrant sovereigns.[43] It has been suggested that five areas are designed to involve co-operation:

(1) the establishment of procedures for replicating claims filed in any one country in all of them;
(2) the sharing of distribution lists by representatives to ensure that later distributions do not go to creditors who have already recovered the full amounts owed to them;
(3) the joint sale of assets, when a joint sale would produce a higher price than separate sales in multiple countries or when the value of assets within a country is not sufficiently large to warrant separate administration;
(4) the voluntary investment by representatives in one country in the debtor's reorganization effort in another; and
(5) the seizure and return of assets that have been the subject of avoidable transfers.[44]

Co-operative territorialism has been alleged to have several advantages. First, it has been argued that the approach of co-operative territorialism solves the problem of the indeterminate standard of 'home country' with regard to which home country is to have jurisdiction over the multinational debtor. It is envisaged that separating the multinational debtors at the national border is unlikely to damage them because a large majority already compartmentalise themselves by country. Second, it maintains the advantages of pure territorialism, such as greater predictability

[39] Adams and Fincke (n 6) 56.
[40] LoPucki, 'Co-operation in International Bankruptcy' (n 11) 724–43.
[41] ibid.
[42] LoPucki, 'Universalism Unravels' (n 11) 162; Adams and Fincke (n 6) 56; D Costa Levenson, 'Proposal for Reform of Choice of Avoidance Law in the Context of International Bankruptcies from a US Perspective' (2002) 10 *American Bankruptcy Institute Law Review* 291, 293.
[43] Biery et al (n 19) 57; Levenson (n 42) 293.
[44] LoPucki, 'Co-operation in International Bankruptcy' (n 11) 750.

and a less complex system than that found under universalism. Finally, among others, it has been argued that the greatest advantage of co-operative territoriality is that its implementation would require only minimal changes to the status quo of current practices in the area of cross-border insolvency; this is due to the fact that 'most countries have in most cases acted territorially with regard to assets within the country at the time of the bankruptcy filing'.[45] However, the most serious flaw with co-operative territorialism appears to be that the co-operative element is not mandatory and is only adopted on a voluntary basis. The purpose of co-operative territorialism may therefore not be achieved as it is based upon the discretion of the forum to decide whether to co-operate with other courts.[46]

ii. Modified Universalism

However, 'modified universalism embraces universalism's core belief of co-operation, but maintains the primacy of local courts' power to exercise discretion with respect to "the fairness of the home country procedures" and with respect to protecting the interests of local creditors'.[47] Under the approach of modified universalism, a local court (the assisting court) agrees that assets should be collected and distributed on a worldwide basis and generally defers to the main proceeding for the purposes of collecting and distributing assets of the insolvency company. However, the assisting court 'does not contemplate a full administration and distribution of the debtor's local assets' but aims primarily to assist the main proceeding in the debtor's home country, such as by issuing injunctions or providing assistance to foreign administrators.[48] The assisting court preserves its discretion to evaluate the fairness of the main proceeding and to protect the interests of local creditors.[49] The most common legal criterion for the local court to determine when considering whether to retain rights to protect local creditors is whether the main insolvency proceeding in another country would alter the legal rights of local creditors or violate the public policy of the assisting country.[50]

The advantage of modified universalism is that it retains the advantage of pure universalism while incorporating flexibility and discretion. The most important advantage of modified universalism over pure universalism envisaged by its supporters is the ability to refuse co-operation that would prejudice local creditors.[51] Modified universalism allows for a flexible approach; whether to co-operate or remain independent depends on the local court's discretion in the particular circumstances of the insolvency proceeding.[52] Thus, modified

[45] LoPucki, 'Co-operation in International Bankruptcy' (n 11) 751–53; see also Tung (n 16) 37.
[46] Clark and Goldstein (n 10) 513.
[47] Adams and Fincke (n 6) 50.
[48] American Law Institute (n 10) 11–12.
[49] Westbrook, 'A Global Solution to Multinational Default' (n 25) 2299–3000.
[50] Adams and Fincke (n 6) 48–49.
[51] Westbrook, 'A Global Solution to Multinational Default' (n 25).
[52] ibid.

universalism would sit comfortably for those who are concerned about relinquishing national sovereignty. Under modified universalism, the local court can examine or even negotiate the treatment of local creditors in the main proceeding before surrendering local assets to the main proceeding.[53] In addition, even though modified universalism is not as efficient as pure universalism, it still, to some extent, limits duplicative administrative expenses while maintaining a harmonised and co-ordinated insolvency proceeding. Finally, modified universalism is independent of international conventions and can, therefore, be unilaterally completed through domestic legislation. It can also be used as 'an interim solution pending movement to true universalism'.[54]

However, opponents argue that this approach sacrifices the advantages of both territorialism and universalism, which results in additional uncertainties for both debtors and creditors.[55] The approach of modified universalism does not address the core problem of identifying the home country that arises from the approach of pure universalism. In addition, it introduces additional uncertainties on the grounds that, 'the regime or regimes that will ultimately distribute the debtor's assets may depend on the country in which the assets are located at the time of bankruptcy' and 'for the lender to predict the regime applicable to distribution at the time of the loan, the lender must guess what intercountry differences in bankruptcy law the forum court will consider substantial'.[56] Moreover, due to deviating from the 'single court' model envisaged by pure universalists, modified universalism may generate a bankruptcy proceeding in every country where the debtor has assets; this sacrifices another main benefit claimed by pure universalism, namely, reducing transaction costs and simplifying international insolvency proceedings.[57] It has been noted that modified universalism distinctly and inevitably involves an aspect of territorialism.[58]

III. The Evolution of Theories and the Status Quo

From the discussions above it can be seen that none of the four theories appear to be perfect, with each having its own advantages and disadvantages. Both universalists and territorialists have proposed modifications to their theories in order to minimise the potential disadvantages. Currently, the problem of cross-border insolvency has not been subjected to a global, mandatory and uniform regime, nor does it have international law to govern the various, unco-ordinated proceedings.

[53] LoPucki, 'Co-operation in International Bankruptcy' (n 11) 728.
[54] See also Westbrook, 'A Global Solution to Multinational Default' (n 25) 2277.
[55] LoPucki, 'Co-operation in International Bankruptcy' (n 11) 729.
[56] ibid.
[57] ibid.
[58] Bufford (n 24) 124; see also Adams and Fincke (n 6) 55.

Since the law of insolvency inherently deals with the issue of distribution of assets and reflects the preferred distributional choices made by a sovereign country, it is inevitable that states prefer to apply their own bankruptcy law to cross-border insolvencies. The application of the local insolvency law reduces the cost of learning foreign bankruptcy law for parties who have entered into a cross-border transaction, as well as the incommensurable cost of relinquishing the preferred distributional outcomes of a state's own insolvency law.[59] In choosing a cross-border insolvency regime, a state needs to balance the protection of local creditors and the interest of co-operation between other states.[60] In addition, the state needs to make a trade-off between increased cross-border economic activity and the application of a less-preferred substantive insolvency law.[61] It has been argued that the exogenous force of economic interdependencies between states has a bearing on the outcome of this trade-off:

> A state may be relatively more dependent ('dependent state') on the economy of another, less dependent, state ('dominant state') than vice versa. To increase its gains from cross-border economic activity with the dominant state, the dependent state has an interest in the dominant state applying territorialism vis-à-vis the dependent state. Moreover, by applying unilateral universalism vis-à-vis the dominant state, the dependent state increases such gains even more. However, a dependent state's preference for the distributional consequences of its own insolvency law may prevent it from applying unilateral universalism vis-à-vis the dominant state.
>
> ....
>
> The world economy consists of different regional economies. Each regional economy has its own dominant state. Accordingly, in different regional economies, alternative dominant states will apply leverage over the issue of which legal rules to place into a uniform bankruptcy law. This means that, as long as international economic integration is not complete, the chances of different substantive insolvency laws converging over time look slim.[62]

Thus, although the current trend seems to be in favour of the idealistic approach of universalism at the theoretical level,[63] it has to be admitted that the approach of universalism may be difficult to institutionalise in the absence of an international insolvency Convention or a centralised enforcement mechanism.[64] Thus, in the interim, countries need to decide 'how to move forward (or not) while awaiting a more decisive shift'.[65] The fundamental controversy lies in the 'modified' versions

[59] Franken (n 4) 98–99.
[60] Wessels et al (n 3) 40.
[61] Franken (n 4) 130.
[62] Franken (n 4) 130.
[63] See Walters (n 10) 49; J Pottow, 'Beyond Carve-Outs and Toward Reliance: A normative Framework for Cross-border Insolvency Choice of Law' (2014) 9 *Brooklyn Journal of Corporate, Financial & Commercial Law* 202, 202.
[64] See eg Westbrook, 'A Global Solution to Multinational Default' (n 25) 2328; Adams and Fincke (n 6) 48–49; Biery et al (n 19) 57; Guzman (n 24); Buxbaum (n 4); Walters (n 10).
[65] Wessels et al (n 3) 70.

of universalism and territorialism in the sense of the extent to which the forum court should embrace comity to the international insolvency system and co-operate with other courts regarding cross-border insolvency cases. Notwithstanding that modified universalism has been criticised with regard to its practical utility and the methodology of institutionalism,[66] as an interim or transitional solution it has currently emerged as the dominant theory in the realm of cross-border insolvency, in recognition of the increasing integration of the world economy.[67]

[66] See eg Tung (n 16); Walters (n 10); Franken (n 4).

[67] See eg Westbrook, 'A Global Solution to Multinational Default' (n 25) 2277; Clark and Goldstein (n 10); American Law Institute (n 10) 18.

4

The UNCITRAL Model Law

In order to resolve the inconsistencies in the realm of cross-border insolvency discussed in Chapter 3, academics, judges, and practitioners have sought to develop a harmonised regime that would govern cross-border insolvencies on a global basis. The achievement was reached on 31 May 1997 by virtue of the United Nations Commission on International Trade Law (UNCITRAL) Model Law on Cross-Border Insolvency (the Model Law).[1] By 2019, 46 states had adopted the Model Law into their respective insolvency statutory regimes.[2]

The Model Law is intended to assist the enacting states to address the cross-border insolvency issue in a more efficient and modern way.[3] The main situation that the Model Law aims to address is where the debtor has assets in different countries or where creditors are domiciled across the world.[4] The Model Law (arguably) represents an attempt to impose a modified universalism approach.[5] Generally, all bankruptcy assets and claims are expected to be administered in the debtor's centre of main interests (COMI) and distributed under the law of COMI, subject to appropriate co-ordination procedures or local public policy exception.[6]

However, the UNCITRAL chose to enact this international instrument on cross-border insolvency in the form of a model law, which is 'a legislative text that is recommended to states for incorporation into their local law'.[7] Unlike a 'take-it-or-leave-it' Convention, the Model Law is a 'soft law' and can be altered to adapt to

[1] S Gopalan and M Guihot, 'Recognition and Enforcement in Cross-Border Insolvency Law: A Proposal for Judicial Gap-Filling' (2015) 48 *Vanderbilt Journal of Transnational Law* 1225, 1229.

[2] 'Status: UNCITRAL Model Law on Cross-Border Insolvency' (UNCITRAL, 1997) uncitral.un.org/en/texts/insolvency/modellaw/cross-border_insolvency/status accessed 5 June 2020; see eg UNCITRAL Secretariat, *UNCITRAL Cross-Border Insolvency Law with Guide to Enactment and Interpretation* (United Nations Office at Vienna, 2014) 20–23; A Walters, 'Modified Universalisms & the Role of Local Legal Culture in the Making of Cross-Border Insolvency Law' (2019) 93 *American Bankruptcy Law Journal* 47, 56 (for a detailed discussion of the origins of the Model Law).

[3] UNCITRAL Secretariat, *Guide to Enactment* (n 2) 19.

[4] ibid.

[5] See eg JL Westbrook, 'A Global Solution to Multinational Default' (2000) 98 *Michigan Law Review* 2276, 2315; E Adams and J Fincke, 'Co-ordinating Cross-Border Bankruptcy: How Territorialism Saves Universalism' (2009) 15 *Columbia Journal of European Law* 43, 61–63; but see S Franken, 'Cross-Border Insolvency Law: A Comparative Institutional Analysis' (2014) 34 *Oxford Journal of Legal Studies* 97, 104 (arguing that the Model Law entails a co-operative territorial approach).

[6] UNCITRAL Model Law on Cross-Border Insolvency (UNCITRAL Model Law), Art 6; UNCITRAL Secretariat, *Guide to Enactment* (n 2) 19.

[7] UNCITRAL Secretariat, *Guide to Enactment* (n 2) 24.

the needs of the enacting states. It is not binding on any state unless incorporated into its domestic law. In making this choice the drafters of the Model Law have attempted to provide a more relaxed regime that will attract more states to adopt it, which is claimed as pragmatic and incremental.[8] As noted by the Model Law: 'It focuses on authorizing and encouraging cooperation and coordination between jurisdictions, rather than attempting the unification of substantive insolvency law, and respects the differences among national procedural laws'.[9] It attempts to overcome judicial and administrative barriers rather than trying to unify the substantive insolvency law. Accordingly, the Model Law is essentially procedural in nature and contains no uniform choice-of-law rule. In addition, 'as the uniform text can be modified locally, the Model Law trades certainty for flexibility and aims at harmonization by softer, non-binding means'.[10] Although the Model Law has been criticised for its non-binding nature, divergence in its implementation and interpretation, and the tendency of potential forum shopping,[11] it is a necessary evil as an interim alternative to the development of a standard regime of cross-border insolvency.[12]

In order to achieve the alleged goal of universalism and to encourage co-operation and co-ordination between member states, UNCITRAL built four foundational principles, which are: (1) access; (2) recognition; (3) relief; and (4) co-operation and co-ordination.[13] These four principles assist the Model Law to realise the goal for which it was designed: promoting legal certainty for trade and investment; dealing with cross-border insolvency proceedings fairly and efficiently; protecting and maximising the pool of debtor's assets; communication and co-operation between local and foreign courts; and, finally, protecting investment and preserving employment.[14] The following sections introduce these four principles in detail.

I. Access

'The provisions on access address both inbound and outbound aspects of cross-border insolvency'.[15] The inbound access means that the assistance is sought in

[8] I Mevorach, 'A Fresh View on the Hard/Soft Law Divide: Implications for International Insolvency of Enterprise Group' (2019) 40 *Michigan Journal of International Law* 505, 508; J Pottow, 'Beyond Carve-Outs and Toward Reliance: A Normative Framework for Cross-Border Insolvency Choice of Law' (2014) 9 *Brooklyn Journal of Corporate, Financial & Commercial Law* 202, 203.

[9] UNCITRAL Model Law, preamble.

[10] Walters (n 2) 59.

[11] See eg Walters (n 2); L LoPucki, 'Global and Out of Control?' (2005) 79 *American Bankruptcy Law Journal* 79.

[12] S Block-Lieb and T Halliday, 'Less is More in International Private Law' (2015) 3 *Nottingham Insolvency and Business Law e-Journal* 43; Mevorach (n 8); G McCormack, 'COMI and Comity in UK and US Insolvency Law' [2012] *LQR* 128, 158.

[13] SE Story, 'Cross-Border Insolvency: A Comparative Analysis' (2015) 32 *Arizona Journal of International & Comparative Law* 431, 436–37.

[14] UNCITRAL Model Law, Preamble.

[15] UNCITRAL Secretariat, *Guide to Enactment* (n 2) 27.

the enacting state by a foreign representative of a foreign proceeding, while the outbound access means that the assistance is sought in a foreign country by the representative of a domestic insolvency proceeding in the enacting state.

Article 9 of the Model Law provides foreign representatives with inbound access 'at the earliest possible time' to the courts in the enacting state where the recognition and relief are sought.[16] Foreign representatives can thereby utilise certain aspects of their legal powers in the assisting jurisdiction.[17] In an insolvency situation, it is essential for foreign representatives to take actions as soon as possible to avoid the dissipation or concealment of debtors' assets.[18] Through the expedited and direct access provided by the Model Law, foreign representatives can avoid relying on formal and time-consuming methods to obtain permission to appear before local courts, such as letters rogatory, consular communications or other forms of diplomatic channels, which may take months.[19]

The Model Law entitles a foreign representative: to apply directly to local courts;[20] to commence a proceeding under the local insolvency law 'if the conditions for commencing such a proceeding are otherwise met';[21] and to participate in an existing local insolvency proceeding upon the recognition of a foreign proceeding.[22] Nevertheless, an application for recognition alone does not subject the foreign representative to the jurisdiction of the local court for any purpose other than this application.[23]

Moreover, Article 5 of the Model Law authorises outbound access, which explicitly allows the representatives appointed in the enacting state to act abroad on behalf of the local assisting proceeding.[24] The rationale of this article is to give domestic representatives the explicit power to act in a foreign jurisdiction should they not otherwise have such power under their domestic laws.[25]

In addition to easy access for foreign representatives, Article 13 provides foreign creditors with the same rights regarding the commencement of, and participation in, an insolvency proceeding as local creditors.[26] Moreover, foreign creditors' claims generally have the same ranking as equivalent local claims.[27]

[16] See UNCITRAL Model Law, Art 9.

[17] Story (n 13) 436–37. See also UNCITRAL Secretariat, *UNCITRAL Model Law on Cross-Border Insolvency: Judicial Perspective* (United Nations Office at Vienna, 2014) 5.

[18] UNCITRAL Secretariat, *Judicial Perspective* (n 17) 14.

[19] B Wessels et al, *International Co-operation in Bankruptcy and Insolvency Matters* (Oxford University Press, 2009) 208. See also Story (n 13) 436–37.

[20] UNCITRAL Model Law, Art 9.

[21] ibid Art 11.

[22] ibid Art 12.

[23] ibid Art 10.

[24] UNCITRAL Model Law, Art 5.

[25] AJ Berends, 'The UNCITRAL Model Law on Cross-Border Insolvency: A Comprehensive Overview' (1998) 6 *Tulane Journal of International and Comparative Law* 309, 335.

[26] UNCITRAL Model Law, Art 13(1).

[27] ibid Art 13(2).

II. Recognition

The second principle is recognition. 'Perhaps the most important feature of the Model Law is the provision for the recognition of a foreign insolvency proceeding and the consequences of such recognition'.[28] The purpose of this 'recognition' principle is to simplify the procedure for recognition of a foreign insolvency proceeding by courts in enacting states and to bring certainty to the recognition process.[29] The Model Law distinguishes foreign main proceedings and foreign non-main proceedings and then triggers different consequences and relief upon recognition.[30] Regardless of this distinction, the Model Law requires the recognition of both foreign main proceedings and non-main proceedings.[31] Subject to the Article 6 public policy exception, as long as the application follows the proper procedural requirements required by Article 15 and the substantive requirements provided by Article 17, recognition should be granted by the local court. There is no requirement of reciprocity, or any consideration of 'whether the foreign proceeding was correctly commenced under applicable law'.[32]

Article 15 establishes the procedural and evidentiary requirements for filing a recognition application of the foreign proceeding under the Model Law.[33] The Model Law is not aimed at encumbering the foreign representative with additional procedural requirements beyond those referred to in Article 15, but to provide a simple, expedited structure to obtain recognition.[34] Moreover, the Model Law presumes that the documents submitted in support of the application are authentic, whether or not they have been legalised.[35] This presumption helps the recognition process to be prompter and easier, thereby further facilitating universalism.

Besides the Article 15 procedural requirements, Article 17 provides substantive requirements for the local court to grant the application for recognition: (1) the proceeding must be a foreign proceeding, which falls within the definition provided in Article 2(a) of the Model Law;[36] (2) the person who applies for the recognition must be a foreign representative within the definition in Article 2(d) of the Model Law;[37] (3) the application was accomplished by the evidentiary requirement set forth in Article 15;[38] and (4) the application was submitted

[28] SL Bufford et al, *International Insolvency* (Federal Judicial Centre, 2001) 61.
[29] Story (n 13) 436–37. See also UNCITRAL Secretariat, *Judicial Perspective* (n 17) 5, 13.
[30] JL Westbrook, 'Multinational Enterprises in General Default: Chapter 15, the ALI Principles, and the EU Insolvency Regulation' (2002) 76 *American Bankruptcy Law Journal* 1, 14. See also UNCITRAL Secretariat, *Judicial Perspective* (n 17).
[31] Westbrook, 'Multinational Enterprises in General Default' (n 30) 14.
[32] UNCITRAL Secretariat, *Judicial Perspective* (n 17) 15.
[33] ibid.
[34] UNCITRAL Model Law, Art 15; UNCITRAL Secretariat, *Guide to Enactment* (n 2) 64.
[35] UNCITRAL Model Law, Art 16.
[36] UNCITRAL Model Law, Arts 2(a), 17(1)(a).
[37] UNCITRAL Model Law, Arts 2(d), 17(1)(b).
[38] UNCITRAL Model Law, Arts 15(2), 17(1)(c).

to the proper court.[39] 'The purpose of Article 17 is to establish that, if recognition is not contrary to the public policy of the enacting state … and if the application meets the requirements set out in the article, recognition will be granted as a matter of course'.[40] That means, if the application meets the requirements laid down in Article 17(1), the local court of the enacting state must grant the recognition. There is no discretionary power for the court to evaluate the merits of the foreign proceedings.[41] Therefore, the Model Law provides a high degree of certainty regarding an application for recognition of foreign proceedings.[42]

Article 18 compels the foreign representative to inform the recognising court 'promptly' of any 'substantial change' in the recognised proceeding.[43] The purpose of this obligation is to allow the court to modify or terminate the consequences of recognition in the event that subsequent changes may affect the court's decision.[44] The Model Law requires the recognition application to be granted at the earliest opportunity. Nevertheless, local courts reserve the discretion to modify or terminate the recognition or the relief granted if later evidence shows that the grounds for recognition or relief have changed or no longer exist.[45]

If the foreign insolvency proceeding is subsequently recognised as a 'foreign main proceeding', an automatic and mandatory moratorium will apply to certain types of creditors' action, including: the commencement of proceedings concerning the debtor company's assets, rights, obligations or liabilities; execution against its assets; and/or transfer or disposal of its assets.[46] In contrast, only discretionary relief provided under Article 21 is available upon the recognition of foreign non-main proceedings.[47]

A. Foreign Proceedings

One of the most important issues for Model Law to settle is: what kind of foreign proceeding should be recognised as an 'insolvency' proceeding (although the notion of 'insolvency' differs between jurisdictions). Article 2(a) of the Model Law defines a foreign proceeding:

> 'Foreign [insolvency] proceeding' means a collective judicial or administrative proceeding in a foreign [s]tate, including an interim proceeding, pursuant to a law relating to insolvency in which proceeding the assets and affairs of the debtor are subject to control or supervision by a foreign court, for the purpose of reorganization or liquidation.[48]

[39] UNCITRAL Model Law, Arts 4, 17(1)(d).
[40] UNCITRAL Secretariat, *Guide to Enactment* (n 2) 73.
[41] Berends (n 25) 354.
[42] Wessels et al (n 19) 214.
[43] UNCITRAL Model Law, Art 18.
[44] UNCITRAL Model Law, Art 18; UNCITRAL Secretariat, *Guide to Enactment* (n 2) 78. See eg *Suk v Hanjin Shipping Co Ltd* [2017] FCA 404.
[45] UNCITRAL Model Law, Art 17(3), (4).
[46] ibid Art 20.
[47] ibid Art 21.
[48] UNCITRAL Model Law, Art 2(a).

Specifically, foreign proceeding consists of six characteristics:

(1) the proceeding is 'collective' in nature; ...
(2) the proceeding has either a judicial or administrative nature ...;
(3) the proceeding has been opened in a foreign [s]tate ...;
(4) the proceeding is pursuant to a law relating to insolvency ...;
(5) the assets and affairs of the debtor are subject to control or supervision by the court ...; and
(6) the aim of the proceeding is a reorganization or a liquidation ...[49]

These six characteristics are cumulative and should be considered as a whole. If a proceeding is consistent with all the characteristics listed above, the recognition, non-discrimination, and co-operation procedures undertaken by the enacting state in adopting the Model Law will extend to such proceedings.[50] The timing for considering whether a foreign proceeding possesses or possessed those characteristics is the date the foreign proceeding is commenced.[51]

It is obvious that reorganisation and liquidation proceedings are covered. The debtor-in-possession procedure in the US and interim proceedings that are commonly found in Commonwealth countries are also included.[52] However, individual actions made by creditors, such as attachment and garnishment, are excluded. Specific entities, such as bank and insurance companies, may be excluded from the scope of the Model Law if the enacting state decides to do so, if these special entities are excluded from the domestic insolvency regime or are subject to a special regulatory regime in the domestic insolvency regime.[53]

When determining whether a foreign insolvency proceeding fits within the definition set out in Article 2 of the Model Law, the name or the type of the

[49] Berends (n 25) 328–29. See also UNCITRAL Secretariat, *Judicial Perspective* (n 17) 14.

[50] Westbrook, 'Multinational Enterprises in General Default' (n 30) 12.

[51] UNCITRAL Secretariat, *Judicial Perspective* (n 17) 25.

[52] Westbrook, 'Multinational Enterprises in General Default' (n 30) 12. A debtor-in-possession (DIP) is a US proceeding where the debtor retains possession and control of its asset while the reorganisation takes place. The Model Law does not require the level of court's control or supervision nor does it require the time at which that control or supervision should arise for a foreign proceeding to be recognised. Though the debtor retains possession and control of its assets in a DIP proceeding, it is still to some extent subject to court's supervision. Therefore, a DIP proceeding will satisfy the 'control or supervision by a foreign court' requirement and can be recognised as a foreign proceeding under the Model Law regime. See eg *In Re 19 Entertainment Ltd* [2016] EWHC 1545 (Ch); *In re Legend International Holdings Inc* [2016] VSC 308; UNCITRAL Secretariat, *Guide to Enactment* (n 2) 40; UNCITRAL Secretariat, *Judicial Perspective* (n 17) 30. In terms of 'interim proceedings', in practice many Commonwealth countries' insolvency proceedings are often commenced on an 'interim' base. The court may appoint an interim (provisional) liquidator before making a formal order confirming the continuation of the insolvency proceedings on a non-interim basis. The Model Law recognised these interim proceedings on the basis that these proceedings are not distinguished from other insolvency proceedings merely because they are of an interim nature. See UNCITRAL Secretariat, *Guide to Enactment* (n 2) 43. See eg Companies Act 1993, s 246 (NZ).

[53] UNCITRAL Model Law, Art 1; UNCITRAL Secretariat, *Guide to Enactment* (n 2) 35–36.

proceeding is not determinative. Instead, courts should look into the substance of the proceeding, namely whether the proceeding meets the six characteristics listed above, especially whether the proceeding is 'collective' in nature. For example, in *Stanford International Bank Ltd*, the English Court held that a receivership order made by a US court was not 'collective' in nature and denied the application of recognition.[54] The English Court explained that the order was made at the request of the US Securities Exchange Commission 'to prevent a massive ongoing fraud'.[55] The purpose of the order was to prevent detriment to investors, rather than to reorganise the corporation or to realise assets for the benefit of all creditors.[56] Similarly, a US Court refused to recognise a receivership commenced under Israeli law in *In Re Gold & Honey Ltd*.[57] The Court reasoned that the proceeding 'did not require the receivers to consider the rights and obligations of all creditors and was designed primarily to allow a certain party to collect its debts'.[58]

B. Foreign Main Proceeding and Foreign Non-Main Proceeding

As mentioned above, the distinction between a foreign main proceeding and a foreign non-main proceeding is important under the Model Law. Recognition of a 'main' proceeding triggers an automatic stay of individual creditors' actions or executions concerning the assets of the debtor and an automatic 'freeze' of those assets, subject to certain exceptions.[59] In contrast, any effects upon the recognition of a foreign non-main proceeding arise only pursuant to court order and any relief granted by the local court is discretionary.[60]

A foreign main proceeding is the proceeding commenced in the state where the debtor has 'the centre of its main interests' (COMI).[61] The COMI of a debtor is a critically important new concept introduced by the Model Law, but the Model Law does not define this term. The Model Law provides a presumption that, absent proof to the contrary, the COMI of a debtor is the state where the debtor's registered office or habitual residence is located.[62]

[54] *In re Stanford International Bank Ltd* [2010] EWCA Civ 137, [25]–[29].
[55] UNCITRAL Secretariat, *Judicial Perspective* (n 17) 27. See also *In re Stanford* (n 54) [25]–[29].
[56] *In re Stanford* (n 54) [25]–[29].
[57] *In Re Gold & Honey Ltd* 410 BR 357 (Bankr ED New York 2009).
[58] UNCITRAL Secretariat, *Judicial Perspective* (n 17) 26–27. See also *In re Gold & Honey* (n 57) 370.
[59] UNCITRAL Model Law, Art 20.
[60] ibid Art 21.
[61] ibid Art 2(b).
[62] ibid Art 16(3). For interpretation of COMI, see eg *In re Stanford* (n 54); *Ackers v Saad Investments Co Ltd* [2010] FCA 1221; *Williams v Simpson* [2011] 2 NZLR 380; *In re SPhinX Ltd* 371 BR 10 (SD New York 2007); *In re Bear Stearns High-Grade Structured Credit Strategies Master Fund Ltd* 389 BR 325 (SD New York 2008).

However, proceedings outside the COMI, 'taking place in a state where the debtor has an establishment', are foreign non-main proceedings.[63] An establishment is broadly defined to include 'any place of operations where the debtor carries out a non-transitory economic activity with human means and goods or services'.[64] If a foreign proceeding is initiated in a state where the debtor has neither a COMI nor an establishment, such as a proceeding commenced solely based on the presence of assets, then this proceeding does not qualify for recognition under the Model Law regime.[65]

Therefore, the determination of COMI, especially the determination of COMI of offshore shipping companies, becomes essentially important. A detailed discussion regarding the interpretation and determination of the COMI is provided in Chapter 12 below.

C. Public Policy Exception

There is little room left for the local court to exercise any discretion to refuse to grant the recognition of the foreign proceedings if all the requirements provided in Article 17 are met.[66] The only exception to the mandatory nature of recognition is Article 6. Article 6 provides that nothing in the Model Law 'prevents a court from refusing to take any action … [that] would be manifestly contrary to the public policy of the state'.[67]

The notion of public policy is based on local domestic law, which varies from state to state; and therefore no uniform definition of public policy is provided by the Model Law.[68] Some states have construed the public policy concept strictly and have invoked public policy exceptions only when the proposed actions impact their own fundamental principles, such as constitutional guarantees. For example, in Australia, the explanatory memorandum states that 'Article 6 is only intended to be invoked under exceptional circumstances concerning matters of fundamental importance for the enacting state'.[69] Other states might have a broader definition and thus invoke the exception as they would for any mandatory rule of domestic law. One example is Japan, where the Japanese enacted version of Model Law (The Law on Recognition of and Assistance in Foreign Insolvency Proceedings) provides that 'the court can refuse recognition of a foreign proceeding if the result of recognition is contrary to the public policy or good customs in Japan'.[70]

[63] UNCITRAL Model Law, Art 2(c).

[64] ibid Art 2(f).

[65] Berends (n 25) 322.

[66] UNCITRAL Model Law, Arts 17, 20, 21.

[67] ibid Art 6.

[68] UNCITRAL Secretariat, *Guide to Enactment* (n 2) 52.

[69] Explanatory Memorandum, Cross-Border Insolvency Bill 2008 (Cth) 21 [21]; *Akers v Deputy Commissioner of Taxation* [2014] FCAFC 57 [40]–[41].

[70] UNCITRAL Secretariat, *Guide to Enactment* (n 2) 52; K Yamamoto, 'New Japanese Legislation on Cross-Border Insolvency as Compared with the UNCITRAL Model Law', available at onlinelibrary.wiley.com/doi/abs/10.1002/iir.98, accessed 5 June 2020.

Nevertheless, the drafters of the Model Law expected that the public policy exception should be strictly interpreted and be rarely used.[71] That is why the word 'manifestly contrary' was added to the text. The Guide to Enactment explains that the word 'manifestly' is to emphasise that public policy exceptions should be interpreted in a more restrictive way.[72] 'Article 6 is only intended to be invoked under exceptional and limited circumstances concerning matters of fundamental importance for the enacting state'.[73]

For example, the public policy exception cannot be invoked simply because differences are found in insolvency schemes.[74] In *Re HIH Casualty and General Insurance*, the English Court held that no public policy of English insolvency law would be offended despite the fact that the Australian insolvency regime was different from the English insolvency regime in terms of the categories of preferential creditors.[75] Similarly, in *In re Ephedra Products Liability Litigation*, the US Court recognised the Canadian insolvency proceeding regardless of the inability to have a jury trial in Canada, though the jury trial is an important constitutional right in the US.[76]

However, US courts will refuse to recognise a foreign proceeding if it is commenced in violation of the automatic stay order under the US Bankruptcy Code. In *In re Gold & Honey Ltd*, the receiver filed a receivership proceeding in Israel and applied for the recognition of the Israeli proceeding in the US Bankruptcy Court for the Eastern District of New York, notwithstanding that a pre-existing reorganisation proceeding had been filed in the US and a worldwide stay order had been granted by the Court.[77] The Court refused to recognise the Israeli receivership proceeding and held that recognition of the Israeli receivership proceeding would constitute a breach of public policy, because it would 'reward and legitimize [the] violation of both the automatic stay and this Court's Orders regarding the stay'.[78]

As discussed above, the public policy exception is generally strictly interpreted and should only be invoked in rare cases.

[71] UNCITRAL Secretariat, *Guide to Enactment* (n 2) 26.

[72] ibid 52.

[73] ibid.

[74] ibid.

[75] *Re HIH Casualty and General Insurance* [2008] UKHL 21.

[76] *In re Ephedra Products Liability Litigation* 349 BR 333, 335–37 (SD New York 2006). See also *In re Fairfield Sentry Ltd* 714 F 3d 127 (2nd Cir 2013) (where the US Court of Appeals found that 'the confidentiality of BVI bankruptcy proceedings does not offend US public policy'); *In re Ernst & Yong Inc* 383 BR 773 (Bankr Dis Colombia 2008) (where the US bankruptcy court held that certain US creditors receiving less in the foreign proceeding than they would receive from a US court was not 'manifestly' contrary to US public policy); *Akers* (n 69) (where the Full Court of the Federal Court of Australia held that inability to enforce tax debts in a foreign proceeding would not be contrary to Australian public policy).

[77] *In re Gold & Honey* (n 57) 371.

[78] ibid. See also *In re Toft* 453 BR 186 (Bankr SD New York 2011); *In re Qimonda AG Bankruptcy Litigation* 433 BR 547 (ED Virginia 2010).

III. Relief

The third important principle is 'relief', which is provided under Articles 19, 20 and 21 of the Model Law. The aim of this principle is to 'create a sufficient freeze or holding of the assets to protect the business interests of the debtor without unnecessarily interfering with the interests of creditors and traders'.[79] There are three types of relief available under the Model Law, according to when relief is sought:

(a) interim (urgent) relief, which can be sought at any time after the application for recognition of a foreign proceeding has been made prior to the formal recognition (Article 19);[80]
(b) automatic and mandatory relief, which arises simultaneously upon the recognition of a foreign main proceeding (Article 20);[81] and
(c) discretionary (additional) relief, which arises after the recognition of a foreign proceeding, whether main or non-main proceeding (Article 21).[82]

A. Article 19: Interim Relief

Article 19 provides foreign representatives with the right to apply for temporary emergency relief while the recognition application is pending. It is at the court's discretion to decide whether to grant such interim relief. The purpose of this provision is to provide foreign representatives with temporary protection if there is any urgent need to protect the assets of the debtor or the interests of the creditors before the recognition decision is made.[83] Interim relief may include, but is not limited to, the following: staying of execution against the debtor's assets; entrusting the debtor's assets to the foreign representative if the assets are perishable or susceptible to devaluation; suspending the debtor's right to transfer; and examining witnesses or discovering evidence regarding the debtor's assets or liabilities.[84]

Consistent with the requirements for recognition, the relief authorised by Article 19 is the type of relief that is usually available only in 'collective' insolvency proceedings, as opposed to the 'individual' relief that may be granted before the commencement of insolvency proceedings under domestic civil procedural rules (ie measures covering specific assets identified by a creditor).[85] Since the relief under Article 19 is only 'of a provisional nature,' the relief granted should,

[79] Wessels et al (n 19) 217.
[80] UNCITRAL Model Law, Art 19.
[81] ibid Art 20.
[82] ibid Art 21.
[83] J Clift, 'The UNCITRAL Model Law on Cross-Border Insolvency – A Legislative Framework to Facilitate Coordination and Cooperation in Cross-Border Insolvency' (2004) 12 *Tulane Journal of International and Comparative Law* 307, 324.
[84] ibid.
[85] UNCITRAL Secretariat, *Guide to Enactment* (n 2) 80.

in principle, be restricted to urgent measures. In addition, once the application for recognition is decided, Article 19 relief terminates automatically.[86] However, the court may extend certain relief to fill the time gap between the temporary relief granted before recognition and substantive discretionary relief issued after recognition, if the court wishes to do so.[87]

B. Article 20: Automatic Relief for Foreign Main Proceeding

Once the assisting court recognises that a foreign proceeding is a foreign main proceeding under Article 17, certain mandatory effects need to be followed by the assisting court under Article 20. While relief provided under Article 19 and Article 21 is discretionary, the effect provided by Article 20 is not. It is 'automatic' and 'mandatory' upon the recognition of a foreign main proceeding.[88]

In addition, Article 20 automatic relief applies only to main proceedings, while discretionary relief provided by Article 19 and Article 21 applies to both main and non-main proceedings. Similarly to a domestic insolvency proceeding, a moratorium order is essential to organise an orderly and fair cross-border insolvency proceeding. Moreover, prompt action is of importance in an international bankruptcy proceeding. Therefore, no time should be wasted and the relief should be granted automatically and mandatorily once the proceeding is recognised as a foreign main proceeding.

Under Article 20(1) of the Model Law, the commencement or continuation of individual actions or individual proceedings concerning the debtor's assets, rights, obligations or liabilities is suspended; execution against the debtor's assets is suspended; and the right to transfer, encumber or otherwise dispose of any assets of the debtor is suspended.[89] Nevertheless, foreign representatives or creditors can always commence a parallel local insolvency proceeding or participate in such a proceeding.[90]

Notwithstanding the 'automatic' and 'mandatory' nature of Article 20 relief, the Model Law emphasises in Article 20(2) that the scope, modification, suspension, or termination of the stay may be subject to local exceptions or limitations that may exist in the enacting states.[91] The exception includes the enforcement of claims by secured creditors.[92] In other words, Article 20(2) offers enacting states the opportunity to preserve the operation of local insolvency laws. The Guide to Enactment suggests the enforcement of a secured claim as an

[86] UNCITRAL Secretariat, *Judicial Perspective* (n 17) 38.
[87] ibid.
[88] UNCITRAL Secretariat, *Judicial Perspective* (n 17) 39.
[89] UNCITRAL Model Law, Art 20.
[90] ibid Art 20(4).
[91] ibid Art 20(2).
[92] ibid.

example of a potential carve-out.[93] Article 20(3) also provides that the stay does not affect the claimant's right to initiate a necessary action to preserve its claim.[94] This protects a creditor's claim from passing the statute of limitation because of the stay: 'Once the claim has been preserved, the [subsequent] action continues to be covered by the stay'.[95]

C. Article 21: Additional Appropriate Relief

Finally, Article 21 forms the last part of the framework for the relief and effects upon recognition. Article 21 deals with post-recognition relief that may be granted for the benefit of a foreign proceeding.[96] The additional appropriate relief is granted at the discretion of the court and is available for both main and non-main proceedings following the recognition. In the case of main proceedings, that discretionary relief would be in addition to the relief available on recognition. Although the Model Law does not define the term 'appropriate', the standard is set out in Article 22(1) of the Model Law, that is, 'the court must be satisfied that the interests of the creditors and other interested persons, including the debtor, are adequately protected'.[97]

In addition, Article 21 lists the seven most frequently granted examples of additional relief, but the list is not exhaustive:

(1) staying the commencement or continuation of individuals action or proceedings;
(2) staying executions against the debtor's asset;
(3) staying the right to transfer;
(4) providing for the examination of witness or discovery of evidence;
(5) entrusting the debtor's asset to a foreign representative;
(6) extending the Article 19 provisional relief; and
(7) any additional relief that may be available under the laws of the enacting states.[98]

IV. Co-operation and Co-ordination

The final principle combines the concepts of co-operation and co-ordination and places the burden on both courts and representatives in different jurisdictions to communicate and co-operate with their best efforts. This co-operation and co-ordination principle is one of the core elements in the Model Law. This principle ensures

[93] UNCITRAL Secretariat, *Guide to Enactment* (n 2) 85.
[94] UNCITRAL Model Law, Art 20(3).
[95] UNCITRAL Secretariat, *Guide to Enactment* (n 2) 85.
[96] ibid 87.
[97] UNCITRAL Model Law, Art 22(1).
[98] UNCITRAL Model Law, Art 21(1).

that the insolvency process can be dealt with in a manner that is best designed for the needs of all creditors.[99] Co-operation and co-ordination can facilitate an efficient and fair administration of debtors' estates and prevent dissipation of assets, thereby maximising creditors' returns and protecting their investments.

Co-operation does not depend upon a previous formal decision on recognition of the foreign proceeding.[100] It may occur at an early stage, even before an application for recognition.[101] Under Article 25 and Article 26, both courts and administrators are specifically authorised to communicate directly with foreign counterparts.[102] In fact, the Model Law not only authorises cross-border co-operation, by providing that the court and the insolvency representative 'shall cooperate to the maximum extent possible', it also gives this principle a mandatory nature.[103] These articles fill the gaps in the domestic law of most countries, especially civil law countries, providing a legal basis for co-operation between local courts and foreign courts in dealing with cross-border insolvencies.[104] Thus, courts in different jurisdictions may 'just pick up the phone' to contact each other, rather than going through the complicated and tedious formalities, such as communication via higher court, letters rogatory, or other diplomatic or consular channels.[105] For example, in *In re Nortel Networks Corporation*, a joint trial was held between the Canadian Court, the US Court, and representatives of all parties in each jurisdiction by a video link conference and the two Courts agreed a joint reorganisation plan pursuant to a protocol between the Canadian and US Courts.[106] Similarly, in *Perpetual Trustee Company Ltd v Lehman Bros Special Financing Inc*, the English Court and the US Court communicated with each other and reached an agreement that the relief would be limited to declaratory relief to avoid conflicting decisions between the two countries.[107]

Finally, Articles 28 and 29 address the issue of co-ordination between concurrent proceedings. The Model Law allows 'the commencement of a local insolvency proceeding concerning the same debtor even after recognition of a foreign main proceeding as long as the debtor has assets in the state'.[108] However, from another perspective, if a foreign proceeding is recognised as a foreign main proceeding, Article 28 also restricts the local court from commencing non-main proceedings unless debtors have assets in the enacting states. This restriction avoids the possibility of a large number of non-main proceedings.

[99] UNCITRAL Secretariat, *Judicial Perspective* (n 17) 66.
[100] ibid 67.
[101] ibid.
[102] See UNCITRAL Model Law, Arts 25–26.
[103] UNCITRAL Secretariat, *Judicial Perspective* (n 17) 66; UNCTIRAL Model Law, Arts 25–26.
[104] ibid.
[105] Wessels et al (n 19) 224.
[106] *In re Nortel Networks Inc* 532 BR 494 (Bankr Delaware 2015); *Re Nortel Networks Corporation* [2015] ONSC 2987.
[107] *Perpetual Trustee Co Ltd v Lehman Bros Special Financing Inc* [2009] EWHC 2953 (Ch); *In re Lehman Bros Holding Inc* 422 BR 407 (Bankr SD New York 2010).
[108] UNCITRAL Secretariat, *Guide to Enactment* (n 2) 100.

5

Maritime Claims: Characteristics, Secured Status and Enforcement Methods

Maritime law is one of the world's oldest areas of law, developed centuries earlier than the bankruptcy regime. It is an ancient and well-established body of law that focuses on the special nature of the international shipping industry and on the enforcement of maritime claims against maritime assets.[1] The cradle of maritime law can be traced back to the Mediterranean Sea, 'where the sea commerce has had a continuous history for nearly five thousand years'.[2]

For centuries, maritime law has developed a 'sophisticated and generally harmonious' system of dealing with the bankruptcy of shipowners. It provides sufficient and special protection for maritime creditors, especially for maritime lien holders, but excludes land-based creditors and other creditors with an insufficiently direct connection with the ship.[3] This generally harmonious system existed for centuries before the 'universalist approach' became a concern in the regime of bankruptcy.[4]

The two devices of admiralty jurisprudence that have been developed in order to achieve the harmonisation of the maritime law regime are 'maritime liens' and 'actions in rem'.[5] Maritime liens provide security to creditors that can give them increased confidence and certainty in maritime commerce, whilst in rem proceedings are a powerful tool to enforce a debt against a vessel itself. Although different jurisdictions have adopted various rules regarding the availability and priorities of maritime liens as well as developing various theories regarding the nature of in rem actions, it seems that the whole maritime industry has already created a coherent and harmonised system for enforcing maritime claims through unique regimes.[6] In particular, maritime creditors are allowed to arrest vessels in

[1] *Holt Cargo Systems Inc v ABC Containerline NV (Trustee of)* [2001] SCC 90, [25].

[2] ibid.

[3] S Rares, 'Ship Arrests, Maritime Liens and Cross-Border Insolvency' [2018] *Lloyd's Maritime and Commercial Law Quarterly* 398, 399; L Athanassiou, *Maritime Cross-Border Insolvency* (Informa Law from Routledge, 2018) 109.

[4] Rares, 'Ship Arrests, Maritime Liens and Cross-Border Insolvency' (n 3) 408–409.

[5] S Rares, 'Admiralty Law – the Flying Dutchman of Cross-Border Insolvency' (FCA) [2009] *Federal Judicial Scholarship* 22, [7]–[8], available at www3.austlii.edu.au/au/journals/FedJSchol/2009/22.html accessed 5 June 2020.

[6] ibid.

rem wherever they are found and to realise their claims from the proceeds of the vessels' judicial sale, regardless of, and independent from, the shipowner's foreign insolvency proceeding.[7] However, creditors and claims without a sufficiently direct connection to the ship and its operation are excluded from this admiralty process.

I. Maritime Liens

Maritime law has its own special system of security, combined with its own method of enforcement.[8] A maritime lien is a privileged claim that is peculiar to maritime law and attaches to the ship, cargo or freight.[9] In *The Bold Buccleugh*, Sir John Jervis provided the first comprehensive and authoritative definition of a maritime lien:

> a maritime lien is well defined … to mean a claim or privilege upon a thing to be carried into effect by legal process … that process to be a proceeding in rem … This claim or privilege travels with the thing into whosesoever possession it may come. It is inchoate from the moment the claim or privilege attaches, and, when carried into effect by legal process by a proceeding in rem, relates back to the period when it first attached.[10]

The regime of maritime liens represents one of the most prominent features of contemporary maritime law and has been described as 'one of the first principles of the law of the sea'.[11] Maritime liens are internationally recognised and are created by operation of law rather than by contract.[12] The basic purpose of the regime of maritime liens is to provide security for a claim while permitting the ship to proceed on its way in order to earn the freight or hire necessary to pay off the claim.[13] For thousands of years, the regime of maritime liens has been understood and heavily relied on by all ships' creditors across the world, especially financiers, who regard the vessel itself as the primary source of security. Creditors know that they can always arrest a vessel and recover their debt from the proceeds of a judicial sale of a vessel, no matter who owns it at any particular moment.[14] When interplayed with bankruptcy, it is crucial to determine whether a maritime lien claim is a secured claim in order that the maritime lien claimant may compete with other ordinary creditors for whatever is left in the debtor's asset pool.

In most countries, the widely recognised maritime claims that can give rise to maritime liens are: wages of the crew and master; salvage; collision and damage done by a ship (tort claim); and, in rare cases, master's disbursements.[15]

[7] M Davies, 'Cross-Border Insolvency and Admiralty: A Middle Path of Reciprocal Comity' (2018) 66 *American Journal of Comparative Law* 101, 101.
[8] W Tetley, *International Maritime and Admiralty Law* (Éditions Yvon Blais, 2002) 473.
[9] See eg DR Thomas, *Maritime Liens* (Stevens & Sons, 1980) 10.
[10] *The Bold Buccleugh* (1851) 7 Moo PC 267, 284–285.
[11] *The Tolten* [1946] P 135, 144; see also Thomas (n 9) 2.
[12] R Force, *Admiralty and Maritime Law*, 2nd edn (Federal Judicial Center, 2013) 173.
[13] ibid.
[14] S Derrington, 'An Introduction to Cross-Border Insolvency' in *CMI Yearbook 2011–2012*, 371, https://comitemaritime.org/wp-content/uploads/2018/06/Yearbook_2011_12.pdf accessed 5 June 2020.
[15] See eg W Tetley, *Maritime Liens and Claims*, 2nd edn (Éditions Yvon Blais, 1998) 419; *The Bold Buccleugh* (n 10).

These types of claim cover the areas that are essential in order for the maritime commerce and shipping industry to operate successfully. In the UK, Australia, Singapore and other Commonwealth countries, most other types of maritime claims can only give rise to statutory rights of action in rem. Usually these claims include: claims for necessaries such as repair, towage, stevedore, pilotage and other supplies furnished to a vessel;[16] claims for personal injury; claims for general average; claims for cargo damage; and claims for breach of charterparties and other contract.[17] However, in the US, the scope of maritime liens is much broader than in the UK and across other Commonwealth countries. In fact, almost all maritime claims will be granted maritime liens in the US; these arise with the relevant claims and travel with the ship.[18] In particular, unlike in the UK and Commonwealth countries (except Canada), contractual claims for 'necessaries', cargo damage, breach of charter parties and general average claims are granted full status as maritime liens, instead of mere statutory rights of action in rem.[19]

A. Legal Characteristics of Maritime Liens

The fundamental legal characteristics of a maritime lien can be summarised as follows:

(1) privileged: a maritime lien is a privileged claim. As discussed below, for reasons of general public policy it ranks in priority above all other claims against the maritime property, namely mortgages, possessory liens and statutory rights of action in rem, whether they arose prior to or subsequent to the attachment of the maritime lien;[20]

(2) indelible encumbrance: a maritime lien attaches to the vessel, cargo or freight in the sense that the lien travels with the *res* regardless of any change of ownership, even if the bona fide purchaser is unaware of the lien.[21] The term 'vessel' can be broad, which includes its appurtenances, such as engines and boilers, as well as the wreck thereof.[22] This characteristic of maritime liens is based on the notion that maritime liens give rights against the ship rather than the shipowner.[23] Accordingly, the sale of a ship per se does not extinguish the lien. The lien can be discharged only when a judicial sale or other methods

[16] However, in Canada, creditors have maritime liens against foreign vessels for claims that arise in respect of necessaries supplied to the foreign vessels. See Marine Liability Act 2001, s 139.

[17] See eg Senior Courts Act 1981, s 20(2)(e)–(r); Admiralty Act 1988 (Cth), ss 17, 19; High Court (Admiralty Jurisdiction) Act (Singapore), s 3.

[18] Federal Maritime Lien Act, 46 USC §§ 31341–31343; Force (n 12) 175–180.

[19] 46 USC § 31301.

[20] Thomas (n 9) 12.

[21] See *The Bold Buccleugh* (n 10); Thomas (n 9) 14; *The Colorado* [1923] P 102.

[22] See eg *The Dundee* (1824) 66 ER 39; *The Aline* (1839) 166 ER 514.

[23] *The Colorado* (n 21).

of extinction occur, such as a payment or bond being provided by the shipowner, or the ship or the cargo where the lien is attached being destroyed;[24]

(3) secret lien: a maritime lien is a secret lien that is inchoate in the vessel from the time the claim occurs. It does not need to be recorded or acknowledged by the claimant. It is perfected and is carried into effect by an action in rem that relates back to the period when it first attached. Accordingly, a maritime lien secretively follows the ship and continues to bind the ship throughout its operation, without anyone knowing the exact extent of this burden until it is carried into effect by legal process, namely, an action in rem.[25] Although the lack of publicity of maritime liens has been widely criticised as being incompatible with the characteristics of contemporary international transactions, namely that rights that are enforceable against third parties must always be public, this characteristic is an historical residue of the customary origin of maritime liens and remains intact at both a national and international level;[26]

(4) non-possessory and non-consensual: a maritime lien is a non-possessory security device that is created by operation of law. Neither the possession of the property nor the consent by the parties is required;[27]

(5) enforced by an action in rem: a maritime lien can only be enforced by legal process by a proceeding in rem against the vessel itself, upon which the lien is perfected and relates back retrospectively to the time when it first attached. In order to realise its maritime lien, a maritime lien holder must initiate a proceeding for the arrest and sale of the relevant vessel in an admiralty court, with its claim satisfied out of the proceeds of the judicial sale.[28]

B. Underlying Nature of Maritime Liens

The issue regarding whether a maritime lien is substantive and proprietary in nature, or procedural and remedial in nature, has been the subject of dispute for many decades. A maritime lien has traditionally been deemed to be a substantive property right and is based on the personification doctrine that can be traced back to the English admiralty courts of the sixteenth century.[29] Under the personification doctrine, a vessel is personified and is held liable for its torts and any contractual obligations undertaken on its behalf to facilitate the accomplishment

[24] J Browne, 'The Extinction of Maritime Liens' [2003] *Lloyd's Maritime and Commercial Law Quarterly* 361.

[25] *The Two Ellens* (1872) LR 4 PC 161, 169; Athanassiou (n 3) 109.

[26] Athanassiou (n 3) 109.

[27] Force (n 12) 173.

[28] *The Tolten* (n 11); *The Cella* (1888) 13 PD 82; Thomas (n 9) 12; Browne (n 24) 366.

[29] See eg *The Bold Buccleugh* (n 10); M Tsimplis, 'Procedures for Enforcement' in Y Baatz (ed), *Maritime Law*, 4th edn (Routledge, 2017) 503, 501; P Herbert, 'The Origin and Nature of Maritime Liens' (1930) 4 *Tulane Law Review* 381.

of its mission.[30] The vessel itself is regarded as the 'wrongdoer' and as a 'distinct juristic entity' in the sense that an in rem action is viewed as an action against the vessel itself for its wrong, independent of the fault of the owner. The vessel can be liable even though the owner has no in personam liability.[31] In the US, the personification doctrine has been taken rather literally and seriously.[32] Under the logic of the personification doctrine, a maritime lien is regarded as a substantive property right that creates an immediate property right when certain services are done to the ship and when certain damage is done by the ship; it remains inchoate at the time the claim is attached.[33] The lien will be carried into effect either by the initiation of a proceeding in rem,[34] or by the subsequent breach,[35] and relates back to the time when it first attached.[36]

However, English courts abandoned the doctrine of personification in the late nineteenth century in favour of what is known as 'the procedural theory'.[37] The procedural theory was first articulated by Jeune J in *The Dictator*, where he held that, 'if the owners do not appear, the action only enforces the lien on the res, but that, when they do, the action in rem … is also a means of enforcing against the appearing owners, if they could have been made personally liable in the Admiralty Court'.[38] Lord Diplock, in a debatable case, *The Halcyon Isle*, further supported the procedural theory by holding that, in order to be consistent with the characterisation of a maritime lien as procedural and remedial in nature, whether a particular class of claim will give rise to a maritime lien shall be determined by English law as the *lex fori*.[39] Subsequently, following the decision of the House of Lords in *The Indian Grace (No 2)*, English courts applied the 'procedural theory' in a particularly radical way. In *The Indian Grace (No 2)*, the House of Lords held that an in rem action was merely a procedural tool for forcing the appearance of the shipowner and, in substance, the owner was the party to an action in rem.[40] Accordingly, under the procedural theory, a maritime lien is regarded as

[30] See eg *The China* 74 US 53 (1986); *Tucker v Alexandroff* 183 US 424 (1902); Force (n 12) 173; M Davies, 'In Defense of Popular Virtues: Personification and Ratification' (2000) 75 *Tulane Law Review* 337, 338.

[31] See eg *The China* (n 30).

[32] See eg *The China* (n 30); *Tucker v Alexandroff* (n 30).

[33] *The Bold Buccleugh* (n 10).

[34] Under the Anglo-common law countries' substantive view of maritime liens, maritime liens are perfected upon the initiation of proceedings in rem. See P Myburgh, 'Richard Cooper Memorial Lecture Admiralty Law – What is it Good For?' (2009) 28(1) *University of Queensland Law Journal* 19, 30; *The Bold Buccleugh* (n 10) 284–85.

[35] Under the US view, a maritime lien attaches at the commencement of the undertaking and any subsequent breach perfecting the lien relates back to that time: *Bank One Louisiana NA v Mr Dean MV* 293 F 3d 830, 834 (5th Cir 2002).

[36] *The Bold Buccleugh* (n 10).

[37] Davies, 'In Defense of Unpopular Virtues' (n 30) 341.

[38] *The Dictator* [1892] P 304, 320–21.

[39] *The Halcyon Isle* [1981] AC 221, 234.

[40] *The Indian Grace (No 2)* [1998] AC 878, 909.

procedural and remedial, and creates no 'immediate property right' at the time the claim attaches.[41] It is only carried into effect by a proceeding in rem and, once carried into effect, dates back to the period when it first attached.[42]

However, the decision in *The Indian Grace (No 2)* has been criticised by many commentators.[43] It is important to note that in *The Indian Grace (No 2)*, what the Court considered was not an in rem claim to enforce a maritime lien, but a claim regarding a statutory right of action in rem (a cargo damage claim) that will be discussed in detail below.[44] Accordingly, it has been argued by many commentators, and I agree, that maritime liens are still substantive and proprietary in nature in the sense that a strong version of personification still persists, with maritime liens being enforceable only against the 'offending' vessel, and only to the extent of the value of the vessel.[45] Maritime liens are no more inchoate than any other substantive rights. 'Prior to the proceedings in rem, it is just as much as an encumbrance on the vessel as is a charge on a fund, or an equitable lien on land or a fund'.[46]

C. Policy Rationale of Maritime Liens and the Doctrine of Personification

The unique regime regarding maritime liens has arisen in order to fit the unique characteristics of the maritime property and shipping industry. 'Centuries ago, ships were literally "floating islands" that traversed the globe, with no way of communicating with their onshore owners or managers, and having to rely entirely on their own resources'.[47] Once a vessel has sailed away from land it is not necessarily in the immediate possession and control of its owner. During the voyage the vessel needs to undertake necessary expenditure and continue its maritime adventure. In addition, the vessel needs to be properly navigated and the cargo professionally managed; this relies upon a proper master and crew to provide essential navigation services.[48] Furthermore, in order to help the voyage go smoothly the vessel will need a 'necessaries assistant' to be responsible for matters such as repairs,

[41] *The Halcyon Isle* (n 39) 235.

[42] *The Halcyon Isle* (n 39) 235; see also DC Jackson, *Enforcement of Maritime Claims*, 4th edn (Routledge, 2005) [18.21].

[43] See eg N Teare, 'The Admiralty Action in Rem and the House of Lords' [1998] *Lloyd's Maritime and Commercial Law Quarterly* 33; BJ Davenport, 'End of an Old Admiralty Belief' (1998) 11 *LQR* 169; Tsimplis (n 29) 501–502; S Rares, 'Maritime Liens, Renvoi and Conflicts of Law' [2014] *Lloyd's Maritime and Commercial Law Quarterly* 183; S Derrington and J Turner, *The Law and Practice of Admiralty Matters*, 2nd edn (Oxford University Press, 2016) ch 2.

[44] *The Indian Grace (No 2)* (n 40); N Meeson and J Kimbell, *Admiralty Jurisdiction and Practice*, 5th edn (Informa Law from Routledge, 2017) 94.

[45] *The Bold Buccleugh* (n 10); Myburgh (n 34) 29; Meeson and Kimbell (n 44) 94.

[46] Jackson (n 42) 480.

[47] Myburgh (n 34) 25.

[48] Rares, 'Ship Arrests, Maritime Liens and Cross-Border Insolvency' (n 3) 399.

stevedoring, towage and supplies. When the vessel is in peril it may need a salvor to assist the vessel, its crew and cargo, which may give rise to a salvage award. Finally, during the voyage, the vessel may commit a tortious act against a crew member, passenger, cargo or even towards another vessel.[49] These potential claimants 'have been perceived, either as providing fundamental service to the vessel, or as victims of maritime tort that must be compensated by the negligent ship'.[50] Due to the mobile nature of ships, who could keep incurring liabilities to the disadvantage of any existing claimants, the interests of these aforementioned claimants were vulnerable and they had less certainty and security of recovering their debt. Therefore, given that these claimants were fundamental to maritime adventures, the regime of maritime liens was developed in order to provide special protection to these claimants and to give priority to their interests.[51]

Moreover, despite the mobile nature of the property, the way that such assets are owned and operated is also a significant factor leading to this special regime of maritime liens and the doctrine of personification. The true ownership of a seagoing vessel is often very difficult to discern as it may be hidden and disguised through a 'one-ship company'.[52] It has been common practice in the shipping industry to register a vessel in the name of a company with no assets other than the particular ship itself; this is despite the fact that these individual ships may have a common parent corporation or holding company and be managed or operated as a fleet together. This arrangement is known as a 'one-ship company' and such companies will often register in an offshore jurisdiction.[53] The system is principally a cost-saving device that permits ships to be registered in states for a lower price. It also permits shipowners to avoid heavier national taxation and employ seafarers at lower pay rates. In addition, by separating their assets into each one-ship company, the beneficial owners can protect their collective investment – the fleet – from the ever-present risks attendant on individual ships.[54] In the absence of evidence of fraud, courts generally refuse to lift the corporate veil to look behind the 'one-ship company' structure for the purpose of identifying the beneficial owner of the company as the responsible party.[55] Accordingly, this arrangement makes the rights of maritime claimants even more uncertain and more easily attacked. Thus, by granting them the right to enforce their claims against the vessel itself, ie the

[49] ibid.

[50] N Letalik, 'Maritime Lien' in E Gold et al (eds), *Canadian Maritime Law*, 2nd edn (Irwin Law, 2016) 363–64.

[51] Rares, 'Ship Arrests, Maritime Liens and Cross-Border Insolvency' (n 3) 399; Letalik (n 50) 363–64.

[52] Davies, 'In Defense of Unpopular Virtues' (n 30) 363; C Schwartz, 'Due Process and Traditional Admiralty Arrest and Attachment Under the Supplemental Rules' (1983) 8 *Maritime Lawyer* 229, 262.

[53] See eg J Ford and C Wilcox, 'Shedding Light on the Dark Side of Maritime Trade – A New Approach for Identifying Countries as Flags of Convenience' (2019) 99 *Marine Policy* 298; GS Egiyan, 'Flag of Convenience or Open Registration of Ships' (1990) 14 *Marine Policy* 106.

[54] ibid.

[55] Meeson and Kimbell (n 44) 106–107.

vessel is personified as the offending defendant, maritime lien holders will not be frustrated by the difficulty of identifying the defendant. Maritime lienholders can always enforce their claims against the vessel directly regardless of who owns the vessel at the moment of enforcement.

D. Secured Status of Maritime Liens

If a maritime lien is regarded as a substantive property right, it is generally accepted that it is, by definition, a secured claim. It is a security interest in the vessel that arises simultaneously upon the services or events giving rise to a maritime lien.[56] Shipowners promise to secure creditors' debts through the vessel itself and, as an interest in the vessel, a maritime lien extends only to the value of the vessel.[57] Although a maritime lien remains inchoate until the lien is carried into effect, either by the initiation of a proceeding in rem, or by the subsequent breach, it retrospectively relates back to the time when it first attached, upon the arrest, the obtaining of security in lieu or the subsequent breach.[58] Therefore, when a claimant enforces its maritime lien, it is, in fact, enforcing a pre-existing proprietary interest in the vessel.[59] In other words, a maritime lien arises upon the claim attaching and is secured simultaneously; the commencement of an action in rem or the subsequent breach is one step further to bringing the maritime lien into effect.[60]

However, if a maritime lien is regarded as a procedural and remedial right, it only becomes secured when an in rem action is commenced. Notwithstanding that under the procedural theory a maritime lien is also carried into effect by a proceeding in rem and, once carried into effect, dates back to the time when it first attached, under the procedural theory a maritime lien creates no immediate

[56] MJ Hafeez-Baig, 'Navigating The Waters Between Admiralty and Cross-Border Insolvency: A Comparison of the Australian, German and French Position' [2018] *Lloyd's Maritime and Commercial Law Quarterly* 97, 115; J Devlin, 'The UNCITRAL Model Law on Cross-Border Insolvency and Its Impact on Maritime Creditors' (2010) 21 *Journal of Banking and Finance Law and Practice* 95, 99–100.

[57] D Skeen, 'Liens and Liquidation: Preferences, Strong Arm Clause, Fraudulent Transfers, Equitable Subordination, Priorities and Other Limitations on Liens Claims' (1985) 59 *Tulane Law Review* 1401, 1423–24.

[58] *The Bold Buccleugh* (n 10); Hafeez-Baig (n 56) 115.

[59] Hafeez-Baig (n 56) 115.

[60] *The Bold Buccleugh* (n 10); *The Heinrich Bjorn* (1885) 10 PD 44; Hafeez-Baig (n 56) 115. An issue may arise, at least in the US, with regard to the trustee's avoiding power to eliminate the secured status of an unperfected lien once a bankruptcy proceeding is commenced. However, it has been argued that trustee's avoiding power did not apply to a maritime lien on the ground that the 'strong-arm power' applied only to judicial liens or liens obtained through a legal or equitable proceeding. Although maritime liens are enforced by judicial proceedings, they arise automatically upon the claim attached. See D Skeen, 'Liens and Liquidation: Preference, Strong Arm Clause, Fraudulent Transfers, Equitable Subordination, Priorities and Other Limitation on Liens Claims' (1984) 59 *Tulane Law Review* 1401, 1405; *In re North Atlantic & Gulf Steamship Co* 204 F Supp 899 (SD New York 1962); *In re H&S Transport Co* 42 BR 164, 167 (Bankr MD Tennessee 1984).

property right at the time the claim attaches.[61] Thus, if a maritime lien is procedural and remedial in nature, it only becomes a secured claim upon the commencement of an in rem action, by which it creates a property right and is carried into effect. However, if for whatever reason the subsequent action in rem cannot be brought, such as the commencement of an insolvency proceeding, the lien remains inchoate and there is no basis for it to obtain secured status.

II. Statutory Rights of Action in Rem

A. Legal Characteristics and Nature of Statutory Rights of Action in Rem

As discussed above, in the UK, Australia, Singapore and other Commonwealth countries, only certain groups of claims can give rise to maritime liens, while most other maritime claims only give rise to statutory rights of action in rem. Therefore, it is necessary to distinguish traditional maritime liens from statutory rights of action in rem.

A statutory right of action in rem resembles a maritime lien in the sense that it involves a proceeding against a *res*, as distinct from a person. However, it differs from a maritime lien in at least four major aspects. First, the underlying nature of a statutory right of action in rem is purely a procedural remedy; the underlying nature of a maritime lien is arguably a substantive remedy. A statutory right of action in rem is simply a right that is granted by statute to arrest a ship in an action in rem in order to obtain security for a maritime claim.[62] It is a way to force the owner of the vessel to appear and be subject to the court's jurisdiction. Second, a statutory right of action in rem does not arise with the relevant claim, but, instead, arises with the issuing of the writ (in the UK)[63] or with the vessel arrest (in Canada)[64] and will be extinguished when the vessel is released or security is provided.[65] Third, it does not 'travel with the ship into a new ownership', but will be extinguished 'if the vessel is sold to another owner before it is arrested'.[66] Finally, in the distribution of the proceeds in a judicial sale of a vessel, a statutory right of action in rem ranks after a ship mortgage, which, in turn, has a lower priority than a maritime lien.[67]

[61] *The Halcyon Isle* (n 39).
[62] W Tetley, 'Arrest, Attachment, and Related Maritime Law Procedures' (1999) 73 *Tulane Law Review* 1895, 1905–1906; Tsimplis (n 29) 477.
[63] *In re Aro Co Ltd* [1980] Ch 196.
[64] *The Monica S* [1968] P 741.
[65] Tetley, *International Admiralty and Maritime Law* (n 8) 491.
[66] ibid.
[67] ibid.

B. Secured Status of Statutory Rights of Action in Rem

A statutory right of action in rem is a kind of hybrid between a maritime lien and a general unsecured claim. It is a right granted to the claimant and will not be vested in the vessel as a property interest until the claimant chooses to exercise that right. Therefore, it is not a secured claim when it arises, but in most cases becomes a secured claim once it is perfected by the issuance of a writ or the arrest of the vessel. Contrary to the security interest created by a maritime lien that retrospectively relates back to the time when the maritime lien first attaches to the vessel, once a subsequent action in rem carries it into effect, the security interest created by a statutory right of action in rem is prospective.[68] In other words, the proprietary consequence of a statutory right of action in rem is the product of the statutory criteria, plus the action in rem, and not because of any pre-existing inchoate lien.

i. Majority Position

The majority position is that a statutory right of action in rem becomes a secured claim once the writ of arresting vessel is issued. In *The Cella*, the UK Court of Appeal held that 'though there may be no maritime lien, yet the moment that the arrest takes place, the ship is held by the Court as a security for whatever may be adjudged by it to be due to the claimant'.[69] Accordingly, a ship can be regarded as security that is reserved primarily for certain kinds of claims provided by statute, namely, statutory rights of action in rem.[70] In addition, Hewson J in *The Zafiro* held that a creditor with a necessaries claim, who had issued its writ in rem for arresting the vessel before the commencement of a winding up of the debtor, should be regarded as a secured creditor and obtain priority over other creditors.[71]

Furthermore, in *The Monica S*, the UK High Court was faced with considerable debate regarding the issue of when a statutory right of action in rem attaches to a relevant vessel, and at what point the creditor with a necessaries claim becomes a secured creditor.[72] In *The Monica S*, the creditor issued a writ in rem against the shipowner and claimed for breach of contract of carriage. However, the ship was sold to a third-party bona fide purchaser before the writ had been served. The Court was asked to decide at what point a statutory right of action in rem becomes effective and attaches to the vessel – when the action is brought or when the vessel is actually caught? The Court ruled in favour of the institution of the suit as the critical time and held that a statutory right of action in rem arose when the writ in rem was issued, rather than when it was served.[73] Thus, the change of ship's

[68] Hafeez-Baig (n 56) 115.
[69] *The Cella* (n 28) 88.
[70] ibid 87.
[71] *The Zafiro* [1960] P 1.
[72] *The Monica S* (n 64).
[73] ibid 770.

ownership between the issuing of the writ in rem and the service of the writ did not prevent the process of the ship's arrest. However, Brandon J noted that the case here dealt with a change of ownership and the answer might have been different for a liquidation or priority case.[74] Finally, the UK Court of Appeal in *Re Aro Co Ltd*, a liquidation case, fixed the answer as to when a statutory right of action in rem claim was considered to be instituted.[75] The plaintiff in *Re Aro Co Ltd* issued a writ in rem before the commencement of a winding-up proceeding of the debtor; however, the writ in rem was served after the winding-up order had been made. The UK Court of Appeal concluded that a statutory right of action in rem became a secured claim once the writ in rem was issued.[76]

Therefore, the position in the UK regarding whether a statutory right of action in rem will become a secured claim is that the crucial time point is when the writ in rem is issued.[77] In other words, a statutory right of action in rem is not a secured claim when it initially arises but will convert to a secured claim when the proceeding is instituted by the issuing of a writ in rem.[78] This view has been adopted in most Commonwealth countries. For example, the Federal Court of Australia in *Danny Morris & Another v The Ship Kiama* held that a statutory right in rem became a secured claim upon the issuing of a writ in rem.[79] In addition, the Singapore Court of Appeal in *Kuo Fen Ching v Dauphin Offshore Engineering & Trading Pte Ltd* adopted the same approach. The Court held that 'the issue of a writ in rem in exercise of the statutory right of action had crucial consequences which ensured to the benefit of the plaintiffs and made them secured creditors'.[80]

ii. Minority Position

On the other hand, the minority position held by the Federal Court of Canada in *The Miss Donna* was that, even by arresting the vessel, a claimant for necessaries does not become a secured creditor within the meaning of section 2 of the Canadian Bankruptcy Act.[81] The claimant remains an ordinary unsecured creditor. The Federal Court of Canada considered that the Court's right to control the assets and the power to sell the vessel through a statutory right of action in rem

[74] ibid 771; see also *The Cella* (n 28); *The Zafiro* (n 71).
[75] *In re Aro Co Ltd* (n 63).
[76] *In re Aro Co Ltd* (n 63).
[77] *The Monica S* (n 64); *In re Aro Co Ltd* (n 63).
[78] *In re Aro Co Ltd* (n 63); see also *The Pacific* (1864) 167 ER 356; *The Two Ellens* (n 25).
[79] *Danny Morris & Another v The Ship Kiama* [1998] FCA 256; see also *Comandate Marine Corp v Pan Australia Shipping Pty Ltd* [2006] FCAFC 192; *Yakushiji v Daiichi Chuo Kisen Kaisha* [2015] FCA 1170.
[80] *Kuo Fen Ching and Another v Dauphin Offshore Engineering & Trading Pte Ltd* [1999] SGCA 95. But see *Seaspan Holdco 1 Ltd v MS Mare Traveller Schiffahrts GmbH (MV Seaspan Grouse)* [2019] ZASCA 02 (where the Supreme Court of Appeal of South Africa refused to follow *The Monica S* and held that the date of the commencement of an action in rem was the date of the arrest).
[81] *The Miss Donna* [1978] 1 FC 379.

is not equal to a true vested right in the ship itself. Addy J explained that, since a statutory right of action in rem is merely procedural, the proceeding of vessel arrest must also be merely procedural: 'it merely provides a remedy and does not create any special legal vested right in the creditor or claimant which did not exist previously'.[82] In other words, the arrest of the ship is merely a procedural method that is used to ensure the execution of the judgment and does not create any privilege or lien vested in the creditor or claimant.[83] A person choosing 'to proceed in rem against the vessel in lieu of merely proceeding in personam against the owner, does not, by so doing, acquire the special status of a secured creditor' and thereafter has priority over other ordinary creditors in the bankruptcy proceeding.[84] Therefore, Addy J concluded that the claimant for necessaries was no different to an ordinary unsecured creditor, and had no right to proceed with the action after the bankruptcy proceeding was initiated.

The majority position has been criticised on the ground that it is inequitable and inconsistent with the nature of a statutory right of action in rem as a purely procedural remedy, rather than a substantive maritime lien.[85] In addition, it will lead to jurisdictional complications when involving the interplay with the International Convention Relating to the Arrest of Sea-Going Ships 1952.[86] Nevertheless, it is widely accepted in most jurisdictions that statutory rights of action in rem arise upon the issuing of a writ and become secured claims from then on.

III. Ship Mortgages

A ship mortgage, similar to other land-based mortgages, is a security interest in the vessel that is contractually granted by a shipowner to a lender or mortgagee as security for a debt.[87] Since the nineteenth century ship mortgages have become a widely-accepted practice in the shipping industry as a source of major financing for shipowners, particularly for the construction or purchase of vessels.[88]

In Commonwealth countries, a ship mortgagee is, by definition, a secured creditor. For example, section 248(a) of the Insolvency Act 1986 defines a 'secured creditor' in relation to a company as 'a creditor of the company who holds in respect of his debt a security over property of the company';[89] and section 248(b)(i) defines 'security' in relation to England and Wales as 'any mortgage, charge,

[82] ibid [22].
[83] ibid [22].
[84] ibid [24].
[85] Tetley, *Maritime Liens and Claims* (n 15) 560.
[86] ibid 560–62.
[87] *Citibank NA v Hobbs Savill & Co Ltd (The Panglobal Friendship)* [1978] 1 Lloyd's Rep 368, 371.
[88] ibid.
[89] Insolvency Act 1986, s 248(a).

lien or other security'.[90] In addition, paragraph 7 of Schedule 1 to the UK Merchant Shipping Act 1995 provides for the creation of a mortgage over a vessel:

> (1) A registered ship, or share in a registered ship, may be made a security for the repayment of a loan or the discharge of any other obligation.
> (2) The instrument creating any such security (referred to in the following provisions of this Schedule as a 'mortgage') shall be in the form prescribed by or approved under registration regulations.[91]

Therefore, by definition, a ship mortgage provides a creditor with security for the repayment of a loan, for the performance of an obligation by the acquisition of a property interest in a ship or for any financial obligations that are involved in the operation of the vessel.[92] Similarly, in the US, courts do not regard a ship mortgage as a maritime contract in the sense that a ship mortgage is treated as an ordinary mortgage agreement.[93] Therefore, undoubtedly, the holders of ship mortgages, by definition, are secured creditors in the US.

The mortgagee can enforce the ship mortgage either through an action in rem or an action in personam. In addition, a ship mortgagee can obtain a higher priority than other general unsecured claimants with regard to the distribution of the proceeds of the sale of a vessel.[94]

One side question regarding the secured status of a ship mortgage is whether the holder of an unregistered ship mortgage can be regarded as a secured creditor. Generally, failure to register does not invalidate the ship mortgage:

> An unregistered mortgage constitutes an equitable mortgage and is effective as between the mortgagor and the mortgagee. However, as against third parties, it will rank after recorded subsequent mortgages and will not be affected by an act of bankruptcy committed by the mortgagor.[95]

Accordingly, once the debtor and the creditor have concluded an enforceable ship mortgage agreement, the security interest becomes attached to the collateral and the ship mortgagee will become a secured creditor. In other words, registration as a method of perfection is merely an additional step that a secured creditor can take in order to strengthen its rights so that it will obtain superior rights over other potential unperfected secured creditors or unsecured creditors. Therefore, the lack of registration will not affect the secured status of a ship mortgage.

Nevertheless, at least in the US, a trustee of the bankruptcy estate may allow an unperfected secured interest to be avoided upon the commencement of an

[90] Insolvency Act 1986, s 248(b)(i).
[91] Merchant Shipping Act 1995, Sch 1, para 7.
[92] G Gilmore and C Black, *The Law of Admiralty*, 2nd edn (Foundation Press, 1975) 568–69.
[93] See eg B Smith, 'Ship Mortgages' (1973) 47 *Tulane Law Review* 608, 608; *Bogart v The Steamboat John Jay* 58 US 399 (1854); *Detroit Trust Co v The Thomas Barlum* 293 US 21 (1934); *The JE Rumbell* 148 US 1 (1893); *The Eclipse* 135 US 599 (1890).
[94] Tetley, *Maritime Liens and Claims* (n 15) 480.
[95] ibid 481.

insolvency proceeding; these are known as 'strong arm powers'.[96] If a trustee exercises its discretion and avoids an unperfected secured interest, the unperfected secured claim will lose its secured status and become a general unsecured claim. Accordingly, if the ship mortgage is not registered, it is not perfected. Although it retains its status as a secured claim in normal circumstances, the trustee has the avoiding power to eliminate the secured status of the unregistered ship mortgage once the bankruptcy proceeding is commenced.[97] Nevertheless, it is very rare in practice that ship mortgages are not registered. Since a ship mortgage is such an important method for financing and providing security, a sophisticated lawyer would always register it at the first opportunity. Therefore, in most cases, a ship mortgagee is a secured creditor.

IV. Conflict of Laws

As discussed above, despite the universally recognised characteristics of maritime liens, there remain significant differences between various countries. The two most important differences involve the scope and ranking of maritime liens.[98] For example, in the US, a maritime lien is granted to those who provide necessary services or supplies to a vessel, whilst a necessaries claim that arises in Australia, Singapore, the UK and other Commonwealth countries (except Canada) only gives rise to a statutory right of action in rem.[99] Accordingly, the question of a conflict of laws regarding maritime liens will arise in the forum where the vessel is arrested.

In fact, three layers of conflict questions need to be considered. First, what law governs the plaintiff's underlying claim, namely, the underlying cause of action of the plaintiff's claim? Second, what law governs the availability of a maritime lien? The forum court needs to decide whether it would recognise a foreign maritime lien against the vessel or other property. Third, what law governs the priority between competing maritime lien claims when the proceeds subsequent to a judicial sale are not enough to pay off all the claims?[100]

It is worth noting that the law governing the underlying claim will not always govern the availability of a maritime lien.[101] In most jurisdictions, such as the

[96] 11 USC § 544.

[97] ibid; see also Skeen (n 59) 1407–1408; *IFG Leasing v Captains Courageous Inc* 21 BR 134 (Bankr ND California 1982).

[98] W Tetley, 'Maritime Liens in Conflict of Laws' in J Nafziger and S Symeonides (eds), *Law and Justice in a Multistate World: Essays in Honour of Arthur T von Mehren* (Brill Nijhoff, 2002) 446–47.

[99] Federal Maritime Lien Act, 46 USC §§ 31341–31343; Senior Courts Act 1981, ss 20(2)(e)–(r); Admiralty Act 1988 (Cth), ss 17, 19; High Court (Admiralty Jurisdiction) Act, s 3.

[100] M Davies, 'Choice of Law and US Maritime Liens' (2009) 83 *Tulane Law Review* 1435, 1436; Tetley, 'Maritime Liens in Conflict of Laws' (n 98) 448, 460.

[101] Davies, 'Choice of Law and US Maritime Liens' (n 100) 1436.

UK,[102] Australia,[103] Singapore,[104] New Zealand,[105] South Africa,[106] Malaysia,[107] and China,[108] courts have held that the *lex fori*[109] (the domestic law of the forum) governs the question of recognition of the status of a foreign maritime claim. In other words, the issue of whether a claimant has a maritime lien is a matter for the *lex fori* alone.[110] The decision reached by the majority is based on the notion that maritime liens are procedural remedies, rather than substantive rights. Therefore, under the majority approach, these jurisdictions refuse to recognise a necessaries claim as giving rise to the type of lien available under US law.[111]

In contrast, in the US and Canada, where the underlying claim is governed by a foreign law that would confer a maritime lien on that kind of claim, the local court will enforce it, regardless of whether there is any connection between the claim and the forum.[112] In other words, the US and Canada hold the view that whether a claim would be conferred as a maritime lien is a matter for the law that governs the underlying claim (the *lex causae*). Thus, when the law of a foreign jurisdiction is found to be the 'proper law' according to the US and Canadian choice of law rules, courts in the US and Canada would recognise foreign maritime lien claims, even though the rights they confer are different in character from those that would arise under the equivalent maritime lien claims under *lex fori*.[113] The reason for the approach of *lex causae* is because, in the US and Canada, maritime liens are regarded as substantive rights for the purpose of a conflict of laws. Nevertheless, in distributing the proceeds of the ship's judicial sale, most countries, whether regarding maritime liens as substantive or procedural remedies, adopt the approach of *lex fori* with regard to the priorities of competing maritime claims.[114]

[102] *The Halcyon Isle* (n 39).

[103] See eg *The Ship Sam Hawk v Reiter Petroleum Inc* [2016] FCAFC 26; *Morlines Maritime Agency Ltd & Others v The Skulptor Vuchetich* [1997] FCA 432.

[104] *The Andres Bonifacio* [1993] SGCA 70; *Precious Shipping Public Co Ltd v OW Bunker Far East* [2015] SGHC 187.

[105] *Ship Betty Ott v General Bills Ltd* [1992] 1 NZLR 655; *ABC Shipbrokers v The Ship Offi Gloria* [1993] 3 NZLR 576; *Fournier v Ship Margaret Z* [1999] 3 NZLR 111.

[106] *Transol Bunker BV v Motor Vessel Andrico Unity* [1989] 4 SA 325.

[107] *Ocean Grain Shipping Pte Ltd v The Dong Nai* [1996] 4 MLJ 454; *The Ocean Jade* [1991] 2 MLJ 386.

[108] The Chinese Maritime Code, Art 272; *Mobil Sales and Supply Corp v The Owners of the Ship Pacific Bear* [1979] HKLR 125.

[109] *Lex fori* is defined as the law of the forum or the 'law of the jurisdiction where the case is pending', whilst the *lex causae* is defined as 'the legal system that governs the dispute'. See *Black's Law Dictionary*, 11th edn (West Group, 2019).

[110] *The Halcyon Isle* (n 39).

[111] See eg *The Halcyon Isle* (n 39); *The Andres Bonifacio* (n 104).

[112] See eg *Ocean Ship Supply Ltd v M/V Leah* 729 F 2d 971 (4th Cir 1984); *The Ioannis Daskalelis* [1974] SCR 1248.

[113] See eg *M/V Leah* (n 112) 973–74; *Trinidad Foundry & Fabricating Ltd v M/V KAS Camilla* 966 F 2d 613 (11th Cir 1992); *Bominflot Inc v The M/V Henrich S* 465 F 3d 144 (4th Cir 2006); *The Ioannis Daskalelis* (n 112) 1259.

[114] *M/V Leah* (n 112); *The Ioannis Daskalelis* (n 112); *The Halcyon Isle* (n 39); Tetley, 'Maritime Liens in Conflict of Laws' (n 98).

V. Enforcement of Maritime Claims

A. Action in Personam

A claimant who seeks to enforce a claim that lies within the admiralty jurisdiction may, depending on the circumstances, commence either an action in personam or an action in rem. An action in personam is based on the personal liability of the defendant, as is the case in an ordinary tort or breach of contract situation. In an action in personam, judgment is entered against the defendant and can be enforced against the entire assets of the defendant.[115]

B. Action in Rem

In addition, a claimant can enforce its maritime claim by an action in rem; this is an action directly against the relevant property, typically a ship that relates to the claim. The regime of action in rem is regarded as one of the most powerful and unique remedies in maritime law.[116]

i. Action in Rem under the Personification Doctrine

As discussed above, in rem actions are based on the fiction of 'personification', in the sense that a ship is deemed to have a legal personality separate from its owner and, as such, is subject to direct legal action. It can be held liable for any tortious act that it has committed as well as for any contract that it may have breached.[117] Thus, in a country that adopts the true personification doctrine, such as the US, courts will generally regard in personam actions and in rem actions as two distinct types of lawsuit.[118] Since the enforcement is against the vessel itself, any judgment is therefore limited to the value thereof, or the value of the bond or stipulation substituted for the res to obtain its release.[119] Sister ship arrest is not permitted due to the consequence of the doctrine of personification on the ground that only the 'offending' vessel itself can be arrested and subject to the in

[115] Force (n 12) 30–31; see also Tetley, *International Maritime and Admiralty Law* (n 8) 406.

[116] Rares, 'Admiralty law the Flying Dutchman of Cross-Border Insolvency' (n 5).

[117] Force (n 12) 31.

[118] See eg *The China* (n 30); *SEL Maduro (Florida) Inc v M/V Antonio de Gastaneta* 833 F 2d 1477, 1481–82 (11th Cir 1987); *The Eastern Shore* 24 F 2d 443, 443 (D Maryland 1928); *Central Hudson Gas and Electric Corp v Empresa Naviera Santa SA* 845 F Supp 150, 152–53 (SD New York 1994); but see *Continental Grain Co v Barge* FBL-585 364 US 19, 25 (1960); *Burns Bros v Central RR* 202 F 2d 910, 912–13 (2d Cir 1953); *Royal School Laboratories Inc v Town of Watertown* 358 F 2d 813, 815 (2d Cir 1966); *Insurance Co of N America v S/S American Argosy* 732 F 2d 299, 302 (2d Cir 1984).

[119] *Central Hudson Gas* (n 118) 364.

rem action.[120] Nevertheless, in the US, a sister ship arrest can be taken by a maritime attachment under Rule B of the Supplemental Rules for Certain Admiralty and Maritime Claims of the Federal Rules of Civil Procedure (known as a Rule B attachment).[121] Accordingly, in the US Rule B attachment forms a third option for claimants to enforce their admiralty claims. It combines the characteristics of both in personam and in rem actions, which is often referred to as an action quasi in rem.[122] On the one hand, it resembles an in rem action in that it is commenced by seizing the vessel when the vessel presents within the geographic boundaries of the federal judicial district where the action is being brought, even if the shipowner itself cannot be found within that district.[123] On the other hand, it is similar to an in personam action in the sense that it is based on the personal liability of the property owner.[124] Accordingly, when a defendant submits itself to the personal jurisdiction of the court, the judgment will extend to all the defendant's assets that are found within the judicial district, whether tangible or intangible.[125] The purpose of a quasi in rem proceeding of attachment is to compel the defendant to personally appear to defend against the claim.[126]

ii. Action in Rem under the Procedural Theory

In the UK, Australia, Singapore and most Commonwealth countries, although in rem enforcement is available for maritime liens, statutory rights of action in rem and ship mortgages, the personification doctrine was largely abandoned in the late nineteenth century and evolved into what is now known as the 'procedural theory'.[127]

As discussed above, in the classical version of the procedural theory articulated in *The Dictator*, 'the action in rem is a different action from one in personam' in the sense that even if an owner puts in an appearance, the action in rem remains against the ship, in addition to the action in personam against the shipowner.[128] If the shipowner does not appear, a default judgment should be entered against the vessel itself as the in rem defendant.[129] Following the logic of *The Dictator*, the personal liability of the owners is not inherent in the action in rem but is added by the owner when the owner chooses to appear.[130] The action in rem still exists

[120] M Davies, 'The Future of Ship Arrest' in P Myburgh (ed), *The Arrest Conventions: International Enforcement of Maritime Claims* (Hart Publishing, 2019) 312.
[121] Fed R Civ P Supp, r B.
[122] Tetley, *International Maritime and Admiralty Law* (n 8) 407–08.
[123] Fed R Civ P Supp, r B(1); *Winter Storm Shipping Ltd v TPI* 310 F 3d 263, 278 (2d Cir 2002), overruled by *Shipping Corp of India v Jaldhi Overseas PTE Ltd* 585 F 3d 58 (2d Cir 2009).
[124] Force (n 12) 31.
[125] ibid 35.
[126] ibid 34.
[127] Davies, 'In Defense of Unpopular Virtues' (n 30) 341.
[128] *The Dictator* (n 38) 320; *The Gemma* [1899] P 285; Myburgh (n 34) 29.
[129] Myburgh (n 34) 28.
[130] Teare (n 43) 35.

against the offending vessel, parallel with the in personam action.[131] Due to the extension of the in rem jurisdiction, a sister ship arrest in rem is permitted under the procedural theory in certain circumstances.[132]

However, subsequently, English courts were inclined to apply the 'procedural theory' in a particularly radical way, as can be seen in *The Indian Grace (No 2)*.[133] In *The Indian Grace (No 2)*, the House of Lords considered a cargo damage claim and held that 'an action in rem is an action against the owners from the moment that the Admiralty Court is seized with jurisdiction. ... From that moment the owners are parties to the proceedings in rem'.[134] Therefore, the 'procedural theory' articulated in *The Indian Grace (No 2)* regards an action in rem as merely a device for forcing the appearance of the shipowner in personam rather than a true action against the ship itself.[135] Accordingly, following the logic of *The Indian Grace (No 2)*, even if the owner does not appear in an in rem action, any judgment in default is not limited to the value of the vessel, but should be enforceable against the shipowners in personam.[136] In other words, 'an action in rem is equally an action in personam from its inception'.[137]

Nevertheless, as discussed above, the decision in *The Indian Grace (No 2)* has been criticised by many commentators.[138] In addition, *The Indian Grace (No 2)* has subsequently been rejected by Australia,[139] and distinguished by Singapore.[140] However, it is worth noting that, in *The Indian Grace (No 2)*, Lord Steyn pointed out that 'this case is not concerned with maritime liens. That is a separate and complex subject which I put to one side'.[141]

[131] *The Dictator* (n 38).
[132] See eg Senior Courts Act 1981, s 21(4)(b)(ii); Federal Court Act RSC 1985, c F-7, s 43(8).
[133] *The Indian Grace (No 2)* (n 40).
[134] ibid 913.
[135] Davies, 'In Defense of Unpopular Virtues' (n 30) 341–42.
[136] Meeson and Kimbell (n 44) 94.
[137] Myburgh (n 34) 31.
[138] See eg Teare (n 43); Davenport (n 45); Tsimplis (n 29) 501–502; Rares, 'Maritime Liens, Renvoi and Conflicts of Law' (n 43); Derrington and Turner (n 43).
[139] *Comandate Marine Corp* (n 79).
[140] *Kuo Fen Ching* (n 80).
[141] *The Indian Grace (No 2)* (n 40) 908.

6

Key Conflicts between the UNCITRAL Model Law and Maritime Practice

As discussed in Chapter 2, the fundamental aims of insolvency law are to provide an 'honest but unfortunate' debtor with a financial 'fresh start', to maximise the value of the assets of the debtor, and to treat equivalent creditors equally. In order to fulfil these underlying aims the law of insolvency provides the mechanism of stay orders on the actions of creditors. Although certain creditors, such as secured creditors, can receive greater protection and higher priority in the sense that they can apply for relief from the stay order and request adequate protection up to their security interests, this does not diminish the basic principle of the law of insolvency – gathering all creditors together in order to share a common pool according to a certain and predictable ranking.[1] This principle was further strengthened by the trend of universalism at the end of the twentieth century, when the problem of cross-border insolvency frequently arose and the Model Law was enacted in order to solve inconsistencies in the realm of cross-border insolvency.[2] The concept of universalism 'calls for courts in other countries to co-operate with the courts in the country of the debtor's insolvency to ensure that all of its assets are distributed to its creditors under a single, orderly, system of distribution'.[3]

The unique regimes provided by maritime law with regard to maritime liens and in rem actions allow local maritime creditors to recover their claims against a vessel in rem regardless of the insolvency of a distant, foreign shipowner.[4] The vessel provides maritime creditors with special security. By arresting the vessel in rem, creditors force the insolvent debtor to either appear in court and answer the suit, or promptly pay off the debt by providing bonds or another form of security.[5] However, an in rem action against the vessel outside of an

[1] JL Westbrook, 'A Global Solution to Multinational Default' (2000) 98 *Michigan Law Review* 2276, 2284.

[2] UNCITRAL Secretariat, *UNCITRAL Cross-Border Insolvency Law with Guide to Enactment and Interpretation* (United Nations Office at Vienna, 2014) 19.

[3] M Davies, 'Cross-Border Insolvency and Admiralty: A Middle Path of Reciprocal Comity' (2018) 66 *American Journal of Comparative Law* 101, 101.

[4] ibid.

[5] *The Dictator* (1892) P 304, 320–21; S Rares, 'Ship Arrests, Maritime Liens and Cross-Border Insolvency' [2018] *Lloyd's Maritime and Commercial Law Quarterly* 398, 399.

insolvency proceeding may, to some extent, impede the insolvency proceeding in the sense that it will reduce or destroy the asset pool of the debtor that is available to other non-maritime creditors. In addition, it may contradict the objectives of the Model Law, which aims to promote a single and orderly system of insolvency as well as co-operation between courts. The concept of universalism and the regime of automatic stay orders that are provided by the Model Law will, in turn, shake the most fundamental and essential regimes of maritime law, namely, maritime liens and in rem actions, which are the underlying basis of the shipping industry that has harmoniously existed for thousands of years.[6]

The conflict between the cross-border insolvency regime and maritime law is therefore obvious. The question that needs to be resolved is how these two vastly different regimes can co-exist in harmony. This chapter outlines three major issues that frequently arise when the Model Law regime is applied to maritime creditors and maritime assets. It also discusses the major arguments that are brought forward by parties regarding each issue. Due to various countries adopting different approaches to each of these issues, Chapters 7, 8, 9 and 10 provide a detailed discussion regarding the position of each selected country on these issues.

I. Treatment of Maritime Creditors under the UNCITRAL Model Law Regime

Under the regime of the Model Law, upon the arresting country recognising a foreign insolvency proceeding as a foreign main proceeding, all claims against the debtor and its assets are suspended by an automatic stay order provided by Article 20(1) of the Model Law; this includes maritime claims.[7] Two main arguments may be raised by maritime creditors in order for them to apply for relief from the automatic stay order. First, they may argue that they should be regarded as secured creditors and should therefore be allowed to proceed if the local insolvency law preserves an exception for secured creditors by virtue of Article 20(2) of the Model Law.[8] Second, maritime creditors may rely on the personification doctrine and argue that the admiralty proceedings are against the vessel itself rather than against the debtor, therefore resulting in them not being subject to

[6] Rares (n 5) 399.

[7] UNCITRAL Model Law on Cross-Border Insolvency (UNCITRAL Model Law), Art 20(1).

[8] See eg *Yu v STX Pan Ocean Co* [2013] FCA 680; *Tai-Soo Suk v Hanjin Shipping Co Ltd* [2016] FCA 1404; *The Sanko Mineral* [2014] EWHC 3927; *Harms Offshore AHT 'Taurus' GmbH&co KG v Bloom* [2009] EWCA Civ 632; *Evridiki Navigation Inc v Sanko SS Co* 880 F Supp 2d 666 (D Maryland 2012); *In re Hanjin Shipping Co* 2016 WL 6681169, [2016] AMC 2113 (District of New Jersey 16 September 2016); *Re Taisoo Suk* [2016] SGHC 195.

the automatic moratorium.[9] This book analyses the question of whether maritime creditors can be exempted from the automatic stay mechanism granted by the Model Law and, if not, whether the Model Law provides an exception for maritime claims to proceed regardless of a foreign insolvency proceeding.

A. Relief from the Automatic Stay

The Model Law regime provides clear and efficient procedures in order to resolve the majority of international insolvencies.[10] However, it is not designed with maritime cross-border insolvency in mind. The most relevant and helpful provision in the Model Law that may be used to resolve conflicts between the cross-border insolvency regime and maritime law appears to be Article 20(2).[11]

Article 20(1) of the Model Law requires the forum to stay all proceedings against a debtor upon the recognition of a foreign proceeding as a foreign main proceeding.[12] In addition, it provides that the mandatory and automatic stay order provided by Article 20(1) is subject to the circumstances identified in Article 20(2), (3) and (4).[13] In particular, Article 20(2) preserves the operation of local insolvency laws and provides that:

> The scope, and the modification or termination, of the stay and suspension referred to in paragraph 1 of this article are subject to … any provisions of law of the enacting State relating to insolvency that apply to exceptions, limitations, modifications or termination in respect of the stay and suspension.[14]

The UNCITRAL Model Law on Cross-Border Insolvency with Guide to Enactment and Interpretation (Guide to Enactment) further explains that 'those exceptions may be, for example, the enforcement of claims by secured creditors'.[15] Therefore, when adopting the Model Law, enacting states can reserve exceptions and limitations to the automatic stay order imposed by Article 20(1) of the Model Law; the scope and effect of the stay order can be subject to the insolvency law of the enacting state with regard to the exceptions and limitations of the stay and suspension, such as the enforcement of secured claims. Accordingly, although the *forum arresti* that adopted the Model Law must respect the existence of the foreign main proceeding in the debtor's home country by imposing an automatic stay order, it can choose to preserve an exception to the stay order for secured

[9] See eg *Yu* (n 8); *Kuo Fen Ching and Another v Dauphin Offshore Engineering & Trading Pte Ltd* [1999] SGCA 95; *Precious Shipping Public Co Ltd v OW Bunker Far East* [2015] SGHC 187; Davies (n 3) 112.

[10] See UNCITRAL Secretariat (n 2) 19–20.

[11] UNCITRAL Model Law, Art 20(2).

[12] UNCITRAL Model Law, Art 20(1).

[13] UNCITRAL Model Law, Art 20(1), (2), (3), (4).

[14] UNCITRAL Model Law, Art 20(2).

[15] UNCITRAL Secretariat (n 2) 85.

creditors.[16] As discussed in Chapter 5, maritime creditors may fall into the category of secured creditors in certain circumstances; therefore they may argue that they can proceed with their secured claims against the insolvent debtor in personam or against the debtor's vessel in rem, regardless of any pending or subsequent insolvency proceeding.[17] Nevertheless, given the nature of the Model Law as a type of 'soft law' that allows enacting states to freely interpret it when it is enacted into domestic legislation in order for it to be legally binding, different jurisdictions have introduced various versions of Article 20(2) in their enacting legislation.[18] Chapters 7, 8, 9 and 10 provide a detailed examination of the approaches that have been adopted by selected countries. Chapter 11 provides a comparative analysis and proposes policy reflections on the treatment of maritime creditors under the Model Law regime.

B. In Rem Claims and the Personification Doctrine

Maritime creditors are used to enforcing their maritime claims through effective admiralty proceedings that are specifically provided by maritime law, namely, an in rem action.[19] As discussed in Chapter 5, the underlying rationale of an in rem action lies in the fiction of 'personification', a doctrine whereby a ship is deemed to have a legal personality separate from its owner and, as such, is subject to legal action directly, being held liable for the torts it has committed and any contracts it has breached.[20] Accordingly, maritime creditors may argue that their in rem actions to enforce a maritime claim are, in fact, against the personified vessel itself rather than against the debtor-shipowner and should therefore be allowed to proceed regardless of any pending or subsequent insolvency proceeding.[21] In other words, an in rem action to enforce a maritime claim is a separate and distinct action from an in personam action.

The Model Law only mentions rights in rem on one occasion, in Article 32.[22] Article 32 of the Model Law provides that:

> Without prejudice to secured claims or rights in rem, a creditor who has received part payment in respect of its claim in a proceeding pursuant to a law relating to insolvency in a foreign State may not receive a payment for the same claim in a proceeding under [identify laws of the enacting State relating to insolvency] regarding the same debtor, so long as the payment to the other creditors of the same class is proportionately less than the payment the creditor has already received.[23]

[16] ibid.
[17] Davies (n 3) 101.
[18] UNCITRAL Model Law, Preamble.
[19] Rares (n 5) 399.
[20] R Force, *Admiralty and Maritime Law*, 2nd edn (Federal Judicial Center, 2013) 31.
[21] See eg *Yu* (n 8); *Kuo Fen Ching* (n 9); *Precious Shipping* (n 9); Davies (n 3) 112.
[22] UNCITRAL Model Law, Art 32.
[23] ibid.

In addition, the Guide to Enactment provides the rationale of Article 32:

> The rule set forth in Article 32 (sometimes referred to as the hotchpotch rule) is a useful safeguard in a legal regime for coordination and cooperation in the administration of cross-border insolvency proceedings. It is intended to avoid situations in which a creditor might obtain more favourable treatment than the other creditors of the same class by obtaining payment of the same claim in insolvency proceedings in different jurisdictions.[24]

Therefore, Article 32 is solely intended to establish the underlying principle of the law of insolvency with regard to equal treatment of creditors of the same class. Secured creditors or creditors with rights in rem are not affected by Article 32 of the Model Law in the sense that they shall not be precluded from getting full payment in concurrent proceedings.[25] However, this provision does not deal with the issues regarding whether in rem actions are enforceable regardless of an insolvency proceeding and whether the doctrine of personification is applicable in the realm of cross-border insolvency.

The personification doctrine has been adopted and taken rather literally and seriously in the US.[26] Conversely, it has arguably been abandoned by the UK and Commonwealth countries, who have, instead, embraced the procedural theory.[27] Therefore, whether the personification arguments succeed depends upon the attitude of forums towards the doctrine of personification. Chapters 7, 8, 9 and 10 examine, in detail, the application of the personification argument in the area of cross-border insolvency in each of the selected countries, whilst Chapter 11 provides a comparative analysis.

II. Determination of the Centre of Main Interest

The second problem is how to determine the 'centre of main interest' (COMI) of the debtor in the realm of maritime cross-border insolvency. COMI is a critically important new concept introduced by the Model Law in the sense that, in order for a foreign insolvency proceeding to be recognised as a foreign main proceeding by a *forum arresti* that has adopted the Model Law, it needs to take place in the COMI of the insolvent debtor.[28]

The adoption of the concept of the COMI under the regime of the Model Law is designed to provide predictability and certainty to both debtors and creditors.

[24] UNCITRAL Secretariat (n 2) 107.
[25] ibid.
[26] *Tucker v Alexandroff* 183 US 424 (1902).
[27] *The Dictator* (n 5); *The Halcyon Isle* [1981] AC 221; *The Indian Grace (No 2)* [1998] AC 878.
[28] UNCITRAL Model Law, Art 2(b).

Accordingly, under the Model Law regime it is envisaged that debtors will be prevented from forum shopping and will be required to commence their insolvency proceedings in the place where they have sufficient connection with the forum.[29] However, the Model Law itself does not define this crucial concept and only provides a rebuttable presumption that, in the absence of proof to the contrary, the debtor's COMI is the state where the debtor's registered office or habitual residence is located.[30]

The presumption of the COMI is not necessarily consistent with the realities of the shipping industry and maritime commercial practice. In practice, shipping companies usually separate their ownership from the ship's management. Most shipping companies are incorporated in offshore jurisdictions or flag of convenience states to evade regulation or taxation.[31] However, the company itself does not usually conduct any business relating to the operation of its vessels in its registered office, but instead assigns the operation of the vessels to a ship management company in a different location. In addition, many shipping companies are operated and arranged in the form of a 'one-ship company'. The only asset of each company is usually a single vessel that is registered in a flag of convenience state.[32] Therefore, given that so many connecting factors are involved, it is often complicated and confusing to determine the COMI of a shipping company, especially an offshore shipping company.

The Model Law provides a presumption of the COMI in favour of the location of the registered office. However, there are obvious concerns regarding the determination of offshore countries as the COMI, namely: (1) whether these countries have bankruptcy systems; (2) whether the bankruptcy systems are effective and efficient; and (3) whether bankruptcy orders or debt collection orders that are issued by the bankruptcy courts in offshore countries are enforceable. In other words, even in the absence of fraud, the COMI of an offshore shipping company may not necessarily be a jurisdiction that is competent to provide an effective liquidation or reorganisation for the company.[33]

It is, therefore, important to examine the issue of the determination of the COMI of a shipping company in the context of maritime cross-border insolvency, specifically with regard to an offshore shipping company; and to what extent the presumption of the COMI in favour of the location of the registered office can be rebutted. A detailed discussion is provided in Chapter 12 below.

[29] JL Westbrook, 'Locating the Eye of the Financial Storm' (2007) 32 *Brooklyn Journal of International Law* 1019, 1022.

[30] UNCITRAL Model Law, Art 16(3).

[31] J Ford and C Wilcox, 'Shedding Light on the Dark Side of Maritime Trade – A New Approach for Identifying Countries as Flags of Convenience' (2019) 99 *Marine Policy* 298; GS Egiyan, 'Flag of Convenience or Open Registration of Ships' (1990) 14 *Marine Policy* 106.

[32] ibid.

[33] J Devlin, 'The UNCITRAL Model Law on Cross-Border Insolvency and Its Impact on Maritime Creditors' (2010) 21 *Journal of Banking and Finance Law and Practice* 95, 111.

III. Scope of Debtor's Assets

The third problem is the scope of a debtor's assets. In order to reduce maintenance costs and meet the commercial need for fleet flexibility, it is common for shipping companies to hire the carrying capacity of vessels that are owned by others, either in whole or in part; this is known as chartering.[34] There are three main categories of charterparties; a voyage charter, a time charter and a bareboat charter.[35] Voyage and time charters usually involve hiring the vessel's carrying capacity for a particular voyage or a specified period of time, while a demise charter involves hiring the whole ship without the master or crew.[36] Specifically, a demise charterer must appoint a master and crew, provide suppliers and bunkers, and run the vessel at its own risk and expense. The demise charterer is also responsible for liabilities that are caused due to the operation of the chartered vessel during the period of the charter.[37] It is widely accepted that a demise charterer is to be treated as the owner of the vessel *pro hac vice* (or owner ad hoc), namely, it stands in the place of the vessel's title owner during the charter period.[38] Therefore, issues that specifically arise in the realm of maritime cross-border insolvency are: whether chartered vessels should be regarded as the debtor's assets and should therefore be included in the asset pool of the debtor for the purpose of liquidation or reorganisation among all creditors under the Model Law regime, and whether chartered vessels should be subject to the Article 20 automatic stay order granted by the Model Law. These issues have not often been brought before the courts and the answers to these questions depend on the nature of the charterparty. Chapters 7, 8, 9 and 10 discuss in detail the approaches that have been adopted by each of the selected countries with regard to the scope of debtor's assets, whilst Chapter 12 discusses policy reflections regarding these issues.

In addition, in order to secure the release of, or to prevent the potential arrest of, a vessel, security may be provided by debtor-shipowners in the form of surety bonds or cash, or by third parties in the form of bank guarantees or Protection and Indemnity Associations (P&I) club letters of undertaking (LOUs).[39]

[34] Force (n 20) 44.

[35] ibid.

[36] ibid.

[37] EW Harper, 'Demise Charters: Responsibilities of Owner or Charterer for Loss or Damage' (1975) 49 *Tulane Law Review* 785; *Fraser v Marsh* (1811) 13 East 238; *Sandeman v Scurr* (1866) LR 2 QB 86; *The Great Eastern* (1868) LR 2 Ad & EC 88; *Fenton v City of Dublin Steam Packet Co* (1838) 8 Ad & E 835; *Burnard v Aaron and Sharpley* (1862) 31 LJCP 334.

[38] See eg SA Gebb, 'The Demise Charter: A Conceptual and Practical Analysis' (1975) 49 *Tulane Law Review* 764; see also *Port Line v Ben Line Steamers* [1958] 2 QB 146; *The Andrea Ursula* [1973] 1 QB 265; *The Tasmania* (1888) 13 PD 110; *Sandeman v Scurr* (n 37); *United States v Shea* 152 US 178 (1894); *Leary v United States* 81 US (14 Wall) 607 (1872).

[39] Similar to a bank guarantee, an LOU is a guarantee that is issued by a P&I club, in which the P&I club agrees to undertake the amount adjudged by the court that the member (the debtor-shipowner) is liable to pay, or the amount agreed under settlement terms. An LOU generally provides that, once the

The security serves as substitute *res* against which the in rem admiralty proceedings are brought.[40] Therefore, this book will examine the question of whether the surety bond or security provided by a debtor or third party for the release of an arrested vessel is regarded as the property of the debtor and therefore included in the asset pool of the debtor for the purpose of liquidation or reorganisation among all creditors. A detailed discussion of this issue is provided in Chapter 12 below.

claimant accepts the LOU as security for his claim, he must release the ship from arrest or agree not to arrest the ship. Compared to a bank guarantee, an LOU is more flexible, and can be easily prepared and quickly issued. See P Myburgh, 'P & I Club Letters of Undertaking and Admiralty Arrests' (2018) 24 *Journal of International Maritime Law* 201, 202.

[40] See eg *The Nied Elwin* (1811) 1 Dods 50, 53; *Mackensworth v SS American Merchant* 28 F 3d 246, 252 (2d Cir 1994); *Petroleos Mexicanos Refinacion v M/T King A* 554 F 3d 99, 104 (3d Cir 2009).

7

Australia

I. Overview

As a large shipping country of the world, courts in Australia have frequently confronted the issue of maritime cross-border insolvency. Australia has adopted the Model Law through the enactment of the Cross-Border Insolvency Act 2008 (Cth) (CBIA) and is willing to promote uniformity and co-operation in the area of cross-border insolvency. Recent decisions illustrate that the Australian courts are willing to take the special nature of maritime law into account and, in certain circumstances, will narrow down the scope of the automatic stay order provided by the Model Law regime for a particular maritime claimant in order to allow it to proceed with its claim. This chapter analyses the Australian approach to maritime cross-border insolvency practice under the Model Law regime, especially with regard to the problems identified in Chapter 6.

II. The Regime of Insolvency and the Secured Status of Maritime Claims in Australia

A. Overview of the Regime of Insolvency

In Australia, bankruptcy and insolvency are two different terms. The term 'bankruptcy' refers to an individual's bankruptcy, governed by the Bankruptcy Act 1966 (Cth), while the term 'insolvency' refers to corporate insolvency, which is governed by the Corporations Act 2001 (Cth) (Corporations Act).[1] Since an individual's bankruptcy is usually irrelevant in the area of maritime cross-border insolvency, this chapter focuses on discussions regarding corporate insolvency. Similar to the regime of corporate insolvency in most Anglo-common law countries, Australia generally provides two mechanisms by which to govern the relationship between insolvent debtors and creditors, namely, winding-up proceedings and restructuring proceedings (including administration and schemes of arrangement).[2]

[1] C Symes et al, *Australian Insolvency Law*, 4th edn (LexisNexis Butterworths, 2019) 2.
[2] See Corporations Act 2001 (Cth), Pts 5.1, 5.3A, 5.4, 5.4B, 5.5, 5.6.

i. Winding-Up Proceedings

The mechanism of winding up a company in Australia is predominantly set out in Part 5.4 of the Corporations Act and can be defined as the statutory process of ceasing the business of a company, realising its assets, discharging its liabilities, settling any questions of account or contribution between its members, and ultimately terminating the existence of the company by deregistration.[3] The Corporations Act provides two types of winding up: voluntary winding up and compulsory winding up.[4]

a. Voluntary Winding Up

A voluntary winding up is a proceeding that allows a company to be wound up voluntarily by its members or creditors under certain circumstances.[5] The commencement of a voluntary winding-up proceeding does not require the approval of a court.

In order to determine which regime of voluntary winding up can be pursued, the solvency position of the company is the crucial factor. If the company is solvent, the winding up will be a members' voluntary winding up.[6] In order to commence a members' voluntary winding up, directors of the company must, after making an inquiry into the affairs of the company, make a written declaration of solvency which states that 'the company will be able to discharge its debts in full within 12 months of the commencement of winding up'.[7] During the meeting of the company's members, a special resolution for voluntary winding up will be proposed and will be passed if more than 75 per cent of the members vote in favour of the resolution.[8] Upon the special resolution being passed, the members shall appoint a liquidator to wind up the company and to collect and distribute its assets.[9]

A creditors' voluntary winding up, on the other hand, arises when the company is actually insolvent.[10] If a liquidator who is appointed pursuant to a members' voluntary winding-up subsequently forms the opinion that the company is, in fact, insolvent, or the directors cannot provide a solvency declaration, then the liquidator will convene a meeting of creditors and change the proceeding from a members' voluntary winding up to a creditors' voluntary winding up.[11] In addition, a creditors' voluntary winding up can commence by a resolution of creditors being passed at a second meeting of creditors during the voluntary administration of the company.[12]

[3] See generally Symes et al (n 1) Ch 9; Corporations Act 2001 (Cth) Pts 5.4B, 5.5.
[4] Corporations Act 2001 (Cth), Pts 5.4B; 5.5.
[5] Corporations Act 2001 (Cth), ss 490, 491; *Re Kyra Nominees Pty Ltd* (1980) 5 ACLR 60.
[6] Corporations Act 2001 (Cth), s 494; *Re Kyra Nominees* (n 5).
[7] Corporations Act 2001 (Cth), s 494(1).
[8] Corporations Act 2001 (Cth), s 249L.
[9] Corporations Act 2001 (Cth), s 495; R Tomasic and K Whitford, *Australian Insolvency and Bankruptcy Law*, 2nd edn (Butterworths, 1997) 326.
[10] *Re Kyra Nominees* (n 5).
[11] Corporations Act 2001 (Cth), ss 497, 499, 500.
[12] Corporations Act 2001 (Cth), s 439C.

b. Compulsory Winding Up

A compulsory winding up is a mechanism provided by the Corporations Act that gives power to a court to grant an order to wind up a company upon an application by an eligible applicant.[13] The court often grants an order when the evidence provided by the applicant shows that the company has become insolvent, ie that the company is unable to pay its debts as and when they fall due.[14] After a winding-up order is granted by the court, the company will cease all its ongoing business operations.[15] In addition, a liquidator will be appointed by the court and take control of the affairs of the insolvent debtor. The liquidator will collect and protect the assets of the insolvent debtor for the purpose of distribution among all the company's creditors.[16]

ii. Administration

The mechanism of administration provides the insolvent debtor, or the about-to-be-insolvent debtor, with some time to rehabilitate its business by maintaining the status quo of the debtor; this provides the debtor's company with an opportunity to possibly survive as a going concern.[17] Part 5.3A of the Corporations Act provides two types of administration – voluntary administration and deeds of company arrangement (DOCA), which are usually initiated by the company itself without the involvement of a court.[18] If a company wants to survive as a going concern, the aim of the voluntary administration process is to enter into a DOCA, which is a separate proceeding between the company and its creditors.[19]

a. Voluntary Administration

The regime of voluntary administration was introduced into the Australian law of insolvency by the Corporate Law Reform Act 1992 (Cth) with effect from 1993.[20] The aim of the regime of voluntary administration is to avoid the unnecessary winding up of debtors and to provide insolvent debtors with a procedure where they can be administered in a way that maximises the chances of the debtors

[13] Corporations Act 2001 (Cth), ss 459A, 459P.

[14] In order to determine whether a company is deemed to be insolvent, Australia adopted a 'cash-flow test', which is an assessment of the ability of a company to pay its debts as they become due and payable. See Corporations Act 2001 (Cth), s 95(A); *Quick v Stoland Pty Ltd* (1998) 29 ACSR 130; *Australian Securities and Investments Commission v Plymin* (2013) 21 ACLC 700.

[15] Corporations Act 2001 (Cth), s 471B.

[16] Corporations Act 2001 (Cth), s 472.

[17] Tomasic and Whitford (n 9) 160; see also Corporations Act 2001 (Cth), Pt 5.3A.

[18] Symes et al (n 1) 288–92.

[19] ibid 286–87.

[20] K Lindgren, 'Voluntary Administration: Current Issues and Proposals for Reform' (FCA) [2006] *Federal Judicial Scholarship* 4, available at classic.austlii.edu.au/au/journals/FedJSchol/2006/4.html, accessed 5 June 2020; KJ Bennetts, 'Voluntary Administration: Shaping the Process Thorough the Exercise of Judicial Discretion' (1995) 3 *Insolvency Law Journal* 135.

continuing to exist.[21] A voluntary administration proceeding begins when an administrator is appointed and usually ends when a DOCA is executed or a resolution is reached by the creditors that the company should be wound up.[22] The administrator can be appointed by the directors of the debtor, its liquidators, provisional liquidators or secured creditors.[23] The administrator will take control of the assets, business and affairs of the debtor upon being appointed.[24] This will involve conducting investigations regarding the business affairs and financial circumstances of the debtor, as well as making recommendations to a meeting of creditors as to whether the debtor should enter into a DOCA approved by its creditors, be wound up or be reverted to normal operation by its directors.[25]

b. Deed of Company Arrangement

If the creditors decide that a company should execute a DOCA, which is a compromise agreement between the debtor and its creditors, the voluntary administration will be terminated upon a DOCA being executed.[26] The execution of the DOCA creates a new legal relationship between the debtor and its creditors with regard to all claims arising on or before the date that is specified in the DOCA.[27] Under the terms of a DOCA, creditors will, to some extent, compromise their claims in order to preserve the company as a going concern; this could involve the suspension of enforcement action for a specified period as well as the payment of debts being deferred or accepted in instalments.[28] There is no role for the courts to play under Part 5.3A unless a person commences a proceeding to terminate the DOCA.[29]

iii. Schemes of Arrangement

A scheme of arrangement is governed by Part 5.1 of the Corporations Act.[30] It is a court-approved compromise or arrangement between a company and its creditors that enables the company to reorganise its debts and capital structure and therefore avoid liquidation.[31] The major difference between a scheme of arrangement under Part 5.1A of the Corporations Act and a voluntary administration

[21] Corporations Act 2001 (Cth), s 435A.
[22] Corporations Act 2001 (Cth), s 435C.
[23] Corporations Act 2001 (Cth), ss 436A, 436B, 436C.
[24] Corporations Act 2001 (Cth), s 437A.
[25] Corporations Act 2001 (Cth), ss 438A, 439C; Lindgren (n 20); Tomasic and Whitford (n 9) 171.
[26] Corporations Act 2001 (Cth), ss 435C, 444A.
[27] Corporations Act 2001 (Cth), ss 444C, 444D.
[28] Corporations Act 2001 (Cth), s 444A; *Advance Healthcare Group Ltd* [2008] FCA 1604.
[29] Corporations Act 2001 (Cth), ss 445D, 600A.
[30] See generally Corporations Act 2001 (Cth), Pt 5.1.
[31] Tomasic and Whitford (n 9) 112–14.

proceeding followed by a DOCA under Part 5.3A is the role played by the courts. A scheme of arrangement requires court approval *before* the scheme becomes effective, whilst a voluntary administration proceeding provides for disallowance by the courts *after* the deed has been made.[32] Therefore, in practice, a scheme of arrangement proceeding for restructuring corporate debts has not been used as frequently as a voluntary administration proceeding; this is due to its implementation involving higher costs and being less efficient than a voluntary administration proceeding, as a result of the involvement of the courts.[33]

B. Stay Provisions under the Corporations Act

The Corporations Act provides different stay and suspension provisions to various types of insolvency proceedings. Under a creditors' voluntary winding-up proceeding, after a resolution for a voluntary winding up has been passed, any actions or proceedings to be continued or commenced against the debtor will be stayed unless leave of the court has been obtained.[34] There is no express exception for secured creditors to proceed with their enforcement action against the property of the debtor.[35] On the contrary, upon a compulsory winding-up order being granted, the commencement of enforcement action against the property of the company will be suspended, except if leave of the court is obtained.[36] Nevertheless, this stay and suspension provision does not affect the right of secured creditors to enforce their security interest against the debtor on the ground that section 471C of the Corporations Act provides an explicit exception for secured creditors to be exempted from the automatic stay order imposed by a court.[37]

Furthermore, under a voluntary administration proceeding, the stay and suspension provisions imposed by the Corporations Act are very broad; these apply to both secured and unsecured creditors.[38] Accordingly, a secured creditor will be prevented from taking any steps to enforce its security interest unless it obtains the consent of the administrator or leave of the court.[39] Thus, the insolvent company would have some 'breathing space' in order to investigate and protect its property.

[32] *Lehman Bros Holdings Inc v City of Swan* (2010) 240 CLR 509, 521.

[33] Symes et al (n 1) 27.

[34] Corporations Act 2001 (Cth), ss 500(1), (2).

[35] Corporations Act 2001 (Cth), s 500(2); S Rares, 'Admiralty Law – the Flying Dutchman of Cross-border Insolvency' (FCA) [2009] *Federal Judicial Scholarship* 22, [26], available at www.austlii.edu.au/au/journals/FedJSchol/2009/22.html, accessed 5 June 2020.

[36] Corporations Act 2001 (Cth), s 471B.

[37] Corporations Act 2001 (Cth), s 471C.

[38] Corporations Act 2001 (Cth), ss 440D, 440F, 440G; Rares, 'Admiralty Law – the Flying Dutchman of Cross-border Insolvency' (n 35) [26].

[39] Corporations Act 2001 (Cth), ss 440D, 440F, 440G.

If, subsequently, a DOCA is proposed and executed, it binds all unsecured creditors, even those who have voted against the deed.[40] Secured creditors who voted in favour of the deed are bound by the deed whilst those who voted against are not.[41] Nevertheless, if the dissent of the secured creditor has a material adverse effect on achieving the purpose of the deed, and the interest of the secured creditor has been adequately protected, the court may step in and prevent the secured creditor from exercising its security.[42]

Finally, unless otherwise provided in the scheme or applied by the company, no automatic stay order on actions against the company will be imposed when a scheme of arrangement has been proposed.[43]

C. Secured Status of Maritime Claims

i. Maritime Liens

The Australian Parliament recognises four types of claims as maritime liens in the Admiralty Act 1988 (Cth). These are:

(a) salvage;
(b) damage done by a ship;
(c) wages of the master, or of a member of the crew, of a ship; [and]
(d) master's disbursements.[44]

The characteristic of a maritime lien was explained by the Full Court of the Federal Court in *Comandate Marine Corp v Pan Australia Shipping Pty Ltd*, where the Court rejected the radical application of the 'procedural theory' that was articulated by the House of Lords in *The Indian Grace (No 2)*.[45] However, the Court referred to the decision of the Privy Council in *The Bold Buccleugh* and described a maritime lien as:

> a non-possessory claim or privilege upon a ship carried into effect by legal process by in rem action. It is inchoate from the time of the events giving rise to it, attaching to the ship, travelling with the ship into anyone's possession (even a bona fide purchaser for value without notice, except a purchaser at an Admiralty Court sale) and perfected by legal process relating back to first attachment.[46]

[40] Corporations Act 2001 (Cth), s 444D(1).
[41] Corporations Act 2001 (Cth), s 444D(2).
[42] Corporations Act 2001 (Cth), s 444F.
[43] Corporations Act 2001 (Cth), s 411(16).
[44] Admiralty Act 1988 (Cth), s 15(2).
[45] *Comandate Marine Corp v Pan Australia Shipping Pty Ltd* [2006] FCAFC 192; *The Indian Grace (No 2)* [1998] AC 878.
[46] *Comandate Marine* (n 45) 112; see also *The Bold Buccleugh* (1851) 7 Moo PC 267; *The Two Ellens* (1872) LR 4 PC 161.

In addition, the Full Court of the Federal Court of Australia in *Yu v STX Pan Ocean Co Ltd* also followed the decision in *The Bold Buccleugh* and regarded a maritime lien as 'an existing security right'.[47] Notwithstanding that the Full Court of the Federal Court of Australia in *The Ship Sam Hawk v Reiter Petroleum Inc* followed the decision of the majority of the Privy Council in *The Halcyon Isle* and adopted the *lex fori* rule in order to decide the availability of a foreign maritime lien,[48] it has been argued that, in Australia, a maritime lien claim is regarded as a secured claim and is secured from the moment the events occur that give rise to the lien.[49] In other words, a maritime lien is a pre-existing security interest that obtains its secured status before the commencement of the action in rem or the arrest of the ship.[50] Accordingly, as a secured claim, a maritime lien can be exempted from a winding up moratorium under section 471B of the Corporations Act and proceed with its enforcement action in rem against the vessels of the debtor.[51] Nevertheless, a maritime lien may still need to be subject to a voluntary administration moratorium and will be prevented from commencing or continuing its in rem action unless it obtains the leave of the court or the consent of the administrator.[52]

ii. *Statutory Rights of Action in Rem*

In addition, sections 4(3) and 17 of the Admiralty Act 1988 (Cth) sets out the claims that give rise to statutory rights of action in rem.[53] These claims include: claims in respect of the supply of goods or services supplied to a vessel for its operation or maintenance; general average; pilotage; loss of cargo; and breach of charterparties etc.[54] Unlike a maritime lien, a statutory right of action in rem does not create any property interest in the vessel upon the occurrence of the events that give rise to the claim, namely, it is 'not secured by, and does not seek to enforce, any pre-existing proprietary or security interest in the ship'.[55] To be specific, it becomes a vested secured interest in the vessel until the claimant

[47] *Yu v STX Pan Ocean Co* [2013] FCA 680, [40]; see also *The Bold Buccleugh* (n 46).

[48] *The Ship Sam Hawk v Reiter Petroleum Inc* [2016] FCAFC 26; *The Halcyon Isle* [1981] AC 221.

[49] MJ Hafeez-Baig, 'Navigating The Waters Between Admiralty and Cross-Border Insolvency: A Comparison of the Australian, German and French Position' [2018] *Lloyd's Maritime and Commercial Law Quarterly* 97, 115; Rares, 'Admiralty Law – the Flying Dutchman of Cross-border Insolvency' (n 35) [42]; J Soars, 'Cross-Border Insolvency and Shipping – A Practical Guide' (7 Wentworth Selborne Chambers Sydney) 29–30, available at https://comitemaritime.org/wp-content/uploads/2018/05/2016-04-11-CBI-and-Shipping-paper-Julie-Soars-.pdf accessed 5 June 2020.

[50] Hafeez-Baig (n 49) 115; Soars et al (n 49) 29–30; *Yu* (n 47) [44]–[41]; *Kim v Daebo International Shipping Co Ltd* [2015] FCA 684, [12].

[51] Hafeez-Baig (n 49) 132–33; Soars et al (n 49) 40; Corporations Act 2001 (Cth), ss 471B, 471C.

[52] Corporations Act 2001 (Cth), s 440D.

[53] Admiralty Act 1988 (Cth), s 17.

[54] Admiralty Act 1988 (Cth), ss 4(3), 17.

[55] Hafeez-Baig (n 49) 115.

chooses to exercise the right by commencing an action in rem; it does not relate back to any earlier period.[56]

For example, in *Danny Morris & Another v The Ship 'Kiama'*, the plaintiffs commenced an action in rem in order to arrest the vessel that was owned by the debtor.[57] The vessel was arrested and eventually sold. The debtor subsequently filed a voluntary administration proceeding under Part 5.3A of the Corporations Act. Thus, the plaintiffs applied to obtain the leave of the court in order to proceed with their enforcement action regardless of the automatic stay order that was imposed by section 440B of the Corporations Act upon the initiation of the administration proceeding. The Court recognised the secured status of the plaintiffs on the ground that, by issuing the writ in rem, they obtained the security interest and had become secured creditors.[58] In addition, in *Kim v Daebo International Shipping Co Ltd*, Rares J held that a claimant who commenced an in rem action against a vessel based on a statutory right of action in rem would obtain 'a secured interest in respect of that claim simply because of the timing of the commencement of the proceeding *in rem*'.[59] Finally, as noted by Allsop CJ in *Yakushiji v Daiichi Chuo Kisen Kaisha*, the filing of a claim in rem may 'be seen to create a form or species of qualified or quasi security'.[60]

Therefore, when interacting with the domestic insolvency regime, if a statutory right of action in rem is initiated before the commencement of a winding-up proceeding, in my view it is a secured claim and can be exempted from a winding-up stay order.[61] However, if a statutory right of action in rem is initiated after the commencement of a winding-up proceeding it will remain unsecured and will not be exempted from a winding-up stay order.[62] Nevertheless, it will generally be subject to a voluntary administration stay order unless the creditor obtains the leave of the court or the consent of the administrator, whether it is initiated before or after the commencement of a voluntary administration proceeding.

III. Cross-Border Insolvency in Australia

A. Overview of Australian Implementation of the Model Law

Australia adopted the Model Law entirely in its 'stand alone' CBIA.[63] Under the CBIA, Australian courts will recognise a foreign insolvency proceeding and

[56] *In Re Aco Co Ltd* [1980] Ch 196; *Yakushiji v Daiichi Chuo Kisen Kaisha* [2015] FCA 1170, [20]; *Kim* (n 50) [8], Soars et al (n 49) 31; Hafeez-Baig (n 49) 115.
[57] *Danny Morris & Another v The Ship 'Kiama'* [1998] FCA 256, 16–17.
[58] *The Ship 'Kiama'* (n 57); see also *The Zafiro* [1960] P 1, 15.
[59] *Kim* (n 50) [8].
[60] *Yakushiji* (n 56) [20].
[61] Hafeez-Baig (n 49) 132.
[62] Hafeez-Baig (n 49) 132; Corporations Act 2001 (Cth), s 471C.
[63] See generally CBIA 2008.

co-operate with foreign courts in order to protect the interests of all creditors and maximise the value of the debtor's assets pool.[64] The competent courts which can perform the functions of the CBIA, such as recognition and co-operation, are the Federal Court of Australia and the Supreme Court of a State and Territory, which also exercises admiralty jurisdiction.[65]

In the realm of corporate insolvency, the scope of the CBIA generally extends to insolvency proceedings arising from Chapter 5 (other than Parts 5.2 and 5.4A) of the Corporations Act.[66] Receiverships involving the private appointment of a controller (Part 5.2 of the Corporations Act),[67] member's voluntary winding-up proceedings (Part 5.5 of the Corporations Act)[68] and winding up by courts other than on the grounds of insolvency (Part 5.4A of the Corporations Act)[69] are excluded from the Model Law and the CBIA. Finally, if any inconsistencies exist between the Model Law and the Corporations Act 2001, ss 21 and 22 of the CBIA provide that the Model Law shall prevail over the Corporations Act to the extent of any inconsistency.[70]

B. Article 20 of the CBIA and the Staying of Proceedings

Under Article 20(1) of Schedule 1 to the CBIA, upon a foreign insolvency proceeding being recognised as a foreign main proceeding, an automatic stay order will be granted simultaneously by the courts that will stay the 'commencement or continuation of individual actions or individual proceedings concerning

[64] CBIA 2008, s 8; Rares, 'Admiralty Law – the Flying Dutchman of Cross-border Insolvency' (n 35) [14]–[15].

[65] CBIA 2008, s 10.

[66] The Parliament of the Commonwealth of Australia, *Cross-Border Insolvency Bill 2008 Explanatory Memorandum*, Ch 1, available at www.legislation.gov.au/Details/C2008B00008/Explanatory%20 Memorandum/Text, accessed 5 June 2020.

[67] Receiverships are excluded because they relate only to a debt owed to the appointer, rather for the benefits of all creditors and therefore cannot be characterised as 'collective' proceedings that need to be subject to 'control or supervision by a foreign court' and 'for the purpose of reorganisation or liquidation': The Parliament of the Commonwealth of Australia (n 66) Ch 1; UNCITRAL Secretariat, *UNCITRAL Model Law on Cross-Border Insolvency: Judicial Perspective* (United Nations Office at Vienna, 2014) 25–28.

[68] Members' voluntary winding-up proceedings are excluded because they do not require companies to be in the situation of 'severe financial distresses'. See eg *Tucker, in the matter of Aero Inventory (UK) Ltd v Aero Inventory (UK) Ltd (No 2)* [2009] FCA 1481 [20]–[22]. But see *In re Betcorp Ltd (in liquidation)* 400 BR 266 (Bankr District of Nevada 2009) (where the US Bankruptcy Court for the District of Nevada held that a voluntary winding-up proceeding that was commenced under Part 5.2 of the Corporations Act was a 'collective' administrative proceeding and fell within the scope of the Model Law). This decision has been criticised by some commentators. See eg LC Ho, 'Recognising an Australian Solvent Liquidation under the UNCITRAL Model Law: In re Betcorp' [2009] *Journal of International Banking Law and Regulation* 418.

[69] Winding up proceedings by courts other than on the grounds of insolvency are excluded because they do not satisfy the element of 'for the purpose of liquidation or reorganisation'. See The Parliament of the Commonwealth of Australia (n 66) Ch 1; UNCITRAL Secretariat (n 67) 31.

[70] CBIA 2008, ss 21, 22; Soars et al (n 49) 10.

the debtor's assets, rights, or obligations or liabilities' and any '[e]xecution against the debtor's assets'.[71]

In enacting the Model Law, Australia chose to preserve the exceptions and limitations to Article 20(1) regarding automatic stays, by referring to its own domestic insolvency laws, namely, the Corporation Act 2001 (Cth) and the Bankruptcy Act 1966 (Cth).[72] Specifically, section 16 of the CBIA provides that:

> For the purposes of paragraph 2 of Article 20 of the Model Law (as it has the force of law in Australia), the scope and the modification or termination of the stay or suspension referred to in paragraph 1 of that Article, are the same as would apply if the stay or suspension arose under:
>
> (a) the Bankruptcy Act 1966; or
> (b) Chapter 5 (other than Parts 5.2 and 5.4A) of the Corporations Act 2001.[73]

This section provides that the scope and effect of the automatic stay order that is granted by Article 20(1) of the Model Law are identical to the stay provisions that would have been imposed if the case had arisen under Australian domestic insolvency proceedings.[74] In other words, whether secured creditors may be permitted to proceed with their rights against debtors would be decided by the same stay provisions applicable to Australian local insolvency proceedings that the foreign proceedings 'most closely resemble'.[75] However, in practice, Article 20(2) can become 'beguilingly ambiguous', because the Corporations Act has various stay provisions that 'differentially affect the position of secured creditors, sometimes at different points in the same overall process'.[76] As discussed above, the local stay provisions in Australia depend on the type of insolvency proceedings:

> (1) Part 5.1 (scheme of arrangement) – no stay applies.
> (2) Part 5.3A (voluntary administration) – ss 440A–440JA provide for stays.
> (3) Part 5.4/Part 5.4B (court-ordered liquidation) – ss 467, 471B and 471C provide for stays ....[77]

However, secured creditors can be exempted from stay orders. As discussed above, in compulsory winding-up proceedings, secured creditors are allowed to proceed with their claims against the debtor regardless of the stay order.[78] In voluntary administration proceedings, on the other hand, the enforcement actions by secured creditors will usually be suspended unless either consent can be obtained from

[71] CBIA 2008, Sch 1, Art 20(1).
[72] CBIA 2008, s 16.
[73] ibid.
[74] See eg *Hur v Samsun Logix Corp* [2009] FCA 372; *Akers v Deputy Commissioner of Taxation* [2014] FCAFC 57; *Yu* (n 47); *Kim* (n 50); S Rares, 'Ship Arrests, Maritime Liens and Cross-Border Insolvency' [2018] *Lloyd's Maritime and Commercial Law Quarterly* 398, 409.
[75] *Tai-Soo Suk v Hanjin Shipping Co Ltd* [2016] FCA 1404, [21].
[76] *Hur* (n 74) [21].
[77] *Tai-Soo Suk* (n 75) [20].
[78] Corporations Act 2001 (Cth), s 471C.

the administrator or the court grants relief; this is so that the corporate debtor can still have some 'breathing space' and the prospect of surviving its insolvency.[79] Therefore, in Australia, if the foreign main proceeding resembles proceedings for a compulsory winding up, secured claimants are exempted from an automatic stay of proceedings and the suspension of the enforcement process. However, if the foreign main proceeding resembles a voluntary administration, secured claimants are not exempted from an automatic stay order, but are prevented from commencing or continuing any enforcement action against the debtor, unless they obtain the consent of the administrator or relief from the court.[80] Secured creditors may apply for the court's permission to be exempted from the administration proceeding, but such relief depends on a case-by-case analysis. Finally, if the foreign main proceeding resembles a scheme of arrangement, no stay orders will be imposed against secured creditors unless otherwise provided in the scheme or applied by the debtor.[81]

C. Application of Article 20 in the Maritime Context

The conflict between maritime law and Australian domestic insolvency law was encountered by the Federal Court of Australia in *Danny Morris & Another v The Ship 'Kiama'*, where the Court held that the arrest of the ship and its subsequent judicial sale would not be characterised as 'a process of execution' within the meaning of section 440G of the Corporations Act; the Court therefore allowed the plaintiffs to proceed with their in rem claim against the proceeds of the judicial sale of the ship.[82] The Court adopted a narrow interpretation of the term 'execution' in the sense that it should be a proceeding that 'succeeds, and does not precede, judgment'.[83] However, in the situation where the arrest of a ship is concerned, 'there is no existing judgment upon which to execute'; therefore, the arrest of the ship does not amount to a process of execution that is against the assets of the debtor.[84] Nevertheless, in the context of cross-border insolvency, the Model Law and CBIA aim to provide a wide scope of moratorium order in order to suspend most of the actions against the debtor's assets, rights, obligations or liabilities. Thus, even if a ship arrest may not amount to an execution in Australia in the sense that it may be outside the scope of the stay order under Article 20(1)(b) of the Model Law, the action of the ship arrest, in any event, will be regarded as the commencement of, or the continuation of, a proceeding 'concerning the debtor's assets, rights, obligations or liabilities' that falls within the meaning of Article 20(1)(a) of the Model Law.[85]

[79] Corporations Act 2001 (Cth), s 440D.
[80] CBIA 2008, s 16; Corporations Act 2001(Cth), ss 440D, 471C; *Yu* (n 75); *Tai-Soo Suk* (n 75).
[81] Corporations Act 2001 (Cth), s 411(16).
[82] *The Ship 'Kiama'* (n 57) [15]–[16].
[83] ibid [16].
[84] ibid [17].
[85] Soars et al (n 49) 16.

Moreover, in the context of maritime cross-border insolvency, a special issue may arise with regard to whether statutory rights of action in rem need to be initiated, ie become secured claims before: (1) the commencement of a foreign insolvency proceeding; or (2) the recognition of a foreign main proceeding in Australia.[86] It is suggested by Rares J in *Kim v Daebo International Shipping Co Ltd* that the recognition of a foreign main proceeding rather than the commencement of a foreign insolvency proceeding might be the crucial point in time; this is on the basis that the Model Law and CBIA would only repeal domestic statutory remedies upon the recognition of a foreign main proceeding.[87] In other words, domestic statutory remedies, including the issue of a writ in rem, would not be affected by a foreign insolvency proceeding unless it is being recognised.[88]

Accordingly, in my view, a claimant with a maritime lien claim is a secured creditor from the moment that the lien is attached, whilst a claimant with a statutory right of action in rem claim would be regarded as a secured creditor if a writ in rem has been issued *before* a foreign insolvency proceeding has been recognised as a foreign main proceeding by the Australian courts.[89] If the writ in rem cannot be issued before the recognition of a foreign insolvency proceeding, the statutory right of action in rem remains inchoate and unsecured. As a result, if the foreign insolvency proceeding resembles a compulsory winding-up proceeding, secured maritime creditors would be able to proceed with their claims regardless of the pending or subsequent insolvency proceeding.[90] However, if the foreign insolvency proceeding resembles a voluntary administration proceeding, secured maritime creditors would be stayed by the voluntary administration moratorium unless they obtain the leave of the court or the consent of the administrator.[91]

i. Yu v STX Pan Ocean

Yu v STX Pan Ocean provides an example of the approach that is adopted by Australia with regard to the application of Article 20(2) of the Model Law.

In *Yu*, STX Pan Ocean (STX), a Korean dry bulk shipping company, commenced a rehabilitation proceeding in the bankruptcy court of South Korea.[92] After examining the relevant evidence submitted by the receiver of STX, the Federal Court of Australia held that the rehabilitation of STX that was initiated in Korea satisfied the requirements under Article 17 of the Model Law and therefore recognised the Korean rehabilitation proceeding as a 'foreign main proceeding'.[93]

[86] ibid 40.
[87] *Kim* (n 50) [14]; Soars et al (n 49) 40.
[88] *Kim* (n 50) [14].
[89] Soars et al (n 49) 29–32; Hafeez-Baig (n 49) 115.
[90] CBIA 2008, s 16; Corporations Act 2001(Cth), s 471C; *Tai-Soo Suk* (n 75).
[91] CBIA 2008, s 16; Corporations Act 2001(Cth), s 440D; *Tai-Soo Suk* (n 75).
[92] *Yu* (n 47) [26].
[93] ibid [27].

In addition to the application for recognition, the receiver of STX asked the Court to grant additional relief pursuant to Article 21(1) of the Model Law whereby the administration and realisation of all assets of STX located in Australia should be entrusted to him and no enforcement action should be allowed to continue or be commenced against the assets of STX.[94] The receiver of STX argued that the additional relief was essential in order to achieve a successful reorganisation of STX; this was on the basis that it would prevent local creditors in Australia from arresting any of its vessels that called in Australian ports and therefore preserve the assets of STX.[95] Further, the receiver of STX explained that the interests of STX would be greatly harmed if the automatic stay order was granted; this was on the grounds that the arrest and delay of ships might give rise to severe liquidation damage payments and the termination of charterparties with major clients of STX, one of the main sources of STX's revenue.[96]

Therefore, the issue before the Court was whether the automatic stay order provided by Article 20 of the Model Law should apply to maritime claimants who had the right to enforce their claims in rem against the vessels of STX.[97] The Court noted that the Australian enacting legislation of the Model Law preserved the operation of local insolvency laws in its Article 20(2), providing that the scope and effect of the automatic stay order were limited to the same extent as if the Corporations Act applied. Under section 471(C) of the Corporations Act, secured creditors are not affected by the automatic stay in a compulsory winding-up proceeding.[98] Buchanan J recognised the secured status of a maritime lien and held that a maritime lien holder had a security interest in the vessel rather than merely an in personam right against the vessel owner; therefore an action in rem to enforce a maritime lien would fall within the operation of section 471C of the Corporations Act.[99] Accordingly, the Court refused to grant a non-discretionary restraining order in order to prevent the arrest of STX's vessels in Australia.[100] Instead, the Court held that whether maritime claimants were allowed to proceed with their enforcement action against the vessels of the debtor, regardless of a pending or subsequent insolvency proceeding, should be examined by a 'Judge of the Court rather than … a Registrar' on a case-by-case basis.[101]

The decision reached by the Federal Court of Australia in *Yu* was based on the stay provision for compulsory winding-up proceedings under Part 5.4 of the Corporations Act, which appears to be inconsistent with Article 16 of the CBIA.[102]

[94] ibid [29].
[95] ibid [31].
[96] ibid [32].
[97] ibid [28].
[98] ibid [37]; Corporations Act 2001 (Cth), s 471C.
[99] M Davies, 'Cross-Border Insolvency and Admiralty: A Middle Path of Reciprocal Comity' (2018) 66 *American Journal of Comparative Law* 101, 112; see also *Yu* (n 47) [41].
[100] *Yu* (n 47) [41]–[43].
[101] *Yu* (n 47) [48]; Soars et al (n 49) 23.
[102] *Yu* (n 47) [37]; Corporations Act 2001 (Cth), s 471C.

The insolvency proceeding that was commenced by STX in Korea was a rehabilitation proceeding, which more closely resembles an Australian voluntary administration proceeding rather than a compulsory winding-up proceeding.[103] Therefore, it would seem that the stay provisions that govern voluntary administration proceedings under Part 5.3A of the Corporations Act should apply; these provide a wider scope of moratorium when compared to a compulsory winding up moratorium, as a voluntary administration moratorium applies to both secured and unsecured creditors.[104] Nevertheless, as mentioned below, the Court was not called upon to identify the issue with regard to which type of proceedings and stay provisions under the Corporations Act should be applied in order to determine the scope and effects of the stay order.[105] In addition, as discussed in Section IV below, it would seem that the Court attempted to get around this inconsistency by strictly construing the doctrine of personification, and held that an in rem action was actually against the vessel itself, rather than the debtor.

ii. *Tai-Soo Suk v Hanjin Shipping Co Ltd*

Similarly, in *Tai-Soo Suk v Hanjin Shipping Co Ltd*, the Federal Court of Australia found that Hanjin's Korean proceeding met all the elements and requirements laid out in Articles 2 and 17 of the CBIA, and therefore recognised Hanjin's rehabilitation proceeding as a foreign main proceeding, granting a stay order preventing maritime creditors from arresting the vessels owned or operated by Hanjin.[106]

Specifically, the Court was asked to identify the specific stay provisions of the Corporations Act that would apply to the foreign proceedings if they were taking place in Australia.[107] The reason for this identification was that, as secured creditors, the treatment of maritime lien claimants would be different under the different types of proceedings. The plaintiff argued that rehabilitation proceedings were more akin to voluntary administration proceedings under Part 5.3A of the Corporation Act, and therefore the stay provisions should not exclude any actions regarding maritime liens held against Hanjin's assets.[108]

Jagot J compared the decision in *Yu* and explained that the reason for Buchanan J reaching his decision in *Yu* (which was based on Part 5.4B of the Corporations Act in respect of winding-up proceedings) was that he was not called upon to consider Part 5.3A of the Corporation Act.[109] Nevertheless, under Article 20(2) of the Model Law and section 16 of the CBIA, the Court did have a duty to determine the type of proceedings that the foreign proceeding

[103] See *Tai-Soo Suk* (n 75).
[104] Corporations Act 2001 (Cth), ss 440D, 440F, 440G, 471B, 471C.
[105] *Tai-Soo Suk* (n 75) [21]–[22].
[106] ibid [16].
[107] ibid [21].
[108] *Tai-Soo Suk* (n 75) [21].
[109] ibid [21], [30].

most closely resembled.[110] The Court would compare the nature of the foreign proceedings with the nature of the proceedings under the relevant parts of the Corporations Act; therefore, the scope of the stay order would be the same as that which is provided for those types of proceedings in the Corporations Act.[111] After examining the evidence submitted by Hanjin's administrator, the Court found that the Korean rehabilitation proceeding more closely resembled an Australian voluntary administration proceeding under Part 5.3A of the Corporations Act, where secured creditors are subjected to an automatic stay, rather than a scheme of arrangement, where no automatic stay would apply.

In addition, the Court held that the automatic stay order did not harm the interests of maritime lien holders, because maritime lien holders could always apply for relief to proceed with their in rem actions simultaneously.[112] On a practical basis, if the relief was granted, maritime lien holders would be in the same position that they would have been if the stay did not apply to their claims.[113] Therefore, the Court concluded that no proceedings to enforce maritime liens could be initiated or continued against vessels owned or chartered by Hanjin unless they were with the debtor's written consent or with the relief of the court.

Thus, in *Tai-Soo Suk*, by identifying that the Korean rehabilitation proceeding was more like a voluntary administration proceeding, the Court issued a wide stay order and prevented maritime creditors from enforcing their claims to further the objective of the Korean rehabilitation proceeding. The stay extended to all vessels owned or chartered by Hanjin, without carving out any pre-arrested vessel.[114]

It is worth noting that approximately five months later, Jagot J in *Suk v Hanjin Shipping Co Ltd* vacated the recognition order and lifted the stay order he had earlier granted.[115] The reason for this termination was that Hanjin's administrator failed to comply with his obligation under Article 18 of the Model Law to inform the Court of a substantial change in the status of the foreign proceeding, whereby Hanjin's Korean rehabilitation proceeding was terminated and converted to a liquidation proceeding, as well as his own loss of status as a foreign representative.[116] Rather than through the application of the debtor or affected creditors, the Court took the initiative to terminate the previous recognition order.[117] Therefore, it is important for foreign representatives to respect their notification obligations under Article 18 of the Model Law, keeping the recognised court updated, so that it can modify the recognition order or stay order accordingly.

[110] ibid [22].
[111] ibid [24].
[112] ibid [51]–[58].
[113] ibid [57].
[114] ibid [51], [65].
[115] *Suk v Hanjin Shipping Co Ltd* [2017] FCA 404.
[116] ibid [11].
[117] ibid; see also *Yakushiji v Kaisha (No 2)* [2016] FCA 1277 (where the debtor brought an application under Article 18 of Schedule 1 to the Model Law after its change of ownership in the Korean rehabilitation proceeding, and accordingly the Federal Court of Australia vacated the original recognition order).

IV. Attitudes of the Courts Toward in Rem Actions and the Personification Doctrine in Australia

As mentioned in Chapter 6, in the area of maritime cross-border insolvency, another argument that may be initiated by maritime creditors in order to be exempted from an automatic stay order under Article 20 of the Model Law is that an in rem action is against the vessel itself as an independent 'wrongdoer', rather than against the insolvent debtor, and as a result the in rem action does not fall within the meaning of Article 20(1) of the Model Law. Whether this argument will succeed depends upon the court's attitude toward the personification doctrine.

It appears that courts in Australia have adopted the procedural theory of actions in rem that was articulated in *The Dictator*.[118] For example, in *Aichhorn and Co KG v The Ship MV Talabot*, the High Court of Australia held that an action in rem is a proceeding directly against a ship; nevertheless 'an action in rem is not simply an action against property – the owner of the property is indirectly impleaded in the action – and that once an appearance is entered the action proceeds as an action in personam'.[119] In addition, in *Caltex Oil (Australia) Pty Ltd v The Dredge Willemstad*, Gibbs J held that:

> An action in rem is an action against the ship itself. However, when the defendants to such an action have entered an appearance, judgment may be enforced against them personally, and to the full extent of the damages proved, even though those damages exceed the value of the ship. After appearances have been entered the action proceeds as if it were an action in personam although it does not cease to be an action in rem.[120]

Finally, as discussed above, in *Comandate Marine*, the Full Court of the Federal Court rejected the radical application of the 'procedural theory' that was articulated by the House of Lords in *The Indian Grace (No 2)*.[121] Therefore, following the decision in *Comandate Marine*, 'under Australian law an action in rem is an action against the ship and not its owner or demise charterer, at least before a relevant person has entered an unconditional appearance'.[122] Notwithstanding that the Full Court of the Federal Court of Australia in *The Ship Sam Hawk* followed the majority decision of the Privy Council in *The Halcyon Isle* and adopted a *lex fori* rule in order to determine the availability of a foreign maritime lien,[123] the Court did not reach the decision on the basis of the procedural nature of a maritime lien; instead, the Court held that the issue with regard to the nature of a maritime lien

[118] See eg *Aichhorn and Co KG v The Ship MV Talabot* [1974] HCA 21; *Comandate Marine* (n 45); *The Dictator* [1892] P 304.

[119] *The Ship MV Talabot* (n 118) [5].

[120] *Caltex Oil (Australia) Pty Ltd v The Dredge Willemstad* [1976] HCA 65, [10].

[121] *Comandate Marine* (n 45); *The Indian Grace (No 2)* (n 45).

[122] Rares, 'Admiralty Law – the Flying Dutchman of Cross-border Insolvency' (n 35) [34].

[123] *The Ship Sam Hawk* (n 48); *The Halcyon Isle* (n 48).

as a substantive or procedural right that had been discussed in *The Halcyon Isle* was a distraction in this case.[124]

In the realm of maritime cross-border insolvency, the argument of 'in rem action being against the vessel independently' seems to be upheld by the Federal Court of Australia in *Yu*, where Buchanan J held that an action in rem is 'an action to obtain a security which will enable a judgment to be satisfied out of the *res*'.[125] It seems that, in the context of a maritime lien, the Court regarded a vessel as a different legal entity from an insolvent debtor in the sense that 'a maritime lien creditor has a secured interest against the ship itself dating from the moment of the event from which the lien arose, rather than merely an in personam right against the ship's owner'.[126] Accordingly, the Court in *Yu* held that an automatic stay order under Article 20(1) of the Model Law should not preclude a claimant from bringing an action in rem to enforce its maritime lien.[127] Nevertheless, this argument was not raised by the maritime creditors of Hanjin in *Tai-Soo Suk*.[128]

In my view, an action in rem to enforce a maritime lien in Australia should be regarded as a separate and distinct action from an action in personam against the insolvent debtor.[129] However, in the area of maritime cross-border insolvency, it is undecided what attitude will be adopted by the Australian courts towards the nature of an in rem action to enforce a statutory right of action in rem.

V. Status of Chartered Vessels in Cross-Border Insolvency

In *Tai-Soo Suk*, the Court extended the automatic stay order to all vessels owned or chartered by Hanjin.[130] However, the Court did not specify the legal basis for extending the stay order to include the chartered vessels of Hanjin, which may not be the property of the debtor in some circumstances.[131] In my view, the stay order granted by the Court in *Tai-Soo Suk*, which included all the chartered vessels of Hanjin, is not consistent with section 440D of the Corporations Act and Article 20(2) of Schedule 1 to the CBIA.[132]

[124] *The Ship Sam Hawk* (n 48) 158–61.
[125] *Yu* (n 47) [40].
[126] Davies (n 99) 112; *Yu* (n 47) [40]–[41].
[127] *Yu* (n 47) [42].
[128] See *Tai-Soo Suk* (n 75).
[129] *Yu* (n 47), *Caltex Oil* (n 20), *The Ship MV Talabot* (n 118); Rares, 'Admiralty Law – the Flying Dutchman of Cross-border Insolvency' (n 35) [33]–[46], Hafeez-Baig (n 49) 108–109; J Turner and S Derrington *The Law and Practices of Admiralty* Matters, 2nd edn (Oxford University Press, 2016) 11–12.
[130] See *Tai-Soo Suk* (n 75) [65].
[131] *Tai-Soo Suk* (n 75) [65].
[132] Corporations Act 2001 (Cth), s 440D, CBIA 2008, Sch 1, Art 20(2).

VI. Summary

Australia has adopted the Model Law entirely and is always willing to promote uniformity and co-operation with regard to cross-border insolvency. Courts in Australia will generally recognise a foreign insolvency proceeding as a foreign main proceeding if it complies with the requirements that are set forth in Article 17 of the Model Law, and will provide proper assistance, as well as remedies, to the foreign representative.[133]

Recent decisions illustrate that the Australian courts always take the special nature of admiralty into account and are willing to narrow down cross-border insolvency in order for a particular maritime claimant to proceed with its claim, despite the automatic stay protection provided by the Model Law.[134] In Australia, if the foreign insolvency proceeding is similar to a compulsory winding-up proceeding, a maritime creditor that has obtained secured status is likely to proceed with its enforcement action against the debtor regardless of any pending or subsequent insolvency proceeding. However, if the foreign insolvency proceeding resembles an Australian administration proceeding, the enforcement action of a maritime creditor is more likely to be subjected to the automatic stay order, in the sense that courts in Australia are more willing to protect the property of the insolvent debtor from arrest in order to achieve the objective of an administration proceeding.[135]

In addition, it seems that courts in Australia regard an action in rem to enforce a maritime lien as a separate and distinct action from an action in personam against the insolvent debtor before the debtor has entered an unconditional appearance.[136] Nevertheless, the attitude of Australian courts towards the nature of an in rem action to enforce a statutory right of action in rem is still untested in the area of maritime cross-border insolvency. Moreover, although the Court in *Tai-Soo Suk* extended the automatic stay order to all vessels that were owned or chartered by the debtor, it did not address the legal basis for extending the stay order beyond the scope of the debtor's property.[137]

[133] CBIA 2008, Sch 1, Art 17.

[134] See eg *Yu* (n 47).

[135] *Tai-Soo Suk* (n 75).

[136] *Yu* (n 47), *Caltex Oil* (n 20), *The Ship MV Talabot* (n 118); Rares, 'Admiralty Law – the Flying Dutchman of Cross-border Insolvency' (n 35) [33]–[46], Hafeez-Baig (n 49) 108–109; Turner and Derrington (n 129) 11–12.

[137] *Tai-Soo Suk* (n 75).

8

United Kingdom

I. Overview

The UK adopted the Model Law and incorporated it into the Cross-Border Insolvency Regulations 2006 with certain modifications. As the leading shipping country of the world, courts in the UK have always been aware of the special nature of maritime claims. This chapter illustrates the specific details regarding the application of the regime of the Model Law in the UK in the context of maritime law.

II. The Insolvency Act 1986 and the Secured Status of Maritime Claims in the UK

A. Overview of the Insolvency Act 1986

In the UK, the legal basis for corporate insolvency is provided by the Insolvency Act 1986.[1] In particular, the Insolvency Act 1986 provides three main insolvency proceedings: winding up, administration and company arrangements.[2]

i. Winding Up

Winding up is the primary procedure that is used to liquidate companies. The purpose of a winding-up proceeding is to collect and realise the assets of a company for the purpose of distribution to its creditors.[3] The commencement of a winding-up proceeding signals 'the beginning of the end of the company's legal existence' in the sense that once the winding-up proceeding has been concluded, the company will be dissolved and its legal personality will be extinguished.[4] Part IV of the Insolvency Act 1986 provides two main types of winding-up procedure: voluntary winding up and compulsory winding up.

[1] See Insolvency Act 1986. In the UK, the term 'bankruptcy' refers to an individual's bankruptcy while the term 'insolvency' is used for corporation insolvency: J Silkenat and C Schmerler, *The Law of International Insolvencies and Debt Restructuring* (Oceana, 2006) 389.
[2] See Insolvency Act 1986, Pts I, II, IV.
[3] Insolvency Act 1986, Pt IV; I Fletcher, *The Law of Insolvency*, 5th edn (Sweet & Maxwell, 2017) 591.
[4] Fletcher, *The Law of Insolvency* (n 3) 594.

A voluntary winding up of a solvent company is known as a 'members' voluntary liquidation' (MVL), whilst a voluntary winding up of an insolvent company is known as a 'creditors' voluntary liquidation' (CVL).[5] If the directors of a company have made a statutory declaration of solvency, that 'the company will be able to pay its debts in full, together with interest, within such period, not exceeding 12 months from the commencement of the winding up' under section 89 of the Insolvency Act 1986, the winding up will take the form of a MVL.[6] In the absence of such a declaration, however, the winding up will take the form of a CVL.[7] Nevertheless, both types of voluntary liquidation are triggered by the actions of the members of the company and by virtue of the passing of a special resolution for a voluntary winding up.[8]

A compulsory winding up is a court-driven proceeding and is usually an insolvent liquidation.[9] It can be commenced by either creditors, directors or shareholders of the company through the presentation of a petition for winding up at court on the ground that the company is unable to pay its debts.[10] Once a court has granted a winding-up order the company will cease to carry on business except to the extent necessary for it to be wound up.[11]

ii. Administration

An administration proceeding is governed by Schedule B1 to the Insolvency Act 1986 and has been substantially reformed by the Enterprise Act 2002.[12] It is a US-Chapter 11-like 'rescue procedure' that provides a way to rehabilitate a company that is in financial difficulty. The first two primary objectives of an administration proceeding are 'rescuing the company as a going concern' and 'achieving a better result for the company's creditors as a whole than would be likely if the company were wound up (without first being in administration)'.[13]

iii. Company Arrangements

It is also possible for a company to voluntarily enter into a compromise arrangement with its creditors in order to deal with its financial difficulties or adapt to changes in market conditions.[14] The purpose of company arrangements is to complement the regime of administration.[15] The two main procedures that are

[5] Insolvency Act 1986, s 90.
[6] Insolvency Act 1986, ss 89, 90.
[7] Insolvency Act 1986, s 90.
[8] Insolvency Act 1986, s 84; V Finch and D Milman, *Corporate Insolvency Law: Perspectives and Principles*, 3rd edn (Cambridge University Press, 2017) 453.
[9] Insolvency Act 1986, s 122.
[10] Insolvency Act 1986, ss 122, 123, 124.
[11] Fletcher, *The Law of Insolvency* (n 3) 677.
[12] See general Insolvency Act 1986, Sch B1; Enterprise Act 2002.
[13] Insolvency Act 1986, Sch B1, para 3.
[14] Finch and Milman (n 8) 409.
[15] Fletcher, *The Law of Insolvency* (n 3) 449.

provided in a voluntary arrangement for companies are: company voluntary arrangements (CVA), as provided in Part I and Schedule A1 to the Insolvency Act 1986, and schemes of arrangement as provided for in section 895 of the Companies Act 2006.[16]

A CVA provides for a debtor to enter into an arrangement with its creditors for a composition of its debts; this usually involves delayed or reduced debt payments or a capital restructuring.[17] If the arrangement is approved by the requisite majority of creditors, it is binding upon the company and all its creditors who are entitled to vote at the meeting, or would have been so entitled if they had had notice of it.[18] However, the right of a secured creditor to enforce its security cannot be affected or modified by the arrangement, unless the consent of the secured creditor is obtained.[19] On the contrary, a scheme of arrangement involves an initial application being made to the court, requiring it to summon a meeting of creditors or classes of creditors to agree to a compromise or arrangement between the company and its creditors.[20] Unlike a CVA, a scheme of arrangement is subject to the approval of the court.[21] Courts will consider the issues of procedural fairness in order to decide whether the proposed scheme is 'fair and reasonable'; for example, 'whether each common interest group … is fairly constituted' and 'whether the class's decision to approve the scheme was one that could reasonably have been made'.[22] Finally, once a scheme of arrangement is approved by the court, it is binding on all affected creditors and may modify the rights of secured creditors without their consent being required.[23]

B. Stay Provisions under the Insolvency Act 1986

With regard to a voluntary winding-up proceeding, no automatic stay order will be granted by the court in order to suspend enforcement actions against the debtor following the commencement of a voluntary liquidation proceeding.[24] The liquidator, the creditors or the members of the debtor must apply to the court for a stay order.[25] Whether such a stay order is granted in order to ensure an equitable distribution of the assets of the debtor is subject to the discretion of the court.[26]

[16] Insolvency Act 1986, Pt I, Sch A1; Companies Act 2006, s 895.

[17] Insolvency Act 1986, Pt I; Finch and Milman (n 8) 417.

[18] Insolvency Act 1986, s 4A(2), (3), (4), (5); Finch and Milman (n 8) 418.

[19] Insolvency Act 1986, s 4(3).

[20] Companies Act 2006, s 896; Finch and Milman (n 8) 410. See generally J Payne, *Scheme of Arrangement: Theory, Structure and Operation* (Cambridge University Press, 2014).

[21] Companies Act 2006, s 896.

[22] Finch and Milman (n 8) 410–11; see also *Re Anglo-Continental Supply Co Ltd* [1992] 2 Ch 723; *Re RAC Motoring Services Ltd* [2000] 1 BCLC 307.

[23] Finch and Milman (n 8) 410–11; *Re Allied Domecq plc* [2000] BCC 582.

[24] Fletcher, *The Law of Insolvency* (n 3) 615–16.

[25] Insolvency Act 1986, ss 112(1), 112(2), 183(1), 183(2)(a).

[26] Insolvency Act 1986, ss 183(1), (2)(a); Fletcher, *The Law of Insolvency* (n 3) 616.

With regard to a compulsory winding-up proceeding, the court will grant an automatic stay that will be imposed against creditors under sections 127 and 128(1), in the sense that 'no action or proceeding shall be proceeded with or commenced against the company or its property, except by leave of the court and subject to such terms as the court may impose'.[27] In addition, any attachment or execution against the insolvent debtor or its assets after the commencement of a compulsory winding-up proceeding is void.[28] However, it is well settled in the UK that a compulsory winding-up stay provision does not affect the rights of secured creditors. Courts will generally grant leave to secured creditors in order that they can proceed with their enforcement actions regardless of any pending or subsequent winding-up proceedings.[29] Furthermore, sections 183(1) and 183(3)(a) provide that if secured creditors have completed execution before the commencement of winding-up proceedings, they are unaffected by the subsequent winding-up proceeding.[30] Therefore, although secured creditors must obtain permission from the court in order to commence or continue with their enforcement actions against the debtor, leave of the court will generally be granted.[31]

Similarly, with regard to administration proceedings, in the UK an automatic stay order will come into effect upon the initiation of an administration proceeding. The stay order will prevent creditors from commencing or continuing to enforce their claims against the debtor or its assets without obtaining the consent of the administrator or the leave of the court.[32] The stay order provides the debtor with breathing space in order to reorganise its business, thereby giving the debtor's business the possibility of surviving as a going concern.[33] However, unlike a compulsory winding-up proceeding, secured creditors will not be exempted from an administration stay order; their actions will also be suspended unless the consent of the administrator or the leave of the court is obtained.[34]

Finally, CVAs and schemes of arrangement do not provide any automatic moratorium to protect the debtor from any enforcement action by its creditors.[35] Nevertheless, in the circumstance of a scheme of arrangement that succeeds an administration proceeding, the company will be able to enjoy the benefit of the

[27] Insolvency Act 1986, s 130(2).

[28] Insolvency Act 1986, ss 127, 128(1).

[29] Insolvency Act 1986, s 183(1), (2)(a); *Re David Lloyd & Co* (1877) LR 6 ChD 339 (CA). See also Fletcher, *The Law of Insolvency* (n 3) 703; *Moor v Anglo-Italian Bank* (1879) 10 ChD 681; *Re Hopkins* (1881) 18 ChD 370; A Keay, *The Law of Company Liquidation*, 4th edn (Sweet & Maxwell, 2017) 835–36; W Tetley, *Maritime Lien and Claims*, 2nd edn (Éditions Yvon Blais, 1998) 1133.

[30] Insolvency Act 1986, s 183(1), (3)(a).

[31] See eg Fletcher, *The Law of Insolvency* (n 3) 703; *Moor* (n 29); *Re Hopkins* (n 29); Keay (n 29) 835–36; Tetley (n 29) 1133–34; *The Constellation* [1965] 2 Lloyd's Rep 538; *Re Rio Grande do Sol Steamship Co* (1877) 5 Ch D 282 (CA).

[32] Insolvency Act 1986, Sch B1, para 44.

[33] Fletcher, *The Law of Insolvency* (n 3) 515–16.

[34] Insolvency Act 1986, Sch B1, para 43; Fletcher, *The Law of Insolvency* (n 3) 516–17.

[35] Finch and Milman (n 8) 414; but see Insolvency Act 1986, s 1A(1), Sch A1 (which enable directors of 'small companies' to take steps to obtain a moratorium for the company when they intend to make a proposal for a CVA).

administration moratorium pending the implementation of the scheme in the sense that the action of a secured creditor will be suspended.[36] Since the Insolvency Act 1986 and the Companies Act 2006 do not provide company arrangements with any mandatory and automatic stay provisions, the following sections will not discuss these proceedings in detail.

C. Secured Status of Maritime Claims

i. Maritime Liens

The claims that give rise to maritime liens in the UK are: salvage; damage done by a ship; seamen's wages; master's wages and disbursements; *bottomry* and *respondentia*.[37] Although the concept of maritime liens has not been defined in legislation, it has been frequently considered by the judiciary. Notwithstanding that the judicial definitions of a maritime lien provided by the courts may differ in terms of formulation and emphasis, 'there has been unanimous agreement as to the essential characteristics of a maritime lien'.[38]

As discussed in Chapter 5, the landmark decision of *The Bold Buccleugh* defined a maritime lien as a claim or privilege upon a ship to be carried into effect via the legal process of a proceeding in rem, which is a process to perfect the claim that is inchoate from the moment the lien attaches.[39] Therefore, under the definition that was provided in *The Bold Buccleugh*, a maritime lien is a substantive security right that obtains its secured status from the time of the accrual of the lien.[40] It remains inchoate until it is perfected by the initiation of a proceeding in rem, by which it retrospectively relates back to the time when it first attached.[41] In other words, a maritime lien is secured before the commencement of the action in rem or the arrest of the ship.[42]

However, courts in the UK gradually shifted to the procedural theory and characterised a maritime lien as being procedural and remedial that creates

[36] Finch and Milman (n 8) 414; *FMS Wertmanagement AÖR v Vietnam Shipbuilding Industry Group & Others* [2013] EWHC 1146 (Comm).

[37] Master's disbursements are the disbursements made by the masters with their own money or obtained on their personal credits, for the emergency necessaries when they are out of touch with the shipowners; *bottomry* is the pledging of a ship by the master as security for payment of repair costs and other necessaries in order to enable the ship to complete a voyage when outside its home port; *respondentia* is the same except the cargo is pledged. See Tetley (n 29) 419; *The Bold Buccleugh* (1851) 7 Moo PC 267.

[38] DR Thomas, *Maritime Liens* (Stevens & Sons, 1980) 10.

[39] *The Bold Buccleugh* (n 37) 284.

[40] *The Bold Buccleugh* (n 37) 284; Tetley (n 29) 1134.

[41] *The Bold Buccleugh* (n 37); *The Tolten* [1946] P 135; MJ Hafeez-Baig, 'Navigating The Waters between Admiralty and Cross-Border Insolvency: A Comparison of the Australian, German and French Position' [2018] *Lloyd's Maritime and Commercial Law Quarterly* 97, 115.

[42] Hafeez-Baig (n 41) 115.

'no immediate right of property' at the time the claim attaches.[43] '[I]t is, and will continue to be, devoid of any legal consequences unless and until it is "carried into effect by legal process, by a proceeding in rem"'.[44] Thus, under the procedural theory, a maritime lien does not create any proprietary right until the lien holder is 'recognised as entitled to proceed in rem against the ship in the court in which he is seeking to enforce his maritime lien'.[45] Put differently, it only becomes secured when an in rem action is commenced and, once carried into effect by the action in rem, dates back to the time when it first attached. However, if for whatever reason the subsequent action in rem cannot be brought, such as the commencement of an insolvency proceeding, the lien remains inchoate and there is no basis for it to obtain secured status.

ii. Statutory Rights of Action in Rem

Except for the five types of claim that are recognised as maritime liens, most maritime claims in the UK only give rise to statutory rights of action in rem. As discussed in Chapter 5, statutory rights of action in rem do not create any property right before the arrest of a ship.[46] In *In Re Aro Co Ltd*, the claimant with a statutory right of action in rem obtained a writ in rem before the commencement of the winding up of the shipowner.[47] However, the relevant ship was already under arrest by another claim and, as a result, the claimant's writ could not be served. The shipowner subsequently went into a compulsory winding up and the claimant sought leave from the court to be exempted from the winding-up moratorium order in order that it could proceed with its action against the ship.[48] The UK Court of Appeal explained that once a writ in rem was issued, the claimant could serve the writ on the ship and arrest it; thus the ship was already effectively encumbered with the claim of the claimant.[49] Accordingly, the Court held that the claimant should be considered as a secured creditor and exercised its discretion in order to grant leave to allow the claimant to proceed with its claim.[50] Therefore, in the UK, a statutory right of action in rem only becomes a secured claim when the writ of arrest has been issued. Nevertheless, unlike a maritime lien, it has no relation back to any earlier period.[51]

[43] *The Halcyon Isle* [1981] AC 221, 234; *The Indian Grace (No 2)* [1998] AC 878; see also DC Jackson, *Enforcement of Maritime Claims*, 4th edn (Routledge, 2005) [18.21].
[44] *The Halcyon Isle* (n 43) 234.
[45] ibid 234.
[46] *The Heinrich Bjorn* (1885) 10 PD 44, 45.
[47] *In re Aro Co Ltd* [1980] Ch 196.
[48] ibid 198.
[49] ibid 209.
[50] ibid 209.
[51] ibid; *The Heinrich Bjorn* (n 46).

iii. Secured Status

When interacting with the law of insolvency, in a compulsory winding-up proceeding, if a claimant has issued a writ in rem (for the purpose of the enforcement of either a maritime lien or a statutory right of action in rem) before the commencement of a compulsory winding-up proceeding, it may realise its security interest regardless of a winding-up stay order.[52] 'Although the claimant must ask for leave to continue the proceedings, it will almost certainly be granted'.[53] If the claimant has not yet enforced its maritime claim by arresting the ship at the time of the commencement of the compulsory winding-up proceeding, the claim will be suspended by the stay order to the same extent as other general unsecured claims. Nevertheless, as pointed out by the decision in *In Re Aro Co*, courts retain a wide discretion when deciding whether to grant leave to claimants; it will depend upon 'what is right and fair in the circumstances'.[54] For example, in *The Bolivia*, claimants issued their writs in rem against a ship of the debtor between the date of the presentation of the winding-up petition and the date that the winding-up order was made. The ship had been arrested by a different creditor before the winding-up petition was presented. Following the decision in *In Re Aro Co*, Arden J exercised her discretion and granted leave to the claimants in order to allow them to proceed with their in rem claims on the ground that an order for sale of the vessel had already been made and the order was to 'convert the company's interest in the ship into a right to receive the balance of the proceeds of sale remaining after satisfaction of the prior claimants'.[55] As a result, the debtor had already ceased to have an interest in the ship and it was unfair to refuse to grant leave merely because the current claimants were not fortunate enough to issue their writs in rem before the commencement of the winding-up proceeding.[56]

Nevertheless, in the case of an administration proceeding, an enforcement action against the assets of the debtor by a claimant who has a maritime claim will automatically be subject to an administration stay order unless the debtor obtains the consent of the administrator or leave of the court; this is the case whether the writ in rem has been issued before the commencement of the administration proceeding or not.[57] Unlike a compulsory winding-up moratorium, the moratorium provided in administration proceedings by paragraph 43 of Schedule B1 to the Insolvency Act 1986 is much broader; in order for the debtor to have breathing space to administer its affairs, the enforcement action of a secured creditor against the debtor will be suspended by the moratorium unless the consent of the administrator or the leave of the court has been obtained.[58]

[52] Insolvency Act 1986, s 285(4); Tetley (n 29) 1134.
[53] Tetley (n 29) 1134–35.
[54] *In re Aro Co Ltd* (n 47) 209; Tetley (n 29) 1136; N Meeson and J Kimbell, *Admiralty Jurisdiction and Practice*, 5th edn (Informa Law from Routledge, 2018) 115–16.
[55] *The Bolivia* [1995] BCC 666, 676.
[56] ibid.
[57] Insolvency Act 1986, Sch B1, para 43; Meeson and Kimbell (n 54) 118–19.
[58] Insolvency Act 1986, s 130(2); Sch B1, para 43.

III. Cross-Border Insolvency in the UK

A. Overview of the Cross-Border Insolvency Regulations 2006

Great Britain took an active role in the development of the Model Law and brought it into force in 2006 by means of the Cross-Border Insolvency Regulations 2006 (CBIR 2006).[59] Similarly, Northern Ireland has parallel legislation, implementing the Model Law: the Cross-Border Insolvency Regulations (Northern Ireland) 2007, which came into force in April 2007.

In addition to the regime of Model Law, the UK provides three other methods in order to assist with the problem of cross-border insolvency, two of which are part of regional or internationally agreed schemes.[60] The first is section 426 of the Insolvency Act 1986, which is a statutory authorisation to assist in insolvency proceedings in designated countries.[61] The second is Regulation (EU) 2015/848 of the European Parliament and of the Council of 20 May 2015 on Insolvency Proceedings Recast (Recast EU Regulation).[62] The Recast EU Regulation applies to insolvency proceedings in respect of debtors who have their centre of main interest (COMI) within the European Union (excluding Denmark), whilst the CBIR 2006 apply to insolvency proceedings where the COMI of debtors are outside the European Union.[63] Finally, the UK common law also empowers courts to recognise and assist in foreign insolvency proceedings.[64] The implementation of the Model Law does not affect the possibility of international recognition and assistance based on the other above-mentioned three principles that are available in the UK.[65] Nevertheless, the following sections will focus on the application of the CBIR 2006 in England and Wales with regard to the area of maritime cross-border insolvency.

The CBIR 2006 include five Schedules, of which Schedule 1 provides the text of the Model Law with certain modifications in order to adapt the Model Law for its application in Great Britain.[66] The courts that are competent to perform the function of recognising foreign insolvency proceedings and co-operating with foreign courts are the High Court (Chancery Division) as regards England and Wales, and the Court of Session as regards Scotland.[67]

[59] I Fletcher, 'Better Late than Never: The UNCITRAL Model Law Enters into Force in Great Britain' (2006) 19 *Insolvency Intelligence* 86, 86.

[60] *Rubin & Another v Eurofinance SA & Others* [2012] UKSC 46, [25].

[61] Insolvency Act 1986, s 426; see eg *In re HIH Insurance Ltd* [2008] 1 WLR 852.

[62] The Recast EU Regulation came into force on 26 June 2015 and applied to insolvency proceedings opened after 26 June 2017, while the insolvency proceedings opened before 26 June 2017 were governed by Council Regulation (EC) No 1346/2000 of 29 May 2000 on Insolvency Proceedings (EC Regulation).

[63] *Rubin & Another* (n 60) [26]–[27].

[64] *Rubin & Another* (n 60) [28].

[65] ibid

[66] CBIR 2006, Sch 1, Art 2.

[67] CBIR 2006, Sch 1, Art 4.

B. Article 20 of Schedule 1 to the CBIR 2006

Article 20(1) of Schedule 1 to the CBIR 2006 provides that, once a foreign proceeding is recognised as a foreign main proceeding, an automatic stay will be triggered in order to protect the debtor's assets, rights, obligations and liabilities.[68] Following the UNCITRAL Model Law on Cross-Border Insolvency with Guide to Enactment and Interpretation (Guide to Enactment),[69] the CBIR 2006 limit the scope and effect of the stay order in Article 20(2):

> 2. The stay and suspension referred to in paragraph 1 of this article shall be—
>
> (a) the same in scope and effect as if the debtor, in the case of an individual, had been adjudged bankrupt under the Insolvency Act 1986 or had his estate sequestrated under the Bankruptcy (Scotland) Act 1985, or, in the case of a debtor other than an individual, had been made the subject of a winding-up order under the Insolvency Act 1986; and
>
> (b) subject to the same powers of the court and the same prohibitions, limitations, exceptions and conditions as would apply under the law of Great Britain in such a case,
>
> and the provisions of paragraph 1 of this article shall be interpreted accordingly.
>
> 3. Without prejudice to paragraph 2 of this article, the stay and suspension referred to in paragraph 1 of this article, in particular, does not affect any right—
>
> (a) to take any steps to enforce security over the debtor's property; …[70]

In other words, Article 20(2) of Schedule 1 to the CBIR 2006 limits the scope and effect of the automatic stay to the same extent as if the case had arisen in a comparable case under the Insolvency Act 1986.[71] To be specific, in *Cosco Bulk Carrier Co v Armada Shipping SA & Another*, the Court explained that Article 20(2) clearly identified English domestic insolvency law as the primary source with regard to the effect and scope of the automatic stay upon the recognition of a foreign main proceeding.[72] Similar to Australia, the Court will compare the nature of the foreign proceedings with the local insolvency proceedings and apply the stay provisions applicable to the most comparable local insolvency proceedings.[73] Although Article 20(3)(a) provides that the automatic stay or suspension does not affect a creditor's right to enforce its security over the debtor's property, Article 20(3) needs to be subject to Article 20(2).[74] Therefore, whether secured creditors can be exempted from automatic stay orders under the CBIR 2006

[68] CBIR 2006, Sch 1, Art 20(1).

[69] UNCITRAL Secretariat, *UNCITRAL Cross-Border Insolvency Law with Guide to Enactment and Interpretation* (United Nations Office at Vienna, 2014).

[70] CBIR 2006, Sch 1, Art 20(2).

[71] CBIR 2006, Sch 1, Art 20(2)(a); see also UNCITRAL Secretariat (n 69) 85.

[72] *Cosco Bulk Carrier Co v Armada Shipping SA& Another* [2011] EWHC 216 (Ch), [45].

[73] ibid.

[74] ibid; see also LC Ho, *A Commentary on the UNCITRAL Model Law*, 4th edn (Globe Law and Business, 2017) 240.

depends on the English domestic stay provisions that apply to the local insolvency proceedings that the foreign proceedings most closely resemble.

Nevertheless, Article 20(4) permits proceedings to be taken to the extent necessary to preserve a claim and Article 20(5) provides that the stay order does not affect the right to request or initiate parallel insolvency proceedings under local insolvency law.[75] In addition, courts always retain discretionary power to modify or terminate their stay orders on the application of the foreign representative, as they think fit.[76] For example, in *Cosco Bulk Carrier* the High Court faced two arbitration claims concerning the debtor's obligations and liabilities that were applied to be exempted from the automatic stay order. The Court suspended the first arbitration claim by virtue of the automatic stay order on the ground that the foreign insolvency proceeding was more analogous to a winding-up proceeding than an administration proceeding and thus, section 130(2) of the Insolvency Act 1986 should be the applicable domestic provision.[77] With regard to the second arbitration claim, the Court exceptionally exercised its discretion and lifted the stay. After balancing the interests of the parties in respect of fairness, convenience and justice, the Court held that it was in favour of the position that the underlying disputes of English shipping law were to be resolved by way of arbitration rather than by a foreign insolvency proceeding.[78]

C. Application of Article 20 in the Maritime Context

In the context of cross-border insolvency, the issue with regard to whether the issuing of a writ in rem needs to take place prior to the commencement of foreign insolvency proceedings or the recognition of foreign insolvency proceedings as foreign main proceedings has not been examined by courts in the UK. In my view, the appropriate relevant time point should be the date of the recognition of the foreign insolvency proceeding on the ground that local creditors will only be bound by foreign insolvency proceedings once they have been recognised as foreign main proceedings in the UK.[79] In other words, the recognition procedure is not automatic under the CBIR 2006, as courts in the UK are not automatically bound by the foreign insolvency order and the CBIR 2006 do not authorise foreign representatives to apply foreign insolvency law directly in UK courts.[80] Thus, it seems that the date of the recognition of foreign insolvency proceedings shall be

[75] CBIR 2006, Sch 1, Art 20(4), (5).
[76] CBIR 2006, Sch1, Art 20(6).
[77] *Cosco Bulk Carrier* (n 72) [45], [53].
[78] *Cosco Bulk Carrier* (n 72) [58].
[79] CBIR 2006, Sch1, Art 15.
[80] CBIR 2006, Sch 1, Art 15; *Rubin & Another* (n 60); G McCormack and WW Yee, 'The UNCITRAL Model Law on Cross-Border Insolvency Comes of Age: New Times or New Paradigms?' (2019) 54 *Texas International Law Journal* 273, 275–76.

the relevant time point before which writs in rem should be issued in order for maritime claims to obtain secured status. Accordingly, a claimant with a maritime lien or a statutory right in rem, who issues a writ in rem before the recognition of a foreign insolvency proceeding shall be regarded as a secured creditor in the UK.[81]

If the foreign insolvency proceeding is more comparable to a compulsory winding-up proceeding that arises under Part IV of the Insolvency Act 1986, the secured maritime claimant shall be allowed to proceed with its in rem claim against the vessel of the debtor regardless of the automatic stay order that is granted by Article 20(1) of Schedule 1 to the CBIR. In addition, if a pre-existing maritime claimant has arrested the vessel, and at the time of the recognition of a foreign insolvency proceeding the admiralty proceeding has already reached the point of judicial sale of the vessel, the claimant can continue to proceed against the proceeds of the judicial sale regardless of the commencement of a subsequent insolvency proceeding.[82] However, if the foreign insolvency proceeding is more comparable to a UK administration proceeding, the secured maritime creditor will be subject to a wide administration moratorium upon the recognition of a foreign main proceeding, and its in rem action against the vessel of the debtor will be suspended.[83]

Furthermore, an issue may arise with regard to whether the arrest of a ship should be regarded as an 'execution' and should therefore be subject to Article 20(1)(b) of Schedule 1 to the CBIR 2006. The position held by courts in the UK is that the arrest of a vessel does not amount to a process of 'execution' but is equivalent to a process of sequestration.[84] Nevertheless, given the broad scope of an automatic stay order that is granted by the Model Law, this argument does not seem relevant in the area of cross-border insolvency in the sense that the arrest of a vessel will nevertheless be regarded as the commencement or continuation of an action concerning the debtor's assets that falls within the meaning of Article 20(1)(a) of the Model Law.

i. Harms Offshore Aht 'Taurus' GmbH & Co Kg & Another v Bloom & Others

In *Harms Offshore*, the case arose from the insolvency of an offshore oil and gas company that had entered into an administration proceeding according to Schedule B1 to the Insolvency Act 1986. The administrator of the debtor was authorised by the Companies Court to enter into a loan agreement with specified lenders and to draw down funds under that agreement for the purpose of

[81] Tetley (n 29) 1134–35; Meeson and Kimbell (n 54) 115–16.

[82] Insolvency Act 1986, s 183(3)(a); M Davies, 'Cross-Border Insolvency and Admiralty: A Middle Path of Reciprocal Comity' (2018) 66 *American Journal of Comparative Law* 101, 107.

[83] See eg Meeson and Kimbell (n 54) 118–19; Insolvency Act 1986, Sch 1, para 43; *Cosco Bulk Carrier* (n 72) [49].

[84] *In re Australian Direct Steam Navigation Co* (1875) LR 20 Eq 325; *The Constellation* (n 31); *The Zafiro* [1960] P 1.

paying off the post-administration liabilities of the debtor.[85] The claimants were pre-administration creditors who time chartered their vessels to the debtor. After the commencement of the administration proceeding, the claimants commenced a Rule B attachment proceeding against the debtor in the US District Court for the Southern District of New York (US District Court), without notice to the administrator or the US District Court, seeking judgment for the charter hire and other payments that were due to them from the debtor.[86] The US District Court subsequently granted ex parte orders and attached the property that was authorised by the Companies Court for the benefit of the administration of the debtor.[87] Thereafter, the administrators of the debtor applied to the Court of Appeal in order to obtain an injunction that required the claimants to use their best efforts to release the attachment and restrained them from taking any steps in the substantive proceedings commenced in New York.[88]

The Court examined the extra-territorial effect of an administration moratorium and found that it had jurisdiction to protect the asset of a company that was subject to an administration proceeding from attachments or executions in foreign jurisdictions.[89] In addition, the Court held that whether it would exercise jurisdiction over the foreign attachment should be determined on a case-by-case basis and tempered by considerations of comity.[90] Notwithstanding that a generous view of comity had to be taken, particularly between the jurisdictions that both adopted the Model Law regime, it might be justified to grant an injunction if the conduct of the creditor was oppressive or vexatious.[91] Therefore, finding that the conduct of the claimant could be considered to be unconscionable, the Court held that it would exercise its jurisdiction and grant the injunction.

In addition to the decision reached by Burnton LJ in *Harms Offshore*, the comments made by him are of prominence in the area of maritime cross-border insolvency. Burnton LJ was aware of the conflicts between admiralty and insolvency proceedings and the issue regarding the secured status of admiralty claimants.[92] He emphasised that:

> The question is not where a dispute as to liability or damages should be determined, but whether the [a]ppellants should be able to continue their proceedings before the District Court so as to secure the benefit of their attachments, and thus promote themselves from unsecured to secured creditors.[93]

Although Burnton LJ did not discuss this issue in depth, it illustrated the court's awareness of the interaction between maritime and insolvency proceedings.

[85] *Harms Offshore Aht 'Taurus' GmbH & Co Kg & Another v Bloom & Others* [2009] EWCA Civ 632, [4].
[86] ibid [7]–[8].
[87] ibid [9].
[88] ibid [15].
[89] ibid [17]–[24].
[90] ibid [25].
[91] ibid [27]–[31].
[92] ibid.
[93] ibid [22].

ii. *The Bank of Tokyo-Mitsubishi UFJ Ltd v The M/V Sanko Mineral and Glencore Ltd*

In *The M/V Sanko Mineral*, Sanko Steamship Co Ltd (Sanko), one of the oldest shipping companies in Japan, entered into a reorganisation proceeding under the Japanese Corporate Reorganisation Act. Its Japanese insolvency proceeding was subsequently recognised by the High Court (Companies Court, Chancery Division) as a foreign main proceeding under the CBIR 2006.[94] Pursuant to the reorganisation plan that was approved by the Japanese bankruptcy court, a ship mortgagee of the debtor was authorised to sell a vessel belonging to Sanko on which it held a mortgage and the proceeds of the judicial sale of the vessel would be paid in satisfaction of finalised secured reorganisation claims.[95] Accordingly, the vessel was arrested and subsequently sold by an Admiralty Marshal with the proceeds of the judicial sale being paid into Admiralty Court; the ship mortgagee was thereafter satisfied from the proceeds of the judicial sale. Being aware of the notice of sale, the claimant issued an application to the Companies Court for permission to commence an in rem action against the vessel in order to join the distribution process in the Admiralty Court and requested the issue of a caution against the release of the proceeds of sale. The claimant argued that it had either a maritime lien claim under US law or a statutory right of action in rem claim under Japanese law, which should take priority over the ship mortgage; therefore it wished to ensure that the subject matter of its asserted secured claim could be preserved.[96] The trustee of Sanko then applied in Admiralty Court for an order to strike out the caution of the claimant and for the residual proceeds that remained in the Court to be paid out to the trustee.[97] The trustee argued that the claimant did not bring any claim against the vessel until the judicial sale of the vessel had finished and therefore the claimant was no longer able to enforce its in rem action against the vessel.[98]

The Court ordered the trustee to preserve the residual proceeds in a separate account for the purpose of the claimant's claim that was pending in the Japanese reorganisation proceeding, even if the claimant did not issue a writ in rem before the foreign insolvency proceeding had been recognised in the UK. The Court explained that it had been well established that, 'when a vessel is sold by the Admiralty Court rights in rem are transferred to the proceeds of sale', and thus the claimant's in rem action could be enforced against the proceeds of the judicial sale within the time provided by the court's order on the sale of the vessel.[99] The judicial sale was permitted by the foreign representative and the Japanese administration

[94] *The Bank of Tokyo-Mitsubishi UFJ Ltd v The M/V Sanko Mineral and Glencore* Ltd [2014] EWHC 3927 (Admlty) [5].
[95] ibid [11]–[13].
[96] ibid [16]–[18].
[97] ibid [15]–[16].
[98] ibid [20].
[99] ibid [41].

proceeding was recognised by the English court; therefore the claimant's statutory right of action in rem could not be lost simply because the writ in rem was issued after the judicial sale of the vessel.[100] The Court thereafter ordered the trustee to preserve the residual proceeds and hold them to the order of the Japanese bankruptcy court.[101]

As can be seen in *The M/V Sanko Mineral*, upon the Japanese reorganisation proceeding being recognised as a foreign main proceeding by the High Court (Chancery Division) under the CBIR 2006, the Court granted a wide stay order to suspend any enforcement action against the insolvent debtor, including enforcement actions that would be taken by secured creditors, except with the consent of the foreign representative or the permission of the Court.[102] The Court did not automatically carve secured creditors out of the automatic stay order that was granted under Article 20 of the Model Law, which is consistent with the CBIR 2006 and the Insolvency Act 1986.[103] Since the Japanese reorganisation proceeding resembled a UK administration proceeding, the scope and the effect of the automatic stay order should be the same as the stay provisions that are applicable to an administration proceeding as it would arise in the UK.[104] Nevertheless, the ship mortgagee obtained the consent of the debtor's trustee and was therefore allowed to enforce their mortgage against the relevant vessel.

However, the decision in *The M/V Sanko* was, in effect, providing an exemption for the claimant to proceed with its enforcement action against the proceeds of the judicial sale of the vessel (if the judicial sale is permitted by the trustee or by law),[105] even if it did not issue a writ in rem before the recognition of a foreign insolvency proceeding. Under the logic of *The M/V Sanko*, it seems that after the satisfaction of the ship mortgage, the residue of the proceeds will not be automatically included in the assets pool of the insolvent debtor and be repaid to the administrator for the purposes of administration or distribution in the bankruptcy proceeding; and that the remaining maritime creditors can bring their in rem claims against the sale proceeds.[106] From this it would seem that the outcome of *The M/V Sanko* is inconsistent with the automatic stay order that was granted by the Companies Court under Article 20 of the Model Law. The trustee of the Sanko only released the ship mortgagee from the stay order and authorised it to enforce its security outside the reorganisation proceeding by judicial sale. The consequences of *The M/V Sanko*, in fact, provided cash security to the claimant for its claim in Japan and allowed the claimant that had an in rem claim, but did

[100] ibid [42].
[101] ibid [49].
[102] ibid [5].
[103] ibid [5].
[104] CBIR 2006, Sch 1, Art 20(2); Insolvency Act 1986, Sch B1, para 43.
[105] Under Insolvency Act 1986, s 183(1) and (3)(a), a claimant can apply for leave to join the admiralty proceeding for the purpose of distribution of the proceeds of judicial sale if its execution is completed before the commencement of insolvency proceeding.
[106] D Osborne et al, *The Law of Ship* Mortgage, 2nd edn (Routledge, 2016) 442.

not issue the writ in rem before the recognition of the insolvency proceeding, to realise its claim outside the reorganisation proceeding. Therefore, in my view, the residue of the proceeds of judicial sale of the vessel should be reverted back to the assets pool of the debtor for the purpose of administration or distribution among all creditors, rather than be reserved for the remaining creditors to enforce their in rem claims against the proceeds.

iii. Ronelp Marine Ltd & Others v STX Offshore & Shipbuilding Co Ltd & Another

In *Ronelp Marine*, the debtor was a Korean shipbuilding company that commenced a rehabilitation proceeding in the bankruptcy court of Korea. The High Court subsequently recognised the Korean rehabilitation proceeding as a foreign main proceeding under the CBIR 2006.[107] The Court found that the Korean rehabilitation proceeding was in the nature of a UK administration proceeding, rather than a winding-up proceeding. It therefore granted a wide automatic stay order to the same extent as the stay order under paragraph 43 of Schedule B1 to the Insolvency Act 1986, and suspended all actions against the debtor unless the consent of the administrator or the permission of the Court was obtained.[108] Accordingly, the claimant asked the Court to allow it to proceed with its contractual dispute with the debtor on the ground that the dispute had been commenced in the Commercial Court before the commencement of rehabilitation.[109]

The Court put the burden of proof on the affected creditor who applied for permission to continue the existing proceeding in order to persuade the Court to grant such relief. In addition, the Court listed three tiers of questions that needed to be proved before the stay could be lifted.[110] First, the affected creditor must identify the nature of the interest that it wished to promote by obtaining such relief.[111] Second, the affected creditor must address the question of whether the achievement of the purpose of the insolvency proceeding would be likely to be impeded if such relief were granted.[112] Third, the courts would balance the interests of the affected creditor and other creditors in order to ensure fairness.[113] The relevant factors that would be taken into account included: the complexity of the claim; the advanced stage of the proceeding before the local court; and the likelihood that the claim would be adjudicated and quantified more speedily in a local court compared to a foreign main proceeding etc.[114]

[107] *Ronelp Marine Ltd & Others v STX Offshore & Shipbuilding Co Ltd & Another* [2016] EWHC 2228 (Ch), [13].
[108] ibid [16].
[109] ibid [14], [16].
[110] ibid [29].
[111] ibid.
[112] ibid.
[113] ibid.
[114] ibid [33], [39], [41].

The Court found that the claim upon which the claimant applied to proceed was an unsecured contract claim for the payment of damage; it is well established and was reaffirmed in *Ronelp Marine* that courts would only grant relief to such a claim in an 'exceptional' case.[115] Nevertheless, the Court granted the relief on the ground that the continuation of the proceeding would not interfere with the Korean rehabilitation proceedings and that, in the balance of interests, it would not unduly advance the interests of the claimant over the interests of other creditors of the debtor.[116] The Court explained that the mere purpose of continuing the proceeding was to obtain an adjudication of the claim, with a view to presenting the outcome to the Korean court.[117] In addition, the claimant had accepted that the judgment that it may obtain from the Commercial Court would not be enforced against the debtor nor would it alter the priority within the Korean insolvency proceeding.[118] Thus, the claimant would continue to have an unsecured claim but it would be one verified and quantified by the Commercial Court; it would then be up to the Korean court to adopt or reject the claim.[119] Accordingly, the Court granted permission to the claimant for it to continue its claim in the Commercial Court.

Therefore, in *Ronelp Marine*, notwithstanding that the Korean rehabilitation proceeding had been recognised as a foreign main proceeding, the Court allowed an unsecured creditor to proceed with its claim to be resolved outside the insolvency proceeding by virtue of being granted leave of the court. The Court emphasised the strong imperative to have all the claims dealt with in a single insolvency proceeding and that a claimant, especially an unsecured creditor, 'must demonstrate a circumstance or combination of circumstances of sufficient weight' to overcome such an imperative.[120] Therefore, in order to grant the relief, the Court carefully examined the issue with regard to whether lifting the stay would impede the achievement of the insolvency proceeding and unduly disadvantage other creditors.[121] In *Ronelp Marine*, Norris J attributed significant weight to the fact that the claimant had a pre-existing proceeding and that a lifting of the stay would actually assist the Korean rehabilitation proceeding rather than impede it.[122] Nevertheless, the claimant in *Ronelp Marine* only applied to proceed with its pre-existing legal proceeding in the Commercial Court in order for it to be verified and quantified, rather than proceeding with an enforcement action against

[115] ibid [31].
[116] ibid [46].
[117] ibid [27].
[118] ibid.
[119] ibid.
[120] ibid [31].
[121] ibid [42], [44], [45].
[122] ibid [42]–[46].

the assets of the debtor. In my view, it would appear that courts would be reluctant to lift a stay order with regard to a claimant with a maritime lien or a statutory right of action in rem in order to enforce its claim against the assets of the debtor, especially when other creditors would be disadvantaged by its enforcement action.

iv. In the Matter of Hanjin Shipping Co Ltd

Finally, in the UK, Hanjin's rehabilitation proceeding was recognised as a foreign main proceeding by an order made by Nugee J in accordance with Article 17 of Schedule 1 to the CBIR 2006 in the High Court (Chancery Division).[123] Finding that Hanjin's proceeding more closely resembled administration proceedings, Nugee J granted a wide automatic stay to suspend all creditors from enforcing any mortgage, lien or other security rights against Hanjin as if it had been entered into administration in England:

> Save for the proceedings identified in the Schedule to this Order, which are permitted to continue to the content identified in the Schedule, no legal process may be instituted or continued against the Company or its property except with the consent of the Administrator or the permission of the Court.[124]

In other words, the stay order issued by the High Court was a wide automatic stay to prevent all parties from enforcing any mortgage, lien or other security over Hanjin's assets except with the consent of the administrator or the permission of the Court.[125] However, in the Schedule to the order, the Court did allow several arbitrations against Hanjin that had already been initiated before the commencement of Hanjin's Korean rehabilitation proceeding or had been given consent by Hanjin's administrator to continue, up to the extent of the specific purposes identified in the Schedule to the order.[126] Nevertheless, the Court emphasised that the claimants were not allowed to take any further steps in those arbitrations or to seek to enforce any award against Hanjin, which the claimants may obtain from those arbitrations.[127]

Thus, similar to Australia, maritime creditors were prevented from arresting Hanjin's vessels in rem to enforce their maritime claims in the UK. Since Hanjin's proceeding was similar to UK administration proceedings, this wide stay order granted by Nugee J was in compliance with the CBIR 2006 and the Insolvency Act 1986.

[123] *In the Matter of Hanjin Shipping Co Ltd* No CR-2016-005448 (High Court of Justice, Chancery Division, Companies Court (6 September 2016)).
[124] ibid para 2(3).
[125] *Hanjin Shipping* (n 123); Insolvency Act 1986, Sch B1, para 43.
[126] *Hanjin Shipping* (n 123), Sch, paras 1–3.
[127] ibid.

IV. Courts' Attitudes Toward in Rem Actions and the Personification Doctrine in the UK

At the outset, it is important to distinguish the two categories of in rem actions – true in rem actions and statutory rights of action in rem. Although they are in the one form of action, namely, in rem, they are in substance two types of in rem actions.[128] To be specific, true in rem claims comprise claims to enforce maritime liens and mortgages, in the sense that they are brought against a ship 'irrespective of her present ownership and irrespective of any link with liability in personam on the part of the owner of the ship at the time the claim is brought'.[129] Conversely, statutory rights of action in rem claims comprise other maritime claims that can be brought by the issue of a writ in rem, but 'which in fact depend upon establishing a link with liability in personam'.[130]

As mentioned above, courts in the UK abandoned the true personification doctrine in the late nineteenth century and thereafter embraced the procedural theory.[131] Nevertheless, in the classic version of procedural theory, a judgment is entered against the vessel itself as the in rem defendant in the absence of the appearance of the shipowner.[132] Only when the shipowner enters an appearance in the court is it considered to 'have submitted to the jurisdiction of the court, and the proceedings continue as an action in personam as well as an action in rem'.[133]

Although in a radical version of the procedural theory in *The Indian Grace (No 2)* the House of Lords characterised an in rem action as a merely procedural device for forcing the appearance of the shipowner in personam (which means that an in rem action is in substance an action against the shipowner), it is worth noting that the decision in *The Indian Grace (No 2)* was not concerned with true in rem claims, but rather statutory rights of action in rem claims.[134]

Thus, in my view, the analysis that was provided by the House of Lords in *The Indian Grace (No 2)* only applies to statutory rights of action in rem claims, and is not applicable to true in rem claims.[135] Therefore, in rem claims to enforce maritime liens and mortgages are indeed against the vessels themselves, which

[128] Meeson and Kimbell (n 54) 88.

[129] ibid.

[130] ibid.

[131] M Davies, 'In Defense of Popular Virtues: Personification and Ratification' (2000) 75 *Tulane Law Review* 337, 341; P Myburgh, 'Arresting the Right Ship: Procedural Theory, the in Personam Link and Conflict of Laws' in M Davies (ed), *Jurisdiction and Forum Selection in International Maritime Law Essay in Honor of Robert Force* (Kluwer Law International, 2005) 286; see also *The Tervaete* [1922] P 259, 270.

[132] *The Dictator* [1892] P 304.

[133] Myburgh (n 131) 283–84; *The Dictator* (n 132); *The August 8* [1983] 2 AC 450 (PC); *The Beldis* [1936] P 51, 75–76; *The Banco* [1971] P 137, 151.

[134] Davies, 'In Defense of Unpopular Virtues' (n 131) 341–42; Myburgh (n 131) 286; *The Indian Grace (No 2)* (n 43).

[135] Meeson and Kimbell (n 54) 89–90; *The Indian Grace (No 2)* (n 43).

are regarded as distinct legal entities, as opposed to the shipowner.[136] However, according to *The Indian Grace (No 2)*, in rem claims in respect of statutory rights of action in rem may actually be regarded as in personam actions against the shipowner. Accordingly, it seems that the personification argument that was mentioned in Chapter 6 may be available for a maritime lien claim to be exempted from an automatic stay of the Model Law, but may be unlikely to be supported by the courts in the UK with regard to a statutory right of action in rem claim.

In the realm of maritime cross-border insolvency, the decision of the High Court in *Stena Bulk AB v Copley* is relevant. In *Stena Bulk AB v Copley*, the shipowner was faced with potentially competing claims from both marine fuel traders, who had an in personam claim according to the fuel supply contract, and physical suppliers who had a statutory right of action in rem claim against the vessels in rem.[137] The High Court was asked to examine the question with regard to whether a statutory right of action in rem claim and an in personam claim were adverse claims arising out of a single obligation, as required by an interpleader proceeding.[138] The High Court held that it had jurisdiction over the interpleader action on the ground that a statutory right of action in rem against the vessels was merely an alternative procedural device to obtaining the same relief with an in rem personam action against the shipowner.[139] In other words, both the in rem action and the in personam action were against the same defendant, namely the shipowner, for the purpose of pursuing the money that was owed for the delivery of the fuel to the vessels of the shipowner. Therefore, in *Stena Bulk AB v Copley*, the Court reaffirmed that the nature of a statutory right of action in rem was, in substance, equal to an in personam action.

V. Status of Chartered Vessels in Cross-Border Insolvency

In *Hanjin Shipping Co Ltd*, the Court granted a general stay order to stay all Hanjin's vessels regardless of whether they were chartered or owned by it.[140] Similar to the Federal Court of Australia in *Tai-Soo Suk v Hanjin Shipping Co Ltd*, the Court did not specify the reason for granting such a wide stay order by including the chartered vessels of Hanjin, which may not be considered to be the property of the debtor in some circumstances.[141]

[136] Meeson and Kimbell (n 54) 88–90.
[137] *Stena Bulk AB v Copley* [2015] 1 Lloyd's Rep 280.
[138] ibid [1]–[2].
[139] ibid [6].
[140] *Hanjin Shipping* (n 123).
[141] *Hanjin Shipping* (n 123); *Tai-Soo Suk v Hanjin Shipping Co Ltd* [2016] FCA 1404.

VI. Summary

The UK adopted a multi-layered system in order to resolve the problem of cross-border insolvency co-operation and assistance. Courts in the UK are always willing to co-operate with a foreign court in order to 'ensure that all the company's assets are distributed to its creditors under a single system of distribution'.[142]

As a leading shipping country, courts in the UK inevitably take the special nature of maritime claims into account. In the case of a winding-up proceeding, courts are willing to narrow down the scope of the automatic stay that is granted by the Model Law for secured admiralty claims to be exempted from the stay order. However, in an administration proceeding, courts are inclined to grant a wide stay order, through which any proceeding against the asset of the debtor will be suspended upon the recognition of a foreign insolvency proceeding. Secured creditors can only proceed with their enforcement actions if they have obtained the consent of the administrator or leave of the court, the latter of which is subject to the discretion of the court.[143]

In addition, since the House of Lords in *The Indian Grace (No 2)* adopted a radical version of the procedural theory, claimants with statutory rights of action in rem who apply to leave the insolvency proceeding, would not be able to argue that their in rem actions are against the vessel itself, which are separate from in personam actions against an insolvent debtor. However, it seems that maritime lien claims and ship mortgagees are not affected by *The Indian Grace (No 2)* and may still utilise this argument. Nevertheless, this argument has not yet been tested in the area of maritime cross-border insolvency in the UK courts.

[142] *In re HIH Insurance Ltd* (n 61) 862.
[143] See eg *Ronelp Marine* (n 107) [29]; *Hanjin Shipping* (n 123).

9

United States

I. Overview

With regard to domestic insolvency proceedings, the US Bankruptcy Code provides a wide and strong automatic stay order in order to stay all the actions against the debtor or the property of the estate once the bankruptcy proceeding has been commenced.[1] In the arena of cross-border insolvency, the US has taken a leading role in encouraging international co-operation, legal certainty, and uniformity.[2] By adding a new chapter, Chapter 15, to the Bankruptcy Code, the US substantially adopted the Model Law.[3] This represents an embrace of universalism by the US. Chapter 15 provides efficient and detailed procedures for dealing with cross-border insolvency issues. Once the foreign insolvency proceeding is recognised as a foreign main proceeding, a broad automatic stay will be issued to stay almost all actions against the debtor's assets, rights, obligations, and liabilities.[4]

From the maritime aspect, the US recognises a much broader scope of maritime liens, compared with other Commonwealth countries. The purpose of recognising a broader scope of maritime liens is to give more protection to creditors, such as cargo owners, bunker suppliers and other necessaries suppliers.[5] However, this purpose probably will be frustrated by the recognition of foreign insolvency proceedings under Chapter 15. The following sections illustrate the application of the Model Law regime to admiralty claimants in the US and discuss the existing conflicts in detail.

II. The Bankruptcy Code of the United States

A. Overview of the Bankruptcy Code

The Bankruptcy Code, deriving from Article I of the US Constitution, is the legal basis of the US bankruptcy law.[6] The Bankruptcy Code provides two major

[1] 11 USC § 362.
[2] 11 USC § 1501.
[3] See The United States House of Representatives, Report No 109-31, part 1.
[4] 11 USC § 1520.
[5] See R Force, *Admiralty and Maritime Law*, 2nd edn (Federal Judicial Center, 2013) 176.
[6] J Silkenat and C Schmerler, *The Law of International Insolvencies and Debt Restructurings* (Oceana, 2006) 409.

insolvency proceedings for business encountering financial difficulties, namely Chapter 7 liquidation and Chapter 11 reorganisation.[7]

In the US, federal courts have exclusive jurisdiction over all bankruptcy cases.[8] Bankruptcy judges are different from Article III judges. They are known as Article I judges, who lack the life tenure and the diminishable salaries enjoyed by Article III judges.[9] Nevertheless, the Amended Bankruptcy Code 1984 granted bankruptcy judges the power to adjudicate 15 types of 'core proceedings', and bankruptcy courts have 'exclusive jurisdiction of all the property wherever located, of the debtor'.[10] Thereby, bankruptcy judges have full authority to administer the debtor's maritime assets, mainly ships. Nowadays, it is well settled that bankruptcy courts have jurisdiction over the validity and priority of maritime liens arising from most maritime claims, such as ship mortgage, necessaries and freight.[11] Bankruptcy courts also have the power to sell a vessel free and clear of all liens.[12] However, this exclusive jurisdiction does not extend to maritime liens arising from seafarers' personal injury or wrongful death claims,[13] because these two claims are not regarded as 'core proceedings', which the Bankruptcy Code empowers bankruptcy judges to adjudicate.[14]

B. Automatic Stay of Proceedings

Section 362(a) of the Bankruptcy Code provides a statutory injunction against creditors' collection actions that rise automatically upon the filing of a bankruptcy petition.[15] The purpose of the automatic stay order is to preserve the status quo once the insolvency proceeding is commenced.[16] The automatic stay order is an essential tool to effectively realise and implement the fundamental goals of a

[7] ibid. See also 11 USC §§ 701–784, §§ 1101–1174.

[8] 28 USC § 1334.

[9] W Tetley, *Maritime Liens and Claims*, 2nd edn (Éditions Yvon Blais, 1998) 1140; *Northern Pipeline Construction Co v Marathon Pipe Line Co* 458 US 50 (1982).

[10] 28 USC § 157(b)(2); TJ Schoenbaum, *Admiralty and Maritime Law*, 6th edn (West Academic Publishing, 2019) 740.

[11] See Tetley, *Maritime Liens and Claims* (n 9) 1144; Schoenbaum (n 10) 740. Under the Amended Bankruptcy Code 1984, bankruptcy judges have jurisdiction over 15 types of 'core proceedings', including 'determinations of the validity, extent or priority of liens'. 28 USC § 157(b)(2)(K). See also *In re Louisiana Ship Management Inc* 761 F 2d 1025, 1985 AMC 2667 (5th Cir 1985); *In re Modern Boats Inc* 775 F 2d 619, 1987 AMC 509 (5th Cir 1985); *In re Topgallant Lines Inc* 208 BR 589, 1997 AMC 1491 (SD Georgia 1996).

[12] R Force et al, *Admiralty and Maritime Law* (Beard Books, 2006) 180; see also *Matter of Buchman* 600 F 2d 160, 165 (8th Cir 1979).

[13] See eg *In re Waterman Steamship Co* 63 BR 435, 436 (SD New York 1986); *In re Mclean Industries Inc* 76 BR 328, 332 (Bankr SD New York 1987).

[14] '"[C]ore proceedings" do not include the liquidation or estimation of contingent or unliquidated personal injury tort or wrongful death claims against the estate for purposes of distribution in a case under Title 11': Tetley, *Maritime Liens and Claims* (n 9) 1145. See also 28 USC § 157(b)(2)(B).

[15] 11 USC § 362(a); CJ Tabb, *Law of Bankruptcy*, 4th edn (West Academic Publishing, 2016) 235.

[16] Tabb (n 15) 236.

bankruptcy case, since the automatic stay ensures a financial fresh start for an honest debtor and an equitable distribution among creditors.[17] On the one hand, it is designed to give debtors a 'breathing spell' from their creditors. Especially in a reorganisation proceeding, the automatic stay enables debtors to develop an effective reorganisation plan and thereby have a better chance for successful reorganisations. On the other hand, the automatic stay protects creditors from one another by putting all creditors on a level playing field, avoiding the chaos of a 'race to the courthouse' and the loss of going-concern value.[18]

The automatic stay is extremely powerful and effective.[19] A US automatic stay order has been held applicable extraterritorially.[20] In addition, the scope of the automatic stay is very wide. Section 362(a)(5) provides that the automatic stay applies to 'any act to create, perfect, or enforce against the property of the debtor any lien to the extent that such lien secures a claim that arose before the commencement of the case'.[21] That is to say, creditors are generally stayed from obtaining possession or exercising control over property of the debtor; creating, perfecting or enforcing liens; or commencing or continuing proceedings to enforce the foreclosing of their mortgages and other liens.[22]

C. Relief from the Automatic Stay

However, upon application, secured creditors may obtain relief to lift the automatic stay if the two grounds for relief under section 362(d) are available. Section 362(d) provides that:

> … The court shall grant relief from the stay provided under subsection (a) of this section, such as by terminating, annulling, modifying, or conditioning such stay:
>
> (1) for cause, including the lack of adequate protection of an interest in property of such party in interest;
>
> (2) with respect to a stay of an act against property under subsection (a) of this section, if
>
> (A) the debtor does not have an equity in such property; and
>
> (B) such property is not necessary to an effective reorganization

These two grounds are separate from and independent of one another. Secured creditors can argue both of them. Since section 362(d)(1) is a more general ground compared to section 362(d)(2), it is usually used as the second shot or

[17] ibid.

[18] J Ayer et al, 'An Overview of the Automatic Stay' (2004) XXII *ABI Journal*, available at www.kirkland.com/siteFiles/kirkexp/publications/2430/Document1/Friedland%20-%20An%20Overview%20of%20the%20Automatic%20Stay.pdf accessed 5 June 2020.

[19] ibid.

[20] *In re Mclean Industries Inc* 74 BR 589 (Bankr SD New York 1987); *United States Lines Inc v GAC Marine Fuels Ltd* 68 BR 690, 694 (Bankr SD New York 1986).

[21] 11 USC § 362(a)(5).

[22] 11 USC § 362(a); Tetley, *Maritime Liens and Claims* (n 10) 1145.

fall-back position of secured creditors.[23] This part of the chapter will analyse first the specific ground under section 362(d)(2), and then the general ground under section 362(d)(1).

i. Lack of Equity in Property that is not Necessary for Reorganisation (section 362(d)(2))

The first ground for obtaining the relief from the stay is that the debtor does not have an equity in the secured property and such property is not necessary to an effective reorganisation.[24] For the purpose of section 362(d), equity – also known as equity cushion – is 'the value, above all secured claims against the property, that can be realised from the sale of the property for the benefit of the unsecured creditors'.[25] In other words, equity is the difference between property value and the total amount of the claims it secures.[26] Thus, in order to obtain the court relief on the basis of the first ground, the secured creditors need to prove that the value of the property is less than the amount of all debts secured by liens on such property.[27]

Then, the debtor or the trustee must show that an effective reorganisation may not occur without the particular piece of property at issue and the planned reorganisation is feasible.[28] In *In re Ritz-Carlton of DC Inc*, the US Bankruptcy Court for the Southern District of New York held that 'this requires is not merely showing that if there is conceivably to be an effective reorganization, this property will be needed for it; but that the property is essential for an effective reorganization that is *in prospect*'.[29] Therefore, the debtor or the trustee is not required to show that its reorganisation plan is confirmable, ie acceptable to its creditors, instead, '[i]t need only determine whether the components of the plan which are to be done after confirmation can be accomplished as a practical matter'.[30]

ii. Lack of Adequate Protection (section 362(d)(1))

The second ground for secured creditors to obtain the relief from the stay is that their interest lacks 'adequate protection' in the secured property.[31] If secured creditors show a risk to their interests that is not adequately protected, courts can grant the relief to lift the stay. The two common types of risks considered to constitute a lack of 'adequate protection' are the loss of the secured property and

[23] D Epstein et al, *Bankruptcy, Practitioner Treatise Series*, vol 1 (West Publishing, 1992) 267.

[24] 11 USC § 362(d).

[25] *In re Mellor* 734 F 2d 1396, 1400 (9th Cir 1984).

[26] *In re New Era Company* 125 BR 725, 728 (SD New York 1991).

[27] Ayer et al (n 18).

[28] Epstein et al (n 23) 275.

[29] *In re Ritz-Carlton of DC Inc* 98 BR 170, 172 (SD New York 1989) (citing *United Savings Association of Texas v Timbers of Inwood Forest Associates Ltd* 484 US 365, 375–76 (1988)).

[30] ibid.

[31] 11 USC § 362(d).

the depreciation of property value; for example, failure to maintain and preserve the secured property, waste or mismanagement and undue delay by the debtor in proposing a reorganisation plan, lack of property casualty insurance and etc.[32] Nevertheless, it should be noted that:

> Adequate protection is never needed or lacking absent a threat to the value of the encumbrance. It is not sufficient either that the debtor lacks an equity in the property or the creditor's claim is undersecured. Even a decline in the collateral's value is not always sufficient, in itself, to trigger adequate protection. The decline must threaten to reduce the value of the creditor's encumbrance.
>
> For this reason, an oversecured creditor is usually denied relief for lack of adequate protection so long as the equity cushion is reasonably thick. Also, a creditor in the opposite position, whose secured claim is zeroed out because of senior encumbrances, get no relief even if the collateral's value begins to fall sharply. The drop could not further reduce the value of her encumbrance.[33]

Therefore, secured creditors are not being harmed until their cushion threatens to disappear, not merely when the value of the property is declining. For an over-secured creditor whose debt is worth less than the value of secured property, it is usually adequately protected and precluded from obtaining relief from stay.[34] In *In re Orlando Coals Inc*, the US Bankruptcy Court for the Southern District of West Virginia refused to grant the relief from stay and found that the creditor was adequately protected because the debtor had a substantial amount of equity in the secured property.[35] Similarly, in *In re Westchase I Associates LP*, the US District Court for the Western District of North Carolina held that the interest of the over-secured creditor was adequately protected because the value of the secured property was stable and, therefore, denied the relief from stay.[36]

For an under-secured creditor whose debt exceeds the property value, in order to constitute a 'lack of adequate protection' and obtain the relief from the stay order, the creditor needs to show that the property is depreciating or has a risk of loss.[37] For example, in *In re Wasserman*, the under-secured creditor was nevertheless not entitled to the relief on the ground that the value of the secured property was not depreciating.[38] However, in *In Re Pittman*, the US Bankruptcy Court for the Southern District of New York noted that, in addition to the fact that the debtor had no equity in the mortgaged property, it was unable to make periodic payments and obtain the fire insurance. The Court, therefore, held that the interest

[32] E Warren et al, *The Law of Debtors and Creditors: Text, Cases, and Problems*, 7th edn (Wolters Kluwer, 2014) 208; Ayer et al (n 18).

[33] Epstein et al (n 23) 275.

[34] R Broude, *Reorganizations Under Chapter 11 of the Bankruptcy Code* (Law Journal Press, 2005) § 4.06 [2]. See also *In re Adams* 27 BR 582, 585 (District Delaware 1983); *In re Rogers Development Corp* 2 BR 679 (Bankr ED Virginia 1980).

[35] *In re Orlando Coals Inc* 6 BR 721 (Bankr SD West Virginia 1980).

[36] *In re Westchase I Associates LP* 126 BR 692 (WD North Carolina 1991).

[37] See eg *In re Cambridge Properties Inc* 82 BR 35 (ED Louisiana 1988).

[38] *In re Wasserman* 122 BR 839, 842–43 (Bankr District Massachusetts 1991).

of the under-secured mortgagee in the property was not adequately protected and granted the relief.[39]

Nevertheless, the scope of the US stay order is very wide and can only be lifted in a few extraordinary cases.[40] In other words, generally, once a bankruptcy proceeding is commenced, a stay order that is issued by a US bankruptcy court would suspend or terminate the enforcement of most maritime creditors against the assets of the debtor.[41] Again, the stay does not apply to seafarer wages claims or pre-petition maintenance and cure claims, as these claims are not considered as 'core proceedings' as discussed above.[42]

III. Cross-Border Insolvency in the United States

A. Chapter 15 Overview and Article 20

The US was active in the development of the Model Law and enacted the Model Law in 2005 as Chapter 15 of the Bankruptcy Code.[43] Chapter 15 adopted the Model Law in text and spirit, but a few alternations were made in order to fit within the existing structure of the Bankruptcy Code.[44] Chapter 15 is primarily procedural in nature.[45] It provides a vehicle for a foreign representative in a foreign insolvency proceeding to obtain the recognition and assistance of the US bankruptcy courts for the purpose of protection or administration the assets of the debtor that are located within the territory of the US.[46] According to section 1515 of Chapter 15, the foreign representative will file a petition in order to commence a proceeding for recognition of the foreign insolvency proceeding by the US bankruptcy court.[47] Moreover, Chapter 15 applies no matter whether a US domestic insolvency proceeding, such as a Chapter 7 proceeding or a Chapter 11 proceeding, is pending concurrently.[48]

Section 1520(a)(1) provides that '[u]pon recognition of a foreign proceeding that is a foreign main proceeding, sections 361 and 362 apply with respect to the debtor and the property of the debtor that is within the territorial jurisdiction of

[39] *In Re Pittman* 7 BR 760 (Bankr SD New York 1980).
[40] Epstein et al (n 23) 93.
[41] See nn 15–22 above and accompanying text.
[42] See nn 13–14 above and accompanying text.
[43] GF Seitz, 'Interaction between Admiralty and Bankruptcy Law: Effects of Globalization and Recurrent Tensions' (2009) 83 *Tulane Law Review* 1339, 1343–44; see also 11 USC § 1506.
[44] LM Clark, *Ancillary and other Cross-Border Insolvency Cases under Chapter 15 of the Bankruptcy Code* (LexisNexis Matthew Bender, 2008) 16; B Wessels et al, *International Co-operation in Bankruptcy and Insolvency Matters* (Oxford University Press, 2009) 245.
[45] Seitz (n 43) 1343–44; see also 11 USC § 1506.
[46] Seitz (n 43) 1344.
[47] See 11 USC § 1515(a).
[48] Silkenat and Schmerler (n 6) 524.

the United States'.[49] Unlike other countries that are discussed in previous chapters, Article 20 of the US enactment of the Model Law does not follow the form suggested by the Model Law. Section 1520(a)(1) of the US Bankruptcy Code combined subsections 1(a) and 1(b) of Article 20 of the Model Law. By reference to the domestic insolvency stay provision, section 1520 imports the protection and limitations for creditors that are set out in section 362 upon the recognition of a foreign main proceeding.[50] The reason for combining the two subsections of the Model Law into section 1520(a)(1) is that section 362 of the US Bankruptcy Code has already imposed the restrictions that are required by those two subsections as well as additional restrictions.[51]

Under section 362(a), the stay is automatic and the scope is very broad. It applies to all the creditors, either secured or unsecured, and either in liquidation or reorganisation proceedings. 'Any act to create, perfect, or enforce against the property of the debtor any lien to the extent that such lien secures a claim that arose before the commencement of the case' will be stayed by the order at the first instance.[52] Although a court may, upon application, grant a creditor relief from the stay if the two grounds under section 362(d) are available, the relief to lift the automatic stay is always hard to obtain.[53] Thus, rather than modifying the automatic stay effect, the Chapter 15 provision actually mandates a stay upon the recognition of a foreign insolvency proceeding.[54]

B. Application of Chapter 15 in the Maritime Context

When adopting the Model Law, the US Congress was not aware of the unique characteristic of maritime claims and, therefore, did not reserve any provision for in rem actions.[55] In the maritime context, upon the recognition of a foreign insolvency proceeding, Chapter 15 provides foreign shipping debtors with sufficient protection through automatic stay orders, which would stay any arrest or attachment proceedings against debtors' assets, obligations and liabilities.[56] Although maritime lien holders are regarded as secured creditors in the US, an automatic stay will be ordered simultaneously notwithstanding the in rem actions. The US courts tend to issue a wide automatic stay order in order to stay all claims against the foreign debtor once courts recognise the foreign insolvency proceeding as a foreign main proceeding, without granting any exception for maritime lien claims.

[49] 11 USC § 1520.
[50] 11 USC §§ 362, 1520.
[51] The United States House of Representatives (n 3) 114–15.
[52] 11 USC § 362(a)(5).
[53] 11 USC § 362(d).
[54] M Davies, 'Cross-Border Insolvency and Admiralty: A Middle Path of Reciprocal Comity' (2018) 66 *American Journal of Comparative Law L* 101, 109; 11 USC §§ 362(a)(5), 1520(a)(1).
[55] See The United States House of Representatives (n 3).
[56] 11 USC § 1520.

However, this approach may raise a concern that if a Chapter 15 petition can exclude a vessel arrest or attachment action so easily, then the arrest or attachment appears to be no longer an effective tool for the enforcement of maritime liens, which is a vital source of rights in admiralty.[57] The following cases illustrate the US application of Chapter 15 in the maritime context.

i. *Evridiki Navigation Inc v Sanko SS Co*

In *Evridiki Navigation Inc v Sanko SS Co*, the US District Court for the District of Maryland vacated a Rule B attachment of vessel after a Japanese insolvency proceeding was recognised by a US bankruptcy court in a Chapter 15 petition.[58] The Court explained that once the Japanese insolvency proceeding was recognised as a foreign main proceeding, control would be transferred to the Japanese court shortly thereafter.[59] Thus, the Court held that it would not exercise jurisdiction over the vessel, even though the vessel was attached and arrested in the US prior to the filing of the Chapter 15 petition.[60]

The Sanko Steamship Co (Sanko) is one of the Japanese oldest and largest steamship companies and its business had been severely affected by the 2008 global financial crisis. After an unsuccessful private alternative dispute resolution (ADR) process with its primary creditors in Japan, Sanko filed for a reorganisation proceeding under the Japanese Corporate Reorganisation Act.[61] Subsequently, Sanko filed a Chapter 15 petition in the US Bankruptcy Court for the Southern District of New York, seeking recognition of the Japanese reorganisation proceeding as a foreign main proceeding. Subsequent to the initiation of the ADR proceeding but prior to the filing of the Japanese reorganisation proceeding and the Chapter 15 petition, the *M/V Sanko Mineral* was arrested and attached by several creditors in Baltimore. Thereafter, the voyage charterer filed an urgent motion asking the District Court of Maryland to vacate the attachment and arrest against the vessel.

The Court explained that, when the arrest and attachment were initially made, Sanko was attempting to rehabilitate itself through a private turnaround ADR process.[62] The ADR process was entirely voluntary and imposed no obstacle to claims of non-participant creditors against the debtor in courts anywhere in the world.[63] Accordingly, at that stage, there was nothing to prevent the Court from exercising jurisdiction over the assets of Sanko and, if necessary, liquidating those

[57] See AJ Falzone III, 'Two Households, Both Alike in Dignity: The International Feud between Admiralty and Bankruptcy' (2014) 39 *Brooklyn Journal of International Law* 1175, 1176.

[58] *Evridiki Navigation Inc v Sanko SS Co* 880 F Supp 2d 666 (D Maryland 2012).

[59] ibid 675.

[60] ibid 674–75.

[61] ibid 668.

[62] ibid 672.

[63] ibid 672.

assets through a judicial sale of the vessel.[64] Nevertheless, the Court acknowledged that Sanko had now filed a formal insolvency proceeding in Japan and the Japanese court had issued a preliminary injunction order to stay all proceedings against Sanko and its assets. In addition, there was a 'substantial likelihood of success' of Sanko's Chapter 15 petition that the Japanese reorganisation proceeding would be recognised as a foreign main proceeding. The District Court of Maryland found that it appeared inevitable that those maritime claims would never be adjudicated in the US, and thereby vacate the arrest and attachment.[65] Notwithstanding the argument of the plaintiffs that they were secured creditors and should therefore be exempted from the stay order, the Court refused this argument by stating that 'attaching parties "may be denied an advantage over the debtor's other previously unsecured creditors is not a valid reason to deny relief to the foreign representative"'.[66]

Sanko is a typical example that illustrates the application of a US Chapter 15 petition in the maritime context. The US has always played an active role in facilitating the uniformity of cross-border insolvency in the sense that US courts would take all efforts necessary to promote a single insolvency proceeding in order to address all assets and liabilities of the debtor in that single proceeding. Thus, it is unsurprising that US courts would preclude vessel arrests or attachments against the insolvent debtor regardless of the secured status of maritime lien claims and transfer the authority over the arrested vessels back to their home jurisdiction to satisfy the outstanding claims.[67] In *Sanko*, the Court even took a step further, where the Court vacated the attachments pre-emptively before the Chapter 15 recognition order had actually been made on the ground of judicial economy.[68] However, the US court in *In re Hanjin Shipping Co* allowed a pre-arrested vessel to proceed on the ground that the claims against the vessel had already been enforceable.[69] The following section discusses *Hanjin Shipping* in detail.

ii. In re Hanjin Shipping Co

After Hanjin Shipping Co filed a rehabilitation proceeding in the Korean Bankruptcy Court due to the financial collapse, the US Bankruptcy Court for the District of New Jersey recognised Hanjin's Korean rehabilitation proceeding as a foreign main proceeding and issued an automatic stay order to stay any pending

[64] ibid 672–73.

[65] ibid 672–73.

[66] ibid 674 (citing *In re Atlas Shipping A/S* 404 BR 726, 742 (Bankr SD New York 2009)).

[67] P Hathorn, 'Cross-Border Insolvency in the Maritime Context: The United States' Universalism vs Singapore's Territorialism' (2013) 38 *Tulane Maritime Law Journal* 239, 262.

[68] *Sanko* (n 58) 674; Davies, 'Cross-Border Insolvency and Admiralty: A Middle Path of Reciprocal Comity' (n 54) 119.

[69] *In re Hanjin Shipping Co Ltd* 2016 WL 6679487, 2016 AMC 2126 (Bankr New Jersey 20 September 2016).

or future actions against Hanjin without preserving a general exemption for maritime actions.[70] In other words, the only recourse for maritime lien holders would be to file a claim in the Korean rehabilitation proceeding.[71] Nevertheless, the Court 'carved out' the arrest of the *M/V Hanjin Montevideo* from the automatic stay on the ground that it was arrested before Hanjin's Chapter 15 petition had been filed.[72]

Unsurprisingly, in *Hanjin Shipping*, the US maritime lien holders opposed the relief and argued that their rights of maritime liens under US law were far superior to those rights recognised in Korea. If the claims of the maritime lien holders were going to be subjected to the Chapter 15 stay order, they had to file their claims under Hanjin's Korean rehabilitation proceeding, and thus, their rights under US law would be severely prejudiced.[73]

The Court did accept the notion that maritime lien claimants, especially necessaries suppliers, were in a better position in the US than they were in Korea,[74] because the Federal Maritime Lien Act created maritime liens for necessaries ordered by authorised vessel agents, while no such liens exist in Korea.[75] However, the Court explained that the goal of universalism is to direct creditors and assets to the foreign main proceeding for the orderly and fair distribution of assets, avoiding the piecemeal seizure of assets by creditors operating outside the jurisdiction of the foreign main proceeding.[76] Therefore, any enforcement of maritime lien claims against vessels would violate Chapter 15's 'clear directive' and would signal an embrace of territorialism.[77] Thus, the Court adhered to the universalist approach under Chapter 15 and refused to grant relief exceptions for maritime lien claimants.[78]

The Court further noted that nothing in the plain language of Chapter 15 or in US public policy would justify allowing the claimants to arrest Hanjin's vessels.[79] In reaching this conclusion, the Court weighed the interest of all parties involved and the practicalities, and was eventually in favour of granting a general stay order without carving out maritime claimants. The Court reasoned that

> if the debtor's vessels were not allowed to dock, unload their cargo, and depart under the protection of a stay, they would potentially avoid ports in the United States, leaving

[70] *Hanjin Shipping* (n 69) 2.

[71] ibid 2.

[72] See *World Fuel Services Inc v M/V Hanjin Montevideo* No 2-16-cv-06584 (CD California 2016).

[73] *In re Hanjin Shipping Co Ltd* No 16-27041 (JKS) 2016 WL 6681169, 2016 AMC 2113 (Bankr New Jersey 16 September 2016).

[74] *Hanjin Shipping* (n 69) 3.

[75] ibid. See also 46 USC § 31342. Korean law only provides claimants with maritime liens when the claims are against the registered owner of the ship. As discussed below in Section V of this chapter, most operating vessels of Hanjin were not owned by Hanjin, but were chartered from third parties, and therefore the claimants would not have maritime liens in Korea: *Hanjin Shipping* (n 69) EFC No 85. See also IH Kim, 'An Overview of Korean Maritime Law' (2012) 10 *Asian Business Law* 35, 58.

[76] *Hanjin Shipping* (n 69) 4 (citing *In re ABC Learning Centres Ltd* 728 F 3d 301, 306–307 (3d Cir 2013)).

[77] *Hanjin Shipping* (n 63) 3.

[78] ibid.

[79] *Hanjin Shipping* (n 69) 6.

delivery of their cargo in limbo and causing BCOs [(The beneficial cargo owners)], port operators and others harm.[80]

Thus, with the interests of Hanjin and all global creditors in mind, the Court held that the automatic stay must forbid admiralty arrests so as to allow Hanjin's vessels to enter the US ports.[81]

Nevertheless, unlike *Sanko*,[82] the Court in *Hanjin Shipping* 'carved out' the arrest of the *M/V Hanjin Montevideo* from the automatic stay.[83] The Court reasoned that the purpose of an automatic stay is to preserve the status quo at the time of the stay and to provide debtors with a 'breathing spell'.[84] The time point of the status quo in *Hanjin Shipping* was the time when the automatic stay was granted. Thus, the lien claims against the *M/V Hanjin Montevideo* were mature and enforceable when the issue was before the Court; this was because the *M/V Hanjin Montevideo* was arrested before Hanjin's Chapter 15 petition had been filed.[85] However, in *Sanko*, the Court vacated the pre-existing vessel arrest on the grounds of judicial economy.[86]

Therefore, *Hanjin Shipping* at least indicates some leeway that the US courts may grant relief for pre-existing vessel arrests by recognising the claims as secured claims. However, in my view, the time at which the vessel was arrested should not affect the treatment of maritime claims in the US courts as a matter of law. In the US, almost all maritime claims are granted maritime liens status. It is a substantive property right inchoate in the vessel given to a creditor as security by the operation of law.[87] It is secured from the moment the maritime lien attached to the vessel, that is, when certain services are rendered to the ship or certain damages are done by the ship.[88] Therefore, maritime claims are secured as long as maritime liens arise before the recognition of a foreign main proceeding, whether the vessel was arrested before or after the recognition. The time at which the vessel has been arrested does not affected the secured status of maritime liens, and therefore all maritime claims against the vessel should receive the same treatment in granting the automatic stay order. Otherwise, it may lead the insolvency proceeding into

[80] *Hanjin Shipping* (n 69) 7. The beneficial cargo owners refer to those cargo owners whose products were stranded in cargo containers at sea, in warehouses and at port facilities because of Hanjin's bankruptcy. The BCOs expressed concern about negative financial impact on their businesses due to the non-delivery or delayed delivery of their goods.

[81] ibid.

[82] *Sanko* (n 58).

[83] *Hanjin Shipping* (n 69) 6; see also *World Fuel Services* (n 72).

[84] *Hanjin Shipping* (n 69) 6.

[85] ibid.

[86] *Sanko* (n 58).

[87] Force (n 5) 173. Unlike the UK and other Commonwealth countries, maritime claims may give rise to statutory rights of action in rem. The treatment of statutory rights of action in rem may be different depending on whether the vessel is arrested before or after the recognition of a foreign main proceeding. Chapters 7, 8 and 10 provide detailed discussions.

[88] Force (n 5) 173.

chaos, with all creditors involved in a 'race to the courthouse' in order to loot the debtor's assets, and the purpose of a single and orderly insolvency proceeding would be undermined. Nevertheless, as further discussed in Chapter 11 below, in my view, maritime liens should be allowed to proceed regardless of the automatic stay order.

IV. US Attitude Towards in Rem Actions and the Personification Doctrine

As mentioned in previous chapters, admiralty creditors may argue that the in rem action is against the vessel itself rather than against the debtor. Whether this argument will succeed depends on the court's attitude towards the personification doctrine.

In the US, courts have traditionally adopted a true personification doctrine and generally deem in personam and in rem actions to constitute two distinct proceedings.[89] For example, in *The China*, one of the leading cases on personification doctrine, the US Supreme Court held that the vessel was liable independently for its acts even though its owner, who had chartered the vessel to another party, could not be held liable in personam.[90] Similarly, in *Tucker v Alexandroff*, the US Supreme Court explained the doctrine of personification doctrines as:

> A ship is born when she is launched, and lives so long as her identity is preserved. Prior to her launching she is a mere congeries of wood and iron – an ordinary piece of personal property … In the baptism of launching she receives her name, and from the moment her keel touches the water she is transformed, and becomes a subject of admiralty jurisdiction. She acquires a personality of her own; becomes competent to contract, and is individually liable for her obligations, upon which she may sue in the name of her owner, and be sued in her own name. Her owner's agents may not be her agents, and her agents may not be her owner's agents. … She is capable, too, of committing a tort, and is responsible in damages therefore. She may also become a quasi bankrupt; may be sold for the payment of her debts, and thereby receive a complete discharge from all prior liens, with liberty to begin a new life, contract further obligations, and perhaps be subjected to a second sale.[91]

There are, however, some courts that have not strictly pursued the personification doctrine and criticise its overly technical application. For example, in the cases of res judicata and interpleader, US courts have approached the doctrine of personification as an equitable principle in the sense that the doctrine may be ignored when it produces an outcome running contrary to the panel's own subjective sense

[89] See eg *The China* 74 US 53, 70–71 (1868); *Tucker v Alexandroff* 183 US 424 (1902).
[90] *The China* (n 89) 70–71.
[91] *Tucker* (n 89) 438; see also P Myburgh, 'Richard Cooper Memorial Lecture: Admiralty Law – What is it Good For?' (2009) 28(1) *University of Queensland Law Journal* 19, 28.

of justice.[92] Nevertheless, with few exceptions, the doctrine of personification is still upheld by the US courts with regard to maritime lien claims, especially in the absence of the appearance of the shipowner.[93]

This personification argument has not yet been fully examined by the US courts in the area of maritime cross-border insolvency. In *Hanjin Shipping*, the Court, as discussed in section III above, stated that '[w]hile it is true that the chartered vessels are not owned by the Debtor, the claims against these vessels are based in part upon liabilities of the Debtor'.[94] The Court, therefore, extended the stay order over Hanjin's chartered vessels based on Hanjin's liability in personam, which seems to completely ignore the personification doctrine.[95] Nevertheless, notwithstanding some criticism, US courts still adhere to the doctrine of personification, especially in the circumstance of the enforcement of maritime liens through in rem actions.[96] Accordingly, in my view, the vessel should be treated as a true defendant in an in rem action, with rights and liabilities separate from those of the insolvent debtor. This issue is discussed further in Chapter 11 below.

V. Status of Chartered Vessels in Cross-Border Insolvency

As mentioned in previous chapters, an issue may be raised regarding the scope of debtors' assets because of the existence of chartered vessels in the maritime context. Whether chartered vessels are regarded as debtors' assets and subject to the automatic stay order depends on the nature of the charterparty.

In *In re Daebo International Shipping Co Ltd*, the US Bankruptcy Court for the Southern District of New York held that a sale-and-leaseback chartered vessel was to be regarded as the debtor's asset.[97] The case involved several US creditors applying for Rule B attachments against a vessel that was 'leased' by Daebo International Shipping Co (Daebo), whose Korean rehabilitation proceeding had

[92] See eg *Burns Bros v Central RR* 202 F 2d 910, 912–13 (2d Cir 1953); *Continental Grain Co v Barge FBL-585* 364 US 19, 25 (1960); *Hapag-Lloyd Aktiengesellschaft v US Oil Trading LLC* 814 F 3d 146, 148 (2d Cir 2016); *Insurance Co of N America v S/S American Argosy* 732 F 2d 299, 302 (2d Cir 1984); see also BJ Schwab, 'Equitable Personification: A Review of Res Judicata's Historical Application to Successive in Personam and in Rem Admiralty Actions in the United States' (2012) 37 *Tulane Maritime Law Journal* 253, 281.

[93] But see *Hapag-Lloyd Aktiengesellschaft v US Oil Trading LLC* 814 F 3d 146 (2d Cir 2016).

[94] *Hanjin Shipping* (n 69) 6.

[95] *Hanjin Shipping* (n 69) 6. See also Davies, 'Cross-Border Insolvency and Admiralty: A Middle Path of Reciprocal Comity' (n 54) 114.

[96] M Davies, 'In Defense of Popular Virtues: Personification and Ratification' (2000) 75 *Tulane Law Review* 337, 345; but see G Gilmore and C Black, *The Law of Admiralty*, 2nd edn (Foundation Press, 1975) 615–16; D Collins, 'Comments on the American Rule of In Rem Liability' (1985) 10 *Maritime Lawyer* 71, 90; G Walker, 'The Personification of the Vessel in United States Civil In Rem Actions and the International Law Context' (1991) 15 *Tulane Maritime Law Journal* 177, 243.

[97] *In re Daebo International Shipping Co Ltd* 543 BR 47 (Bankr SD New York 2015).

been recognised as a foreign main proceeding by the US bankruptcy court. Prior to its Chapter 15 petition, the vessel was under a 'sale and leaseback' arrangement that Daebo entered into with one of its creditors, whereby Daebo had sold its vessel to the creditor, and then leased it back as a means of repaying the debt.[98]

The creditors, Rule B plaintiffs, argued that they were entitled to arrest the leased vessel, and that the court's stay order prevented them from exercising their rights.[99] The creditors further alleged, inter alia, that the charterparty was a 'sham', and the transaction between the debtor and its creditor was actually a secured financing, and that the vessel should thus be regarded as the debtor's property.[100] In rejecting the creditors' claims, the Court held that a previously-granted Chapter 15 stay prevented the Rule B claimants from arresting the vessel.[101] However, the Court did not give a definite answer to this 'lease recharacterisation' claim argument. The Court reasoned that this argument did not provide any support for the creditors' contention that the attachments should be permitted.[102] Therefore, the Court held that even if this argument is correct and the chartered vessel belongs to debtor's asset, the previously-granted Chapter 15 stay order prevented the Rule B claimants from arresting the vessel.[103] Nevertheless, the Court noted that several cases has recognised that a 'sale and leaseback agreement' more closely resembled a secured debt in the context of leveraged lease financing transactions; on this analysis, the debtor would be likely to retain the ownership of the vessel for the benefit of all creditors.[104]

Moreover, in *Hanjin Shipping*, the Court granted a stay order in order to prevent the arrest of Hanjin's vessels even if they were only chartered, not owned by Hanjin.[105] In Hanjin's shipping practice, most of its operating vessels were not owned by Hanjin but chartered from third parties. Those chartered vessels were under either a time-charter agreement or a bareboat charter hire purchase agreement (BBCHP).[106] The BBCHP agreement is a convenient and practical method of ship financing commonly used in South Korea. It provides a means for shipping companies, over a certain period of time, to purchase vessels via charter hires.[107]

[98] ibid 55. See also Davies, 'Cross-Border Insolvency and Admiralty: A Middle Path of Reciprocal Comity' (n 54) 112.
[99] *Daebo* (n 97) 55.
[100] ibid 51.
[101] ibid 54–56.
[102] ibid 55.
[103] ibid 54.
[104] ibid 55. See also eg *In re PCH Associates* 804 F 2d 193 (2d Cir 1986) (considering the 'economic realities' of a transaction and concluding that a purported lease was really a secured financing); *United Airlines Inc v HSBC Bank USA NA* 416 F 3d 609 (7th Cir 2005) (noting that US courts look to the economic substance of a transaction, rather than its label, in deciding whether a transaction constitutes a lease or a secured loan); *Liona Corp v PCH Associates* 949 F 2d 585, 600 (2d Cir 1991); *In re Moreggia & Sons Inc* 852 F 2d 1179 (9th Cir 1988).
[105] *Hanjin Shipping* (n 69) 6.
[106] In Hanjin's practice, 54 vessels of the 61 allegedly-owned vessels (Hanjin's crew on board) were under BBCHP agreement. See H Kim, 'Korean Maritime Case Update: 2015/2016' (2017) 48 *Journal of Maritime Law & Commerce* 211, 222.
[107] Kim, 'Korean Maritime Case Update: 2015/2016' (n 106) 222.

Under the BBCHP structure, the bank establishes a special purpose corporation (SPC) and provides the SPC with capital sufficient to build a vessel.[108] Once the vessel is constructed, the SPC charters the vessel to shipping companies under a BBCHP agreement. While the SPC retains title to the vessel, the shipping company is able to use the vessel for the duration of the BBCHP agreement, and, at the end of the designated charter period, may purchase the vessel 'at a nominal price'.[109]

The Court noted that Hanjin's chartered vessels were not Hanjin's property, and thus were not the property of the debtor as discussed in Chapter 15 of the US Bankruptcy Code.[110] Despite this finding, the Court extended the stay order to these vessels, observing that, as the maritime lien claims were based on Hanjin's liabilities, as long as these vessels were chartered by Hanjin, 'its property rights are impacted'.[111] The Court in *Hanjin Shipping*, therefore, treated all chartered vessels, both BBCHP vessels and time-chartered vessels, as protected property interests and included them in the stay order.[112] In addition, the Court was concerned about the interests of third-party beneficial cargo owners, who stood to lose amounts of money if the chartered vessels were seized, and found that the interests of all involved parties weighed heavily in favour of ordering a broad stay order protecting Hanjin's ships, both owned and chartered.[113]

Notably, the US stay order on the insolvency proceeding of Hanjin is even broader than the Korean stay order, the order in the foreign main proceeding. In Korea, maritime lien holders would not be able to assert maritime liens against the debtor's chartered vessels (neither BBCHP-chartered nor time-chartered vessels) and the stay order would not include chartered vessels.[114] Thus, to some extent, it is illogical that the US stay order is even broader than the Korean order to include both owned and chartered vessels. As Martin Davies criticised:

> It is ironic, to say the least, that a court in the United States, the home of the doctrine of personification, should consign maritime lien claimants to participation in the Korean rehabilitation proceedings arising from the Hanjin insolvency, when a Korean court decided not do so.[115]

Similarly, in *In re STX Pan Ocean Co Ltd* and *In re Korea Line Corp*, courts also extended the stay order to all vessels 'owned, operated or otherwise leased or chartered' by debtors.[116] However, unfortunately, in those two cases, courts did not cite any specific justification or case law to explain why chartered vessels should be included.

[108] ibid 223.
[109] ibid.
[110] *Hanjin Shipping* (n 69) 6.
[111] ibid.
[112] ibid.
[113] ibid.
[114] Changwon District Court Decision 17 October 2016, Docket No 2016taki227. See also Kim, 'Korean Maritime Case Update: 2015/2016' (n 106) 221–22.
[115] Davies, 'Cross-Border Insolvency and Admiralty: A Middle Path of Reciprocal Comity' (n 54) 115.
[116] *In re STX Pan Ocean Co Ltd* No 13-12046 (Bankr SD New York 1 July 2013); *In re Korea Line Corp* No 11-10789 (Bankr SD New York 20 April 2011).

From the above analysis, in my view, time-chartered or voyage-chartered vessels are not assets of the insolvent debtor, because a time charterer or a voyage charterer has only the carrying capacity of the chartered vessel, but 'no right of property in, or to possession of, the vessel'.[117] However, whether a bareboat-chartered vessel or a BBCHP-chartered vessel is the asset of a debtor should depend on the economic substance of the charterparty. In other words, if the bareboat charterparty or the BBCHP charterparty can be recharacterised as a security interest, the chartered vessel will be regarded as the property of the debtor. This issue is discussed further in Chapter 12 below.

VI. Summary

The US is a jurisdiction that favours a universalist approach, which encourages protection of the interests of debtors' global rehabilitation and creditors as a whole. Courts will generally provide assistance to the foreign main proceeding absent plain language to the contrary or a vital public policy concern.[118]

Although in some cases courts did consider the interests of maritime lien holders, they are more inclined to interpret Chapter 15 in a 'universalist' way, in order to avoid 'the piecemeal seizure and distribution of assets by individual nations'.[119] In addition, the prejudices to the rights of maritime lien holders do not amount to a vital public policy concern.[120] So far, US courts tend to issue a wide automatic stay order to stay all claims against the foreign debtor once they recognise the foreign insolvency proceeding as a foreign main proceeding, without granting any exception for maritime lien claims.[121] However, it is controversial that when Chapter 15 of the US Bankruptcy Code works to preclude a vessel arrest or attachment, maritime creditors are denied any recovery from the debtor, resulting in unjust treatment of these creditors in the insolvency proceedings.[122]

In addition, notwithstanding that US courts have traditionally adopted the doctrine of personification doctrine, the personification argument has not yet been fully examined by US courts in the area of maritime cross-border insolvency. Moreover, all chartered vessels, even time chartered vessels, are subject to the stay order and are protected from being arrested.[123] In any case, the overall goal of US courts is to direct creditors and assets to the foreign main proceeding for orderly and fair distribution of assets and to avoid the seizure of assets by local creditors.

[117] W Tetley, *International Maritime and Admiralty Law* (Éditions Yvon Blais, 2002) 126. See also *Port Line v Ben Line* [1958] 2 QB 146, 163.

[118] See 11 USC § 1506.

[119] *Hanjin Shipping* (n 69) 4.

[120] See *Hanjin Shipping* (n 69) 6.

[121] See *Sanko* (n 58); *Hanjin Shipping* (n 69) 2.

[122] See Falzone (n 57) 1176–77.

[123] *Hanjin Shipping* (n 69) 6.

10

Singapore

I. Overview

To strengthen Singapore as an international debt restructuring hub, the Parliament of Singapore passed the Companies (Amendment) Act 2017 (the Companies Act) on 10 March 2017, which later came into force on 23 May 2017.[1] The Companies Act formally embraced modified universalism by adopting the Model Law and abolishing the traditional 'ring-fencing' rule in the winding up of foreign companies.[2] The aim of the Companies Act was to enhance the legal framework of restructuring, creating a restructuring-friendly ecosystem and addressing the perception gap on the strength of Singapore's insolvency regime.[3] By adopting the Model Law, the Companies Act provides a clear, harmonised and fair procedural framework for the recognition of foreign insolvency proceedings in Singapore.[4] As a leading shipping centre in Asia, it is essential to review Singapore's application of maritime law and practice in the area of cross-border insolvency in order to afford shipowners and creditors more predictability within the Asia Pacific region. This chapter examines the considerations taken into account by the Ministry of Law of Singapore (Ministry of Law) when adopting the Model Law and analyses the influence of the approach of Singapore to maritime cross-border insolvency practice after the Model Law has been adopted. The application of the Model Law regime to admiralty claimants in Singapore will now be discussed in detail.

[1] I Rajah, 'Enhancing Singapore as an International Debt Restructuring Centre for Asia and Beyond', available at app.mlaw.gov.sg/files/NoteonDebtRestructuring.pdf/, accessed 6 June 2020.

[2] Companies Act (2006 rev ed), s 377(3)(c); Rajah (n 1).

[3] Insolvency Law Review Committee, 'Report of the Insolvency Law Review Committee' (2013 Report), available at www.mlaw.gov.sg/files/news/public-consultations/2013/10/RevisedReportoftheInsolvencyLawReviewCommittee.pdf, accessed 6 June 2020; Committee to Strengthen Singapore as an International Centre for Debt Restructuring, 'Report of the Committee' (2016 Report), available at www.esquireglobalcrossings.com/wp-content/uploads/sites/21/2016/06/2016-04-Singapore-Committee-Report.pdf accessed 6 June 2020.

[4] ibid.

II. The Regime of Insolvency and Secured Status of Maritime Claims in Singapore

A. Overview of the Regime of Insolvency

The main legislation that governs the regime of corporate insolvency in Singapore is the Companies Act (Cap 50).[5] The insolvency provisions in the Companies Act that regulate both Singaporean and foreign companies were derived from the UK Companies Act 1948[6] and the UK Insolvency Act 1986.[7] Similar to the insolvency regime in the UK, the insolvency regime of Singapore has traditionally been perceived as 'creditor friendly' or, more particularly, 'secured creditor friendly'.[8] Nevertheless, the amended Companies Act, which draws upon the recommendations provided in the Report of the Insolvency Law Review Committee 2013 (2013 Report)[9] and the Report of the Committee to Strengthen Singapore as an International Centre for Debt Restructuring 2016 (2016 Report),[10] has shifted towards creating a climate conducive to corporate rescue. The amended Companies Act provides mechanisms for winding up and restructuring (including judicial management and schemes of arrangement).[11] In addition, with regard to the issue of jurisdiction, Singapore does not have specialised insolvency courts that deal exclusively with insolvency matters. Applications for the commencement of insolvency proceedings are exclusively heard by the Singapore High Court.[12]

i. Winding Up

The mechanism of winding up a company in Singapore is mainly set out in Part X of the Companies Act.[13] The winding up of a company can be either voluntary (voluntary winding up) or by the court (compulsory winding up).[14] A voluntary winding up can be initiated by the members of the company or its creditors passing a special resolution, whereas a compulsory winding up is initiated by the making of an application to the court by a person who is entitled to do so, such as the

[5] Companies Act.

[6] Companies Act 1948 (Cap 38).

[7] Insolvency Act 1986 (Cap 45); see also SK Chan, 'Cross-border Insolvency Issues' (2011) 23 *Singapore Academy of Law Journal* 413, 417.

[8] WY Wan and G McCormack, 'Transplanting Chapter 11 of the US Bankruptcy Code into Singapore's Restructuring and Insolvency Laws: Opportunities and Challenges' (2018) *Journal of Corporate Law Studies* 1, 5.

[9] 2013 Report (n 3).

[10] 2016 Report (n 3).

[11] See Companies Act, Pts VII (schemes of arrangement), VIIIA (judicial management), X (winding up).

[12] Companies Act, s 4.

[13] Companies Act, Pt X; see also CH Tan (ed), *Walter Woon on Company Law*, rev 3rd edn (Sweet & Maxwell, 2009) 596–789 (for general discussion on the regime of winding up in Singapore).

[14] Companies Act, s 247.

insolvent company or its creditors.[15] Upon the commencement of a winding-up proceeding, the company ceases to carry on its business. Its assets will be collected by the liquidator and be used to satisfy the claims of its creditors. Any remaining balance will be distributed pro rata among the shareholders of the company.[16]

ii. *Judicial Management*

The regime of judicial management was introduced in Singapore in 1987 and is based upon the regime of administration in the UK.[17] It offers an alternative to winding up and provides distressed companies with breathing space to reorganise and restore themselves to profitability.[18] The rationale of the regime of judicial management is that a successful judicial management will be in the interests of or benefit to most creditors and members of the company when compared to a premature compulsory liquidation.[19] Section 227B of the Companies Act provides that the court may make a judicial management order if 'the company is or is likely to become unable to pay its debts'.[20] According to this section, the order, if made, would be likely to achieve one or more of the following outcomes: (1) the survival of the company as a going concern; (2) the approval of a scheme of arrangement between the company and its creditors; or (3) a more advantageous realisation of the company's assets than would occur in a winding-up proceeding.[21]

iii. *Scheme of Arrangement*

The regime of the scheme of arrangement was introduced in Singapore in 1967 and became a predominant corporate rescue regime over subsequent years.[22] A scheme of arrangement is a compromise arrangement between a distressed company and its creditors under which the creditors compromise and agree to give up or reschedule all or part of their debts while allowing the company to continue

[15] Companies Act, ss 253, 254, 291, 293; see also Tan (n 13) 695.
[16] Companies Act, ss 272(1), 292(1).
[17] 2013 Report (n 3) 81.
[18] See Tan (n 13) paras 16.22–16.73 (for general discussion on the regime of judicial management in Singapore).
[19] ibid para 16.23.
[20] Companies Act, s 227B(a); *cf* Companies Act (2006 rev ed), s 227(a) (the 2017 amendment of the Companies Act lowered the threshold requirements for courts to make judicial management orders in the sense that companies and creditors can now can access the mechanism of judicial management easier and earlier. Before the amendment, s 227(a) of the Companies Act (2006 rev ed) provided that a judicial management order would be made by the court only if 'the company is or will be unable to pay its debts'. In other words, previously, a company had to show that the company was actually insolvent before a judicial management order could be made.).
[21] Companies Act, s 227B(b).
[22] Companies Act, ss 210, 211; 2013 Report (n 3) 135; see also Tan (n 13) paras 16.1–16.21 (for general discussion on the regime of the scheme of arrangement in Singapore).

its business.[23] A scheme of arrangement can assist a company to come up with an overall plan to deal with all creditors at the same time.

Prior to the 2017 amendment of the Companies Act, Singapore closely followed the UK's scheme of arrangement regime. The amended Companies Act introduced a number of new provisions, including a mechanism of cross-class cram-down of dissenting classes,[24] which is based on the concepts that can be found in Chapter 11 of the US Bankruptcy Code.[25] Through a mechanism of cross-class cram-down, courts can overcome the difficulty of obtaining the unanimous consent of all creditors and members, enabling the corporate debtor to implement a debt restructuring regardless of the minority non-consenting creditors.[26] After approval by the requisite majority and subject to the confirmation of the court, the arrangement shall be binding on all creditors and members of a company.[27]

B. Moratorium under the Companies Act

In Singapore, different types of insolvency proceedings have different rules with regard to the scope and effect of a moratorium. In the case of a winding-up proceeding, the insolvent company or its creditors may apply to the court to restrain any proceedings pending against the company after a winding-up petition is presented but before a court order has been made.[28] Upon a winding-up order being made by the court, an automatic moratorium comes into effect in the sense that no actions or proceedings shall be proceeded with or commenced against the company unless leave of the court is obtained.[29] Although no specific provisions are available for secured creditors to be exempt from the winding-up moratorium under section 262(3) of the Companies Act, it is well settled in the common law of Singapore that courts would generally exercise their discretion to grant leave and allow secured creditors to enforce their security regardless of the pending or subsequent winding-up proceedings.[30]

[23] Tan (n 13) paras 16.1–16.3; *Re Savoy Hotel Ltd* [1981] Ch 351.

[24] The Court may, on the application of the company, approve a compromise or arrangment and force one or more dissenting classes of creditors to be bound by the compromise or arrangement as long as 'the compromise or arrangement does not discriminate unfairly between two or more classes of creditors, and is fair and equitable to each dissenting class': see Companies Act, s 211H.

[25] P Apáthy and E Chua, 'Singapore's New "Supercharged" Scheme of Arrangement' (2017) 5 *Butterworths Journal of International Banking and Financial Law* 282.

[26] Companies Act, s 211H.

[27] Companies Act, s 210(3AA).

[28] Companies Act, s 258.

[29] Companies Act, ss 262(3), 299(2).

[30] Tan (n 13) para 17.133; LS Lin Joyce, 'Is Singapore's Insolvency Regime Excessively Pro-creditor' (2003) 12 *International Insolvency Review* 37; *Re David Lloyd & Co* (1877) LR 6 ChD 339 (CA); *Korea Asset Management v Daewoo Singapore Pte Ltd* [2004] 1 SLR 671; *Hickley Singapore Trading Pte Ltd v Sogo Department Stores (S) Pte Ltd* [2001] 4 SLR 154; *QCD(M) Sdn Bhd v Wah Nam Plastic Industry Pte Ltd* [1997] 2 SLR 544.

In the case of a judicial management proceeding, a statutory moratorium against the enforcement actions of creditors automatically comes into effect upon the judicial management application being filed, and continues to be effective during the time that the application hearing is pending and a judicial management order is in force.[31] No legal proceedings, executions, enforcement of securities or any other legal proceedings shall be commenced or continued against the insolvent company or its assets except with the leave of the court or with the consent of the judicial manager.[32] The Court of Appeal in *Hickley Singapore Trading Pte Ltd v Sogo Department Stores (S) Pte Ltd* followed *In re Atlantic Computer Systems*,[33] the leading English authority, and differentiated between the effect of making a winding-up order and a judicial management order:

> In the former case, where an insolvent company is concerned, the object is to achieve an equal distribution of the company's assets among the unsecured creditors. So in respect of a secured creditor, who wishes to enforce his security, leave would normally be granted. In contrast, a [judicial management] is intended only to be an interim and temporary regime. It is really to provide some breathing space to the company, which is or will be unable to pay its debts and, under the new temporary management of the administrator, to seek to achieve one or more of the following purposes …:
>
> (a) the survival of the company, or the whole or part of its undertaking as a going concern;
> (b) the approval of a compromise or arrangement between the company and its creditors/members;
> (c) a more advantageous realisation of the company's assets would be effected than on a winding up.
>
> Therefore, the effect of the making of … a judicial management order, is that there is a moratorium on the enforcement of debts and rights, proprietary or otherwise, against the company, so as to give the administrators/judicial managers time to formulate proposals and lay them before the creditors, and then implement any proposals approved by the creditors.[34]

Therefore, secured creditors are usually subject to the judicial management moratorium under section 227D(4) of the Companies Act and are prohibited from enforcing their securities over the assets of the company unless they obtain the leave of the court or the consent of the judicial manager.[35] In deciding whether to grant leave under section 227D(4), courts will balance the interests of the applicant who seeks to leave the moratorium, the interests of other creditors who seek to give effect to the objectives of the judicial management, the purpose of the moratorium, the likelihood of adverse consequences to the interested parties and all

[31] Companies Act, ss 227C, 227D; Tan (n 13) para 16.43.
[32] Companies Act, ss 227C, 227D.
[33] *In re Atlantic Computer Systems* [1992] Ch 505.
[34] *Hickley* (n 30) [8].
[35] Companies Act, s 227D(4); *Electro Magnetic (S) Ltd v Development Bank of Singapore* [1994] 1 SLR 734.

the other circumstances of the case.[36] Courts will maintain the moratorium if a substantially greater loss will be caused to the company by the grant of leave, or any loss will be out of all proportion to the benefit conferred on the applicant by the grant of leave.[37] Nevertheless, as the Singapore Court of Appeal explained in *ElectroMagnetic (S) Ltd (under judicial management) v Development Bank of Singapore Ltd*, section 227D(4) of the Companies Act is procedural in nature, as it imposes only a moratorium on the enforcement of the secured creditors' rights but does not destroy them.[38]

Finally, in cases where there is a scheme of arrangement, there is no automatic statutory moratorium when a scheme of arrangement has been proposed. Nevertheless, the insolvent company or its creditors may apply for a moratorium order to restrain the commencement or continuation of any proceedings and the taking of any step to enforce any security over any property of the company when a scheme of arrangement has been proposed or is intended to be proposed.[39] The Companies Act, however, provides an automatic 30-day interim moratorium upon the application for a moratorium order.[40] The automatic moratorium is available only once within a 12-month period.[41] The rationale for this 12-month period requirement is to prevent abuse through repeated filings. The 30-day automatic moratorium applies only to actions of any person in Singapore and will cease 30 days after the application for a moratorium order or until the application is decided by the courts, whichever is earlier.[42] Moreover, related companies, such as subsidiaries or holding companies, can also apply for a moratorium regardless of whether or not they are located in Singapore, if they play a necessary and integral role in the arrangement and where an action being taken against the related companies will frustrate the scheme.[43] Finally, if, following an application in a scheme of arrangement, the 30-day automatic stay is granted, the criteria for granting leave in a scheme moratorium are consistent with those applicable in a judicial management situation.[44]

C. Secured Status of Maritime Claims

The Companies Act will not change the secured status of maritime claims.[45] Maritime claims can become secured claims in certain circumstances.

[36] *Hickley* (n 30); *In re Atlantic* (n 33).
[37] Tan (n 13) para 16.48; *Hickley* (n 30) [10].
[38] *Electro Magnetic* (n 35).
[39] Companies Act, s 211B.
[40] Companies Act, s 211B(8), (13).
[41] Companies Act, s 211B(9).
[42] ibid.
[43] Companies Act, s 211C; Apáthy and Chua (n 25) 282–85.
[44] Rajah (n 1).
[45] ibid.

The following section discusses the secured status of maritime claims when companies become insolvent. If maritime claims can be regarded as secured claims, as discussed above, they will generally not be affected by a winding-up moratorium but will be stayed by a judicial management moratorium unless leave of the court or consent of the judicial manager is obtained.

i. Maritime Liens

Singapore recognises maritime liens for claims involving salvage, seafarer's wages, master's wages and disbursements, and damage done by a ship.[46] Similar to most other Commonwealth countries, courts in Singapore followed the Privy Council in *The Halcyon Isle* and regarded the nature of a maritime lien as procedural in the sense that a maritime lien accrues at the time the claim is attached; however, it creates no immediate property right until it is carried into effect by an action in rem.[47] Accordingly, a maritime lien only creates a property right on the vessel (namely, becomes a secure claim) by a proceeding in rem,[48] and once an action in rem has been commenced, it retrospectively relates back to the time the lien first attached.[49] Thus, in Singapore, if a maritime lien holder takes an in rem action to enforce its claim before the commencement of an insolvency proceeding, it becomes a secured creditor for the purpose of the Companies Act and its secured status dates back to the time when it first attached.[50]

Accordingly, in my view, in the case of a winding-up proceeding, a claim for a maritime lien that brings an action in rem before the commencement of the winding-up proceeding will not be affected by the subsequent winding-up moratorium.[51] The maritime lien holder can rely on section 262(3) of the Companies Act to apply for the leave of the court and proceed with its in rem action regardless of the winding-up moratorium.[52] Given its status as a secured creditor, courts would ordinarily exercise their discretion to grant the leave.[53] However, if the action in rem has not been initiated before the winding-up proceeding is commenced, the maritime lien remains inchoate and there is no basis for it to obtain secured status;

[46] *The Halcyon Isle* [1980] SGPC 3; *The Vinalines Pioneer* [2015] SGHC 278.

[47] *The Ocean Jade* [1991] SGHC 33; *The Halcyon Isle* [1981] AC 221; KS Toh, *Admiralty Law and Practice*, 3rd edn (LexisNexis, 2017) 277; *Precious Shipping Public Co Ltd v OW Bunker Far East (Singapore) Ptd Ltd* [2015] SGHC 187, [51].

[48] *The Halcyon Isle* (n 47) 235; *The Fesco Angara* [2010] EWCA Civ 1050; Toh (n 47) 277.

[49] *The Bold Buccleugh* (1851) 7 Moo PC 267, 285.

[50] B Ang, 'Arrest and Cross-Border Insolvency: The Singapore Experience' in P Myburgh (ed), *The Arrest Conventions: International Enforcement of Maritime Claims* (Hart Publishing, 2019) 215; see ZH Ji, 'Cross-Border Rehabilitation: An Impediment to Ship Arrest in Singapore?' CML Working Paper Series, No 17/04, March 2017, available at papers.ssrn.com/sol3/papers.cfm?abstract_id=2933955, accessed 6 June 2020.

[51] Companies Act, s 262(3).

[52] Companies Act, s 262(3); High Court Admiralty Jurisdiction Act (HCAJA), s 4(3).

[53] Ang (n 50) 215.

thus, it has to be subject to the winding-up moratorium.[54] In the case of a judicial management proceeding, all claims (including secured claims) are subject to a judicial management moratorium.[55] Thus, even though the maritime lien holder initiates its action in rem before the commencement of the judicial management proceeding, it will usually be prohibited from enforcing its maritime lien claim, unless it obtains the leave of the court or the consent of the judicial manager. In determining whether to grant the leave, courts will consider the relevant facts and make a case-by-case decision.[56] Finally, in the case of a scheme of arrangement, if a 30-day automatic moratorium is granted upon an application, maritime lien holders will be subject to the moratorium. The criteria for courts to grant leave in a scheme moratorium are the same as that in a judicial management situation.[57]

ii. Statutory Rights of Action in Rem

As a Commonwealth country, Singapore adopts the concept of statutory rights of action in rem, which refers to the rights of claimants to invoke the courts' admiralty jurisdiction by exercising in rem proceedings.[58] In Singapore, claims for statutory rights of action in rem are set out in section 3 of the High Court (Admiralty Jurisdiction) Act (HCAJA).[59] With regard to the secured status of statutory rights of action in rem, courts in Singapore have followed the Australian and UK position and held that claimants with statutory rights of action in rem will become secured creditors when actions in rem are commenced, namely, when writs in rem are issued.[60] Unlike a maritime lien, the security interest created by a statutory right of action in rem is prospective.[61]

In *Lim Bock Lai v Selco (Singapore) Pte Ltd*, the plaintiff sought to be exempted from the moratorium in the compulsory winding-up proceeding and to pursue its action in rem for the unpaid bunker.[62] The writ in rem had been filed and issued, but not served, before the commencement of the winding-up proceeding. The High Court of Singapore followed the leading English authority *In Re Aro Co Ltd* and considered the plaintiff to be a secured creditor.[63] The Court held that the plaintiff, with a statutory right of action in rem, would become a secured creditor upon the commencement of an action in rem, that is, the time when the writ in rem was issued.[64] The plaintiff, therefore, obtained the leave of the Court under

[54] *The Hull 308* [1991] SGCA 34.
[55] Companies Act, ss 227C, 227D.
[56] Companies Act, ss 227D, 210(10); *Re Taisoo Suk* [2016] SGHC 195.
[57] Rajah (n 1).
[58] HCAJA, s 3.
[59] Typical examples of claims for statutory rights of action in rem in Singapore are claims for loss or damage to cargo, general average, towage, pilotage ect. See HCAJA, s 3.
[60] *Lim Bock Lai v Selco (Singapore) Pte Ltd* [1987] SGHC 35; *In Re Aro Co Ltd* [1980] Ch 196.
[61] See eg *In Re Aro Co* (n 60); *Lim Bock Lai* (n 60).
[62] *Lim Bock Lai* (n 60).
[63] *Lim Bock Lai* (n 60).
[64] ibid [11]–[12].

section 262(3) to proceed with its action in rem, notwithstanding that the writ was not served prior to the winding up.

Similarly, in *Kuo Fen Ching and Another v Dauphin Offshore Engineering & Trading Pte Ltd*, the respondent obtained a judgment in rem and arrested the relevant ship in order to enforce his claim for materials supplied and repair services performed on the vessel.[65] The vessel was released after security was provided in the form of a letter of guarantee issued by Citibank. However, the shipowner was dissolved and liquidated after it entered an appearance to the in rem action and filed its defence. The Court found that a writ in rem had been issued before the shipowner was wound up; this created a statutory right of action in rem in favour of the respondent.[66] The security provided by Citibank was in lieu of the arrested ship and represented pre-judgment security that turned the respondent into a secured creditor of the shipowner. Therefore, the Court of Appeal exercised its discretion under section 262(3) of the Companies Act and allowed the in rem action of the respondent to proceed against the insolvent shipowner despite the winding-up order being made.[67]

In *The Hull 308*, however, the writ in rem was issued *after* the winding up of the insolvent company had been commenced and therefore the Singapore Court of Appeal refused to grant leave for the plaintiffs' in rem actions against the ship to proceed.[68] The Court compared *Lim Bock Lai* and *In re Aro* and explained that, in both cases, the plaintiffs obtained leave from the courts on the ground that their in rem writs against the ships were issued *before* the commencement of the winding up of the respective owners and that they both, therefore, became secured creditors of the insolvent debtors.[69] However, the plaintiffs in *The Hull 308*, who supplied necessaries for the construction of the vessel of the insolvent shipowner, commenced an in rem action one month *after* the commencement of the winding up of the defendants and thus should not be regarded as secured creditors.[70] The Court, therefore, did not grant the leave and held that 'should leave in such circumstances be granted, it would confer upon the plaintiffs a security on an asset of the defendants which the plaintiffs otherwise did not have and could not have', which would be unfair to other unsecured creditors.[71]

As discussed above, in the scenario of a compulsory winding-up proceeding, it seems clear that a claim for a statutory right of action in rem will become secured upon the issue of a writ in rem. In *The Oriental Baltic*, the Singapore High Court extended this principle to a voluntary winding up scenario under section 299(2) of the Companies Act.[72] Since the Companies Act will not change the secured

[65] *Kuo Fen Ching and Another v Dauphin Offshore Engineering & Trading Pte Ltd* [1999] SGCA 95 [1].
[66] ibid [8].
[67] ibid [28]; see also *In Re Aro* (n 60); *Lim Bock Lai* (n 60); *The Hull 308* (n 54).
[68] *The Hull 308* (n 54).
[69] ibid [13].
[70] ibid [1].
[71] ibid [14].
[72] *The Oriental Baltic* [2011] SGHC 75.

status of maritime claims, it is likely that courts in Singapore will also extend this principle to the scenarios of judicial management and schemes of arrangement.[73]

Therefore, in my view, with regard to a winding-up proceeding, if creditors have claims for statutory rights of action in rem and issue writs in rem prior to the commencement of the winding up, they can be exempted from a winding-up moratorium under section 262(3) of the Companies Act.[74] If the writs in rem have not been issued before the commencement of the winding up, creditors with statutory rights of action in rem will remain unsecured and their in rem actions would be stayed by the winding-up moratorium.[75] As for both judicial management proceedings and scheme of arrangement proceedings, claims for statutory rights of action in rem will be suspended by a judicial management or scheme moratorium, even though the writs in rem are issued before the commencement of the judicial management and scheme proceedings. Nevertheless, claimants may apply to be exempted from the moratorium and courts will decide whether to grant leave based on a case-by-case analysis.[76]

III. Cross-Border Insolvency in Singapore

A. Overview of Singapore's Implementation of the Model Law and Its Article 20

Before the 2017 amendment of the Companies Act, courts in Singapore gave limited judicial co-operation or co-ordination to foreign courts with regard to the recognition of foreign insolvency proceedings and the remittance of the assets of a foreign insolvent company.[77] The traditional 'ring-fencing' rule of the winding up of foreign companies provides that a liquidator shall first realise and satisfy the claims of local creditors, and then turn over the remaining assets of the foreign debtor to be administered in the home jurisdiction of the debtor.[78] The 'ring-fencing' rule represents a typical approach of territorialism in the area of cross-border insolvency, which is 'contrary to internationally-accepted standards

[73] See *Re Taisoo Suk* (n 56).

[74] Companies Act, s 263(3); *Lim Bock Lai* (n 60); SMLA's Reply to the Comité Maritime International's International Working Group on Cross-Border Insolvency Questionnaire (2012) para 34, available at comitemaritime.org/work/cross-border-insolvencies/, accessed 6 June 2020.

[75] *The Hull 308* (n 54).

[76] Companies Act, ss 227D, 211B.

[77] See Companies Act (2006 rev edn), s 377(3) (Singapore); *Re HIH Casualty & General Insurance Ltd* [2008] UKHL 21; *Singularis Holdings Ltd v PricewaterhouseCoopers* [2014] UKPC 36; *Beluga Chartering GmbH (in liquidation) v Beluga Projects (Singapore) Ptd Ltd (in liquidation)* [2014] SGCA 14; *Re Opti-Medix Ltd (in liquidation)* [2016] SGHC 108; SMLA's Reply (n 74) para 6; Chan (n 7) [21]; Ang (n 50) 201.

[78] Companies Act (2006 rev ed), s 377(3).

of a fair and equitable cross-border insolvency regime'.[79] By abolishing the general 'ring-fencing' rule[80] and adopting the Model Law on Cross-Border Insolvency as the 10th Schedule to the Companies Act, Singapore abandoned the traditional approach of territorialism and embraced the approach of modified universalism. Upon the adoption of the Model Law, the process of recognising foreign insolvency proceedings will be more certain and straightforward. Furthermore, it will be easier for foreign companies and their representatives to obtain access and assistance from courts in Singapore in order to liquidate or administer their assets that are located in Singapore.[81]

Nevertheless, Singapore adopted the Model Law with modifications and exclusions.[82] The language of Article 20 of the 10th Schedule to the Companies Act is similar to Article 20 of Schedule 1 to the Cross-Border Insolvency Regulations 2006, which is the enacted version of the Model Law in the UK.[83] Article 20(1) of the Schedule provides that an automatic stay will come into force upon a foreign proceeding being recognised as a foreign main proceeding in the sense that:

> (a) commencement or continuation of individual actions or individual proceedings concerning the debtor's property, rights, obligations or liabilities is stayed;
> (b) execution against the debtor's property is stayed; and
> (c) the right to transfer, encumber or otherwise dispose of any property of the debtor is suspended.[84]

Furthermore, Article 20(2) and (3) limit the scope and effects of the automatic stay, providing that:

> (2) The stay and suspension mentioned in paragraph 1 of this Article are —
>
> (a) the same in scope and effect as if the debtor had been made the subject *of a winding-up order under this Act*; and
> (b) subject to the same powers of the Court *and the same prohibitions, limitations, exceptions and conditions as would apply under the law of Singapore in such a case*, and the provisions of paragraph 1 of this Article are to be interpreted accordingly.
>
> (3) Without prejudice to paragraph 2 of this Article, the stay and suspension mentioned in paragraph 1 of this Article do not affect any right —
>
> *(a) to take any steps to enforce security over the debtor's property*;
>
> ... (emphasis added)[85]

[79] 2013 Report (n 3) 240.
[80] However, the rule of 'ring-fencing' has been retained for specific financial institutions, such as banks and insurance companies. See Companies Act, s 377(14).
[81] 2013 Report (n 3) 234–235; Ang (n 50) 208.
[82] Companies Act, Sch 10.
[83] Companies Act, Sch 10, Art 20; Cross-Border Insolvency Regulation 2006, Sch 1, Art 20.
[84] Companies Act, Sch 10, Art 20(1).
[85] ibid Art 20(2).

The Model Law is procedural in nature and is not intended to change the substantive insolvency law of Singapore.[86] Thus, Article 20(2) expressly limits the scope and effect of the automatic stay imposed by Article 20(1) to the same extent as that provided for a winding-up proceeding or a most closely resembled local insolvency proceeding in Singapore.[87] In other words, 'the stay under Article 20(a) subjects the ... debtor to the same protection and the same disabilities as apply to a company undergoing liquidation [or resembled local insolvency proceedings] in Singapore'.[88] The scope and effects of an Article 20 automatic stay granted under the Model Law will therefore not go beyond the moratorium order that is available in the Companies Act. In order to determine the scope and effects of an Article 20 automatic stay order upon the recognition of a foreign main proceeding, courts will look into the nature of the foreign insolvency proceeding and identify the type of local insolvency proceedings under the Companies Act that it most closely resembles; they will thereafter apply the same stay order as that which is provided for in local proceedings under the Companies Act.[89] In addition, without prejudice to Article 20(2), the scope and effect of the automatic stay are further curtailed by Article 20(3) which points out that the stay and suspension 'do not affect any right to take any steps to enforce security over the debtor's property'.[90] Nevertheless, since Article 20(3) provides that 'without prejudice to paragraph 2 of this article ...', in my view, it is merely declaratory and does not operate as an exception to Article 20(1) and (2).[91]

B. Application of Article 20 in the Maritime Context

The version of the Model Law that was enacted in Singapore does not impose a specific provision to carve out in rem actions from Article 20 automatic stays; instead, it refers to local insolvency provisions and established case law with regard to the scope and effect of stay orders.[92]

When adopting the Model Law it seems that the Ministry of Law was not aware of the conflicts between the admiralty regime and the international insolvency regime.[93] However, after the 2017 amendment of the Companies Act was passed in Parliament, the Ministry of Law received public consultations on Article 20 of the Act.[94] A number of maritime stakeholders suggested that the Ministry of Law

[86] 2013 Report (n 3) 231; Ang (n 50) 218; Rajah (n 1).
[87] ibid.
[88] Ang (n 50) 211.
[89] See *Cosco Bulk Carrier Co v Armada Shipping SA& Another* [2011] EWHC 216 (Ch).
[90] Companies Act, Sch 10, Art 20(3).
[91] *Cosco Bulk Carrier* (n 89).
[92] Ministry of Law, 'Supplementary Response to Feedback Received on Companies (Amendment) Act 2017 to Strengthen Singapore as an International Centre for Debt Restructuring', available at www.mlaw.gov.sg/news/public-consultations/supplementary-response-to-feedback-received-on-companies--amendm/, accessed 6 June 2020.
[93] See 2013 Report (n 3); 2016 Report (n 3).
[94] Ministry of Law (n 92).

should consider carving out the admiralty in rem proceedings from Article 20 automatic stays under the enacted version of the Model Law in Singapore. Notwithstanding that the Ministry of Law in its response acknowledged the importance of the maritime industry and the unique features of maritime claims, it did not provide a 'carve-out' provision for maritime claims.[95] The Ministry of Law explained that 'the Model Law moratorium cross-refers to the winding up and judicial management moratoriums and similar principles of the granting of leave would apply' and 'there is established case law as to when leave will be granted in winding up and judicial management situations'.[96] Therefore, the Ministry of Law was of the view that there was no need to add a new specific exception provision for in rem actions.[97] Furthermore, the Ministry of Law emphasised that the purpose of a moratorium is not to prevent the bringing of claims per se, but rather to place a discretion in the hands of the courts who can then decide whether or not leave should be granted in order for claimants to bring or, if already begun, to proceed with their claims. This mechanism of moratorium is a measure of respite in the sense that it gives courts time to consider whether a grant of leave will be helpful to the restructuring.[98] Nevertheless, as further discussed in Chapter 11 below, in my view, a maritime lien holder should be allowed to proceed with its enforcement action regardless of any pending or subsequent insolvency proceeding on the ground that its interest can be significantly infringed by a long and complicated bankruptcy proceeding due to the delay of recovery, especially regarding the interests of crew members in recovering their wages. However, the commencement or continuation of a statutory right of action in rem, or a ship mortgage, should be based on a case-by-case analysis.

Although Singapore did not set forth a specific provision to carve out maritime claims, by integrating provisions of its local insolvency law into the Model Law maritime claimants may, in certain circumstances, be able to enforce their in rem actions against the relevant vessels regardless of the pending or subsequent foreign insolvency proceedings.[99] The amendment of the Companies Act does not change the local law in relation to the pursuit of maritime claims in winding up and judicial management situations.[100] As discussed in Section II above, the principles on how courts deal with applications for leave regarding maritime claims in local insolvency situations have been (arguably) established.[101] Therefore, as the Model Law moratorium cross-refers to rules in local insolvency proceedings, maritime claimants may rely on the similar principles of the granting of leave in the cross-border insolvency area.[102]

[95] ibid.
[96] ibid.
[97] ibid.
[98] ibid.
[99] See Companies Act, s 262(3); Sch 10, Art 20(2).
[100] Rajah (n 1); Ang (n 50) 218.
[101] Nevertheless, the treatment of maritime claims in administration proceedings remains untested with regard to applications for leave of court to be exempted from mortoriums.
[102] Ministry of Law (n 92).

To be specific, a claimant with a maritime lien claim or a statutory right of action in rem claim who issues a writ in rem *before* the commencement of a foreign insolvency proceeding, would be regarded as a secured creditor in Singapore.[103] If the foreign main proceeding resembles a winding-up proceeding, secured admiralty creditors would be able to proceed with their claims regardless of the pending insolvency proceeding.[104] However, if the foreign main proceeding resembles a judicial management proceeding, the enforcement actions of creditors (including secured admiralty creditors) would be stayed by the automatic judicial management moratorium unless the leave of the court or the consent of the judicial manager has been obtained.[105]

i. *Re Taisoo Suk*

The High Court in *Re Taisoo Suk* illustrates how Singapore applies common law in the area of cross-border insolvency.[106] At the time of the decision of *Re Taisoo Suk*, Singapore had not formally adopted the Model Law. The High Court of Singapore, pursuant to its inherent power under the common law, recognised the Korean rehabilitation proceeding of Hanjin Shipping (Hanjin) and granted the stay order. The stay order was a general order that suspended all pending, contingent or fresh proceedings against Hanjin, its Singapore subsidiaries and its assets.[107]

In granting the order, the High Court relied on the Singapore Court of Appeal's decision in *Beluga Chartering GmbH (in liquidation) v Beluga Projects (Singapore) Pte Ltd (in liquidation)*, where the Court recognised the benefits of a universalist approach in winding-up proceedings and noted that courts in Singapore could render assistance to foreign winding-up proceedings in certain circumstances.[108] In *Re Taisoo Suk*, the High Court of Singapore extended *Beluga*'s approach to other forms of insolvency proceedings, including restructuring and rehabilitation proceedings.[109] The High Court listed three factors that needed to be considered in determining whether recognition of foreign rehabilitation proceedings should be granted:

(a) the connection of the company to the forum in which the rehabilitation proceedings are taking place and to the place of rehabilitation;
(b) what the rehabilitation process entails, including its impact on domestic creditors and whether it is fair and equitable in the circumstances; and
(c) whether there are any strong countervailing reasons against recognition of the foreign rehabilitation proceedings.[110]

[103] See *Lim Bock Lai* (n 60).
[104] See Companies Act, s 262(3); Sch 10, Art 20(2).
[105] See Companies Act, ss 227C, 227D; Sch 10, Art 20(2); *Re Taisoo Suk* (n 56) [14].
[106] *Re Taisoo Suk* (n 56).
[107] ibid [14].
[108] ibid [15]; see also *Beluga Chartering* (n 77).
[109] *Re Taisoo Suk* (n 56) [16].
[110] ibid [18].

The court was satisfied with all three factors when considering the application of recognising the Korean rehabilitation proceeding of Hanjin: (1) Hanjin's common law centre of main interest was in Korea, which provided a strong connecting factor between Hanjin and the Korean court;[111] (2) the Korean rehabilitation process would treat all creditors in the same class fairly and equitably, whether local or foreign creditors;[112] (3) there were no strong countervailing reasons against recognition of the foreign rehabilitation proceedings.[113]

Regarding the third factor, namely, the 'countervailing reasons against recognition of foreign insolvency proceedings', Hanjin's creditors argued that the Court should exercise its admiralty jurisdiction under the HCAJA in reaching its decision that related to stays of the arrest of vessels.[114] In addition, a general stay order would have an adverse impact on the admiralty creditors who sought to arrest the vessels that were owned by Hanjin in Singapore.[115] However, the High Court rejected these two arguments. The Court held that the HCAJA did not carve out ship arrests as being exclusive to admiralty jurisdiction, and thus the court could properly order a stay over the arrests.[116] In addition, the Court was of the view that 'the inability of individual creditors to obtain security was a necessary consequence of universal collection and marshalling of assets'.[117] Therefore, in addition to recognising the Korean rehabilitation proceeding of Hanjin, the Court granted a restraint and stay order to the extent of preventing the arrest of ships that were beneficially owned or chartered by Hanjin and its subsidiaries. The Court noted that the importance of there being an orderly rehabilitation proceeding, and the need to protect the assets of Hanjin, provided sufficiently strong grounds for granting such relief.[118]

However, the stay order granted by the High Court did not apply to the *M/V Hanjin Rome*, which had been arrested before the application for recognition was filed by the administrator of Hanjin. Notwithstanding that this 'carve-out' arose out of a concession by Hanjin's administrator,[119] it has been argued that, in Singapore, if maritime claimants take steps to commence their in rem actions, and do so before the commencement of the recognition petition by foreign trustees or administrators, they will be allowed to proceed with these actions regardless of the subsequent insolvency proceedings.[120] This argument ignores the fact that different types of insolvency proceedings have different rules of moratorium with regard to secured creditors. If the foreign insolvency proceeding resembles a winding-up proceeding, the carve-out of pre-arrest vessels seems consistent with

[111] ibid [19].
[112] ibid [21].
[113] ibid [22]–[31].
[114] ibid [24].
[115] ibid [30].
[116] ibid [25]–[26].
[117] ibid [31].
[118] ibid [32].
[119] ibid [35].
[120] Ang (n 50) 201.

the *Lim Bock Lai* and *Kuo Feng Ching*, as the claimants will be regarded as secured claimants for the purpose of the Companies Act and can be exempted from the winding-up moratorium.[121] However, if the foreign insolvency proceeding resembles a judicial management proceeding, the pre-arrest vessels cannot be carved out unless leave of the court or consent of the judicial manager is obtained.

IV. Courts' Attitudes Towards in Rem Actions and the Personification Doctrine in Singapore

As mentioned in Chapter 6, maritime creditors may argue that their enforcement actions are against relevant vessels in rem rather than against insolvent debtors in personam. Therefore, the attitude of courts towards the nature of in rem actions may be decisive when determining whether maritime creditors can proceed with their in rem actions against vessels that are owned by shipping companies, regardless of the pending or subsequent insolvency proceedings of the companies.

The issue regarding the nature of in rem actions was first encountered by the Singapore Court of Appeal in *The Kusu Island*, where the appellants entered a conditional appearance to the in rem actions against three of their vessels initiated by the respondents, and argued that 'in an admiralty action in rem the defendant is the res itself and not the owner of or party interested in the res'.[122] The Court held the view that when a shipowner entered an unconditional appearance to an admiralty action in rem, the shipowner was effectively submitting itself to the jurisdiction of the court in personam and was thereby subject to personal liability if it was not successful in defending the action.[123] On the contrary, 'if no appearance is entered by the defendants to such an action, judgment when entered is enforceable only against the res, and no more, and the defendant in such an action will not suffer any personal liability'.[124] Nevertheless, the action in rem and the action in personam remained separate. The entry of a defendant's appearance did not result in the fusion of the two proceedings. Therefore, the Court held that upon the shipowner entering into an unconditional appearance to an action in rem, the action continued as an action in rem and in personam.[125]

Similarly, the Court of Appeal in *The Fierbinti* confirmed, upon the appearance of the defendant, that the in rem jurisdiction was actually against the defendant.[126] The effect of the appearance was that, thenceforth, the action, which started as an in rem action, would proceed and continue as an action in personam against the defendant and as an action in rem against the ship.[127]

[121] *Lim Bock Lai* (n 60); *Kuo Fen Ching* (n 65).
[122] *The Kusu Island* [1989] SGCA 11 [18].
[123] ibid [22].
[124] ibid [26].
[125] ibid.
[126] *The Fierbinti* [1994] SGCA 74 [18].
[127] ibid; see also *The Capricorn* [1998] SGHC 366.

Furthermore, the Court of Appeal in *Kuo Fen Ching* distinguished *The Indian Grace (No 2)* that was decided by the House of Lords in the UK.[128] The Court explained that if it followed the reasoning of the House of Lords in *The Indian Grace (No 2)*, it would lead to a result that 'the defendant to the action in rem is not the ship but the shipowners, whether or not the shipowners had entered an appearance in the in rem action as the owner is in fact directly impleaded as a defendant once the ship has been served with the writ'.[129] The Court, however, distinguished the facts in *The Indian Grace (No 2)* and held the view that:

> after the owners of the vessel have entered an appearance to the action, the action continues as a parallel in rem and in personam action. The in rem characteristics of the action do not become subsumed by the additional in personam characteristics. … Otherwise, this would defeat the whole point and the advantages of taking out an action in rem.[130]

Finally, in the area of cross-border insolvency, the High Court of Singapore in *Precious Shipping Public Co Ltd v OW Bunker Far East (Singapore) Pte Ltd* reiterated its attitude towards the nature of admiralty in rem actions in Singapore.[131] In *Precious Shipping*, upon the bankruptcy of OW Bunker Group, the shipowners faced in personam claims for payments of bunker initiated by ING Banks acting as the assignee of the OW Bunker Group, and in rem claims for enforcing maritime liens against their vessels initiated by physical bunker suppliers. In order to protect themselves from potential risks of vessel arrest and double payment, the shipowners sought interpleader relief from the High Court. The Court explained that interpleader relief could be granted so long as the claims are 'competing claims', which needed to be 'adverse to and independent of one another'.[132] However, the Court in *Precious Shipping* chose to focus on the technical equivalence of the claims and held that the in personam action against the vessel owners and the in rem action against the vessels were of a different nature and did not concern the same debt.[133] The Court stated that even if it were to accept that the physical suppliers have a maritime lien against the vessel, the shipowner's acknowledgment of liability would not extinguish the maritime liens because they arise by operation of law regardless of any in personam liability. Therefore, the Court concluded that the claims were not adverse to one another and dismissed the request for interpleader relief.[134]

As discussed above, in my view, it seems clear that courts in Singapore have refused to adopt the extreme proceduralism of *The Indian Grace (No 2)*.[135]

[128] *Kuo Fen Ching* (n 65) [19]; see also *Republic of India v India Steamship Co Ltd (The Indian Grace (No 2))* [1998] AC 878.
[129] *Kuo Fen Ching* (n 65) [23].
[130] ibid [32].
[131] *Precious Shipping* (n 47).
[132] ibid [58].
[133] ibid [83].
[134] ibid [84].
[135] *The Indian Grace (No 2)* (n 128).

Although an in rem action and an in personam action may involve the same cause of action, courts in Singapore generally regard these two types of proceedings as separate and distinct and as being against different parties.[136] Thus, in my view, maritime claimants (with either maritime liens or statutory rights of action in rem) may be able to argue that their in rem actions are indeed against the vessels in rem, rather than against the insolvent shipowners in the absence of the appearance of the shipowners and, therefore, they should not be subject to the automatic stay order under Article 20 of the Model Law. Nevertheless, this argument has not yet been fully examined by courts in Singapore in the area of maritime cross-border insolvency.

V. Status of Chartered Vessels in Cross-Border Insolvency

In *Re Taisoo Suk*, the Court ordered a wide stay order to prevent 'any enforcement or execution against the vessels beneficially owned or chartered by Hanjin and its subsidiaries'.[137] Similar to courts in Australia, the UK and the US, courts in Singapore extended the stay protection to all vessels that were owned and chartered by Hanjin, which was even broader than that imposed in the main rehabilitation proceeding in Korea.[138] However, there is no explicit reasoning in *Re Taisoo Suk* regarding why the Court extended the scope of the stay order to all owned and chartered vessels by Hanjin.

However, this stay order was later tested before the duty registrar of the Supreme Court of Singapore when the arrest of the *M/V Hanjin New York* was sought on 6 October 2016.[139] The duty registrar allowed the arrest despite the stay order issued by the High Court freezing the actions of creditors against Hanjin on the grounds that the registered owner of the *M/V Hanjin New York* was a Panamanian entity, not Hanjin. Nevertheless, the vessel was released from arrest following a settlement between the parties, and proceedings have since been discontinued.[140] Thus, whether chartered vessels should be subject to the Article 20 automatic stay mechanism provided by the Model Law, is still undecided.

[136] See eg *Precious Shipping* (n 47); *The Kusu Island* (n 122); *The Fierbinti* (n 126); *Kuo Fen Ching* (n 65); *cf The Indian Grace (No 2)* (n 128).

[137] *Re Taisoo Suk* (n 56).

[138] See Chapter 7 Section V; Chapter 8 Section V, Chapter 9 Section V (for discussion of the status of Hanjin's chartered vessel in Australia, the UK and the US); Changwon District Court Decision Docket No 2016-taki-227 (17 October 2016); IH Kim, 'Korean Maritime Case Update: 2015/2016' (2017) 48 *Journal of Maritime Law & Commerce* 211, 211–12.

[139] Ang (n 50) 208.

[140] ibid.

VI. Summary

Singapore embraced modified universalism and adopted the Model Law in order to achieve the goal of strengthening Singapore as an international debt restructuring hub. The enactment of the Model Law streamlines and clarifies the process of recognising foreign insolvency proceedings in Singapore, thereby providing debtors and creditors with a certain and efficient legal framework of cross-border insolvency.[141] Although as a shipping centre within the Asia Pacific region, Singapore was not aware of the conflicts between the admiralty regime and the international insolvency regime and did not carve out admiralty in rem proceedings from the automatic stay under Article 20 of the Model Law. Instead, the enacted version of the Model Law in Singapore refers to local insolvency law and limits the scope and effect of the automatic stay to the most closely resembled local insolvency proceedings.[142] Nevertheless, the treatment of maritime claims in the area of cross-border insolvency depends on when a writ in rem is issued, and which type of local insolvency proceeding the foreign insolvency most closely resembles.[143] In addition, although it seems clear that courts in Singapore generally regard an in personam action and an in rem action as separate and distinct, and as being against different parties before a relevant person has entered an unconditional appearance, the personification argument has not yet been fully examined by the Singapore courts in the area of maritime cross-border insolvency.[144]

[141] Rajah (n 1).
[142] Companies Act, Sch 10, Art 20(2).
[143] Companies Act, s 263(3); Sch 10, Art 20(2); *Lim Bock Lai* (n 60); *Kuo Fen Ching* (n 65).
[144] *Re Taisoo Suk* (n 56).

11

Policy Reflections on the Treatment of Maritime Creditors under the UNCITRAL Model Law Regime

Maritime law and insolvency law have never been compatible,[1] especially in the context of cross-border insolvency where conflicts between the two regimes have become ever more complicated. The most controversial issue in the context of maritime cross-border insolvency is whether maritime creditors are allowed to proceed with separate in rem actions in the admiralty courts regardless of any pending or subsequent insolvency proceedings.

From the point of view of the Model Law and bankruptcy practitioners, the answer seems to be no.[2] Under the Model Law regime, upon the recognition of a foreign main proceeding in the arresting country, all claims against debtors and their assets would be suspended by the Article 20 automatic stay, including the suspension of maritime claims.[3]

However, maritime practitioners would strongly disagree with this position. They believe that, due to the special enforcement mechanism empowered by admiralty law, admiralty creditors should, to some extent, receive some 'special treatment'.[4] Accordingly, two main arguments may arise from admiralty creditors in order to obtain relief from the automatic moratorium imposed by Article 20 of the Model Law. First, admiralty creditors may rely on Article 20(2) of the Model Law, arguing that they should be regarded as secured creditors and should be allowed to proceed if the local insolvency law preserves an exception for secured creditors. Second, admiralty creditors may rely on the personification doctrine,

[1] DR Thomas, *Maritime Liens* (Stevens & Sons, 1980) [99].

[2] See eg LC Ho, 'Anti-Suit Injunctions in Cross-Border Insolvency: A Restatement' (2003) 53 *International and Comparative Law Quarterly* 52, 697; UNCITRAL Model Law on Cross-Border Insolvency (UNCITRAL Model Law), Art 20.

[3] UNCITRAL Model Law, Art 20.

[4] See eg M Davies, 'Cross-Border Insolvency and Admiralty: A Middle Path of Reciprocal Comity' (2018) 66 *American Journal of Comparative Law* 101; MJ Hafeez-Baig, 'Navigating The Waters Between Admiralty and Cross-Border Insolvency: A Comparison of the Australian, German and French Position' [2018] *Lloyd's Maritime and Commercial Law Quarterly* 97; B Ang, 'Arrest and Cross-Border Insolvency: The Singapore Experience' in P Myburgh (ed), *The Arrest Conventions: International Enforcement of Maritime Claims* (Hart Publishing, 2019); J Soars et al, 'Cross-Border Insolvency and Shipping – A Practical Guide', www.fedcourt.gov.au/__data/assets/pdf_file/0013/31153/Julie-Soars-20150423.pdf accessed 4 June 2020.

arguing that the admiralty proceedings are against the vessel itself rather than against the debtor and, therefore, not subject to the automatic moratorium.[5]

When applying the Model Law some enacting countries, such as Australia and the UK, were aware of the unique features of maritime claims,[6] whilst other countries, such as the US, applied the Model Law with little regard to in rem proceedings.[7] Nevertheless, none of the enacting countries specifically carved out maritime claims from the mandatory stay under Article 20 of the Model Law. Instead, they referred this issue back to their local insolvency proceedings regarding whether secured creditors are allowed to leave the stay orders.[8]

As can be seen from the discussion in previous chapters, the current situation with regard to this issue is that, in order to decide the scope and effect of Article 20 of the Model Law, courts that adopted the regime of the Model Law would refer to their own local substantive insolvency law, resulting in different approaches in different jurisdictions. The fundamental reason for these divergences is due to the nature of the Model Law as a type of 'soft law' that allows enacting states to freely interpret it when it is enacted into domestic legislation in order for it to be legally binding.[9] As a consequence of enacting the Model Law as a 'soft law', and given the great divergences in domestic insolvency law combined with the divergences in the application of maritime law, the treatment of maritime creditors in the area of cross-border insolvency becomes further complicated.

No clear answer was given by courts around the world and decisions made by the courts could be inconclusive, even within one jurisdiction. For example, the Federal Court of Australia in *Yu* recognised the South Korean rehabilitation proceeding that was initiated by STX Pan Ocean as a foreign main proceeding and allowed maritime claimants to proceed to enforce their in rem rights by arresting the debtor's vessel in Australia.[10] Conversely, in *Tai-Soo Suk v Hanjin Shipping Co Ltd*, Hanjin Shipping also commenced a rehabilitation proceeding in the bankruptcy court of South Korea. However, the Federal Court of Australia held that the mandatory stay order under Article 20 of the Model Law should be of the same scope as the voluntary administration proceedings under Part 5.3 of the Corporations Act – therefore maritime lien holders could not proceed to enforce their liens unless they obtained the court's relief or the debtor's consent.[11]

[5] See Ch 6 for further discussion.

[6] See eg *Yu v STX Pan Ocean Co* [2013] FCA 680; *Tai-Soo Suk v Hanjin Shipping Co Ltd* [2016] FCA 1404; *The Bank of Tokyo-Mitsubishi UFJ Ltd v The M/V Sanko Mineral and Glencore Ltd* [2014] EWHC 3927 (Admlty); *Harms Offshore Aht 'Taurus' GmbH & Co Kg & Another v Bloom & Others* [2009] EWCA Civ 632; see also Chs 7 and 8 for further discussion.

[7] See eg *Evridiki Navigation Inc v Sanko SS Co* 880 F Supp 2d 666 (D Maryland 2012); *In re Hanjin Shipping Co Ltd* 2016 WL 6679487, 2016 AMC 2126 (Bankr New Jersey 20 September 2016); see also Ch 9 for further discussion.

[8] See Cross-Border Insolvency Regulations 2006, Sch 1, Art 20(2); Cross-Border Insolvency Act 2008 (Cth), Sch 1, Art 20(2); 11 USC § 1520(a)(1); Companies Act 2017 (Singapore), Sch 10, Art 20(2).

[9] UNCITRAL Model Law, Preamble.

[10] *Yu* (n 6).

[11] *Hanjin Shipping* (n 6).

Similarly, the US District Court for the District of Maryland in *Evridiki Navigation Inc v Sanko SS Co* vacated the Rule B attachment of vessel after the reorganisation proceeding commenced by Sanko in Japan was recognised by the Bankruptcy Court for the Southern District of New York in a Chapter 15 petition.[12] The court held that control of the vessel would be transferred to the Japanese court upon the recognition of Sanko's Japanese reorganisation proceeding. Accordingly, it would not exercise its jurisdiction over the vessel, even though the vessel was attached in the US prior to the filing of the Chapter 15 petition.[13] However, in *Hanjin Shipping*, the US Bankruptcy Court for the District of New Jersey carved out a pre-arrested vessel from the automatic stay order, noting that the lien claims against the vessel were mature and enforceable.[14]

The reason for these conflicting decisions is that courts always lump all in rem actions together, without differentiating between maritime liens and statutory rights of action in rem. In addition, when courts grant automatic stay orders to debtors upon the recognition of foreign insolvency proceedings, they often ignore the type of insolvency proceedings that have been commenced in foreign countries and the examination of which local insolvency proceedings they most closely resemble.

Thus, in order to examine the treatment of maritime claims in the area of cross-border insolvency this chapter divides maritime claims into three typical types: (1) maritime lien claims; (2) claims involving statutory rights of action in rem; and (3) claims involving ship mortgages. This chapter provides policy reflections on the treatment of each type of maritime claim under the Model Law regime. In addition, as discussed in Chapter 5, different countries have different maritime liens and statutory rights of action in rem in terms of their nature and content. In the US, virtually all maritime claims can give rise to maritime liens.[15] However, in the UK, Australia and Singapore, only certain categories of maritime claims are secured by maritime liens, while most other maritime claims merely give rise to statutory rights of action in rem.[16] Accordingly, an examination of the issue of conflict of laws will be provided at the end of this chapter. For the purpose of discussion in this chapter, liquidation proceedings (US) and winding up proceedings (Australia, the UK and Singapore) are hereinafter collectively referred to as 'liquidation proceedings'; and reorganisation proceedings (US), administration proceedings (the UK and Australia), and judicial management proceedings (Singapore) are hereinafter collectively referred to as 'reorganisation proceedings'.

[12] *Evridiki Navigation Inc* (n 7).

[13] ibid 674–75.

[14] *In re Hanjin* (n 7) 2114 (noting that 'the lien claims against *The Montevideo* were mature and enforceable when the issue was before the Court'); see also *World Fuel Services Inc v M/V Hanjin Montevideo* No 2-16-CV-06584 (CD California 2016).

[15] See eg R Force, *Admiralty and Maritime Law*, 2nd edn (Federal Judicial Centre, 2013) 175–76; Federal Maritime Lien Act, 46 USC §§ 31341–43.

[16] See eg *The Bold Buccleugh* [1851] 7 Moo PC 267.

I. Maritime Liens

In my view, maritime lien holders should be permitted to enforce their maritime liens against a vessel regardless of any pending or subsequent insolvency proceedings in the circumstance when the insolvent debtor is unable to continue performing their obligations. Alternatively, they should be permitted to obtain security posted by the insolvent debtor as substitute protection for their liens. The reasons for this view are as follows: (1) a maritime lien claim shall be regarded as a substantive property right and is secured from the moment the claim arises in the sense that the initiation of an action in rem or subsequent breach enforces the existing (albeit inchoate) substantive right, whereas with a statutory right of action in rem, commencing an action in rem creates the property right prospectively.[17] Thus, a maritime lien holder should be allowed to obtain the leave of the court from the automatic stay order on the grounds that the delay imposed by the bankruptcy proceeding prejudices the maritime lien holder; (2) an in rem action to enforce a maritime lien is a true in rem action and should be regarded as against the personified vessel itself, rather than the shipowner.[18] Therefore, a maritime lien holder should be allowed to proceed with an expeditious enforcement action outside the insolvency proceeding.

A. Secured Claims

First, from my point of view, a maritime lien claim is a secured claim that is secured from the moment the claim arises.[19] As a secured creditor the maritime lien holder generally has a better chance to lift the stay order granted by bankruptcy courts.

As discussed in Chapter 5 above, whilst the US adopted a true personification doctrine, the English courts gradually abandoned it in the mid-nineteenth century and embraced a so-called 'procedural theory'.[20] In *The Halcyon Isle*, Lord Diplock characterised a maritime lien as merely a procedural remedy, which is inchoate at the time the claim attaches and creates no 'immediate property right'.[21] It is only

[17] *The Bold Buccleugh* (n 16); *The Heinrich Bjorn* (1885) 10 PD 44; *In re Aro Co Ltd* [1980] Ch 196; Hafeez-Baig (n 4) 115; J Devlin, 'The UNCITRAL Model Law on Cross-Border Insolvency and Its Impact on Maritime Creditors' (2010) 21 *Journal of Banking and Finance Law and Practice* 95, 99–100; see also Ch 5 for further discussion.

[18] *The Bold Buccleugh* (n 16); *The China* (1986) 74 US 53; *Tucker v Alexandroff* 183 US 424 (1902); M Davies, 'In Defense of Popular Virtues: Personification and Ratification' (2000) 75 *Tulane Law Review* 337, 338; M Tsimplis, 'Procedures for Enforcement' in Y Baatz (ed), *Maritime Law*, 4rd edn (Routledge, 2017) 503, 501; N Meeson and J Kimbell, *Admiralty Jurisdiction and Practice*, 5th edn (Informa Law from Routledge, 2018) 88.

[19] *The Bold Buccleugh* (n 16) 284–85; Hafeez-Baig (n 4) 115; Tsimplis (n 18) 501.

[20] P Myburgh, 'Richard Cooper Memorial Lecture: Admiralty Law – What is it Good For?' (2009) 28(1) *University of Queensland Law Journal* 19, 23; *The Bold Buccleugh* (n 16); *The Dictator* [1892] P 304; *The Halcyon Isle* [1981] AC 221; *The Indian Grace (No 2)* [1998] AC 878.

[21] *The Halcyon Isle* (n 20).

carried into effect by a proceeding in rem and dates back to the period when it first attached.[22] This 'procedural theory' has been followed by most Commonwealth countries, such as Australia,[23] Singapore,[24] New Zealand[25] etc.

However, many commentators, with whom I agree, criticised this view by arguing that maritime liens are substantive property rights.[26] It is worth emphasising the distinction between maritime liens (or what are known as 'true actions in rem') and statutory rights of action in rem (or what are known as 'actions quasi in rem'). As Paul Myburgh pointed out:

> There are, and have always been, two distinct admiralty laws: a maritime liens law, which predates the Victorian statutes, and is based on the strong personification doctrine, and a statutory jurisdiction of rights of action in rem, which dates from the Victorian codifications and extensions of admiralty jurisdiction, and is based squarely on procedural theory.[27]

If we adopt the substantive nature of a maritime lien, it is, by definition, a secured claim.[28] It is secured from the moment the maritime lien attaches to the vessel, that is, when certain services are rendered to the ship or certain damages are done by the ship.[29] As explained by Fry LJ in the Court of Appeal in *The Heinrich Bjorn*, 'a maritime lien arises the moment the event occurs which creates it; the proceeding in rem which perfects the inchoate right relates back to the period when it first attached'.[30] Therefore, it does not matter when the maritime lien holder takes action to enforce its claim because, once the maritime lien is perfected, either by the initiation of a proceeding in rem,[31] or by the subsequent breach,[32] it relates back to the time when it first attached.[33]

[22] ibid 235; see also DC Jackson, *Enforcement of Maritime Claims*, 4th edn (Routledge, 2005) [18.21].

[23] *The Ship Sam Hawk v Reiter Petroleum Inc* [2016] FCAFC 26; but see Hafeez-Baig (n 4) 115.

[24] *The Ocean Jade* [1991] SGHC 33.

[25] *The Betty Ott v General Bills Ltd* [1992] 1 NZLR 655.

[26] See eg S Rares, 'Maritime Liens, Renvoi and Conflicts of Law' [2014] *Lloyd's Maritime and Commercial Law Quarterly* 183; S Derrington and J Turner, *The Law and Practice of Admiralty Matters*, 2nd edn (Oxford University Press, 2016) ch 2.

[27] Myburgh, 'Richard Cooper Memorial Lecture Admiralty Law' (n 20) 32.

[28] *The Bold Buccleugh* (n 16) 284–85.

[29] Force (n 15) 173.

[30] *The Heinrich Bjorn* (n 17) 45.

[31] Under the Anglo-common law countries' substantive view of maritime liens, maritime liens are perfected upon the initiation of proceedings in rem. See Myburgh, 'Richard Cooper Memorial Lecture Admiralty Law' (n 20) 30; *The Bold Buccleugh* (n 16) 284–85.

[32] Under the US view, a maritime lien attaches at the commencement of the undertaking and any subsequent breach perfecting the lien relates back to that time: *Bank One Louisiana NA v Mr Dean MV* 293 F 3d 830, 834 (5th Cir 2002).

[33] An issue may arise, at least in the US, with regard to the trustee's avoiding power to eliminate the secured status of an unperfected lien once a bankruptcy proceeding is commenced. However, it has been argued that trustee's avoiding power did not apply to a maritime lien on the ground that the 'strong-arm power' applied only to judicial liens or liens obtained through a legal or equitable proceeding. Although maritime liens are enforced by judicial proceedings, they arise automatically upon the claim attached. See D Skeen, 'Liens and Liquidation: Preference, Strong Arm Clause, Fraudulent Transfers, Equitable Subordination, Priorities and Other Limitation on Liens Claims' (1984) 59 *Tulane Law Review* 1401, 1405; *In re North Atlantic & Gulf Steamship Co* 204 F Supp 899 (SD New York 1962); *In re H&S Transport Co* 42 BR 164, 167 (Bankr MD Tennessee 1984).

B. Relief from the Automatic Stay

Since maritime liens are secured claims under the substantive view of maritime liens, maritime lien holders should be permitted to obtain leave from the insolvency proceeding by arguing the exception under Article 20(2) of the Model Law, or, in the alternative, permitted to obtain security posted by the insolvent debtor as a substitute protection for their liens.

Most domestically enacted versions of Article 20(2) of the Model Law limit the scope and effect of the automatic stay to the same situation as if the case arose under the local insolvency proceeding that the foreign insolvency proceeding most closely resembles.[34] In other words, the treatment of secured creditors depends on the domestic automatic stay provisions of each enacting state. For example, as discussed in previous chapters, the Corporations Act 2001 (Cth) in Australia provides that secured claimants are allowed to proceed against debtors' assets notwithstanding pending or subsequent liquidation proceedings. Conversely, in reorganisation proceedings, they are subject to the moratoriums and suspended from commencing or continuing any enforcement action against the debtor, unless they have obtained the consent of the administrator or the relief of the court.[35] In the UK and Singapore, in direct contrast to the provisions in the Australian Companies Act 2001 (Cth), no explicit provision is provided to exempt secured creditors from the moratoriums in liquidation proceedings. Nevertheless, it is well settled in the common law of both the UK and Singapore that secured creditors are not affected by the moratoriums in liquidation proceedings. Although secured creditors must ask for the court's permission to leave the moratoriums, it is almost certain that this relief will be granted. As for reorganisation proceedings, no creditors, including secured creditors, are allowed to proceed with their claims against the company without first obtaining the consent of the administrator or relief from the court.[36] On the contrary, the US has a relatively strong and broad automatic stay provision, where secured creditors would be stayed from obtaining possession or exercising control over the estate in either liquidation or reorganisation proceedings.[37] The relief for claimants to leave the stay is hard to obtain. However, the stay does not apply to claims involving seafarer wages or pre-petition maintenance and cure since these claims are not regarded as 'core proceedings' for a bankruptcy proceeding to adjudicate on.[38]

[34] See eg Cross-Border Insolvency Regulations 2006, Sch 1, Art 20(2); Cross-Border Insolvency Act 2008 (Cth), Sch 1, Art 20(2); 11 USC §§ 362, 1520(a)(1); Companies Act 2017 (Singapore), Sch 10, Art 20(2).

[35] See Cross-Border Insolvency Act 2008 (Cth), s 16; Corporations Act 2001(Cth), ss 440B, 440D, 440F, 440G, 471B, 471C; *Yu* (n 6) [40].

[36] See Cross-Border Insolvency Regulations 2006, Art 20(2); Insolvency Act 1986, ss 183(1), 2(a); Sch B1; *The Sanko Mineral* (n 6); Companies Act 2017 (Singapore), sch 10, Art 20(2); ss 262(3), 227D, 299(2); *Re Taisoo Suk* [2016] SGHC 195.

[37] See 11 USC § 362; *Evridiki Navigation Inc* (n 7); *In re Hanjin* (n 7)

[38] W Tetley, *Maritime Liens and Claims*, 2nd edn (Éditions Yvon Blais, 1998) 1145. Similarly, in Japan and South Africa, their enacting legislations also make an explicit provision that no exception exists for

Therefore, in certain circumstances, maritime lien holders will need to join the pending or subsequent insolvency proceedings and be subject to any stay order granted by the bankruptcy court unless they obtain consent from the liquidator or leave from the court. In order to obtain leave from the courts, secured creditors have to show that the stay will cause a significant loss to them or that the value of the secured property is decreasing, and that lifting the moratorium would not cause any significant impediment to the purpose of the liquidation or reorganisation proceedings.[39] However, bankruptcy courts, in deciding the issue of the enforcement of maritime liens in the area of cross-border insolvency, often ignore the 'highly mobile' nature of the assets and suspend the enforcement action for maritime liens, which significantly infringes the interests of maritime lien holders.

First, the interests of maritime lien holders can be infringed by a long and complicated bankruptcy proceeding due to the delay of recovery, especially regarding the interests of crew members in recovering their wages. A bankruptcy court usually adjudicates issues at a slower pace than a court acting under admiralty law.[40] The delay imposed by a bankruptcy proceeding is expensive for maritime lien holders.

On the one hand, if enforcement actions are suspended due to a pending or subsequent insolvency proceeding, ships will be stalled in port and be under the custody of marshals, sheriffs or third-party custodian companies that are designated by the court, pending the insolvency proceeding before the bankruptcy court. Ships stranded in the port can accumulate expensive custodial expenses. The longer the ships are detained, the more substantial the custodial expenses will be. The custodial expenses may include wharfage, maintenance, bunkers, suppliers, crew wages and repatriation charges as well as other expenses necessary to preserve the ship. As custodial expenses will usually be paid in priority to all lien holders, either in bankruptcy proceedings or admiralty proceedings, the substantial custody fee will erode the residual value of a ship.[41] For example, in *Coastal Marine Management LLC v Additional Return LLC*, the vessel was abandoned and moored at Boston Harbour for approximately three years.[42] The vessel was sold for US$100,000, while the custodial expenses accrued for wharfage, storage

pre-existing secured creditors. See Act of Recognition of and Assistance for Foreign Insolvency Proceedings, Law No 129 of 2000, ss 27–29 (Japan); Cross-Border Insolvency Act 2000, s 20(2) (South Africa).

[39] See eg E Bailey and H Groves, *Corporate Insolvency: Law and Practice* (LexisNexis, 2014) 520–21; 11 USC § 362(d)(2).

[40] M Alwang, 'Steering The Most Appropriate Course Between Admiralty and Insolvency: Why An International Insolvency Treaty Should Recognise the Primacy of Admiralty Law Over Maritime Assets' (1996) 64 *Fordham Law Review* 2613, 2637–38.

[41] ibid 2638; S Psarellis, 'Bet Your Lien and Roll the Dice: Maritime Liens and Riverboat Gambling' (1993) 6 *University of San Francisco Maritime Law Journal* 49, 71 (where the author shared the experience that expenses incurred while a vessel is in the custody of the court can exceed 40% of the ship's value).

[42] *Coastal Marine Management LLC v Additional Return LLC* CV-No 16-11616-NMG (District of Massachusetts 2018).

and the safekeeping of the vessel amounted to US$282,100. Another example can be found in the case of *In re Qinzhou Guiqin Shipping Group Co*,[43] where *M/V ShengAnda 68* was arrested by the Ningbo Maritime Court of the PRC before the debtor filed a reorganisation petition in the Qinzhou Intermediate Court of the PRC (Bankruptcy Court). The enforcement action against the vessel was suspended, and the vessel was kept by a third-party custodian company appointed by the Maritime Court for more than two years, pending negotiations between relevant parties and the bankruptcy court's order to approve the reorganisation plan. The vessel was eventually sold for approximately US$ 890,000 but the custody expenses that arose because of the delay imposed by the bankruptcy proceeding amounted to more than US$ 300,000.[44] Therefore, as has been mentioned above, the custody expenses incurred can erode a substantial part of the bankruptcy estate, which will harm not only the interest of maritime lien holders but also all other creditors. In contrast, admiralty proceedings can quickly sell vessels and distribute the proceeds of judicial sales to maritime creditors. In the absence of the interference of a bankruptcy court, maritime lien holders can immediately arrest the relevant vessels under admiralty law and promptly realise their claims.[45]

On the other hand, if a ship has not been arrested before the commencement of insolvency proceedings, usually in the circumstance of a reorganisation proceeding, and a stay order has been imposed to prevent further enforcement action against the ship, the vessel will continue to operate. Allowing ships to continue operating will generate certain amount of freight revenue, which will raise the value of a bankruptcy estate. However, despite the improvement in modern navigational technology and skill, ships are still exposed to high risks during navigation due to the inherent nature of the perils of the sea. These perils, which include stranding, sinking, collision, piracy, explosion, heavy waves, and high winds, are much higher and more incalculable than the risks faced by land-based assets.[46] Therefore ships, as the secured assets of maritime lien holders, are easily lost or depreciate in value in the course of an operation. Even worse, the rights of maritime liens on the vessel will be extinguished if the relevant vessel itself is destroyed.[47] Furthermore, bad-faith insolvent shipowners may even use the reorganisation proceeding as a delaying tactic by hiding the vessel in order to evade the repayment of debts. Another unique problem faced by maritime lien holders, mainly in the US, is that, in the circumstance where the proceeds of the judicial sale of the vessel are insufficient to satisfy all maritime lien claims, later liens in the same class will take

[43] [2014] Yong Ningbo Maritime Ct First No 63; [2015] Zhe Higher Ct Maritime Final No 169; [2015] Zhe Higher Court Execution No 45.

[44] ibid.

[45] Alwang (n 40) 2623.

[46] E Gold, *Maritime Transport: The Evolution of International Marine Policy and Law* (Lexington Books, 1981) 118–19.

[47] J Browne, 'The Extinction of Maritime Liens' [2003] *Lloyd's Maritime and Commercial Law Quarterly* 361, 365; *The Sydney Cove* (1815) 165 ER 1399; see also *The Neptune* (1824) 166 ER 81.

priority over earlier liens in the process of distribution; this is known as the 'inverse order' rule.[48] The rationale for this rule is that the latest service performed is held to contribute not only to the preservation of the vessel, but also to keeping the vessel on its course as an instrument of navigation and commerce.[49] Consequently, vessels that continue to operate during a reorganisation proceeding may continue to accumulate maritime liens. If the reorganisation proceeding has later been terminated and converted to a liquidation proceeding, the later liens may take priority over the pre-petition maritime lien holders who could have been entitled to adequate protection from the bankruptcy court.[50] Thus, unless the interests of pre-petition maritime lien holders are protected, such as by being provided with security, their enforcement actions against the ship should be allowed to proceed, regardless of the subsequent insolvency proceeding.

Furthermore, there is a tendency for a ship's value to depreciate after the shipping company goes bankrupt. The shipping market is more vulnerable because of the high leverage ratio and the special character of shipping finance.[51] Shipping companies usually go bankrupt because of general declines in the market.[52] A depressed market will also cause a decline in the value of the ship since there are few buyers.[53] During the trough cycle, the market value of a second-hand ship tends to reach the scrap price.[54] Thus, during a recession in the shipping trade, the value of the vessel may be even lower than the total amount of maritime lien claims which, thereby, to some extent, renders some of the maritime lien holders under-secured.[55]

In addition, maritime courts will provide purchasers with clean title against the whole world, free from all existing liens, charges and other maritime claims,

[48] *The Lyrma No 2* [1978] 2 Lloyd's Rep 30; *The Selina* (1842) 2 NC 18; Notes, 'Priorities of Maritime Liens' (1956) 69 *Harvard Law Review* 525; G Price, 'The Priority of Maritime Liens' (1942) 24 *Journal of Comparative Legislation and International Law* 38. In the US, this inverse order, however, has certain exceptions. For example, courts might decide not to apply the inverse order rule to wage claims. See Force (n 15) 183. However, in the UK, the reverse order rule only applies to maritime liens for salvage claims; other maritime liens in the same category rank pari passu. *The Stream Fisher* [1927] P 73; *The Mons* [1932] P 109; *The Ruta* [2000] 1 WLR 2068. See also *The Posidon* [2017] SGHC 138.

[49] Price (n 48).

[50] G Rutherglen, 'Admiralty and Bankruptcy Revisited: Effects of the Bankruptcy Reform Act of 1978' (1991) 65 *Tulane Law Review* 503, 527.

[51] 'Leverage … is a measure of the percentage of a company's capital provided by debt. Highly leverage companies are perceived to be vulnerable to cash flow volatility or raised interest rates. … The shipping industry has the advantage of an established secondary market for all but the most specialised vessels and advantage of an established secondary market for all but the most specialised vessel and adjustment for fleet market value is commonly added. … In a market downturn, however, it creates a risk of dramatic increases in leverage and a breach that may be difficult to remedy' (quoting from Stephenson Harwood, *Shipping Finance*, 3rd edn (Euromoney Institutional Investor, 2006) 84).

[52] Rutherglen, 'Admiralty and Bankruptcy Revisited' (n 50) 525.

[53] ibid 525–26; M Vaughn, 'Maritime Evaluation of Commercial Ships', www.maritimelawcenter.com/html/market_evaluation.html accessed 4 June 2020; M Stopford, *Maritime Economics*, 3rd edn (Routledge, 2009) 98.

[54] Stopford (n 53) 98.

[55] ibid 266.

and reduce the risk of the refusal of foreign courts to recognise the legal effect of a judicial sale; it is, at the very least, controversial whether judicial sales of vessels by bankruptcy courts will discharge all the existing liens, especially maritime liens.[56] In addition, the clean title obtained by judicial sale by maritime courts will very likely increase the sale price of vessels, which will, in turn, increase the asset pool for the benefit of all creditors.[57]

Finally, if leave is granted by a court, there is no substantially greater loss caused to other creditors. When granting leave, courts need to balance the interests of secured creditors with other creditors in order to ensure that the enforcement of maritime claims does not affect the interests of other creditors in the insolvency proceeding.[58] In the case of liquidation proceedings, since bankruptcy courts will most probably treat maritime lien holders as secured creditors and give them priority over other unsecured creditors in the distribution process, allowing them to proceed earlier outside of liquidation proceedings would not materially impede the purpose of the liquidation proceeding and the interests of other creditors. In the case of reorganisation proceedings, even if the vessel is sold first to satisfy the claims of maritime lien holders, any remaining proceeds can be returned back to the bankruptcy court.[59] Furthermore, since maritime liens are much more preferential rights than other land-based rights and statutory rights of action in rem, in most Commonwealth countries they are subject to strict construction and only a small number of claims can give rise to maritime liens.[60] Thus, when granting the leave of the court, the interests of most other creditors of the insolvent debtor will not be materially impeded, and, in the meantime, the interests of maritime lien holders will also be protected; to do otherwise would significantly infringe their interests.

Allowing a maritime lien holder to proceed with its enforcement action will not contradict the modified universalism regime imposed by the Model Law. As discussed in previous chapters, although the Model Law aims to achieve legal harmonisation and proposes a modified universalism approach in the area of cross-border insolvency, the drafters of the Model Law chose to take a form of 'soft law' rather than one in the form of a binding international treaty. In making this choice the drafters of the Model Law have attempted to provide a more relaxed regime that will attract more states to adopt it.[61] However, the fundamental core

[56] L Bleyen, *Judicial Sales of Ships* (Springer, 2016) 153; P Myburgh, 'Satisfactory for Its Own Purposes: Private Direct Arrangements and Judicial Vessel Sales' (2016) 22 *Journal of International Maritime Law* 355–69; S Rares, 'Admiralty Law the Flying Dutchman of Cross-Border Insolvency' [2009] *Federal Judicial Scholarship* 22. However, it is accepted, in the US, that if a vessel is sold by a bankruptcy court in an insolvency proceeding, the vessel is sold with a clean title as well. See *In re Millenium Seacarriers Inc* 419 F 3d 83, 95 (2d Cir 2005).

[57] Bleyen (n 56) 153.

[58] See eg *Lazari GP Ltd v Jervis* [2012] EWHC 1466 (Ch).

[59] Alwang (n 40) 2645.

[60] See eg *The Bold Buccleugh* (n 16).

[61] I Mevorach, 'A Fresh View on the Hard/Soft Law Divide: Implications for International Insolvency of Enterprise Group' (2019) 40 *Michigan Journal of International Law* 505, 508.

of the regime of insolvency lies in the distribution of assets where 'different jurisdictions may assign different weights and values to different considerations in the assets distribution process dependent upon their view as to social and economic policy'.[62] For example, the economic interdependencies between states may affect the choice made by the enacting states when deciding whether to adopt a modified universalism proposed by the Model Law, or to what extent the local courts should transfer their jurisdiction over assets located in their territory to foreign courts where the main insolvency proceedings are located.[63] Thus, even states that choose to implement the Model Law may implement it differently into their enacting legislation.[64] In fact, the Model Law deliberately left the scope and effects of the automatic stay orders to enacting countries. Thus, in maritime lien claims, the leave of the court granted by the *forum arresti* will not contradict the modified universalism regime imposed by the Model Law as it is, in fact, consistent with the regime of the Model Law.

As discussed above, the interest of maritime lien holders can be significantly infringed by the intervention of bankruptcy proceedings; this is due to the delay in the recovery of a ship and the value of the ship tending to decrease upon the commencement of bankruptcy proceedings. Therefore, in my view, the leave of the court should be granted to maritime lien holders in order to allow them to proceed to earlier and more expeditious enforcement action.

C. In Rem Claims and the Personification Doctrine

In maritime law, the rationale of the long-existing personification doctrine lies in the legal fiction that a ship has 'rights and obligations separate from those of its owner'.[65] As discussed above, in my view, maritime liens are substantive property rights and are based on the true personification doctrine.[66] Accordingly, an in rem action to enforce a maritime lien is a separate and distinct action from an in personam action. Put differently, an in rem action to enforce a maritime lien is against the personified vessel, not the insolvent debtor, and should be allowed to proceed regardless of any pending or subsequent insolvency proceeding, either in liquidation or reorganisation proceedings.

Whether this argument can be upheld depends upon the court's attitude toward the doctrine of personification. The doctrine of personification is fundamental to in rem claims and has been controversial; it therefore remains under attack in

[62] G McCormack, 'COMI and comity in UK and US insolvency Law' [2012] *LQR* 128, 158.

[63] See SM Franken, 'Cross-Border Insolvency Law: A Comparative Institutional Analysis' (2014) 34 *Oxford Journal of Legal Studies* 97 (where the author discusses how economic interdependencies between states will affect the choices of enacting states when adopting the Model Law).

[64] McCormack (n 662) 158.

[65] Davies, 'In Defense of Popular Virtues' (n 18) 338.

[66] See Tsimplis (n 18) 501; Jackson (n 22) Ch 17.

modern times.[67] The doctrine has its supporters[68] and opponents.[69] Justifications that are commonly raised to support the doctrine of personification include: the historical distinction of admiralty actions; the unique character of maritime commerce; the exceptional mobile nature of the asset; and the peculiar risks and perils faced by maritime ventures.[70] However, these justifications have been faced with challenges and have been held to be no longer logical due to the development of technology since the twentieth century and the improvements in litigation practices.[71] Nevertheless, it has been argued that the justifications for this doctrine still lie in the way that vessels are owned and operated, and that the joint venture vehicle is the ship itself.[72]

In my view, the doctrine of personification arguably exists in respect of maritime lien claims in the sense that an action to enforce a maritime lien claim is against the vessel itself rather than against the owner.[73] The US courts have traditionally adopted a true personification doctrine and generally regard in personam and in rem actions as two distinct types of proceedings.[74] The vessel can be held liable even though the owner has no in personam liability.[75] With few exceptions, the doctrine of personification is still upheld by the US courts with regard to maritime lien claims.[76]

In Commonwealth jurisdictions, the procedural theory was first articulated by Jeune J in *The Dictator* in the late nineteenth century.[77] Jeune J held that:

> if the owners do not appear, the action only enforces the lien on the res, but that, when they do, the action in rem … is also a means of enforcing against the appearing owners, if they could have been made personally liable in the Admiralty Court.[78]

Subsequently, following the decision of the House of Lords in *The Indian Grace (No 2)*, English courts applied the 'procedural theory' in a particularly radical way. In *The Indian Grace (No 2)*, the House of Lords held that an in rem action was merely a procedural tool for forcing the appearance of the shipowner and, in substance, 'an action in rem is equally an action in personam from its inception'.[79]

[67] Myburgh, 'Richard Cooper Memorial Lecture Admiralty Law' (n 20) 28.

[68] See eg Davies, 'In Defense of Unpopular Virtues' (n 18) 345; *The China* (n 18); *Tucker v Alexandroff* (n 18).

[69] See eg *The Dictator* (n 20), *The Indian Grace (No 2)* (n 20); Myburgh, 'Richard Cooper Memorial Lecture Admiralty Law' (n 20); G Gilmore and C Black, *The Law of Admiralty*, 2nd edn (Foundation Press, 1975) 616.

[70] Myburgh, 'Richard Cooper Memorial Lecture Admiralty Law' (n 20) 25.

[71] G Rutherglen, 'The Contemporary Justification for Maritime Arrest and Attachment' (1989) 30 *William & Mary Law Review* 541.

[72] Davies, 'In Defense of Unpopular Virtues' (n 18) 362–66.

[73] *The Bold Buccleugh* (n 16).

[74] *The China* (n 18); *Tucker* (n 18).

[75] *The China* (n 18); Note, 'Personification of Vessels' (1964) 77 *Harvard Law Review* 1122, 1125.

[76] But see *Hapag-Lloyd Aktiengesellschaft v US Oil Trading LLC* 814 F 3d 146 (2d Cir 2016).

[77] *The Dictator* (n 20).

[78] ibid 320–21.

[79] *Indian Grace (No 2)* (n 17); Myburgh (n 20) 31.

This decision has been criticised by many commentators.[80] It is important to note that in *The Indian Grace (No 2)*, what the court considered to be a claim regarding a statutory right of action in rem (a cargo damage claim), was not a true in rem claim. Thus, I would argue that the radical procedural theory adopted in *The Indian Grace (No 2)* only applies to statutory rights of action in rem and not to maritime liens. In other words, actions to enforce maritime liens are actions against the relevant vessels only, and only to the extent of the value of the vessels, in the sense that the personified vessels are defendants rather than insolvent debtors.[81]

Furthermore, *The Indian Grace (No 2)* has subsequently been rejected by the Full Court of the Federal Court of Australia in *Comandate Marine Corp v Pan Australia Shipping Pty Ltd*.[82] In the area of cross-border insolvency, the Federal Court of Australia in *Yu v STX Pan Ocean Co Ltd* upheld the doctrine of personification and allowed the enforcement of a maritime lien to proceed on the ground that the claim was actually against the vessel itself rather than merely an in personam right against the vessel owner.[83] Similarly, *The Indian Grace (No 2)* has also been distinguished by the Court of Appeal of Singapore in *Kuo Fen Ching and Another v Dauphin Offshore Engineering & Trading Pte Ltd*, where the Singapore Court of Appeal allowed the in rem action to proceed, despite the dissolution of the shipowner, on the grounds that the admiralty action in rem in the present case was an action against the vessel itself rather than an action against the shipowner.[84] Similarly, in *Precious Shipping Public Co Ltd v OW Bunker Far East*, the High Court of Singapore reiterated its attitude towards admiralty in rem actions, namely, that actions in rem and actions in personam are two separate claims.[85]

As above, the personification doctrine is still applicable to maritime liens in the sense that in rem actions to enforce maritime liens are against the 'offending' vessels only; these are separate and distinct from in personam actions against insolvent debtors. Therefore, in light of the secured status of maritime lien holders and the significant damage caused by bankruptcy proceedings to the delay of its claims and the personification doctrine of maritime liens, maritime lien holders should be allowed to proceed earlier and use expeditious enforcement action to protect themselves, regardless of the insolvency proceedings. The proceeds of a judicial sale of the vessel will first satisfy the claims of maritime lien holders; thereafter, any remaining proceeds would be returned back to the FMP court.

[80] See eg N Teare, 'The Admiralty Action in Rem and the House of Lords' [1998] *Lloyd's Maritime and Commercial Law Quarterly* 33; BJ Davenport, 'End of an Old Admiralty Belief' (1998) 11 *LQR* 169; Tsimplis (n 18) 501–502.

[81] See *The Bold Buccleugh* (n 16); Tsimplis (n 18) 503; Meeson and Kimbell (n 18) 94.

[82] *Comandate Marine Corp v Pan Australia Shipping Pty Ltd* [2006] FCAFC 192.

[83] *Yu* (n 6) 40–41; Davies, 'Cross-Border Insolvency and Admiralty' (n 4) 112.

[84] *Kuo Fen Ching and Another v Dauphin Offshore Engineering & Trading Pte Ltd* [1999] SGCA 95.

[85] *Precious Shipping Public Co Ltd v OW Bunker Far East* [2015] SGHC 187.

II. Statutory Rights of Action in Rem

In most Commonwealth jurisdictions, in addition to maritime liens, there is another category of maritime claim that involves a wide variety of claims; these are known as statutory rights of action in rem. Since there is no such category of maritime claim available in the US, the discussion in this section only applies to Commonwealth jurisdictions. In my view, an admiralty proceeding to enforce claims for statutory rights of action in rem does not always prevail over the pending or subsequent insolvency proceeding, but should be based on a case-by-case analysis. The treatment of claims for statutory rights of action in rem should depend upon various factors, including: the type of pending or subsequent insolvency proceedings; the arresting country's enacting legislation of the Model Law; the scope and effect of the stay provisions that are provided in the arresting country's local insolvency law; and the court's attitude towards in rem actions.

A. Secured Status

As discussed above, claims involving statutory rights of action in rem are based upon procedural theory, where the property interests are not vested in the vessel until a claimant chooses to exercise that right by virtue of the procedure of the action in rem. That is to say, statutory rights of action in rem are not secured claims when they originally arise. Nevertheless, in most cases, they become secured claims once they are perfected by the issuing of a writ in rem.[86]

B. Time Point

In order to obtain secured status in the area of cross-border insolvency a timing issue may arise with regard to claims involving a statutory right in rem, namely, whether the writ of arrest has been issued: (1) before the foreign proceeding was commenced in the home country (commencement point); or (2) before the assisting country recognised the foreign proceeding (recognition point).

Although this issue has not yet been fully considered by courts across the world, courts tend to favour the date of recognition as being the relevant time point.[87] For example, in *Kim v Daebo International Shipping Co Ltd*, the Australian

[86] Courts in England, Australia and Singapore have held that a statutory right of action in rem becomes a secured claim upon the issue of a writ in rem; see eg *In re Aro* (n 17); *Danny Morris & Another v The Ship Kiama* [1998] FCA 256; *Kuo Fen Ching* (n 84); *cf* Canadian courts, on the other hand, which have held that a statutory right in rem remains unsecured even when the writ in rem is issued and the vessel is arrested: see *The Miss Donna* [1978] 1 FC 379 [22].

[87] See eg M Brown, 'Overview of the English Framework for Cross-Border Insolvency' (March 2012), www.mayerbrown.com/public_docs/Overview_English_Legal_Framework.pdf accessed 4 June 2020; Soars (n 4) [106.3]; *Kim v Daebo International Shipping Co Ltd* [2015] FCA 684 [14].

court suggested that the date of commencement of the foreign proceedings was not relevant.[88] Similarly, the Singapore Court of Appeal in *Beluga Chartering GmbH (in liquidation) v Beluga Projects (Singapore) Pte Ltd* held that it is recognised that assisting courts are not automatically bound by a foreign insolvency order.[89] Only when the assisting court has recognised the foreign insolvency proceeding might it choose to render assistance to the foreign representative.[90] Thus, it is likely that, in order for the holder of a statutory right of action in rem to obtain the benefits of secured status, the writ of arrest should be issued before the recognition of the foreign proceeding under the Model Law.

C. Factors Needing to be Considered

Since 'necessaries claims' (such as claims for repair, towage, stevedore, pilotage and other supplies furnished to a vessel) seem to be those that appear most frequently in practice, the following section uses 'necessaries' as an example for discussion purposes.[91] In this example, an admiralty proceeding is brought by a bunker supplier in Country A (the arresting country), while an insolvency proceeding is filed in Country B (the home country). Country A has enacted the Model Law and recognises Country B's proceeding as a foreign main proceeding. Whether the bunker supplier can proceed to arrest the vessel regardless of Country B's insolvency proceeding depends on many considerations, including:

(1) Is the pending or subsequent insolvency proceeding in Country B a liquidation or reorganisation proceeding?
(2) Is the 'necessaries claim' classified as a claim involving a statutory right in rem in Country A?
(3) If the 'necessaries claim' is classified as a claim involving a statutory right in rem in Country A, is the writ of arrest issued before the recognition of the foreign main proceeding? In other words, is the 'necessaries claim' secured in Country A before Country B's proceeding is recognised as a foreign main proceeding?
(4) Does Country A's enacting legislation of the Model Law preserve any exception for an in rem action or refer back to Country A's local insolvency law?
(5) Does Country A's most closely resembled local insolvency proceeding provide any exception for secured creditors to lift the stay order?
(6) Does Country A, the arresting country, recognise the true personification doctrine or merely the 'procedure theory'?

[88] *Daebo* (n 87) [14].
[89] *Beluga Chartering GmbH (in liquidation) v Beluga Projects (Singapore) Ptd Ltd (in liqudation)* [2014] SGCA 14.
[90] UNCITRAL Model Law, Arts 19, 20, 21.
[91] In most Commonwealth countries, a necessaries claim will give rise to a statutory right in rem. However, in Canada, creditors have maritime liens against foreign vessels for claims that arise in respect of necessaries supplied to the foreign vessels. See Marine Liability Act 2001, s 139.

In recent case law many countries have already followed this pattern in their analysis of cross-border insolvency cases in a maritime context. In the UK, Australia and Singapore, their enacting legislation of the Model Law limits the scope and effects of the automatic stay to the extent that the situation is the same as if the case had arisen under local insolvency law. In addition, in these countries, claims by bunker suppliers will give rise to statutory rights of action in rem instead of maritime liens.[92] Thus, following the above-suggested pattern of analysis, the suggested outcome for these countries will be whether or not the bunker supplier could obtain secured status before the recognition of a foreign main proceeding; if it can, it would be permitted to proceed to enforce its claim notwithstanding any pending or subsequent liquidation proceedings. However, if the proceeding is a reorganisation proceeding, even if its claim is secured before the recognition of a foreign main proceeding, it has to remain subject to the stay order unless it obtains the consent of the administrator or relief from the court.[93] If, after the above analysis, the bunker supplier is not allowed to proceed with its admiralty claim in Country A, then it has to participate in the main insolvency proceeding in Country B.

D. Rationale

There are three main reasons why statutory rights of action in rem should be treated differently from maritime liens and why there is no need to provide an explicit exception for them to be unaffected by the insolvency proceeding.

First, there are obvious differences between a statutory right in rem that is provided by statutes conferring jurisdiction on the court, and a maritime lien that has its origins in the inherent jurisdiction of the admiralty court and general maritime law.[94] For example: a statutory right in rem only arises from the time that the writ of arrest is issued,[95] whereas under the majority view of commentators and this book, a maritime lien arises from the moment the claim arises;[96] a statutory right in rem does not travel with the ship, whereas a maritime lien will not be extinguished even if the shipowner has changed; and a statutory right in rem ranks after a traditional maritime lien, whereas a maritime lien has higher priority in the distribution process. To some extent, a statutory right in rem has always received less protection than a traditional maritime lien. Accordingly, compared with a maritime lien, a statutory right of action in rem is less infringed by the intervention of an insolvency proceeding, especially when the writ in rem is issued after the commencement of the insolvency proceeding.

[92] See Ch 5 for further discussion.

[93] See eg *Hanjin Shipping* (n 6); *The Sanko Mineral* (n 6) [5]; *Re Taisoo Suk* (n 36) [35]; see Chs 7, 8, 10 for further discussion.

[94] W Tetley, *International Maritime and Admiralty Law* (Éditions Yvon Blais, 2002) 482; Tsimplis (n 18) 480.

[95] Courts in the UK hold this view; see eg *In Re Aro* (n 17).

[96] See nn 26–33 and the accompanying text.

Second, when balancing the interests of statutory rights of action in rem with other claims, the worldwide threat of vessel arrest tends to obstruct a successful insolvency proceeding, especially in an international shipping reorganisation, and may affect the interests of other creditors in the insolvency proceeding.[97] A reorganisation is more likely to succeed if a single forum can protect all of a debtor's assets, as it could avoid the cost of duplicative proceedings. Moreover, a natural economic unit would be sold at a higher price than a piecemeal dismemberment of the company, which, in turn, greatly increases the return to creditors.[98] Thus, in order to achieve a successful reorganisation, the company is often required to use any assets necessary for its ongoing operations, free from financial pressures.[99] The most important and valuable assets of a shipping company are its vessels. Ships travel internationally and when creditors learn that a company has been, or is about to be, subjected to an insolvency proceeding, they will try their best to locate and arrest the debtor's vessels in order to realise their claims outside the insolvency proceeding. As a result, it would be difficult to keep vessels operating and thereby maintain the debtor's business. In particular, due to the wide range of statutory rights of action in rem and the high frequency of this kind of claim occurring in practice, if these claims were allowed to prevail over bankruptcy each time, a successful restructuring would be even more difficult to achieve and the interests of other creditors in the insolvency proceeding would be affected.

Third, in Commonwealth jurisdictions, unlike a maritime lien, a statutory right of action in rem is not regarded as substantive security against the vessel unless the claimant chooses to exercise the right by commencing an action in rem; it is seen as a procedural tool for forcing the appearance of the elusive shipowner to facilitate the collection of debts.[100] Once the shipowner enters an appearance to defend its ship, the owner is deemed to have submitted to the in personam jurisdiction and is subject to full personal liability.[101] Therefore, the personification argument in support of a maritime lien claim is not strongly in favour of a claim for a statutory right in rem.

Therefore, in my view, claims for statutory rights of action in rem should not invariably prevail over bankruptcy proceedings, but be subject to the type of pending or subsequent insolvency proceedings, the arresting country's legislation that enacts the Model Law, as well as the scope and effect of the stay provisions that

[97] Rutherglen, 'Admiralty and Bankruptcy Revisited' (n 50) 532.

[98] Alwang (n 40) 2643; see also J Westbrook, 'Theory and Pragmatism in Global Insolvencies: Choice of Law and Choice of Forum' (1991) 65 *American Bankruptcy Law Journal* 457, 461, 465.

[99] Alwang (n 40) 2643.

[100] *The Indian Grace (No 2)* (n 20); *The Halcyon Isle* (n 20).

[101] See eg *The Dictator* (n 20); *The Indian Grace (No 2)* (n 20); *Comandate Marine* (n 82); *Kuo Fen Ching* (n 84); *Raukuna Moana Fisheries Ltd v The Ship Irina Zharkikh* [2001] 2 NZLR 801. The difference between *The Indian Grace (No 2)* and other cases is that *The Indian Grace (No 2)* held that once the owner entered an appearance, the in rem action ceased to exist. However, several countries distinguished this radical 'procedural' view, and held that when the vessel owner has entered an appearance, the action continues as a parallel in rem action and in personam action; the in rem action did not cease. See eg Myburgh, 'Richard Cooper Memorial Lecture Admiralty Law' (n 20) 29.

are provided in the arresting country's local insolvency law and the court's attitude towards in rem actions. For example, if creditors issue writs of action in rem after the recognition of a foreign main proceeding, it is certain that statutory rights of action in rem are not permitted to proceed. In other circumstances, courts should decide the issue based on the six factors discussed above. Nevertheless, it is worth noting that even if statutory rights of action in rem are stayed to proceed on the merits of their claim by the arresting country, it does not preclude the claimant from commencing an action to preserve its claim under Article 20(3) of the Model Law.[102]

III. Ship Mortgages

In practice, ship mortgagees are less active than other maritime claimants when it comes to the financial distress of shipowners.[103] Commencing court proceedings to enforce a ship mortgage is, for any lender, an option of last resort.[104] Usually, a lender and a borrower will co-operate together to seek a consensual restructuring of the debt.[105] This is typically achieved by an orderly open market sale through a memorandum of agreement (MOA).[106] The purpose of this private arrangement is to reduce expenses and achieve a higher resale value, without involving a protracted and costly court process.[107] As explained by Charles Buss, in practice, the lender will only enforce in three situations:

> The first is where the borrower is refusing to cooperate, hoping either that a market recovery is imminent or that he can pressurise the lender into accepting an unrealistic loan restructuring ….
>
> Second, … the borrower is unable to pay off or secure the claims of other maritime creditors who have already arrested his ship, leaving the mortgagee no option but to finance the ship's release or to accelerate the loan and join in the Admiralty process. …
>
> The third case is where the mortgagee believes that a court sale is required to give the purchaser 'clean' title.[108]

[102] '[Article 20(1a)] … does not affect the right to commence individual actions or proceedings to the extent necessary to preserve a claim against the debtor': UNCITRAL Model Law, Art 20(3); Cross-Border Insolvency Act 2008 (Cth), Sch 1, Art 20(3); Cross-Border Insolvency Regulations 2006, Sch 1, Art 20(4); 11 USC § 1520(b); Companies Act 2017 (Singapore), Sch 10, Art 20(4).

[103] C Buss, 'Ship Mortgagees: Enforcement and Remedies' in B Soyer and A Tettenborn (eds), *Ship Building Sale and Finance* (Informa from Routledge, 2016) 150; see also D Osborne et al, *The Law of Ship Mortgages*, 2nd edn (Informa Law from Routledge, 2016) 378; but see *The Sertao* [2018] EWHC 1013 (Admlty) (where ship mortgagees took action due to the industry downturn).

[104] Buss (n 103) 149.

[105] A debt restructuring is a method used by companies with outstanding debt obligations to alter the terms of the debt agreements, usually lengthening the due date for the principal payment on a debt contract or modifying the frequencies of interest payments. The distressed company can then improve or restore the liquidity so that it can continue its operations.

[106] Buss (n 103) 149.

[107] ibid 149.

[108] ibid 149–50.

Nevertheless, if ship mortgagees do initiate admiralty proceedings before or during the insolvency proceedings, their treatment should not be different from other land-based secured creditors. Ship mortgages provide the lender with security and the lender can enforce its security by repossessing the vessel.[109] It has been well established that ship mortgages, like other land-based mortgages, are secured claims.[110] A ship mortgage becomes secured when the mortgage agreement is concluded and it subsequently perfects upon the registration of the ship mortgage. Thus, the treatment of ship mortgages should be subject to the type of pending or subsequent insolvency proceeding, the arresting country's enacting legislation of the Model Law, as well as in accordance with its local insolvency law.

The determinative considerations may include:

(1) Is the pending or subsequent insolvency proceeding in the foreign main proceeding a liquidation or reorganisation proceeding?;
(2) Is the ship mortgage registered before the recognition of the foreign main proceeding?;
(3) Does the arresting country's enacting legislation preserve any exception for in rem actions or refer back to its local insolvency law?;
(4) Does the most comparable local insolvency proceeding provide an exception for secured creditors to leave the stay order?; and
(5) Does the arresting country recognise the personification argument?

For example, Australia, the UK and Singapore would allow a ship mortgagee to proceed in a liquidation proceeding but stay the enforcement of a mortgage in a reorganisation proceeding, unless consent from the administrator has been given or leave of the court has been obtained.[111] However, in the US the enforcement of a mortgage will usually be stayed by the US court and the arrested ship would be returned to the foreign representative for the benefit of the foreign proceeding.[112] Thus, as for a ship mortgage claim, each enforcement case should be decided on a case-by-case analysis. Further, an issue may arise in a financing lease

[109] ibid 484.

[110] See eg Insolvency Act 1986, s 248(a) defines 'secured creditor', in relation to a company, as 'a creditor of the company who holds in respect of his debt a security over property of the company.' Section 248(b)(i) defines 'security,' in relation to England and Wales, as 'any mortgage, charge, lien or other security'. Mortgagees of a ship or shares in a ship are therefore secured creditors, as are maritime lien holders from the time the claim giving rise to the maritime lien arises (quoting W Tetley, 'Conflicts of Law Between the Bankruptcy Courts in Admiralty: Canada, United Kingdom, United States, and France' (1996) 20 *Tulane Maritime Law Journal* 257, n 69). The Canadian Bankruptcy and Insolvency Act, Art 2 defines 'secured creditor' as 'a person holding a mortgage, hypotec, pledge, charge, lien or privilege on or against the property of the debtor …'; the US Uniform Commercial Code (UCC), Art 9–102(73) defines 'secured party' as '(A) a person in whose favo[u]r a security interest is created or provided for under a security agreement, whether or not any obligation to be secured is outstanding'.

[111] See eg Cross-Border Insolvency Act 2008 (Cth), s 16; Corporations Act 2001 (Cth), ss 471B, 471C; Insolvency Act 1986, s 183(1), (3)(a); Cross-Border Insolvency Regulations 2006, Sch 1, Art 20(2)(a); Companies Act (2017), s 262(3); Companies Act 2017 (Singapore), Sch 10, Art 20(2).

[112] 11 USC §§ 362, 1520.

as to whether the lease is regarded as a 'true lease' or a security agreement, and thereby included in the debtor's estate. This issue is discussed in Chapter 12 below.

IV. Conflict of Laws

A. Conflict of Laws in the Arresting Countries

Since different arresting countries have different scopes of maritime liens, a long-standing question of conflict of laws regarding the availability of maritime liens will inevitably be involved when the *forum arresti* decides whether to grant leave of the court to maritime claims. Put differently, in order to decide the treatment of maritime claims in the *forum arresti*, the court needs to decide whether the claim before the court is a maritime lien claim, a claim for a statutory right of action in rem or a general non-maritime claim. In addition, if the *forum arresti* decides to proceed with the enforcement of a maritime claim, a complex issue regarding the priority between competing maritime claims will also be in the domain of the conflicts rule. In fact, as explained by Martin Davies, there are three layers of conflicts questions that need to be considered in the *forum arresti*:

> First, there is the question of what law governs the plaintiff's underlying claim, the cause of action that is the basis for its claim to redress. Second, there is the question of what law governs access to a maritime lien, the right to bring suit in rem on that claim against a ship or other property. Third, there is the question of what law should govern priority between competing maritime liens, the order in which the claims should be paid if the fund available in court is insufficient to satisfy them all in full.
>
> … In many cases, perhaps most, the answer to the first two questions will be the same, with the result that the law governing the underlying claim also governs the availability of maritime lien. Nevertheless, it is a mistake to think this must necessarily be so.[113]

With regard to the availability of maritime liens, there are usually two types of conflicts approaches that are adopted by Anglo-common law jurisdictions, namely the *lex causae* and the *lex fori*. The US and Canada hold the view that whether a claim would be conferred as a maritime lien is a matter for the law that governs the underlying claim (the *lex causae*), on the ground that maritime liens are regarded as substantive rights for the purpose of a conflict of laws in the US and Canada. In contrast, the UK,[114] Australia,[115] Singapore,[116] New Zealand,[117] South Africa,[118]

[113] M Davies, 'Choice of Law and US Maritime Liens' (2009) 83 *Tulane Law Review* 1435, 1436.

[114] *The Halcyon Isle* (n 20).

[115] See eg *The Sam Hawk* (n 23); *Morlines Maritime Agency Ltd & Others v The Skulptor Vuchetich* [1997] FCA 432.

[116] *The Andres Bonifacio* [1993] SGCA 70; *Precious Shipping* (n 85).

[117] *Ship Betty Ott v General Bills Ltd* [1992] 1 NZLR 655; *ABC Shipbrokers v The Ship Offi Gloria* [1993] 3 NZLR 576 (NZ); *Fournier v Ship Margaret Z* [1999] 3 NZLR 111 (NZ).

[118] *Transol Bunker BV v Motor Vessel Andrico Unity* [1989] 4 SA 325.

Cyprus,[119] Malaysia,[120] China[121] and many other jurisdictions have adopted a *lex fori* rule, namely, that the availability of the maritime liens is regarded as a matter of procedure and should therefore be governed exclusively by the law of the forum.[122]

Nevertheless, regarding the priority to be given to the maritime claims, most Anglo-common law countries agree that it should be governed, for practical reasons, by the *lex fori*.[123] In other words, if the *forum arresti* allows the enforcement of maritime claims outside the insolvency proceeding, and thereafter sells the arrested vessel, the law that governs the priority between competing maritime claims is the *lex fori*.

With regard to the existence of maritime liens, the choices between *lex fori* and *lex causae* have long been discussed by courts and academic scholars. Thus, it would be redundant to deal with this issue any further. Nevertheless, it seems that courts in most jurisdictions have adopted the *lex fori* view, notwithstanding that many scholars and commentators argued for the propriety of *lex causae*.[124] The reasons for commentators criticising the *lex fori* rule are summarised as follows. First, application of the *lex fori* misconstrues the maritime lien as a matter of procedure, which completely ignores its substantive characteristics.[125] Commentators who argue for this position believe that a maritime lien is a substantive property right that originates from general maritime law. It exists before the arrest and survives changes of ownership. Second, adopting a *lex fori* rule promotes forum shopping in the sense that creditors may arrest the ship in the jurisdiction that is most favourable to them. It also increases uncertainty for creditors, especially for necessaries claimants, since whether their liens are available remains unknown at the time when the service is rendered.[126] Academic commentators have argued that the *lex causae* rule is more predictable and consistent with the substantive nature of the maritime lien.

However, it is also obvious why the *lex fori* rule is widely adopted in the majority of jurisdictions. First, the general approach of English law, and the law in its former colonies, regards a maritime lien (actually, a statutory right in rem) as

[119] *Hassanein v The Hellenic Island* [1989] 1 CLR 406.

[120] *Ocean Grain Shipping Pte Ltd v The Dong Nai* [1996] 4 MLJ 454; *The Ocean Jade* [1991] 2 MLJ 386.

[121] Maritime Code of the People's Republic of China, Art 272 (1993); *Mobil Sales and Supply Corp v The Owners of the Ship Pacific Bear* [1979] HKLR 125.

[122] See eg W Tetley, 'Maritime Liens in Conflict of Laws' in J Nafziger and S Symeonides (eds), *Law and Justice in a Multistate World: Essays in Honour of Arthur T von Mehren* (Brill Nijhoff, 2002) 448; M Davies, 'Maritime Liens and Choice of Law' (2018) 42 *Tulane Maritime Law Journal* 269, 270.

[123] Davies 'Maritime Liens and Choice of Law' (n 122).

[124] See eg Rares, 'Maritime Liens, Renvoi and Conflicts of Law' (n 26) 190; Jackson (n 22) [17.57]–[17.58]; Thomas (n 1) [371]–[374]; Lord Collins of Mapesbury and J Harris (eds), *Dicey, Morris and Collins on The Conflict of Laws*, 15th edn (Sweet & Maxwell, 2012) [7-018]; Tetley, 'Maritime Liens in Conflict of Laws' (n 122) 448; Derrington and Turner (n 26) [4.50]–[4.51]; Davies, 'Choice of Law and US Maritime Liens' (n 113) 1436.

[125] See eg Jackson (n 22) [17.57]–[17.58]; Thomas (n 1) [371]–[374]; Tetley, 'Maritime Liens in Conflict of Laws' (n 122) 448; but see *The Halcyon Isle* (n 20).

[126] ibid.

a matter of procedure, rather than substance.[127] Second, a maritime lien arises only by the operation of law and should be strictly construed; this is because it is a much more preferential right than other land-based rights. Thus, courts are reluctant to expand maritime liens by judicial exposition, which means that they tend to adhere to locally recognised maritime liens and defeat the expectations of foreign maritime lien holders, such as US suppliers, who should have been entitled to maritime liens in the US courts.[128] Third, another policy reason for courts to adopt a *lex fori* rule is to protect mortgagees from claims from ship suppliers.[129] As explained by Michael Cohen, courts did so:

> for reasons of economic policy in order to protect banks against impairment of their security. Doing so makes the forum attractive to financial institutions on the theory that they will then be motivated to make credit more available on easier terms, especially for the merchant marine.[130]

B. Conflict of Laws in the Foreign Main Proceeding

i. *The Availability of Lien Status*

As discussed above, I argue that, with regard to claims arising from maritime liens, the *forum arresti* should allow the ship arrest and proceed to sell the vessel. In such circumstances the ship will be sold by the *forum arresti* under admiralty law. On the contrary, with regard to claims arising from statutory rights of action in rem, including ship mortgages, I argue that the treatment of these claims depends on the discretion of the *lex fori arresti* to decide whether the insolvency proceedings prevail over the admiralty action in rem. If the *forum arresti* decides that the insolvency proceeding prevails over the admiralty in rem action and releases the vessel, the ship will be returned to the foreign representative and included in the debtor's asset pool. In the case of a liquidation, the admiralty claimants would need to join the home country's foreign main proceeding (FMP) for the purpose of distribution, whereas in the case of a reorganisation they need to join the FMP for the purpose of a creditors' meeting or approval of a reorganisation plan.[131]

[127] Thomas (n 1) [371]–[374].

[128] Rares, 'Maritime Liens, Renvoi and Conflicts of Law' (n 26) 190; *The Sam Hawk* (n 23) (where Court held that the wider class of maritime liens for necessaires in the US were not likely to be classified as maritime liens under Australian law).

[129] M Marks Cohen, 'In Defense of the Halcyon Isle' [1987] *Lloyd's Maritime and Commercial Law Quarterly* 152.

[130] Conversely, 'a jurisdiction like the United States, which allows maritime liens to proliferate and thereby expands the remedy of arrest, is clearly motivated by Benthamite populism and seeks to promote the maritime interests of many small local suppliers of goods and services over the interests of the relatively few, large and somewhat remote financial institutions holding ship mortgages': Cohen (n 129) 154.

[131] For example, in the US, in case of a liquidation, after the ship is sold, all maritime liens holders against this ship can claim distribution from the sale proceeds. The vessel is sold with clean title. In case of a reorganisation, the debtor is likely to create a separate class for each group of creditors asserting a lien against each vessel. In some countries, the debtor may even further classify the claimants

In these circumstances, the forum in which the foreign main proceeding has been brought under the Model Law (the FMP court) may likewise face a choice-of-law question. All these procedures require the FMP court to determine the classification of involved maritime claims (ie secured or unsecured claims); in other words, whether the FMP court would confer on admiralty claims the same secured creditor status as they may have in the arresting country. In addition, as maritime claimants will inevitably compete with each other and with other non-maritime creditors in order to obtain the most favourable treatment under the proceeding, the FMP court also needs to determine, for the purposes of distribution, the respective ranking and priority of various lien claims.[132] For example, suppose that the FMP court is in Korea, and *forum arresti* A is in the US hearing Claim A that has been filed by necessaries suppliers. In addition, suppose that *forum arresti* B is in the UK and is hearing Claim B filed by necessaries suppliers. Moreover, suppose that the FMP forum also hears a claim, Claim C, filed by necessaries suppliers. If *fora arresti* A and B transfer Claim A and Claim B back to the FMP (Korea) for distribution or reorganisation, together with Claim C,[133] the FMP court in Korea will need to hear three necessaries claims: Claim A (from the US); Claim B (from the UK); and Claim C (from Korea). However, claims by necessaries suppliers can give rise to maritime liens under US law, whereas, under English law, claims by necessaries suppliers only give rise to statutory rights of action in rem. Under Korean law, they are neither maritime liens claims nor claims for statutory rights of action in rem. Accordingly, the Korean court faces the question: which conflict of laws should it apply in determining the status of these three claims in the process of distribution and reorganisation – *lex fori* or *lex causae*?

I would argue that, despite the disparate treatment regarding the nature of a maritime lien, when considering the FMP court's recognition and distribution in the context of maritime cross-border insolvency, the *lex fori* rule appears to be more appropriate and pragmatic.

The rationale for this is that, first, in my view, a maritime lien claim should be allowed to proceed regardless of any pending or subsequent insolvency proceedings. In addition, ship mortgages are undoubtedly considered to be secured claims across the world. Therefore, in my proposed regime, only claims for statutory rights of action in rem may have the possibility of being returned back to the FMP court. When determining whether a lien is attached to a claim and the resulting right of security, the subject that the FMP court will need to determine

against vessels according to the type of lien (true maritime lien or statutory right in rem). See G Seitz, 'Interaction between Admiralty and Bankruptcy Law: Effects of Globalisation and Recurrent Tensions' (2009) 83 *Tulane Law Review* 1339, 1371; S Peck, 'Navigating the Murky Waters of Admiralty and Bankruptcy Law' (2013) 87 *Tulane Law Review* 955, 990.

132 Peck (n 131) 990.

133 Although I argue that maritime lien holders should be permitted to enforce their maritime liens against a vessel, in the insolvency of Hanjin, courts in the US and UK granted stay orders to prevent maritime lien holders from arresting Hanjin's vessels and ordered them to join Hanjin's insolvency proceeding in Korea. See *In re Hanjin* (n 7); *In the Matter of Hanjin Shipping Co Ltd* No CR-2016-005448, in the High Court of Justice, Chancery Division, Companies Court (6 September 2016).

is the claim for statutory rights of action in rem. Although many commentators are critical of the fact that the *lex fori* rule mistreats the in rem right as procedural in nature, it is undeniable that the procedural view of a statutory right in rem has been widely adopted in most Commonwealth jurisdictions.[134] Accordingly, the *lex fori* approach would reinforce the 'procedural' view of a statutory lien in the majority of jurisdictions.[135]

Second, commentators have criticised the *lex fori* rule for inviting forum shopping; this means that creditors will arrest a ship in the jurisdiction that is most favourable to them. There is no such concern under the Model Law regime. If claims for statutory rights of action in rem do not prevail over insolvency law in the arresting country, those claimants will be transferred back to the FMP. Consequently, claimants cannot choose the forum that would be favourable to them. Instead, under the Model Law regime, the FMP is actually designed to prevent forum shopping.[136] In order to become an FMP, the insolvency proceeding has to be opened where the debtor's centre of main interest (COMI) is located. The COMI is, to some extent, predictable and presumed to be the location of the debtor's registered office. Therefore, the application of the *lex fori* rule in the FMP does not involve the same concerns regarding the forum shopping of creditors for which the *forum arresti* has been criticised.

Furthermore, on the one hand, the *lex fori* rule provides a more harmonised and pragmatic solution, which ensures that all claims are subject to the same treatment with regard to their existence and ranking in the FMP. On the other hand, it can also echo the goal of universalism, that is, a single proceeding governing the entire insolvency proceeding under a single controlling law.

The scenario mentioned above illustrates a weakness in the *lex causae* rule regarding the area of maritime cross-border insolvency. This is because it may lead to inconsistent treatment between foreign and domestic creditors of the same kind. If the FMP court applies a *lex causae* rule,[137] Claim A would be recognised as a maritime lien in the same way as it would be conferred by US law. However, Claim B and Claim C would (arguably) be regarded as general unsecured claims.[138] Thus, it may lead to an outrageous result that US suppliers would be classified as secured creditors, while UK and domestic suppliers would be classified as

[134] See Davies, 'Choice of Law and US Maritime Liens' (n 113) 1436; Tetley, 'Maritime Liens in Conflict of Laws' (n 122) 443.

[135] Tetley, 'Maritime Liens in Conflict of Laws' (n 122) 443.

[136] A Ragan, 'COMI Strikes a Discordant Note: Why US Courts Are Not in Complete Harmony Despite Chapter 15 Directives' (2010) 27 *Emory Bankruptcy Development Journal* 117, 132 (citing P Wood, *Principles of International Insolvency* (Sweet & Maxwell, 1995) 291).

[137] Actually, Korea adopts the rule of *lex navis*, which refers to the law of the flag state to decide whether a claim would be conferred a maritime lien. See CW Lee, D Kim, ICLG Shipping Law, Korea, Shipping 2019, iclg.com/practice-areas/shipping-laws-and-regulations/korea, accessed 4 June 2020. In addition, Greece is another civil law country that adopted the *lex navis* for the recognition and ranking of foreign maritime claims; see Greek Code of Private Maritime Law, Art 9. Since this rule has not been adopted in the Commonwealth countries and the US, I will not discuss it in detail.

[138] See Lee and Kim (n 137).

unsecured creditors, despite the fact that they are the same type of claimants in nature. Thus, the FMP court would be confused if, because of the different *lex causae*, several claims were of the same kind but classified into different categories in the same jurisdiction. Accordingly, they would also be given different priority for the purposes of distribution, due to the different classification of the same kind of creditors. This problem has indeed arisen in reality. In *The Ioannis Daskalelis*, US creditors were given greater rights in Canada than domestic creditors.[139] This disadvantage to local creditors may lead to the FMP court being reluctant to adopt the *lex causae* rule.

Undeniably, it may be argued that suppliers of necessaries may have commercial expectations when they engage in business activities.[140] As commercial suppliers of necessaries they should know whether or not they can be conferred with maritime liens. Accordingly, it seems fair for the Korean FMP to apply the *lex causae* rule and treat the suppliers differently due to the Korean supplier of necessaries having no expectation of maritime liens; this is in contrast to the US supplier of necessaries who may have such an expectation. However, I would argue that the lien status that the US supplier of necessaries expects to obtain is not from a Korean court, but from a US admiralty court. In other words, a reasonable commercial expectation of a US supplier of necessaries is to obtain a maritime lien by filing an in rem action against the ship under US admiralty law when the ship arrives at a US port. Conversely, when a US supplier enters into a supply contract with a shipowner, for example, Hanjin Shipping, they do not have an expectation that a Korean bankruptcy court will grant their maritime lien status in a bankruptcy proceeding. Instead, they would know that they do not have maritime liens in a Korean court. Therefore, I would argue that the *lex fori* rule is more appropriate and pragmatic.

ii. Priorities

As discussed above, if a ship is to be sold by the *forum arresti* under admiralty law, the *forum arresti* shall distribute the proceeds to pay off the relevant maritime liens first; after satisfying the maritime court's cost of arrest, custody and sale, the *forum arresti* would transfer the remaining proceeds back to the FMP court for the purpose of distribution or reorganisation. With regard to the priorities of competing maritime liens, it has been widely accepted that they are to be determined by the *lex fori* rule.[141] This rule is both a matter of principle, in the sense that it

[139] *The Ioannis Daskalelis* [1974] SCR 1248; see Cohen (n 129).

[140] *Liverpool & London Steamship Protection & Indemnity Association v Queen of Leman MV* 480 F 2d 1024 (2d Cir 1973).

[141] Rares, 'Maritime Liens, Renvoi and Conflicts of Law' (n 26) 190; Jackson (n 22) [17.57]–[17.58]; Thomas (n 1) [371]–[374]; Collins and Harris (n 124) [7-018], [70041]; Tetley, 'Maritime Liens in Conflict of Laws' (n 122) 448; Derrington and Turner (n 26) [4.50]–[4.51]; Davies, 'Choice of Law and US Maritime Liens' (n 113) 1436.

is ultimately the *forum arresti* that confers the lien status, and a matter of practical necessity, in that it is impossible to apply the *lex causae* rule to determine the priorities.[142] The *forum arresti* has no justifiable reason to choose one country over another.[143] Therefore, it must apply its own ranking to secure greater uniformity.

If a ship is going to be sold by the FMP court, the proceeds of the judicial sale will be distributed among all creditors of the insolvent debtor, whether maritime or non-maritime creditors. Under this circumstance, the priority of these competing claims shall also be governed by the *lex fori* rule on the ground that it is seen as a matter of procedure.[144] In addition, the rule of *lex fori* can echo the fundamental purpose of the Model Law and universalism, namely that the entire insolvency proceeding shall be governed by a single controlling law, including the issue of priority.

V. Summary

In my view, from the above analysis, a maritime lien holder should be allowed to proceed with its enforcement action regardless of any pending or subsequent insolvency proceeding. However, a statutory right of action in rem, or a ship mortgage, should not always prevail over an insolvency proceeding but be based on a case-by-case analysis. Their treatment should depend on the arresting country's scope of maritime liens, its enacting legislation of the Model Law, the scope and effect of the stay provisions that are provided in the arrest country's local insolvency law, and the court's attitude towards in rem actions. With regard to the conflict-of-laws issue that may occur in the FMP court, the *lex fori* rule is a more appropriate and pragmatic rule for the purpose of the FMP court's recognition of lien status and distribution.

[142] Davies, 'Choice of Law and US Maritime Liens' (n 113) 1457.
[143] ibid.
[144] See eg A Ehrenzweig, 'The Lex Fori: Basic Rule in the Conflict of Laws' (1960) 58 *Michigan Law Review* 637; J Carruthers, 'Substance and Procedure in the Conflict of Laws: A Continuing Debate in Relation to Damages' (2004) 53 *The International Comparative Law Quarterly* 691.

12

Policy Reflections on the Determination of the Centre of Main Interest and the Scope of Debtor's Assets

I. Determination of the Centre of Main Interest of Shipping Companies

The concept of the 'centre of main interest' (COMI) is important under the regime of Model Law.[1] The Model Law adopted this concept for the purpose of recognition of foreign insolvency proceedings as foreign 'main' proceedings, in the sense that foreign insolvency proceedings will be recognised as foreign main proceedings if they are initiated in the place where debtors have their COMI.[2] More importantly, upon courts recognising foreign proceedings as foreign main proceedings, they are bound to issue automatic and mandatory stay orders to protect debtors' assets, rights, obligations or liabilities from any individual actions or executions.[3]

As discussed in Chapter 4, Section II, the Model Law does not provide a definition of COMI, but only a rebuttable presumption that the state where the registered office or habitual residence of the debtor is located is presumed to be the COMI of the debtor, unless proved otherwise.[4] The adoption of the concept of the COMI under the regime of the Model Law is designed to provide predictability and certainty to both debtors and creditors. Accordingly, it is envisaged that debtors will be prevented from forum shopping and will be required to commence

[1] UNCITRAL Secretariat, UNCITRAL Model Law on Cross-Border Insolvency Law with Guide to Enactment and Interpretation (United Nations Office at Vienna, 2014) 70.

[2] The concept of COMI was draw from the EU Convention on Insolvency Proceedings (the European Convention). The European Convention subsequently lapsed for lack of ratification by all Member States. See UNCITRAL Secretariat, UNCITRAL Model Law on Cross-Border Insolvency: Judicial Perspective (United Nations Office at Vienna, 2012) 28; G Moss et al, *The EC Regulation on Insolvency Proceedings: A Commentary and Annotated Guide*, 3rd edn (Oxford University Press, 2016) 1.01–1.25; UNCITRAL Model Law on Cross-Border Insolvency (UNCITRAL Model Law), Art 17.

[3] UNCITRAL Model Law, Art 20(1)(a).

[4] UNCITRAL Secretariat, Judicial Perspective (n 2) 28. The reason why the Model Law is silent about the definition of the COMI is that no agreement was reached at the UNCITRAL meetings. See A Berends, 'The UNCITRAL Model Law on Cross-Border Insolvency: A Comprehensive Overview' (1998) 6 *Tulane Journal of International and Comparative Law* 309, 330.

their insolvency proceedings in the jurisdiction with which they have sufficient connections under the Model Law regime.[5]

However, the lack of clarity regarding the definition of the COMI has led to the determination of the COMI being inconclusive and has left courts with the task of formulating the definition of the COMI on their own. Especially in the context of shipping practice, shipping companies usually conduct business in various locations, with ownership separated from ship management.[6] To be more specific, shipping companies are often special purpose companies (SPCs) that have been incorporated in offshore jurisdictions such as Panama, the Cayman Islands, the Marshall Islands or Liberia, where companies do not actually conduct any business relating to the operation of their vessels.[7] Each shipping company often owns a single ship and are known as a 'one-ship' company. Its vessel may be registered in a country that operates open registry,[8] while the operation of the fleet is usually assigned to a ship management company in a different location, such as London, Greece or the US, for the purpose of technical and commercial management.[9] Furthermore, several one-ship companies may be owned by the same shipping group and under the operation of the same ship management company.[10] In other words, these one-ship companies may have common shareholders and ultimately be controlled by the same beneficial owners.[11] Thus, the presumption of the determination of the COMI does not necessarily comport with the realities of maritime commercial practice. The determination of the COMI in the maritime context, therefore, seems difficult because of the common use of offshore companies and one-ship companies in commercial shipping practice.

The interpretation of the COMI under the Model Law was largely influenced by the interpretation of the COMI under Regulation (EU) 2015/848 of the European Parliament and of the Council of 20 May 2015 on Insolvency Proceedings Recast (Recast EU Regulation).[12] However, as mentioned below, the concepts of the

[5] JL Westbrook, 'Locating the Eye of the Financial Storm' (2007) 32 *Brooklyn Journal of International Law* 1019, 1022.

[6] D Osborne et al, *The Law of Ship Mortgage*, 2nd edn (Informa Law from Routledge, 2016) 387.

[7] ibid.

[8] The term 'open registry' is also known as 'flag of convenience', which signifies 'the ability of a shipowner to register a vessel in a particular flag State regardless of his own nationality as a determining factor in the grounds of his qualification or entitlement to do so. These flag States permit registration for reasons of commercial expediency rather than any prerequisite sentimental, patriotic or naturally domiciled allegiance': E Watt and R Coles, *Ship Registration: Law and Practice*, 3rd edn (Informa from Routledge, 2019) 45.

[9] J Ford and C Wilcox, 'Shedding Light on the Dark Side of Maritime Trade – A New Approach for Identifying Countries as Flags of Convenience' (2019) 99 *Marine Policy* 298; GS Egiyan, 'Flag of Convenience or Open Registration of Ships' (1990) 14 *Marine Policy* 106.

[10] See eg Ford and Wilcox (n 9); Egiyan (n 9); *Re Northsea Base Investment Ltd & Others* [2015] EWHC 121 (Ch).

[11] Ford and Wilcox (n 9); Egiyan (n 9).

[12] The Recast EU Regulation came into force on 26 June 2015 and applied to insolvency proceedings opened after 26 June 2017, while insolvency proceedings opened before 26 June 2017 were governed by Council Regulation (EC) No 1346/2000 of 29 May 2000 on Insolvency Proceedings (EC Regulation); see also G McCormack, 'COMI and Comity in UK and US Insolvency Law' [2012] *LQR* 140, 142–43; UNCITRAL Secretariat, Guide to Enactment (n 1) 44.

COMI in these two instruments serve different purposes. Therefore, this section begins with a brief overview of the interpretation of the COMI under the Recast EU Regulation. The section then examines, in detail, the determination of the COMI of shipping companies under the Model Law regime, with a focus on offshore shipping companies.

A. The Recast EU Regulation

The notion of the COMI under the Recast EU Regulation and the Model Law shares the same origin, namely, the Convention on Insolvency Proceedings of the European Union (the European Convention), which did not come into force and subsequently lapsed due to lack of ratification by all Member States.[13] Subsequently, the concept of the COMI was inherited by the European Council Regulation No 1346/2000 of 29 May 2000 on Insolvency Proceedings (the EU Regulation) from the European Convention. However, the EU Regulation remained silent on the definition of the COMI and provided the same presumption of the COMI as the Model Law, namely, the COMI of debtors is presumed to be the place of their registered offices.[14] Finally, the Recast EU Regulation codified the definition of the COMI in Article 3, which provides: 'The centre of main interests shall be the place where the debtor conducts the administration of its interests on a regular basis and which is ascertainable by third parties'.[15]

The definition of the COMI in the Recast EU Regulation is thus premised on three specific elements: (1) the place of the debtor's main interests; (2) where the administration of the debtor is conducted on a regular basis; and (3) the need for predictability for third parties.[16] In determining the COMI of the debtor, the Recast EU Regulation focuses on the pre-insolvency activities of debtors as they appear to a third party.[17] The leading decision with respect to the determination of COMI under the EU Regulation (now Recast EU Regulation) is *In re Eurofood IFSC Ltd*, where the European Court of Justice gave the COMI presumption significant weight.[18] In *Eurofood*, the European Court of Justice held that the COMI presumption in favour of the registered office of the debtor applied even if the company had a parent company with a registered office in a different State. The presumption could only be rebutted 'if … factors which are both objective and ascertainable

[13] UNCITRAL Secretariat, Judicial Perspective (n 2) 32.
[14] EC Regulation, Art 3(1). See Berends (n 4) 330.
[15] Recast EU Regulation, Art 3; EC Regulation, recital 13. (Article 3 of the Recast EU Regulation adopted the same statement in recital 13 of the EC Reguation, which states 'the "centre of main interests" should correspond to the place where the debtor conducts the administration of his interests on a regular basis and is therefore ascertainable by third party'.).
[16] L Athanassiou, *Maritime Cross-Border Insolvency* (Informa Law from Routledge, 2018) 132.
[17] B Rochelle, 'Cross-border Insolvency in the US and UK: Conflicting Approaches to Defining the Locus of a Debtor's Centre of Interests' (2017) 50 *International Law* 391, 397.
[18] Case C-341/04 *In re Eurofood IFSC Ltd* [2006] ECR I–3854.

by third parties enable it to be established that an actual situation exists which is different from that which locating it at that registered office is deemed to reflect'.[19] The European Court of Justice suggested that in the case of a 'letterbox company' that has no business at the place where it is registered, the presumption could be rebutted. However, if the company carried out its business in the place where the registered office is located, 'the mere fact that its economic choices are or can be controlled by a parent company in another Member State is not enough to rebut the presumption laid down by the Regulation'.[20]

In the maritime context, the English High Court in *Re Northsea Base Investment Ltd & Others* was asked to examine the concept of the COMI and its presumption under the EU Regulation.[21] In *Northsea Base Investment*, the administrators of eight affiliated companies sought a declaration that the COMI of each company was England. Six of the eight shipping companies were SPCs and each company owned a single ship in the fleet. The six SPCs were themselves 100 per cent owned by the immediate parent company, Baltic Tanker Holding Ltd, which in turn was itself 100 per cent owned by the ultimate parent company, Northsea Base Investment Ltd (NSBI). All eight companies were incorporated in Cyprus under the same corporate form and shared a common registered office. They all appointed the same English company, Marine Cross, to perform management and operating services. Moreover, the eight shipping companies were the only client of Marine Cross. Thereafter, Marine Cross entered into a service agreement with Scorpio Group (Scorpio), which was a company based in India and the UK, and assigned the commercial, operational and technical management of each of the companies to the Scorpio.[22]

The Court followed the interpretation of the COMI in *Eurofood* and relied heavily on the factors that were both objective and ascertainable by third parties. The Court found that Marine Cross provided services exclusively to the shipowning companies; all the creditors of the eight ship owning companies were paid by Marine Cross as agents; charterparties were operated by both Marine Cross and Scorpio; and external queries from third parties were passed on to Marine Cross.[23] The Court regarded the involvement of the ship agent as 'critical' to the operation of the company and that it was ascertainable by third parties.[24] In other words, when third parties dealt with each of the shipping companies, they assumed that they were dealing with Marine Cross in England rather than the SPCs in Cyprus. Thus, taking into account the overall facts and paying particular attention to the objective factors ascertainable by third parties, the Court rebutted the presumption in favour of the registered office of eight applicant companies, namely, Cyprus, and held that that those eight companies had their COMI in England.[25]

[19] *Eurofood* (n 18) 34; McCormack (n 12) 144.
[20] *Eurofood* (n 18) 36; see also McCormack (n 12) 144.
[21] *Northsea Base Investment* (n 10).
[22] ibid 18.
[23] ibid 22–25.
[24] *Northsea Base Investment* (n 10).
[25] ibid 21–29.

By focusing on the objective ascertainability of third parties, the decision to rebut the presumption in *Northsea Base Investment* is consistent with the function of the COMI under the Recast EU Regulation, which provides certainty and foreseeability for company creditors. Factors are only to be counted as ascertainable if they are in the public domain and would be perceived by a typical third party in the ordinary course of business with the debtor.[26] Therefore, in order to ensure legal certainty and foreseeability, it was necessary for the court in *Northsea Base Investment* to rebut the COMI presumption by emphasising the importance of the perception of third parties in the determination of COMI. As Gerard McCormack has noted, 'there would be a quite unrealistic burden if every transaction had to be preceded by a set of inquiries to establish whether the underlying reality differed from the apparent facts'.[27] Thus, where offshore shipping companies organise their operations in a comparable way to the eight companies in *Northsea Base Investment*, and where the regime of the Recast EU Regulation applies, the COMI of those offshore shipping companies is likely to be identified as the place where their ship agents operate.

B. The Model Law

i. The Interpretation of the COMI

The concepts of the COMI under the Model Law and the Recast EU Regulation serve different purposes. The concept of the COMI under the Model Law determines 'the nature of the foreign insolvency proceedings for recognition purposes', and thereby, upon recognition, determines the relief available to assist the foreign insolvency proceeding.[28] The presumption of COMI in the Model Law is designed to 'expedite the evidentiary process' with the aim of 'speed and convenience of proof where there is no serious controversy'.[29] Under the Recast EU Regulation, by contrast, the concept of COMI is used to determine the proper place where the insolvency proceeding should be commenced and, accordingly, to designate the law that should be applicable to the insolvency proceeding. All other EU Member States (except Denmark) are obliged to automatically recognise an insolvency proceeding once it is commenced under the law of the Member State where the COMI of the debtor is situated.[30] In other words, the recognition under the Model

[26] LC Ho, 'Cross-Border Fraud and Cross-Border Insolvency: Proving COMI and Seeking Recognition under the UK Model Law' (2009) *Butterworths Journal of International Banking and Financial Law* 537, 538.

[27] McCormack (n 12) 146.

[28] Ho (n 26) 538.

[29] UNCITRAL Secretariat, Guide to Enactment (n 1) 61; United States House of Representatives Report No 109-31, 113–14 (2005).

[30] UNCITRAL Secretariat, Guide to Enactment (n 1) 69; Recast EU Regulation, Arts 3, 20; Athanassiou (n 16) 131.

Law is not automatic and the concept of the COMI does not determine where insolvency proceedings should be commenced.

Although the drafters of the Model Law noted the different purposes of the COMI under these two instruments, they were of the view that the interpretation of the COMI in the Model Law should be modelled on the interpretation of COMI in the Recast EU Regulation.[31] The analysis of the COMI begins with the presumption in Article 16(3) of the Model Law that, 'in the absence of proof to the contrary, the debtor's registered office … is presumed to be the centre of the debtor's main interests'.[32] The opposing party who seeks to rebut the presumption bears the burden of proof to persuade the court that the location of the COMI is elsewhere.[33] In such circumstances, the UNCITRAL Model Law on Cross-Border Insolvency Law with Guide to Enactment and Interpretation (Guide to Enactment) proposes two principal factors that are relevant to the determination of the debtor's COMI, namely: '(a) where the central administration of the debtor takes place, and (b) which is readily ascertainable by creditors'.[34] Further, the Guide to Enactment lists several additional factors that may need to be considered when the above two factors do not provide a conclusive answer, including:

> [T]he location of the debtor's books and records; the location where financing was organized or authorized, or from where the cash management system was run; the location in which the debtor's principal assets or operations are found; the location of the debtor's primary bank; the location of employees; the location in which commercial policy was determined; the site of the controlling law or the law governing the main contracts of the company; the location from which purchasing and sales policy, staff, accounts payable and computer systems were managed; the location from which contracts (for supply) were organized; the location from which reorganization of the debtor was being conducted; the jurisdiction whose law would apply to most disputes; the location in which the debtor was subject to supervision or regulation; and the location whose law governed the preparation and audit of accounts and in which they were prepared and audited.[35]

The above-mentioned factors are not exhaustive. The Guide to Enactment indicates that, in order to determine the location of the COMI of the debtor, the relevant factors should be considered as a whole. In addition, which factors should be given a greater or lesser weight is at the discretion of the courts.[36] Nevertheless, the question of where the COMI of the debtor is actually located will always be a question of fact.[37] In addition, with respect to the appropriate date at which the above-mentioned factors should be examined, the Guide to Enactment suggests

[31] UNCITRAL Secretariat, Guide to Enactment (n 1) 70.
[32] UNCITRAL Model Law, Art 16(3).
[33] UNCITRAL Secretariat, Guide to Enactment (n 1) 70; McCormack (n 12) 146; *In Re Stanford International Bank Ltd* [2010] EWCA Civ 137.
[34] UNCITRAL Secretariat, Guide to Enactment (n 1) 70.
[35] ibid.
[36] ibid 71.
[37] P Smart, *Cross-border Insolvency*, 2nd edn (LexisNexis UK, 1998) 162.

that the COMI of the debtor should be determined at the time of the commencement of foreign insolvency proceedings.[38] This approach is also influenced by the Recast EU Regulation due to the concept of the COMI being used to determine where the main insolvency proceedings should be commenced under the regime of the Recast EU Regulation.[39] It has been argued that this approach can provide greater certainty and predictability for international insolvencies because it can prevent debtors from moving their COMI closer to the commencement of the insolvency proceedings for the purpose of thwarting the legitimate expectations of creditors or third parties.[40]

However, the fact that the concepts of the COMI under the Model Law and the Recast EU Regulation share a common origin does not necessarily signify that their meanings under these two instruments are identical.[41] In my view, the interpretation of the COMI and the weight of the COMI presumption in the Model Law may not be the same as those applied in the Recast EU Regulation, even though the wording and the historical origin of these two instruments are shared.[42] As explained by Look Chan Ho, the COMI presumption in the Model Law should be afforded less weight than that contained in the Recast EU Regulation:

> First, … it is important to predict with certainty the jurisdiction in which insolvency proceedings may be opened so that relevant local advice may be sought *ex ante* (in advance). But creditors are usually much less concerned with the assistance local insolvency proceedings may obtain abroad, the realm of the Model Law.
>
> Secondly, foreign main proceedings (wherever located) are entitled to essentially the same recognition and assistance under the Model Law. If creditors need to predict the assistance to be granted under the Model Law, it may be irrelevant *ex ante* where the debtor's COMI is located because provided the debtor is subject to foreign main proceedings somewhere, the same assistance may be obtained under the Model Law.
>
> Thirdly, provided a foreign proceeding may be recognised as either a main or a nonmain proceeding under the Model Law, there is plenty of scope for the recognising court to tailor its relief according to the circumstances of the case.[43]

Nevertheless, despite the clear guidance in the Guide to Enactment, countries that adopted the Model Law appear to have diverged in their interpretations of the COMI. Some countries that adopt the Model Law, such as the UK and Australia, follow the guidance in the Guide to Enactment when interpreting the concept of

[38] UNCITRAL Secretariat, Guide to Enactment (n 1) 71; *In re Videology Ltd* [2018] EWHC 2186 (Ch); Stanford (n 33).

[39] S Coleman and J Johnson, 'Journey to the Centre of the Economic Universe: How the Current US COMI Timing Determination Misses the Mark' (2014) 23(6) *Norton Journal of Bankruptcy Law and Practice* Art 4.

[40] UNCITRAL Secretariat, Guide to Enactment (n 1) 75; Videology (n 38); Stanford (n 33); *In re Millennium Global Emerging Credit* 458 BR 63 (SD New York 2011).

[41] McCormack (n 12) 151; Ho (n 26) 538–39; Westbrook, 'Locating the Eye of the Financial Storm' (n 5) 1034.

[42] See eg Ho (n 26) 538; McCormack (n 12) 151; Westbrook, 'Locating the Eye of the Financial Storm' (n 5) 1034.

[43] Ho (n 26) 539.

the COMI, drawing on the reasoning and analysis in *Eurofood*.[44] In other words, courts in the UK and Australia have created a substantive presumption in favour of the state of incorporation in the sense that the presumption of the COMI is a rebuttable presumption, and the party opposing the recognition bears the onus of rebutting the presumption on the balance of probabilities.[45] To be more specific, the English Court of Appeal in *In re Stanford International Bank Ltd*, referring to the EU Regulation and *Eurofood*, held that the presumption in favour of the registered office of the debtor could be rebutted only if 'factors which are both objective and ascertainable by third parties enable it to be established that an actual situation exists which is different from that which locating it at that registered office is deemed to reflect'.[46] The English Court of Appeal explained that the adoption of the approach of the 'objective third party test' was necessary in order to be consistent with the interpretation of the COMI in the EU Regulation as both the Model Law and the EU Regulation applied in England.[47] Similarly, the Federal Court of Australia in *Ackers v Saad Investments Co Ltd* expressly followed the 'objective third party test' that was adopted in *Eurofood* and *Stanford*, and held that 'the factors relevant to a rebuttal of the presumption must be both objective and ascertainable by third parties, being matters already in the public domain'.[48] The Federal Court of Australia explained that this approach would help to ensure legal certainty and foreseeability.[49]

By contrast, courts in the US have adopted a more pragmatic approach, which appears to equate the concept of the COMI with the US legal conception of 'principal place of business'.[50] The term 'principal place of business' was discussed by the US Supreme Court in *Hertz Corp v Friend*, where the Court concluded that a company's principal place of business is its headquarters or 'nerve center', namely, 'the place where a corporation's officers direct, control and coordinate the corporation's activities'.[51] In addition, US courts have regarded the COMI presumption of a registered office as merely a factor to be considered, rather than a 'rebuttable presumption' in the sense that the registered office only has 'evidentiary value and

[44] Stanford (n 33); *Ackers v Saad Investments Co Ltd* [2010] FCA 1221; *Wild (Foreign Representative) v Coin Co International plc (Administrators Appointed)* [2015] FCA 354.

[45] Stanford (n 33) [35]; *Videology* (n 38) [31]; *Wild* (n 44) [66]; *Ackers* (n 44) [45]–[49]; McCormack (n 12) 151.

[46] Stanford (n 33) [42] (citing *Eurofood* (n 18) [34]); see also *Videology* (n 38) [31].

[47] Stanford (n 33) [54].

[48] *Ackers* (n 44) [44]; see also *Wild* (n 44) [66]; *Moore v Australian Equity Investors* [2012] FCA 1002 [19]; *Legend International Holdings Inc (as debtor in possession of the assets of Legend International Holdings Inc) v Legend International Holdings Inc* [2016] VSC 308 [96].

[49] Stanford (n 33) [54]; *Ackers* (n 44) [49].

[50] See eg *Hertz v Friend* 559 US 77, 91–92 (2009); *In re Tri-Continental Exchange* 349 BR 627, 635 (ED California 2006); *In re Fairfield Sentry Ltd* 440 BR 60, 65 (SD New York 2010), aff'd 714 F 3d 127 (2d Cir 2013); J Westbrook, 'A Global Solution to Multinational Default' (2000) 98 *Michigan Law Review* 2276, 2316.

[51] *Hertz* (n 50) 91–92; see also *Fairfield* (n 50) 64–65.

does not shift the risk of non-persuasion'.[52] In other words, it is the foreign representative that bears the burden of proof to persuade courts by a preponderance of evidence that the COMI is in the same country as the registered office. Therefore, it has been argued that US courts have attached less weight to the presumption of COMI under the Model Law than UK and Australian courts.[53] The inconsistency with respect to the interpretation of the COMI between the US approach and the UK or Australian approach is due to the 'minor changes' of the legislative language in 11 USC § 1516(3).[54] Specifically, in enacting the equivalent provision of Article 16 of the Model Law into Chapter 15 of the US Bankruptcy Code, the US Congress changed the language of the COMI presumption from 'absence of *proof* to the contrary' (emphasis added) to 'in the absence of *evidence* to the contrary' (emphasis added).[55] Thus, the use of the US terminology, 'evidence' in 11 USC § 1516(3) has made it clear that the ultimate burden of proof is on foreign representatives.[56] Therefore, in addition to the factor of 'the location of the registered office of debtors', the Bankruptcy Court for the Southern District of New York in *Bear Stearns* has listed various pieces of evidence that would be relevant to determine the COMI of debtors, including: the location of the headquarters of debtors; the principal place of business of debtors; the location of the main assets of debtors; the location of the majority of the debtors' creditor; and the jurisdiction whose law would apply to most disputes.[57] Courts in the US will consider all the relevant evidence to determine the true COMI of debtors and give limited weight to the COMI presumption.

Finally, Singapore courts adopt an intermediate position. The Singapore High Court in *Re Zetta Jet Pte Ltd* held that it followed the English and Australian position in the sense that the presumption of the COMI in Article 16(3) of Singapore's implementation of the Model Law can be rebutted by factors that are 'objectively ascertainable by third parties, generally, with a focus on creditors and potential creditors in particular'.[58] However, with respect to the weight of the presumption, the Singapore High Court seems to follow the approach of the US. Abdullah J explained:

> I regard the presumption under Art 16 to operate as a starting point subject to displacement by other factors depending on the circumstances of the specific case. Art 16 refers to 'the absence of proof to the contrary', which to my mind does not require proof on the balance of probabilities; it allows for the presumption to be rebutted simply on the presence of proof, ie, evidence, to the contrary.[59]

[52] *Tri-Continental Exchange* (n 50) 635; *In re Bear Stearns High-Grade Structured Credit Strategies Master Fund Ltd* 374 BR 122, 130 (SD New York 2007) aff'd 389 BR 325 (SD New York 2008); Westbrook, 'A Global Solution to Multinational Default' (n 50) 2316.

[53] McCormack (n 12) 145; Westbrook, 'Locating the Eye of the Financial Storm' (n 5) 1024.

[54] US House of Representatives Report No 109-31, 112–13 (2005); *Bear Stearns* (n 52) 130; Westbrook, 'Locating the Eye of the Financial Storm' (n 5) 1024; Ho (n 26) 539.

[55] 11 USC § 1516(3); UNCITRAL Model Law, Art 16.

[56] US House of Representatives Report No 109-31, 112–13 (2005); *Bear Stearns* (n 52) 130; Westbrook, 'Locating the Eye of the Financial Storm' (n 5)1024; Ho (n 26) 539.

[57] *Bear Stearns* (n 52) 128.

[58] *Re Zetta Jet Pte Ltd* [2019] SGHC 53 [76].

[59] ibid [31].

Thus, Singapore courts do not seem to regard the COMI presumption as a rebuttable presumption of law that must be disproved on the balance of probabilities. Instead, the presumption can be rebutted if 'other factors point the COMI away from the place of registration to some other location'.[60] The Singapore High Court did not explicitly answer the issue regarding who should bear the risk of non-persuasion. Nevertheless, in determining the COMI of debtors, the Court emphasised the importance of predictability from a creditor standpoint and focused on the factors that were objectively ascertainable by third parties, such as: the location from where control and direction was administered; the location of clients, creditors and employees; the location of operations; and the governing law.[61]

As discussed above, the interpretation of the COMI under the Model Law regime is not conclusive, as different jurisdictions may assign different weights and values to different factors depending upon their view of social and economic policies.[62] Nevertheless, in practice, it seems that the different approaches that have been articulated by courts in the UK, Australia, the US and Singapore may not necessarily lead to different results in most cases.[63] It has been argued that at least in the circumstance of fraud, where debtors intended to engineer a public perception that their business is operated from their registered offices, the abovementioned approaches may produce different outcomes.[64] In such a circumstance, UK, Australian and Singapopre courts may feel bound by the 'smoke and mirrors' due to them being required to focus more on the factors that are objectively ascertainable by third parties, whereas US courts may feel free to determine the true location of the COMI of the debtor.[65]

The determination of the COMI is always a matter of fact and is left to the discretion of the courts, especially when the ownership of a debtor-shipowner is registered in an open registry country but its management is entrusted to a third management company located elsewhere.[66] The fact sensitivity of the COMI inquiry always leaves a certain degree of uncertainty and ambiguity, no matter which approach is applied. Nevertheless, in such a situation, I argue that the location of the registered office may not always be the COMI of debtors. The rationale of the COMI presumption in the Model Law is designed for the purpose of 'speed and convenience of proof where there is no serious controversy', rather than aiming to provide a 'preferred alternative where there was a separation between

[60] ibid [76].
[61] ibid [85].
[62] McCormack (n 12) 145.
[63] McCormack (n 12) 146.
[64] Ho (n 26) 538–39.
[65] See Ho (n 26) 538–39; *In re Ernst & Young Inc* 383 BR 773 (District of Colorado 2008) (where Look Chan Ho uses *Ernst & Young* as an example and provided detailed discussion with respect to the potential different outcomes that may arise in the application of different approaches of the Recast EU Regulation and the Model Law, in the circumstance were the business of debtors is fraudulent).
[66] Smart (n 37) 162.

a corporation's jurisdiction of incorporation and its "real seat".[67] In addition, a major concern for rigidly recognising an offshore jurisdiction as the COMI of the debtor is whether the regime of insolvency in an offshore country is efficient and fair enough to perform the basic functions of bankruptcy law, namely, the maximisation of the value of the debtors' assets and adequate protection of the interests of all creditors. As Jay Lawrence Westbrook says:

> we must not adopt a COMI rule that is likely to permit havens to serve often as the COMI of a corporation whose headquarters and operations are elsewhere. Yet a strong presumption in favor of jurisdiction of incorporation might have just that effect.[68]

In the maritime context, the connecting factors that may be relevant to the determination of the COMI of debtors include: the registration office of the shipping company; the flags of vessels; the place where the management and operation of the shipping company are conducted; the place where the meetings of the board of directors and shareholders are held; and the place where the essential decisions are made and principal contracts are approved (for example, the purchase and disposal of ships, the conclusion of ship mortgages, ship financing, charterparties and insurance policies).[69]

Among the above-mentioned factors, courts should pay more attention to those that are ascertainable to third parties, such as the place where the actual management, supervision and operation of the shipping company are conducted, and the place where the essential decisions are made or principal contracts are approved.[70] Notwithstanding that Australian, UK, US and Singapore courts have given different weight to the presumption of the COMI, courts generally tend to consider relevant factors that are objectively ascertainable to third parties when determining the COMI of debtors. In addition, although US courts equate the concept of the COMI with the concept of 'principal of business' or 'headquarter', the location of the COMI of the debtor is still fairly predictable to third parties.[71] Thus, in determining the weight of the relevant factors, courts should focus more on the factors that are ascertainable to third parties.

For example, vessels can be moveable across the world as part of the operation process of shipping companies. A reasonable third-party creditor may not regard the location of vessels as being significant when conducting business with shipping companies. In such a situation, the location of a shipping company's fixed assets will, in turn, play a more significant role in determining the COMI of the company.[72] Similarly, the place where vessels are registered is not a crucial factor because vessels are often registered in open registry countries, such as Panama

[67] Westbrook, 'Locating the Eye of the Financial Storm' (n 5) 1033.
[68] ibid 1032–33.
[69] Athanassiou (n 16) 151.
[70] ibid 160.
[71] Westbrook, 'Locating the Eye of the Financial Storm' (n 5) 1038.
[72] *Zetta Jet* (n 58) [78].

and Liberia, which are chosen for reasons associated with tax, chartering cost, and maintenance conditions.[73] From the perspective of third-party creditors, the location where vessels are registered will not necessarily be linked to the state where the shipping company carries out its core business.[74] Furthermore, the location of board meetings is not to be regarded as being of great significance because, from the point of view of factors ascertainable by a third party, a third party will not have any knowledge of the location where directors' meetings are held.[75] Therefore, factors such as the place where the actual management, supervision and operation of the shipping company are conducted, and the place where the essential decisions are made or principal contracts are approved, should be more crucial in determining the true COMI of debtors.

ii. Relevant Date for the Determination of the COMI

A debtor may shift its COMI for its own reasons. For example, a shift of the COMI may be intended to enable the debtor to have access to a specific insolvency process and to enjoy the benefit of that specific insolvency regime, such as reorganisation.[76] In addition, the shift of the COMI can be driven by rules of procedure, legal costs, the speed and mode of litigation and the quality and ability of the judiciary and legal professions in the target jurisdiction.[77] Furthermore, the shift of the COMI can sometimes be for the purpose of fraud, concealing assets, evading debts or liabilities of debtors, or thwarting the legitimate expectations of creditors.[78]

In some instances, a debtor may shift its COMI to a target jurisdiction prior to the commencement of insolvency proceedings in that target jurisdiction and then get the insolvency proceedings recognised in a third jurisdiction in order to obtain assistance and relief from courts in that third jurisdiction.[79] In other instances, a debtor may commence an insolvency proceeding in the target jurisdiction before it gradually moves its COMI to that target jurisdiction; this may be because some jurisdictions do not require a jurisdictional nexus in order to file an insolvency application in that jurisdiction. The debtor will then apply to recognise its insolvency proceeding in a third country and obtain assistance from

[73] Ford and Wilcox (n 9); Egiyan (n 9).

[74] Athanassiou (n 16) 160.

[75] *Northsea Base Investment* (n 10) [27].

[76] See eg *In re Ocean Rig UDW Inc* 585 BR 31, 36 (SD New York 2018) aff'd 764 F App'x 46 (2d Cir 2019) (Ocean Rig Group migrated its COMI from the Marshall Islands to the Cayman Islands in order to take advantage of the reorganisation mechanism that is available under the law of the Cayman Islands, but not available in the Marshall Islands).

[77] A Bell, *Forum Shopping and Venue in Transnational Litigation* (Oxford University Press, 2003) 24.

[78] ibid.

[79] See eg *Ocean Rig* (n 76) (Ocean Rig Group shifted its COMI to the Cayman Islands before it filed a reorganisation proceeding in the Cayman Islands. It then filed an application of recognising its Cayman Islands insolvency proceeding in the US Bankruptcy Court).

that third country.[80] Therefore, a side issue with respect to the relevant date at which to determine the COMI of debtors has come before courts across the world. Countries have adopted different approaches in order to deal with this issue.

The English approach is laid down in *Stanford*, where the English Court of Appeal held that the COMI of the debtor was to be determined at the date of the commencement of a foreign insolvency proceeding.[81] The English Court of Appeal again followed the approach of the Recast EU Regulation and the Guide to Enactment of the Model Law.

However, US and Singapore courts determined the COMI of the debtor as at the date the application for recognition was filed.[82] The US Courts of Appeal for the Second Circuit in *In re Fairfield Sentry Ltd* held that it would determine the location of the debtor's COMI by looking at relevant factors present or immediately preceding the time when the debtor filed its recognition petition and would not look at the prior operational history of the debtor.[83] Furthermore, the Second Circuit also considered the activities that occurred during the extended period of post-insolvency, even if they had been conducted only in connection with liquidation or reorganisation.[84] Nevertheless, the Second Circuit noted that the period between the commencement of the foreign insolvency proceeding and the filing of the application for recognition might also need to be taken into consideration in order to ensure that the debtor had not manipulated its COMI in bad faith.[85] Similarly, the Singapore High Court in *Zetta Jet* chose to follow the US approach and held that 'determining the COMI of the debtor as at the date the recognition application is filed provides greater certainty and better accords with commercial realities, given the possible vagaries of hearing diaries in all jurisdictions'.[86] The primary reason given by US and Singapore courts for adopting this approach is the use of the present tense in Article 17(2)(a) of the Model Law, which is a textualist approach.[87] Article 17(2)(a) of the Model Law provides that a foreign proceeding is to be recognised as a main proceeding 'if it *is* taking place in the State where

[80] See eg *In re Suntech Power Holdings Co Ltd* 520 BR 399 (SD New York 2014) (Suntech Power Holding Co Ltd (Suntech) filed a liquidation proceeding in the Cayman Islands, while its COMI was in China at the time of the commencement of the liquidation proceeding. Suntech then moved its COMI from China to the Cayman Islands before it filed a recognition application in the US Bankruptcy Court).

[81] Stanford (n 33); see also *Videology* (n 38); but see *Re Toisa Ltd* (an unreported case of English High Court (Commercial Division) that was decided by Burton J orally in April 2019). In *Toisa*, Burton J moved away from the approach adopted in Videology and held that the appropriate date on which COMI should be determined was the date that the application for recognition was filed. A report of *Toisa* is available at www.globalrestructuringwatch.com/2019/04/clarity-on-cross-border-conundrum/, accessed 6 June 2020.

[82] See eg *Fairfield* (n 50); *In re Ran* 607 F 3d 1017, 1025 (5th Cir 2010); *Suntech* (n 80); *Ocean Rig* (n 76); *Zetta Jet* (n 58).

[83] *Fairfield* (n 50) 135; Coleman and Johnson (n 39).

[84] *Fairfield* (n 50) 138.

[85] ibid 135.

[86] *Zetta Jet* (n 58) [53], [61].

[87] *Fairfield* (n 50); *Zetta Jet* (n 58).

the debtor *has* the centre of its main interests' (emphasis added).[88] Therefore, US and Singapore courts held that the use of the present tense required the court to view the COMI determination in the present, namely, at the time the petition for recognition is filed.

Furthermore, the Federal Court of Australia in *Moore* held that the COMI of the debtor is to be determined at the time that the court is called upon to make a relevant decision, which is the date of the hearing of the recognition application.[89] Under the Australian approcah, the COMI of the debtor will be examined at a slightly later stage than the approach adopted in the US and Singapore, and the recognising courts are given greater leeway in ascertaining the COMI of the debtor. However, unlike the position in the US and Singapore, 'historical facts that have led to the position as it is at the time for determination' will be examined under the Australian position.[90] Nevertheless, the Federal Court of Australia did not provide any specific reasons as to why it adopted this approach.[91]

Compared with the above-mentioned three alternative dates that are currently adopted by courts in practice, in my view, the date of the commencement of foreign insolvency proceedings is more appropriate. First, the Model Law regime is not applicable from the commencement of foreign insolvency proceedings, but comes into force from the moment that foreign proceedings have been recognised.[92] Therefore, 'the date of the application for recognition is mere happenstance' and may take place at any time after the commencement of the foreign proceedings.[93] For example, in *Millennium Global*, the debtor did not file an application for recognition in the US Bankruptcy Court for the Southern District of New York until three years after its insolvency proceeding in the Cayman Islands had been commenced.[94] Therefore, selecting the date at which the recognition application is filed as the relevant date might encourage an arbitrary choice of time to apply for recognition.[95] In addition, in cases where there were multiple applications for recognition of the same foreign proceeding in different countries at different times, using the date when the application for recognition was filed as the relevant date may lead to different outcomes in different courts.[96] Furthermore, after the commencement of an insolvency proceeding, it is the liquidating or reorganising entity, not the debtor, that continues to have a COMI.[97] The post-insolvency

[88] UNCITRAL Model Law, Art 17(2).

[89] *Moore* (n 48) [18]–[19]; *Legend* (n 48); *Wood v Astra Resources Ltd (UK Company No 07620218)* [2016] FCA 1192; But see *Kapila in the matter of Edelsten* [2014] FCA 1112, [35]–[39]; *King in the matter of Zetta Jet Pte Ltd* [2018] FCA 1932, [11] (Beach and Perram JJ held that the relevant date for determining the COMI should be the date of the commencement of the foreign proceeding).

[90] *Moore* (n 48) [19].

[91] ibid [18]–[19].

[92] Athanassiou (n 16) 131.

[93] *Millennium Global* (n 40) 72.

[94] ibid.

[95] UNCITRAL Secretariat, Judicial Perspective (n 2) 44.

[96] *Kapila* (n 89) [37].

[97] *Millennium Global* (n 40) 73; UNCITRAL Secretariat, Judicial Perspective (n 2) 44.

activities that are conducted only in connection with the liquidation or reorganisation of the business should not be regarded as a suitable factor ascertainable to third parties.[98] Therefore, the date of the commencement of a foreign proceeding should be the proper date for the determination of a debtor's COMI in the sense that it can provide more certainty and predictability.

Nevertheless, it is worth noting that the concern of forum shopping may occur at any stage of the proceeding, even if the COMI is to be determined at the date of the commencement of insolvency proceedings. In my view, instead of focusing on the relevant date for the determination of the COMI, courts should focus more on the manipulation test as to how to regulate the abusive shift of the COMI when the shift is in bad faith.[99] However, given the difficulty of proving subjective bad faith, it is difficult to ascertain whether the COMI shift is abusive, especially where the shift is to the detriment of some creditors but to the benefit of others.[100]

II. Scope of Debtor's Assets

A. Chartered Vessel: Debtor's Assets?

Many international shipping companies only own a few vessels. Instead, they charter most of their fleet from third parties in order to reduce the cost of maintenance and meet the need for flexibility of business operations. For example, Hanjin Shipping Co Ltd (Hanjin), prior to its bankruptcy, was the largest container shipping line in Korea and the seventh largest in the world. However, of its 61 operating vessels, 54 vessels were chartered, rather than owned.[101] Therefore, as illustrated in Chapter 6, Section III, in the area of maritime cross-border insolvency, there is an issue that frequently arises in practice: should chartered vessels (whether demise, time or voyage chartered) be regarded as the debtor's assets and thereby be included into the asset pool of the debtor for the purpose of liquidation or reorganisation among all creditors? Should chartered vessels be subjected to the Article 20 automatic stay order granted by the Model Law? In my view, the answer to this issue depends on the nature of the charterparty, which will now be discussed in detail.

[98] *Millennium Global* (n 40) 73.

[99] See eg *Fairfield* (n 50), *Suntech* (n 80), *Zetta Jet* (n 58). In these cases, courts mentioned the manipulation test as a safeguard against abusive COMI shifts. However, the manipulation test has been left largely undefined. For a general discussion regarding the manipulation test see J Hallock, 'Time Out: The Problematic Temporality of COMI Analysis in Chapter 15 Bankruptcy Cases in the Second Circuit' (2015) *Columbia Business Law Review* 1074, 1107–11.

[100] Hallock (n 99) 1108–10.

[101] IH Kim, 'Korean Maritime Case Update: 2015/2016' (2017) 48 *Journal of Maritime Law & Commerce* 211, 216.

i. Time or Voyage Chartered Vessels

In the case of a time or voyage charterparty, it is well established across the world that a shipowner remains in control of the ship and carries all the risk and costs of running the ship. However, the time or voyage charterer only has the right to use the ship, but 'no right of property in, or to possession of, the vessel'.[102] Therefore, in the event that a time or voyage charterer files for bankruptcy protection, the time or voyage chartered vessel should not be regarded as the asset of the charterer in the sense that it will not be included into the asset pool of the debtor for the purpose of liquidation or reorganisation. However, a potential or actual arrest against a chartered vessel can be regarded as an action concerning the 'rights, obligations or liabilities' of debtors in terms of Article 20(1)(a) of the Model Law, and therefore the chartered vessel will be subject to the protection of the Article 20 stay order granted under the Model Law regime.[103] As discussed in Chapters 7–10, Australia, UK, US and Singapore courts all granted a general stay order that applied to all vessels owned or chartered by Hanjin, even time or voyage chartered vessels.[104] Although no explanation was provided by those courts, it seems that they regarded the claims against the chartered vessels of Hanjin as 'rights, obligations or liabilities' of Hanjin and therefore prevented third-party creditors from enforcing their claims against those vessels.[105]

ii. Demise Chartered Vessels

However, it is widely accepted that a demise charterer is to be treated as the owner *pro hac vice* (or owner ad hoc).[106] Under a demise charterparty, a charterer is hiring the whole ship without the master or crew. A demise charterer must appoint the master and crew, provide suppliers and bunkers, as well as run the vessel at its own

[102] *The Hill Harmony* [2011] 1 Lloyd's Rep 147, 156; *The Berge Tasta* [1975] 1 Lloyd's Rep 422, 424; see also B Eder et al, *Scrutton on Chapterparties and Bill of Lading*, 23rd edn (Sweet & Maxwell, 2015) 2–3; H Bennett (ed), *Carver on Chapterparties* (Sweet & Maxwell, 2017) 3–11; T Coghlin et at, *Time Charters*, 7th edn (Informa Law from Routledge, 2014) 1–2; W Tetley, *International Maritime and Admiralty Law* (Éditions Yvon Blais, 2002) 126; R Force, *Admiralty and Maritime Law*, 2nd edn (Federal Judicial Center, 2013) 44; G Gilmore and C Black, *The Law of Admiralty*, 2nd edn (Foundation Press, 1975) paras 4–1, 4–24.

[103] *In re Hanjin Shipping Co Ltd* 2016 WL 6679487, [2016] AMC 2126 (Bankr District of New Jersey 20 September 2016); *Kim and Yu v STX Pan Ocean Co Ltd* [2014] NZHC 845 [18].

[104] See Chapter 7, Section V; Chapter 8, Section V, Chapter 9, Section V; Chapter 10, Section V (for discussion of the status of Hanjin's chartered vessel in Australia, the UK, the US, and Singapore respectively); *Tai-Soo Suk v Hanjin Shipping Co Ltd* [2016] FCA 1404; *In the Matter of Hanjin Shipping Co Ltd* No CR-2016-005448, High Court of Justice (Chancery Division), Companies Court (6 September 2016); *In re Hanjin Shipping* (n 103); *Re Taisoo Suk* [2016] SGHC 195.

[105] Nevertheless, as discussed in Chapter 11, claims against the chartered vessels can be allowed to proceed regardless of the Art 20 stay order under certain circumstances, subject to the secured status of the claims and the court's attitude towards in rem actions. For further discussion see Chapter 11.

[106] A demise charterer stands in the place of the vessel's title owner during the charter period. See eg *Port Line v Ben Line Steamers* [1958] 2 QB 146; *The Andrea Ursula* [1973] 1 QB 265; *The Tasmania* (1888) 13 PD 110; *Sandeman v Scurr* (1866) LR 2 QB 86; *United States v Shea* 152 US 178 (1894).

risk and expense.[107] Nevertheless, they are liable for liabilities that are caused due to the operation of the chartered vessel.[108] However, demise charterers are not the legal or equitable owners of the vessels.[109] Therefore, it seems that in the event that a demise charterer files for bankruptcy protection, the demise chartered vessels should not be treated as the assets of the debtor.

As the underlying nature of a demise charterparty may be a finance lease between a charterer and the true shipowner (usually banks), a more complex situation occasionally arises, where the demise charterer may be exposed to the possibility of recharacterisation as the beneficial owner of the chartered ship. The structure of a financing arrangement in the shipping industry is not novel and the vehicle of a bareboat charter is frequently used as part of financing transactions, which has been a common method of ship financing since World War II.[110] However, courts are inconclusive as to whether a demise charterparty that contains a hire-purchase agreement (or other similar forms, such as sale and lease back agreement or conditional sale) can be recharacterised as a disguised security agreement, and therefore can result in the charterer being regarded as a beneficial owner of the chartered vessel.

The US approach with respect to recharacterisation is explained by Simon Baughen:

> Under US law, an agreement in the form of a lease which vests most of the economic benefits in the lessee may be recharacterised by the courts, particularly in bankruptcy, as in reality a security agreement. If the courts determine that the named lessor does not truly retain the economic benefits of the property ownership, but rather appears to be a creditor secured by its possession of title to the assets, the nominal lessee may be deemed the owner of the asset.[111]

In the US, whether a transaction in the form of a lease can create a security interest is a matter of fact and is decided on a case-by-case basis. UCC § 1-203(b) provides a bright line test in order to make an initial determination with respect to whether a lease is a 'true' lease or a disguised security agreement:

> A transaction in the form of a lease creates a security interest if the consideration that the lessee is to pay the lessor for the right to possession and use of the goods is an obligation for the term of the lease and is not subject to termination by the lessee, and:
>
> (1) the original term of the lease is equal to or greater than the remaining economic life of the goods;

[107] Eder et al (n 102) 3–4; Bennett (n 102) 12; SA Gebb, 'The Demise Charter: A Conceptual and Practical Analysis' (1975) 49 *Tulane Law Review* 764; see also *Port Line* (n 106); *The Andrea Ursula* (n 106); *The Tasmania* (n 106); *Sandeman* (n 106).

[108] Eder et al (n 102) 5; Bennett (n 102) 523; *Fraser v Marsh* (1811) 13 East 238; *Sandeman* (n 106); *The Great Eastern* (1868) LR 2 Ad & EC 88; *Fenton v City of Dublin Steam Packet Co* (1838) 8 Ad & E 835; *Burnard v Aaron and Sharpley* (1862) 31 LJCP 334.

[109] *The Andrea Ursula* (n 106); Eder et al (n 102) 523.

[110] *In re Lykes Bros SS Co Inc* 196 BR 574, 580 (MD Florida 1996); Gilmore and Black (n 102) 704–05.

[111] B Soyer and A Tettenborn, *Ship Building, Sale and Finance* (Informa Law from Routledge, 2016) 210; see eg *In re Pillowtex Inc* 349 F 3d 711 (3d Cir 2003); *Lykes* (n 110).

(2) the lessee is bound to renew the lease for the remaining economic life of the goods or is bound to become the owner of the goods;
(3) the lessee has an option to renew the lease for the remaining economic life of the goods for no additional consideration or for nominal additional consideration upon compliance with the lease agreement; or
(4) the lessee has an option to become the owner of the goods for no additional consideration or for nominal additional consideration upon compliance with the lease agreement.[112]

The four factors provided by UCC § 1-203(b) focus on the fact of whether the lease demonstrates that the lessor is retaining a substantial residual interest in the leased property.[113] If this bright line test has not been met, the court will then look at the 'economic substance' or 'economic realities' of each transaction, by examining the underlying factual characteristics of a transaction to discern its true intent.[114]

Applying this test in the maritime context, the factors in favour of recharacterisation usually include, but are not limited to: (1) the term of the charter being equal to or greater than the remaining economic life of the vessel;[115] (2) the debtor-charterer having an option to renew the charter or being bound to become the owner of the vessel for no or nominal additional consideration at the expiration of the charter;[116] (3) the charter hire appearing to be based upon a calculation designed to ensure a return on investment, not on market rate;[117] (4) the debtor-charterer being responsible for all maintenance, repairs, insurances, liabilities occurred during the operation and tax of the 'leased' vessel;[118] (5) any surplus proceeds of the vessel sale after a termination event being paid to the debtor-charterer;[119] (6) after a termination event, the owner transferring the vessel to the debtor-charterer if the debtor-charterer or its guarantor makes payments;[120] (7) the initial purchase price, in a sale and leaseback transaction, being related to the value of the assets;[121] (8) the equipment having been selected by the lessor or having been custom designed for the use of the lessee and the equipment having significant value to the lessee rather than the lessor;[122] (9) the lessor not regularly being in the

[112] UCC § 1-203(b) provides what has been characterised as a 'bright line' test for making an initial determination of whether a transaction cast as a lease is in fact a security interest.

[113] *In re WorldCom Inc* 339 BR 56, 65 (SD New York 2006).

[114] *Lykes* (n 110) 581.

[115] UCC § 1-203(b).

[116] ibid.

[117] *Lykes* (n 110) 583; *In re PCH Associates* 804 F 2d 193 (2d Cir 1986).

[118] Even though this is a common feature of bareboat charters, it has been considered by bankruptcy courts as a factor in recharacterisation. See *Lykes* (n 110) 582; *Matthews v CTI Container Transport International Inc* 871 F 2d 270 (2d Cir 1989); *Orix Credit Alliance Inc v Pappas* 946 F 2d 1258 (7th Cir 1991).

[119] *Lykes* (n 110) 582; *PCH Associates* (n 117); *Orix* (n 118).

[120] *Lykes* (n 110) 583; *Matthews* (n 118).

[121] *Lykes* (n 110) 583; *PCH Associates* (n 117).

[122] *Lykes* (n 110) 583; *Orix* (n 118); *National Equipment Rental Ltd v Priority Electronics Corp* 435 F Supp 236 (ED New York 1977).

business of leasing.[123] As mentioned in Chapter 9, Section V, in the area of maritime cross-border insolvency, in *In re Daebo International Shipping Co Ltd* the US Bankruptcy Court for the Southern District of New York vacated the claims for attachments and held that it appeared from evidence at trial that the involved sale and lease back arrangement was to be treated as a secured loan.[124] Thus, there is a great chance that the Court will treat the vessel as the asset of the debtor.[125]

Accordingly, in the US, on the one hand, if courts decide that the transaction is a disguised security agreement, the chartered vessel will be deemed to be the property of the debtor-charterer. Under this circumstance, the financing lessor cannot repossess the vessel because it is not the owner of the vessel. Instead, it only has a secured interest against the vessel and becomes a ship mortgagee. The problem that the financing lessor will encounter under such a circumstance is that, if the mortgage has not been perfected upon the commencement of the bankruptcy proceeding – namely, no relevant registration has been filed – the mortgage of the financing lessor can be voided by the trustee;[126] however, many flag states do not provide legal methods for a financing lessor to perfect a security interest in vessels to which it held title.[127] On the other hand, if the courts decide that the transaction is not a disguised security agreement but a true lease, the chartered vessel will not be deemed as the asset of the debtor-charterer in the sense that the lessor can repossess the vessel if the trustee of the debtor does not assume the lease.[128]

UK courts, however, are hesitant to recharacterise the 'financing nature' contained in a demise charterparty as a security interest. The English Court of

[123] *Lykes* (n 110) 582; *Matthews* (n 118).

[124] *In re Daebo International Shipping Co Ltd* 543 BR 47, 55 (SD New York 2015); see also eg *PCH Associates* (n 117); *United Airlines Inc v HSBC Bank USA NA* 416 F 3d 609 (7th Cir 2005); *Liona Corp v PCH Associates* 949 F 2d 585 (2d Cir 1991); *In re Moreggia & Sons Inc* 852 F 2d 1179 (9th Cir 1988).

[125] *Daebo* (n 124) 55; M Davies, 'Cross-border Insolvency and Admiralty: A Middle Path of Reciprocal Comity' (2018) 66 *American Journal of Comparative Law* 101, 111.

[126] 11 USC §544 (a); J Ashmead et at, 'The Intersection of Maritime Law and the United States Bankruptcy Code' (2016) 28 *University of San Francisco Maritime Law Journal* 117, 132–33.

[127] Nevertheless, in 2013, the Marshall Islands became the first flag state to pass legislation allowing a finance lessor to perfect a security interest in vessels to which it held title. Section 302(A) of the Republic of the Marshall Islands Maritime Act provides that either a financing charterer or a documented owner is allowed to file a financing charter with the Marshall Islands registry. If a financing charter is properly registered, the documented owner will obtain a preferred mortgage on the vessel. However, the law of the Marshall Islands provides that the mere registration or recording does not constitute evidence that the contract does, in fact, create a security interest. '[E]ven if the owner and the charterer agree in the charter that the charter constitutes a "financing charter", this declaration alone is not binding on third parties or courts hearing the question'. Therefore, there still remains the possibility to argue that the charterparty is a true lease, but in the circumstance where courts recharacterise the charter into a financing lease, the financing lessor is entitled to a preferred mortgage under the law of Marshall Islands: The Republic of the Marshall Islands Maritime Act, s 302(A)(4); Soyer and Tettenborn (n 111) 211.

[128] See 11 USC § 365 (where the trustee has an option to either assume or reject any executory contract or unexpired lease of the debtor); see also M Howard, 'Equipment Lessors and Secured Parties in Bankruptcy: An Argument for Coherence' (1991) 48 *Washington and Lee Law Review* 253, 266.

Appeal in *Welsh Development Agency v The Export Finance Company Ltd* paid closer attention to the legal form or label chosen by the parties than to the economic substance of the transaction.[129] The underlying reason explained by Dillon LJ was that parties have the autonomy to decide on the form of finance that they want to use unless the transaction is deemed to be a mere sham.[130] Thus, in a compulsory winding-up proceeding of a demise charterer, a finance lessor can exercise its right to repossess the vessel regardless of the winding-up proceeding of the debtor, since the vessel is regarded as the asset of the finance lessor, rather than the debtor.[131] In an administration proceeding, the administrator of the debtor has an option with regard to whether to cancel the demise charter. If the administrator chooses to cancel the charter and hand the ship over to the finance lessor, the damages thereafter caused by the cancellation are classified as general unsecured claims. However, if the administrator is willing and able to carry on performing the obligations under the charter, the court will prevent the finance lessor from repossessing the ship.[132]

The demise charterparty involved in the bankruptcy of Hanjin is a special scheme of charterparty, which is known as bareboat charter hire purchase (BBCHP). As mentioned in Chapter 9, Section V, the BBCHP is a popular method for ship financing in Korea. Under the BBCHP agreement, Hanjin was able to use the vessel for the duration of the charter period and at the end of the designated charter period had the option of purchasing the vessel 'at a nominal price'.[133] Courts in Australia, the UK, the US, and Singapore all granted a general stay order that applied to all vessels owned or chartered by Hanjin. However, in all those cases, the courts did not explicitly give reasons regarding why the orders were so broad as to include the BBCHP chartered vessels.[134] On the contrary, in Korea, where the main insolvency proceeding of Hanjin was initiated, the Changwon District Court of Korea held that BBCHP chartered vessels with registration in Panama were not owned by Hanjin and were not subject to the stay order.[135] The Changwon District Court of Korea explained that under the BBCHP agreement 'Hanjin has only the expectation right to obtain the title at the end of the charter period on the condition that it pays the charter hire completely without fail'.[136]

[129] *Welsh Development Agency v The Export Finance Co Ltd* [1992] BCC 270.

[130] ibid; *Ensign Tankers (Leasing) Ltd v Stokes (Inspector of Taxes)* [1992] 1 AC 665.

[131] Soyer and Tettenborn (n 111) 209; *General Share & Trust Co v Wetley Brick & Pottery Co* (1882) ChD 260; *Re Blue Jeans Sales Ltd* [1979] 1 All ER 641.

[132] Soyer and Tettenborn (n 111) 209; *Transag Haulage Ltd v Leyland DAF Finance Ltd* [1994] BCC 356.

[133] IH Kim, 'Legal Implication of Hanjin Shipping's Rehabilitation Proceeding' [2017] *Hong Kong Law Journal* 915, 928.

[134] See Chapter 7, Section V; Chapter 8, Section V, Chapter 9, Section V; Chapter 10, Section V (for discussion of the status of Hanjin's chartered vessel in Australia, the UK, the US, and Singapore respectively).

[135] *Changwon District Court Decision Docket No 2016-taki-227* (17 October 2016); See Kim, 'Korean Maritime Case Update: 2015/2016' (n 101) 211–12.

[136] Kim, 'Korean Maritime Case Update: 2015/2016' (n 101) 222.

The charter period had not ended and, therefore, the title of the vessel remained in the SPC in Panama. Even though the Changwon District Court of Korea noted the strong necessity to maximise the assets of the debtor for the benefit of creditors, it held that regarding BBCHP chartered vessels as assets of Hanjin under its rehabilitation proceeding might significantly affect the foreseeability and legal stability of the claimants in the international transaction.[137]

As mentioned above, courts reached conflicting decisions with regard to whether the BBCHP chartered vessels were to be regarded as assets of Hanjin, and whether BBCHP chartered vessels should be subjected to the automatic stay order granted by the Model Law. In addition, these conflicting decisions seem to have led to an odd situation: Australia, the UK, the US and Singapore refused to arrest Hanjin's chartered vessel and asked maritime lien claimants to participate in the Korean rehabilitation proceeding. However, the Korean court, where the foreign main insolvency proceeding occurred, actually allowed the arrest of the chartered vessels.

In my view, whether BBCHP chartered vessels will be regarded as Hanjin's property depends on whether the court is willing to recharacterise the legal nature of the BBCHP. If the charterparty can be recharacterised as a security agreement, the charterer will become the beneficial owner of the chartered vessel. Therefore, the chartered vessel will be deemed to be the property of the debtor-charterer, whereas the financing lessor, usually the bank, has a secured claim against the vessel and becomes the ship mortgagee. The chartered vessel will be included in the asset pool of the debtor and the financing lessor will not be allowed to repossess the vessel from the charterer. If the transaction is characterised as a true lease, the chartered vessel will not be regarded as the property of the debtor in the sense that it will not be included in the asset pool of the debtor for the purpose of liquidation or reorganisation among all creditors. However, in any sense, as mentioned above, it seems that a potential or actual arrest against a demise chartered vessel concerns the 'rights, obligations or liabilities' of a debtor in terms of Article 20(1)(a) of the Model Law, and therefore the claims against the demise chartered vessel will be subject to the scope of the Article 20 stay order granted under the Model Law regime.[138]

In order to determine the legal nature of a demise charterparty, courts should look into the economic substance of the charterparty, rather than its label.[139] Although the approaches of Korean (and possibly UK) courts can provide more predictability and certainty to debtors and creditors, the true nature of the transaction should never be concealed by how it is labelled. Especially in the circumstance

[137] ibid. Nevertheless, IH Kim argues that there is a tendency in Korea that the BBCHP vessel will be regarded as being actually owned by the Korean charterer.

[138] *In re Hanjin Shipping* (n 103); *Kim and Yu* (n 103) [18]. Nevertheless, as discussed in Chapter 11, claims against the chartered vessels can be allowed to proceed regardless of the Art 20 stay order under certain circumstances, subject to the secured status of the claims and the court's attitude towards in rem actions. For further discussion see Chapter 11.

[139] See *Daebo* (n 124).

of bankruptcy, blindly pursuing certainty but sacrificing the true nature of the transaction will damage the interests of both debtors and creditors. Although it must be admitted that the interest of a financing lessor has indeed been compromised in the circumstance of a recharacterisation, it seems that the interests of the insolvent debtor and its creditors need more protection. As can be seen from the example of Hanjin's bankruptcy, 54 out of 61 of its operating vessels were under BBCHP charterparties. This kind of operating strategy is commonly used in shipping practice. If a disguised demise charterparty is determined as a 'true lease', as it is labelled, the rehabilitation of the debtor would be severely hampered due to the potential threat of ship arrest against its operating vessels, especially if a large number of its operating vessels are operated under this kind of disguised demise charterparty.[140] If these vessels are not regarded as the assets of the debtor and are not subject to the protection of an Article 20 automatic stay order granted by the Model Law, claimants may take every opportunity to arrest these vessels in order to enforce their claims. Therefore, it will be difficult for the debtor to have a 'breathing space' to successfully rehabilitate its business. An unsuccessful rehabilitation of a debtor will then, in turn, have a significant impact on the entire shipping industry, including shippers, consignees, stevedores, pilots and crew members. Therefore, the economic substance of a demise charterparty should prevail over its label. In determining whether to recharacterise the demise charterparty the courts should examine all economic factors that drive the transaction, which are the prime impetus to the ultimate decision to enter into the transaction, and which constitute the reasons for structuring the transaction as it was effected.[141] Nevertheless, chartered vessels (either demise, time or voyage chartered) should be subject to the scope of the Article 20 automatic stay order.

B. Security to Release from Ship Arrest

Debtors or third parties, such as banks or mutual Protection and Indemnity Associations (P&I clubs), may provide surety bonds or security in order to prevent vessels that are owned by debtors from being arrested or to secure the release of the arrested vessels.[142] The amount of security is usually agreed by the parties. However, if the parties fail to reach an agreement with regard to the amount of the security, it will be decided by the courts at an amount that is sufficient to cover the claimant's 'best reasonably arguable claim, together with interest and costs'.[143]

[140] Kim, 'Korean Maritime Case Update: 2015/2016' (n 101) 223.
[141] *Lykes* (n 110) 580.
[142] Athanassiou (n 16) 252.
[143] N Meeson and J Kimbell, *Admiralty Jurisdiction and Practice*, 5th edn (Informa Law from Routledge, 2017) 167; *The Moschanty* [1971] 1 Lloyd's Rep 37, 44; *The Tribels* [1985] 1 Lloyd's Rep 128, 130; *FSL-9 Pte Ltd v Norwegian Hull Club (The FSL New York)* [2016] EWHC 1091 (Comm); see also Force (n 102) 39; Federal Rules of Civil Procedure, supp r E(5)(a); P Myburgh, 'P & I Club Letters of Undertaking and Admiralty Arrests' (2018) 24 *Journal of International Maritime Law* 201.

The question that will be discussed in this section is whether the security provided by a debtor or third party for the release of an arrested vessel or the avoidance of a potential vessel arrest, is to be regarded as the property of the debtor.[144] If the security is to be regarded as the asset of the debtor, the security will be protected by the automatic stay order granted by the Model Law regime and will be included in the estate of the debtor for the purpose of liquidation or reorganisation among all creditors. Conversely, if the security is not to be regarded as the asset of the debtor, it is not bound by the bankruptcy proceeding and can be provided to the specific creditor for the realisation of that specific claim.

i. *Security Provided by Debtors*

It is rare in practice that debtor-shipowners will provide surety bonds or cash for refraining from arresting relevant vessels, or releasing vessels that have been arrested, in the circumstance when debtors are on the brink of insolvency or have commenced insolvency proceedings. Therefore, detailed discussions of this circumstance will not be provided. However, it should be noted that if debtors provide surety bonds or cash during the preference period before a bankruptcy petition has been filed, such a transfer may constitute voidable preferences, which can then be set aside at the discretion of the liquidator or administrator.[145] In other words, the surety bonds or cash provided by debtors within the preference period will be included in the asset pool of the debtor for the purpose of liquidation or reorganisation among all creditors.

ii. *Security Provided by Third Parties*

In practice, in order to secure the release of a vessel or prevent the potential vessel arrest, it is more frequently the case that the security will be provided by third parties in the form of bank guarantees or P&I club letters of undertaking (LOUs),[146] which are nowadays the most routinely and ubiquitously used form of security in shipping practice.[147] The security serves as substitute *res* against which

[144] Given the insolvency of debtors, security may rarely be provided, especially by third parties; thus, this issue may not occur frequently in practice. Nevertheless, it is worth discussing it in detail.

[145] See D Skeen, 'Liens and Liquidation: Preferences, Strong Arm Clause, Fraudulent Transfers, Equitable Subordination, Priorities and Other Limitations on Liens Claims' (1985) 59 *Tulane Law Review* 1401, 1411; J Landers, 'The Shipowner Becomes A Bankrupt' (1972) 39 *University of Chicago Law Review* 490 (provides detail discussion on the avoidance of preference with respect to payment of maritime claims in bankruptcy proceedings).

[146] Similar to a bank guarantee, an LOU is a guarantee that is issued by a P&I club, in which the P&I club agrees to undertake the amount adjudged by the court that the member (the debtor-shipowner) is liable to pay, or the amount agreed under settlement terms. An LOU generally provides that, once the claimant accepts the LOU as security for his claim, he must release the ship from arrest or agree not to arrest the ship. Compared to a bank guarantee, an LOU is more flexible, can be easily prepared and quickly issued. See Myburgh (n 143) 202.

[147] Myburgh (n 143) 201.

the in rem admiralty proceedings are brought.[148] It is usually claim and party specific, in the sense that it only undertakes to pay a specified claim asserted by a specified plaintiff.[149] When security is properly posted and the vessel is released, the plaintiff no longer has an in rem action on the vessel; instead, the in rem action will be transferred to proceed against the security. The security will be forfeited to pay the plaintiff's claim if the plaintiff's claim turns out to be successful. However, the security does not support in rem actions or undertake any other claims that are asserted by other parties, in the sense that other parties cannot pursue the security for the satisfaction of their claims.[150]

Two questions arise on of the insolvency of shipowners. First, when a debtor is on the brink of insolvency, will the security provided by a bank or a P&I club for the release of vessel arrest be regarded as the property of the debtor? Second, if a debtor subsequently commences an insolvency proceeding, will its P&I club be obliged to provide an LOU upon the commencement of its insolvency and, if so, will the LOU be regarded as the asset of the debtor?

First, if a bank guarantee or LOU is issued before the commencement of an insolvency proceeding, it is not an asset of the debtor on the ground that the underlying nature of the bank guarantee or LOU is a private arrangement between the parties which is not transferable and is not for the benefit of all creditors. As explained by Martin Davies:

> Although the Club's undertaking to satisfy claims against the shipowner is obviously an asset in one sense, in that it relieves the shipowner of an obligation that it would otherwise have, it is not a fungible, transferable asset that can be realized by anyone other than the admiralty claimant, or in any place other than in the jurisdiction where it was given. Among other consequences, this means that the Club undertaking is not an asset that the court could entrust to the foreign representative to be brought into the [foreign main proceeding], under Article 21(1)(e) of the Model Law.[151]

Therefore, bank guarantees or LOUs are undertakings by banks or P&I clubs to pay certain claimants for certain claims and are only effective in a certain jurisdiction.[152] Given the fact that undertakings provided by third parties cannot be transferred to the foreign main proceedings of debtors and cannot be realised by any creditors other than the specific admiralty creditors that are specified in the guarantees or LOUs, they cannot be regarded as assets of debtors under the framework of the Model Law.[153]

[148] See eg *The Nied Elwin* (1811) 1 Dods 50, 53; *Mackensworth v SS American Merchant* 28 F 3d 246, 252 (2d Cir 1994); *Petroleos Mexicanos Refinacion v M/T King A* 554 F 3d 99, 104 (3d Cir 2009).

[149] Force (n 102) 39; Myburgh (n 143) 202–203; *The Nied Elwin* (n 148).

[150] Force (n 102) 39; Davies (n 125) 111.

[151] Davies (n 125) 111.

[152] ibid; Myburgh (n 143) 203.

[153] Davies (n 125) 111; B Ang, 'Arrest and Cross-Border Insolvency: The Singapore Experience' in P Myburgh (ed), *The Arrest Conventions: International Enforcement of Maritime Claims* (Hart Publishing, 2019) 217; *Kuo Fen Ching and Another v Dauphin Offshore Engineering & Trading Pte Ltd* [1999] SGCA 95.

Second, in practice, it seems that banks will usually not provide any guarantees if bankruptcy proceedings have been commenced by shipowner-debtors. However, it is not conclusive with regard to the issue of whether P&I clubs are obliged to continue to provide LOUs upon the commencement of a debtor's bankruptcy proceedings. Notwithstanding that a 'cesser clause' (also known as an 'ipso facto clause') exists in almost all P&I Club Rules (Club Rules), which provides that the insurance cover of shipowners automatically terminates upon their commencement of insolvency proceedings, it may or may not be enforceable in the arresting country.[154] In the UK it has been concluded that a 'cesser clause' is valid and effective. The UK Supreme Court in *Belmont Park Investments Pty Ltd v BNY Corporate Trustee Services Ltd* explained that it will, as far as possible, be deferential to party autonomy.[155] Thus, if the Club Rules are governed by UK law, P&I clubs can refuse to provide LOUs if aware of the commencement of a shipowner's insolvency proceedings. Conversely, the US Bankruptcy Court for the Southern District of New York in *In re Probulk Inc* held that the insurance right of the debtor continued after its petition for bankruptcy, despite the cesser clause in the Club Rules.[156] Therefore, in the US, the cesser clause is invalid and P&I clubs are restrained from terminating coverage, in the sense that they are bound to continue to provide security for the (potential) ship arrests that may occur after the commencement of insolvency proceedings.[157] Therefore, if the Club Rules are governed by US law and an LOU is provided by a P&I club, it will not be regarded as the asset of a debtor, but will only satisfy the specific claim that is undertaken by the LOU for the specific claimant outside of the bankruptcy proceeding.

III. Summary

The interpretation of COMI under the Model Law regime is not conclusive, as different jurisdictions may assign different weights and values to different factors dependent upon their view of social and economic policies. The fact sensitivity of the COMI inquiry always leaves a certain degree of uncertainty and ambiguity. In my view, the location of the registered office may not always be the COMI of debtors, especially with offshore shipping companies. In determining the COMI of a shipping company, courts should pay more attention to the factors that are

[154] See eg UK P&I Club Rules & Articles, available at www.ukpandi.com/fileadmin/uploads/uk-pi/LP%20Documents/2018/RULES/Final_Rulebook_2018.pdf, accessed 6 June 2020; American P&I Club Rules, available at www.american-club.com/files/files/1819.pdf, accessed 6 June 2020.

[155] *Belmont Park Investment Pty Ltd v BNY Corporate Trustee Services Ltd* [2011] UKSC 38; see also *Re Pan Ocean Co Ltd* [2014] EWHC 2124 (Ch); Davies (n 125) 117.

[156] *In re Probulk Inc* 407 BR 56, 61 (SD New York 2009); see also *In re Government Securities Corp* 972 F 2d 328, 329–30 (11th Cir 1992); *In re Lehman Bros Holdings Inc* 422 BR 407 (SD New York 2010); 11 USC § 541(c)(1)(B).

[157] Davies (n 125) 118; *Probulk* (n 156).

ascertainable to third parties, such as the place where the actual management, supervision and operation of the shipping company is conducted, and the place where the essential decisions are made or principal contracts are approved.[158] In addition, whether a chartered vessel (either demise, time or voyage chartered) can be regarded as the asset of the debtor depends on the nature of the charterparty. In determining whether to recharacterise the demise charterparty, courts should examine the 'economic substance' of each transaction. Finally, bank guarantees or LOUs are not regarded as assets of debtors and can satisfy specific claims that are undertaken by bank guarantees or LOUs outside bankruptcy proceedings.

[158] Athanassiou (n 16) 160.

BIBLIOGRAPHY

Books

American Law Institute, *Transactional Insolvency: Co-operation among the NAFTA Countries, Principles of Cooperation Among the NAFTA Countries* (Juris Publishing, 2003).

Athanassiou, L, *Maritime Cross-Border Insolvency* (Informa Law from Routledge, 2017).

Bailey, E and Groves, H, *Corporate Insolvency: Law and Practice* (LexisNexis, 2014).

Bell, A, *Forum Shopping and Venue in Transnational Litigation* (Oxford University Press, 2003).

Bennett, H (ed), *Carver on Chapterparties* (Sweet & Maxwell, 2017).

Black's Law Dictionary, 11th edn (West Group, 2019).

Bleyen, L, *Judicial Sales of Ships* (Springer, 2016).

Broude, R, *Reorganizations under Chapter 11 of the Bankruptcy Code* (Law Journal Press, 2005).

Bufford, SL et al, *International Insolvency* (Federal Judicial Centre, 2001).

Clark, L, *Ancillary and other Cross-Border Insolvency Cases under Chapter 15 of the Bankruptcy Code* (LexisNexis Matthew Bender, 2008).

Coghlin, T et al, *Time Charters*, 7th edn (Informa Law from Routledge, 2014).

Collins, L and Harris, J (eds), *Dicey, Morris and Collins on The Conflict of Laws*, 15th edn (Sweet & Maxwell, 2012).

Derrington, S and Turner, J, *The Law and Practice of Admiralty Matters*, 2nd edn (Oxford University Press, 2016).

Eder, B et al, *Scrutton on Chapterparties and Bill of Lading*, 23rd edn (Sweet & Maxwell, 2015).

Epstein, D et al, *Bankruptcy, Practitioner Treatise Series* vol 1 (West Publishing, 1992).

Finch, V and Milman, D, *Corporate Insolvency Law: Perspectives and Principles*, 3rd edn (Cambridge University Press, 2017).

Fletcher, I, *Insolvency in Private International Law*, 2nd edn (Oxford University Press, 2007).

—— *The Law of Insolvency*, 5th edn (Sweet & Maxwell, 2017).

Force, R, *Admiralty and Maritime Law*, 2nd edn (Federal Judicial Centre, 2013).

Force, R et al, *Admiralty and Maritime Law* (Beard Books, 2006).

Gilmore, G and Black, C, *The Law of Admiralty*, 2nd edn (Foundation Press, 1975).

Gold, E, *Maritime Transport: The Evolution of International Marine Policy and* Law (Lexington Books, 1981).

Gross, K, *Failure and Forgiveness: Rebalancing the Bankruptcy System* (Yale University Press, 1999).

Ho, LC, *A Commentary on the UNCITRAL Model Law*, 4th edn (Globe Law and Business, 2017).

Jackson, DC, *Enforcement of Maritime Claims*, 4th edn (Routledge, 2005).

Jackson, T, *The Logic and Limits of Bankruptcy Law* (Harvard University Press, 1986).

Keay, A, *The Law of Company Liquidation*, 4th edn (Sweet & Maxwell, 2017).

Meeson, N and Kimbell, J, *Admiralty Jurisdiction and Practice*, 5th edn (Informa Law from Routledge, 2017).

Moss, G et al, *The EC Regulation on Insolvency Proceedings: A Commentary and Annotated Guide*, 3rd edn (Oxford University Press, 2016).

Osborne, D et al, *The Law of Ship Mortgage*, 2nd edn (Informa Law from Routledge, 2016).

Payne, J, *Scheme of Arrangement: Theory, Structure and Operation* (Cambridge University Press, 2014).

Philip, S, *Cross-border Insolvency*, 2nd edn (Lexisnexis UK, 1998).

Schoenbaum, T, *Admiralty and Maritime Law*, 6th edn (West Academic Publishing, 2019).

Silkenat, J and Schmerler, C, *The Law of International Insolvencies and Debt Restructurings* (Oceana TM, 2006).
Soyer, B and Tettenborn, A, *Ship Building, Sale and Finance* (Informa Law from Routledge, 2016).
Stephenson Harwood, *Shipping Finance*, 3rd edn (Euromoney Institutional Investor, 2006).
Stopford, M, *Maritime Economics*, 3rd edn (Routledge, 2009).
Sullivan, T et al, *As We Forgive Our Debtors: Bankruptcy and Consumer Credit in America* (Oxford University Press, 1989).
Symes, C et al, *Australian Insolvency Law*, 4th edn (LexisNexis Butterworths, 2019).
Tabb, C, *Law of Bankruptcy*, 4th edn (West Academic Publishing, 2016).
Tan, CH (ed), *Walter Woon on Company Law*, rev 3rd edn (Sweet & Maxwell, 2009).
Tetley, W, *International Maritime and Admiralty Law* (Éditions Yvon Blais, 2002).
—— *Maritime Liens and Claims*, 2nd edn (Éditions Yvon Blais, 1998).
The Parliament of the Commonwealth of Australia, Cross-Border Insolvency Bill 2008 Explanatory Memorandum.
Thomas, DR, *Maritime Liens* (Stevens & Sons, 1980).
Toh, KS, *Admiralty Law and Practice*, 3rd edn (LexisNexis, 2017).
Tomasic, R and Whitford, K, *Australian Insolvency and Bankruptcy Law*, 2nd edn (Butterworth, 1997).
UNCITRAL Secretariat, *UNCITRAL Cross-Border Insolvency Law with Guide to Enactment and Interpretation* (United Nations Office at Vienna, 2014).
—— *UNCITRAL Model Law on Cross-Border Insolvency: Judicial Perspective* (United Nations Office at Vienna, 2014).
Warren, E et al, *The Law of Debtors and Creditors: Text, Cases, and Problems*, 7th edn (Wolters Kluwer, 2014).
Wessels, B et al, *International Cooperation in Bankruptcy and Insolvency Matters* (Oxford University Press, 2009).
Westbrook, J et al, *A Global View of Business Insolvency Systems* (Martinus Nijhoff, 2010).

Articles

Adams, E and Fincke, J, 'Co-ordinating Cross-Border Bankruptcy: How Territorialism Saves Universalism' (2009) 15 *Columbia Journal of European Law* 43.
Adler, B et al, 'Regulating Consumer Bankruptcy: A Theoretical Inquiry' (2000) 29 *Journal of Legal Studies* 585.
Alwang, M, 'Steering The Most Appropriate Course Between Admiralty and Insolvency: Why An International Insolvency Treaty Should Recognise the Primacy of Admiralty Law Over Maritime Assets' (1996) 64 *Fordham Law Review* 2613.
Ang, B, 'Arrest and Cross-Border Insolvency: The Singapore Experience' in P Myburgh (ed), *The Arrest Conventions: International Enforcement of Maritime Claims* (Hart Publishing, 2019).
Apáthy, P and Chua, E, 'Singapore's New 'Supercharged' Scheme of Arrangement' (2017) 5 *Butterworths Journal of International Banking and Financial Law* 282.
Ashmead, J et al, 'The Intersection of Maritime Law and the United States Bankruptcy Code' (2016) 28 *University of San Francisco Maritime Law Journal* 117.
Bebchuk, L and Fried, J, 'The Uneasy Case for the Priority of Secured Claims in Bankruptcy' (1996) 105 *Yale Law Journal* 857.
Bebchuk, L and Guzman, A, 'An Economic Analysis of Transactional Bankruptcy' (1999) 42 *The Journal of Law & Economics* 775.
Bennetts, KJ, 'Voluntary Administration: Shaping the Process Thorough the Exercise of Judicial Discretion' (1995) 3 *Insolvency Law Journal* 135.
Berends, A, 'The UNCITRAL Model Law on Cross-Border Insolvency: A Comprehensive Overview' (1998) 6 *Tulane Journal of International and Comparative Law* 309.

Biery, E et al, 'A Look at Transnational Insolvencies and Chapter 15 of the Bankruptcy Abuse Prevention and Consumer Protection Act of 2005' (2005) 47 *Boston College Law Review* 23.

Block-Lieb, S and Halliday, T, 'Less is More in International Private Law' (2015) 3 *Nottingham Insolvency and Business Law e-Journal* 43.

Browne, J, 'The Extinction of Maritime Liens' [2003] *Lloyd's Maritime and Commercial Law Quarterly* 361.

Bufford, S, 'Global Venue Controls Are Coming: A Reply to Professor Lopucki' (2005) 79 *American Bankruptcy Law Journal* 105.

Buss, C, 'Ship Mortgagees: Enforcement and Remedies' in B Soyer and A Tettenborn (eds), *Ship Building Sale and Finance* (Informa from Routledge, 2016).

Buxbaum, H, 'Rethinking International Insolvency: The Neglected Role of Choice of Law Rules and Theory' (2000) 36 *Stanford Journal of International Law* 23.

Carruthers, J, 'Substance and Procedure in the Conflict of Laws: A Continuing Debate in Relation to Damages' (2004) 53 *The International Comparative Law Quarterly* 691.

Chan, SK, 'Cross-Border Insolvency Issues Affecting Singapore' (2011) *Singapore Academy of Law Journal* 413.

Clark, L and Goldstein, K, 'Sacred Cows: How to Care for Secured Creditors' Rights in Cross-Border Bankruptcies' (2011) 46 *Texas International Law Journal* 513.

Clift, J, 'The UNCITRAL Model Law on Cross-Border Insolvency – A Legislative Framework to Facilitate Coordination and Cooperation in Cross-Border Insolvency' (2004) 12 *Tulane Journal of International and Comparative Law* 307.

Cohen, MM, 'In Defense of the Halcyon Isle' [1987] *Lloyd's Maritime and Commercial Law Quarterly* 152.

Coleman, S and Johnson, J, 'Journey to the Centre of the Economic Universe: How the Current US COMI Timing Determination Misses the Mark' [2014] 23 No 6 *Norton Journal of Bankruptcy Law and Practice* Art 4.

Collins, D, 'Comments on the American Rule of In Rem Liability' (1985) 10 *Maritime Lawyer* 71.

Davenport, BJ, 'End of an Old Admiralty Belief' (1998) 11 *LQR* 169.

Davies, M, 'Choice of Law and US Maritime Liens' (2009) 83 *Tulane Law Review* 1435.

—— 'Cross-Border Insolvency and Admiralty: A Middle Path of Reciprocal Comity' (2018) 66 *American Journal of Comparative Law* 101.

—— 'In Defense of Popular Virtues: Personification and Ratification' (2000) 75 *Tulane Law Review* 337.

—— 'Maritime Liens and Choice of Law' (2018) 42 *Tulane Maritime Law Journal* 269.

—— 'The Future of Ship Arrest' in P Myburgh (ed), *The Arrest Conventions: International Enforçement of Maritime Claims* (Hart Publishing, 2019).

Dean, M, 'International Insolvencies: The Difficulties, The Traditional Solution and The Ideal' (2001) 9 *Insolvency Law Journal* 88.

Devlin, J, 'The UNCITRAL Model Law on Cross-Border Insolvency and Its Impact on Maritime Creditors' (2010) 21 *Journal of Banking and Finance Law and Practice* 95.

Drobnig, U, 'Secured Credit in International Insolvency Proceedings' (1998) 22 *Texas International Law Journal* 53.

Egiyan, GS, 'Flag of Convenience or Open Registration of Ships' (1990) 14 *Marine Policy* 106.

Ehrenzweig, A, 'The Lex Fori: Basic Rule in the Conflict of Laws' (1960) 58 *Michigan Law Review* 637.

Eisenberg, T, 'Bankruptcy Law in Perspective' (1981) 28 *UCLA Law Review* 953.

Falzone, AJ, 'Two Households, Both Alike in Dignity: The International Feud between Admiralty and Bankruptcy' (2014) 39 *Brooklyn Journal of International Law* 1175.

Fletcher, I, 'Better Late than Never: The UNCITRAL Model Law Enters into Force in Great Britain' (2006) 19 *Insolvency Intelligence* 86.

Ford, J and Wilcox, C, 'Shedding Light on the Dark Side of Maritime Trade – A New Approach for Identifying Countries as Flags of Convenience' (2019) 99 *Marine Policy* 298.

Franken, S, 'Cross-Border Insolvency Law: A Comparative Institutional Analysis' (2013) *Oxford Journal of Legal Studies* 97.
Gebb, SA, 'The Demise Charter: A Conceptual and Practical Analysis' (1975) 49 *Tulane Law Review* 764.
Gopalan, S and Guihot, M, 'Recognition and Enforcement in Cross-Border Insolvency Law: A Proposal for Judicial Gap-Filling' (2015) 48 *Vanderbilt Journal of Transnational Law* 1225.
Guzman, A, 'International Bankruptcy: In Defense of Universalism' (2000) 98 *Michigan Law Review* 2177.
Hafeez-Baig, MJ, 'Navigating The Waters between Admiralty and Cross-Border Insolvency: A Comparison of the Australian, German and French Position' [2018] *Lloyd's Maritime and Commercial Law Quarterly* 97.
Hallinan, C, 'The Fresh Start Policy in Consumer Bankruptcy: A Historical Inventory and an Interpretative Theory' (1986) 21 *University of Richmond Law Review* 49.
Hallock, J, 'Time Out: The Problematic Temporality of COMI Analysis in Chapter 15 Bankruptcy Cases in the Second Circuit' (2015) *Columbia Business Law Review* 1074.
Harper, E, 'Demise Charters: Responsibilities of Owner or Charterer for Loss or Damage' (1975) 49 *Tulane Law Review* 785.
Hathorn, P, 'Cross-Border Insolvency in the Maritime Context: The United States' Universalism vs Singapore's Territorialism' (2013) 38 *Tulane Maritime Law Journal* 239.
Herbert, P, 'The Origin and Nature of Maritime Liens' (1930) 4 *Tulane Law Review* 381.
Ho, LC, 'Anti-Suit Injunctions in Cross-Border Insolvency: A Restatement' (2003) 53 *International and Comparative Law Quarterly* 52.
—— 'Cross-Border Fraud and Cross-Border Insolvency: Proving COMI and Seeking Recognition under the UK Model Law' [2009] *Butterworths Journal of International Banking and Financial Law* 537.
—— 'Recognising an Australian Solvent Liquidation under the UNCITRAL Model Law: In re Betcorp' [2009] *Journal of International Banking Law and Regulation* 418.
Howard, M, 'Equipment Lessors and Secured Parties in Bankruptcy: An Argument for Coherence' (1991) 48 *Washington and Lee Law Review* 253.
Hurd, H, 'The Virtue of Consumer Bankruptcy' in R Brubaker et al (eds), *A Debtor's World: Interdisciplinary Perspectives on Debt* (Oxford University Press, 2012).
Jackson, T, 'The Fresh-Start Policy in Bankruptcy Law' (1985) 98 *Harvard Law Review* 1393.
—— 'Bankruptcy, Nonbankruptcy Entitlements, and the Creditors' Bargain' (1982) 91 *Yale Law Journal* 857.
Ji, ZH, 'Cross-Border Rehabilitation: An Impediment to Ship Arrest in Singapore?' CML Working Paper Series, No 17/01, March 2017.
Kim, IH, 'An Overview of Korean Maritime Law' (2012) 10 *Asian Business Law* 35.
—— 'Korean Maritime Case Update: 2015/2016' (2017) 48 *Journal of Maritime Law & Commerce* 211.
—— 'Legal Implication of Hanjin Shipping's Rehabilitation Proceeding' [2017] *Hong Kong Law Journal* 915.
King, J, 'Moving Beyond the Hard–Easy Tug of War: A Historical, Empirical and Theoretical Assessment of Bankruptcy Discharge' (2004) 28 *Melbourne University Law Review* 654.
Kraft, T and Aranson, A, 'Transnational Bankruptcies: Section 304 and Beyond' (1993) *Columbia Business Law Review* 329.
Landers, J, 'The Shipowner Becomes a Bankruptcy' (1972) 39 *University of Chicago Law Review* 490.
Lee, SLJ, 'Is Singapore's Insolvency Regime Excessively Pro-creditor' (2003) 12 *International Insolvency Review* 37.
Letalik, N, 'Maritime Lien' in E Gold et al (eds), *Canadian Maritime Law*, 2nd edn (Irwin Law, 2016).
Levenson, D, 'Proposal for Reform of Choice of Avoidance Law in the Context of International Bankruptcies from a US Perspective' (2002) 10 *American Bankruptcy Institute Law Review* 291.
Lindgren, K, 'Voluntary Administration: Current Issues and Proposals for Reform' (FCA) [2006] *Federal Judicial Scholarship* 4.

LoPucki, L, 'Co-operation in International Bankruptcy: A Post-Universalist Perspective' (1999) 84 *Cornell Law Review* 696.

—— 'Global and Out of Control?' (2005) 79 *American Bankruptcy Law Journal* 79.

—— 'Universalism Unravels' (2005) 79 *American Bankruptcy Law Journal* 143.

Mann, R, 'Explaining the Pattern of Secured Credit' (1997) 110 *Harvard Law Review* 625.

Martin, N, 'The Role of History and Culture in Developing Bankruptcy and Insolvency Systems: The Perils of Legal Transplantation' (2005) 28 *Boston College International and Comparative Law Review* 1.

McCormack, G, 'COMI and Comity in UK and US Insolvency Law' [2012] *LQR* 140.

—— 'Universalism in Insolvency Proceedings and the Common Law' (2012) 32 *Oxford Journal of Legal Studies* 325.

McCormack, G and Wan, WY, 'The UNCITRAL Model Law on Cross-Border Insolvency Comes of Age: New Times or New Paradigms?' (2019) 54 *Texas International Law Journal* 273.

Mevorach, I, 'A Fresh View on the Hard/Soft Law Divide: Implications for International Insolvency of Enterprise Group' (2019) 40 *Michigan Journal of International Law* 505.

Myburgh, P, 'Arresting the Right Ship: Procedural Theory, the in Personam Link and Conflict of Laws' in M Davies (ed), *Jurisdiction and Forum Selection in International Maritime Law Essay in Honor of Robert Force* (Kluwer Law International, 2005).

—— 'P & I Club Letters of Undertaking and Admiralty Arrests' (2018) 24 *Journal of International Maritime Law* 201.

—— 'Richard Cooper Memorial Lecture Admiralty Law – What is it Good For?' (2009) 28(1) *University of Queensland Law Journal* 19.

—— 'Satisfactory for Its Own Purposes: Private Direct Arrangements and Judicial Vessel Sales' (2016) 22 *Journal of International Maritime Law* 355.

Notes, 'Priorities of Maritime Liens' (1956) 69 *Harvard Law Review* 525.

Peck, S, 'Navigating the Murky Waters of Admiralty and Bankruptcy Law' (2013) 87 *Tulane Law Review* 955.

Pottow, J, 'Greed and Pride in International Bankruptcy: The Problems of and Proposed Solutions to Local Interests' (2006) 104 *Michigan Law Review* 1899.

—— 'Beyond Carve-Outs and Toward Reliance: A Normative Framework for Cross-border Insolvency Choice of Law' (2014) 9 *Brooklyn Journal of Corporate, Financial & Commercial Law* 202.

Price, G, 'The Priority of Maritime Liens' (1942) 24 *Journal of Comparative Legislation and International Law* 38.

Psarellis, S, 'Bet Your Lien and Roll the Dice: Maritime Liens and Riverboat Gambling' (1993) 6 *University of San Francisco Maritime Law Journal* 49.

Ragan, A, 'COMI Strikes a Discordant Note: Why US Courts Are Not in Complete Harmony Despite Chapter 15 Directives' (2010) 27 *Emory Bankruptcy Development Journal* 117.

Rares, S, 'Admiralty Law the Flying Dutchman of Cross-Border Insolvency' (FCA) [2009] *Federal Judicial Scholarship* 22.

—— 'Consistency and Conflict – Cross-Border Insolvency' [2015] *Federal Judicial Scholarship* 14.

—— 'Maritime Liens, Renvoi and Conflicts of Law' [2014] *Lloyd's Maritime and Commercial Law Quarterly* 183.

—— 'Ship Arrests, Maritime Liens and Cross-Border Insolvency' [2018] *Lloyd's Maritime and Commercial Law Quarterly* 398.

Rasmussen, R, 'A New Approach to Transactional Insolvencies' (1997) 19 *Michigan Journal of International Law* 1.

Rochelle, B, 'Cross-border Insolvency in the US and UK: Conflicting Approaches to Defining the Locus of a Debtor's Centre of Interests' (2017) 50 *Int'l L* 391.

Rutherglen, G, 'Admiralty and Bankruptcy Revisited: Effects of the Bankruptcy Reform Act of 1978' (1991) 65 *Tulane Law Review* 503.

—— 'The Contemporary Justification for Maritime Arrest and Attachment' (1989) 30 *William & Mary Law Review* 541.

Seitz, G, 'Interaction between Admiralty and Bankruptcy Law: Effects of Globalization and Recurrent Tensions' (2009) 83 *Tulane Law Review* 1339.

Schwab, B, 'Equitable Personification: A Review of Res Judicata's Historical Application to Successive in Personam and in Rem Admiralty Actions in the United States' (2012) 37 *Tulane Maritime Law Journal* 253.

Schwartz, A, 'A Theory of Loan Priorities' (1989) 18 *Journal of Legal Studies* 209.

Schwartz, C, 'Due Process and Traditional Admiralty Arrest and Attachment under the Supplemental Rules' (1983) 8 *Maritime Lawyer* 229.

Skeen, D, 'Liens and Liquidation: Preferences, Strong Arm Clause, Fraudulent Transfers, Equitable Subordination, Priorities and Other Limitations on Liens Claims' (1985) 59 *Tulane Law Review* 1401.

Smith, B, 'Ship Mortgages' (1973) 47 *Tulane Law Review* 608.

Soars, J, 'Cross-Border Insolvency and Shipping – A Practical Guide' 7 Wentworth Selborne Chambers Sydney.

Story, S, 'Cross-Border Insolvency: A Comparative Analysis' (2015) 32 *Arizona Journal of International & Comparative Law* 431.

Teare, N, 'The Admiralty Action in Rem and the House of Lords' [1998] *Lloyd's Maritime and Commercial Law Quarterly* 33.

Tetley, W, 'Arrest, Attachment, and Related Maritime Law Procedures' (1999) 73 *Tulane Law Review* 1895.

—— 'Conflicts of Law between the Bankruptcy Courts in Admiralty: Canada, United Kingdom, United States, and France' (1996) 20 *Tulane Maritime Law Journal* 257.

—— 'Maritime Liens in Conflict of Laws' in J Nafziger and S Symeonides (eds), *Law and Justice in a Multistate World: Essays in Honour of Arthur T von Mehren* (Brill Nijhoff, 2002).

Tsimplis, M, 'Procedures for Enforcement' in Y Baatz (eds), *Maritime Law* (4rd edn, Routledge 2017).

Tung, F, 'Is International Bankruptcy Possible?' (2001) 23 *Michigan Journal of International Law* 31.

Walker, G, 'The Personification of the Vessel in United States Civil In Rem Actions and the International Law Context' (1991) 15 *Tulane Maritime Law Journal* 177.

Walters, A, 'Modified Universalisms & the Role of Local Legal Culture in the Making of Cross-Border Insolvency Law' (2019) 93 *American Bankruptcy Law Journal* 47.

Wan, WY and McCormack, G, 'Transplanting Chapter 11 of the US Bankruptcy Code into Singapore's Restructuring and Insolvency Laws: Opportunities and Challenges' (2018) *Journal of Corporate Law Studies* 1.

Warren, E, 'A Principled Approach to Consumer Bankruptcy' (1997) 71 *American Bankruptcy Law Journal* 483.

—— 'Bankruptcy Policymaking in an Imperfect World' (1993) 92 *Michigan Law Review* 336.

Westbrook, J, 'A Global Solution to Multinational Default' (2000) 98 *Michigan Law Review* 2276.

—— 'Developments in Transnational Bankruptcy' (1995) 39 *St Louis University Law Journal* 745.

—— 'Locating the Eye of the Financial Storm' (2007) 32 *Brooklyn Journal of International Law* 1019.

—— 'Multinational Enterprises in General Default: Chapter 15, the ALI Principles, and the EU Insolvency Regulation' (2002) 76 *American Bankruptcy Law Journal* 1.

—— 'Theory and Pragmatism in Global Insolvencies: Choice of Law and Choice of Forum' (1991) 65 *American Bankruptcy Law Journal* 457.

INDEX

A

Abdullah J 173

access to proceedings

Model Law principle of 6, 28–29

Ackers v Saad Investments Co Ltd 172

Addy J 51

administration proceedings

appointment of administrator 69

Australia 12n, 66, 68–69, 70–71, 72, 73, 79, 80, 83, 141

company arrangements and 85–86, 87–88

deed of company arrangement (DOCA) 68–69, 71

demise-chartered vessels 184

disallowance by court 70

generally 12n

objectives 68, 85

security for release 187

Singapore, judicial management regime 12n, 121, 122, 123, 141

stay orders 7, 87–88, 90

United Kingdom 12n, 85, 87–88, 90, 94–95, 97–100, 103, 141

voluntary 68–69, 70, 72, 73, 79

winding-up proceedings and 67, 70–71

administrator

co-operative territorialism 6, 22

company reorganisations 13

territorialism 18–19

admiralty law *see* **maritime law**

Aichhorn and Co KG v The Ship MV Talabot 81

Allsop CJ 73

Arden J 90

Aro Co Ltd 50, 89, 90, 127, 128

arrest of vessel

admiralty law, generally 2–3

Australia 72, 73, 76, 78, 83

change of ownership before 48

chartered vessels 180

conflict of laws 3, 40–41, 53–54, 76

custodial expenses following 145–146

different creditor, by 90

forum arresti 3, 59, 60, 62–63, 149, 158–160, 163–164

generally 2–3, 40–41, 64–65

in rem actions 2, 7, 40–41, 43, 48–51, 57, 58–59, 72–73, 89, 96–100

international 3

International Convention Relating to the Arrest of Sea-Going Ships 51

judicial sale 2, 43, 160

lex causae rule 159, 162–163

lex fori rule 158–160

maritime liens 2–3, 40–41, 43, 47, 53, 72, 76, 88, 89, 141

prevention 64–65, 70, 71, 72, 78, 79, 80, 87, 100, 117, 132, 134, 137, 146, 186–189

ranking of claims 48, 52, 158, 161

recognition of foreign main proceeding 5, 59, 60–61, 76–80, 139–140

Rule B attachment 56, 95, 111, 116–117

security for maritime claim 48

security for release *see* security for release of vessel

Singapore 128, 134–135, 136, 137, 180

sister ships 55–56, 57

stay order (moratorium) *see* stay order

timing of writ 152–153

United Kingdom 88, 89, 90, 94, 100

United States 110, 111–115, 117, 119

assets

arrest, subject to *see* arrest of vessel

asset collection and realisation 12, 67, 84

avoidable transfer, seizure and return where 22

chartered vessels *see* chartered vessel

common pool 11, 14, 28, 58–59, 64

company liquidations 12

company reorganisations 12

cross-border insolvencies, generally 16

depreciation in value 36, 107–108, 146, 147, 149

distribution *see* distribution of assets

entrusting to foreign representative 36, 38

evidence regarding, uncovering 36, 38

freezing 2, 33, 36

going concerns, preservation 10

grab rule *see* territorialism

joint sale, co-operative territorialism 22
maritime, generally 2–4
maximisation of value 10–11, 13–14, 18, 20, 58
mobile nature of shipping 3, 145, 146, 175–176
modified universalism 23–24
multiple states, in 27
new pragmatism 21–24
non-exempt 10
perishable 36
presence of 34
scope of debtor's assets 5, 64–65, 179–190
secured creditors *see* creditor
security for release, whether asset of debtor 5, 65, 187–190
single court adjudicating all claims 11–12
stay of proceedings against *see* stay order
suspension of right to transfer 36, 38
territorialism *see* territorialism
universalism *see* universalism
unsecured creditors 14–15, 110
vessels, generally 3

Atlantic Computer Systems 124

attachment
foreign proceedings and 32
Rule B 56, 95, 111, 116–117, 141

Australia
Ackers v Saad Investments Co Ltd 172
administration proceedings 12n, 66, 68–69, 72, 73, 79, 80, 83, 141
Admiralty Act 1988 71, 72
Aichhorn and Co KG v The Ship MV Talabot 81
arrest of vessel 72, 73, 76, 78, 83
automatic stay order 66, 73, 74–76, 78, 80, 81–83, 154
bankruptcy, generally 66
Bankruptcy Act 1966 66, 75
Caltex Oil (Australia) Pty Ltd v The Dredge Willemstad 81
centre of main interest of debtor 171–172, 173, 174, 178
chartered vessels 82, 180
Comandate Marine Corp v Pan Australia Shipping Pty Ltd 71, 81–82, 151
conflict of laws 76–80
Corporate Law Reform Act 1992 68
Corporations Act 2001 66, 67, 68, 69, 70–71, 73, 74, 75, 78–80, 82, 144
Cross-Border Insolvency Act 2008 66, 73–80
Danny Morris & Another v The Ship 'Kiama' 50, 73, 76
deed of company arrangement 68–69, 71
foreign main proceedings 74–76, 77–79, 83
foreign proceedings in Australia 79–80
in rem actions 7, 50, 56–57, 72–73, 77, 78, 81–82, 83, 141, 154
insolvency regime, generally 66–70, 73–74, 75
Kim v Daebo International Shipping Co Ltd 73, 77, 152–153
lex fori rule 158
maritime liens 42, 48, 53, 71–72, 77, 78, 79–80, 81–82, 141
Model Law, adoption 7, 66, 73–75, 83, 140
Moore v Australian Equity Investors 178
personification doctrine 79, 81–82
procedural theory 56–57, 71, 81–82, 151
public policy exception 34
receivership 74
recognition of foreign claims 54
recognition of foreign proceedings 74–76, 77–79, 83
restructuring proceedings 66
schemes of arrangement 66, 69–70, 71, 75
secured claims 71–73
secured creditors 15, 71, 75–77, 79–80, 83, 144
ship mortgages 157
The Ship Sam Hawk v Reiter Petroleum Inc 72, 81
stay provisions 66, 70–83, 144, 154
Tai-Soo Suk v Hanjin Shipping Co Ltd 79–80, 82, 83, 140
unsecured creditors 71
winding-up proceedings 12n, 66–68, 72, 73, 74, 78–79, 83, 141
Yakushiji v Daiichi Chuo Kisen Kaisha 73
Yu v STX Pan Ocean Co Ltd 72, 77–79, 82, 140, 151

B

bank guarantee
security for release of vessel 8, 64, 128, 186–189

bankruptcy law
aim 9–10, 58
assets *see* assets
Australia 66, 75
conflict with maritime law 1, 3, 4, 5, 58–65, 76–80, 95, 131, 139–141
creditor *see* creditor

debtor *see* debtor
discharged debts 10, 12, 13
distribution *see* distribution of assets
equivalent creditors, equal treatment 1, 11–12, 58
fresh start policy 9–10, 13, 58
fundamental aims 9–12
insolvency *see* insolvency
liquidation 12
maximisation of asset value 10–11, 13–14, 18, 20, 58
national variations 1, 6, 9, 12, 12n
overall interests of all creditors 11
ranking claims *see* ranking of claims
reorganisation 12
secured creditors 5
single court adjudicates all claims 11–12
US Bankruptcy Code 8, 104–115, 119, 173

bareboat charter *see* **chartered vessel**
bareboat charter hire purchase agreement (BBCHP) 8, 117–119, 184–185
Baughen, Simon 181
Bear Stearns 173
Belmont Park Investments Pty Ltd v BNY Corporate Trustee Services Ltd 189
Beluga Chartering GmbH v Beluga Projects Pte Ltd 133, 153
The Bold Buccleugh 41, 71–72, 88
The Bolivia 90
Brandon J 50
breach of contract
charterparty claims 42, 72
maritime liens 44, 47, 142–143, 143n
in personam actions 55
in rem claims 42, 55–56, 61
Buchanan J 78, 79
Burnton LJ 95
Buss, Charles 156

C

Caltex Oil (Australia) Pty Ltd v The Dredge Willemstad 81
Canada
in rem actions 48, 50–51
lex causae rule 158, 163
maritime liens 42
The Miss Donna 50
recognition of foreign claims 54
cargo
damage, in rem actions 42
lien *see* maritime lien
loss, in rem actions 72
tortious act by vessel 46
The Cella 49
centre of main interest (COMI) of debtor
Australia 171–172, 173, 174, 178
change of 176–177
charterparties 168
conflict of laws 62–63
date for determination 176–179
determination 5, 8, 33–34, 62–63, 165–179, 189–190
distribution of assets 27
flag of convenience/open registry 63, 166, 166n, 175–176
foreign main proceedings 33–34, 62–63, 162, 165
forum shopping 63, 165
fraud 174
habitual residence 5, 8, 33, 63, 165
letterbox companies 168
management and ownership, separation 63, 166, 174–176
Model Law 5, 27, 33–34, 62–63, 165–167, 169–176, 189–190
offshore registration 63, 166, 168–169, 175, 189
one-ship companies 63, 166, 168
principal place of business 20, 172–173
proceedings outside 34
purpose of rule 62–63
Recast EU Regulation 91, 166–172, 177
registered office 5, 8, 33, 63, 165, 167–168, 170, 172–176, 189
Regulation (EU) 2015/848 166–167
Singapore 173–174, 177–178
United Kingdom 171–172, 173, 174, 177
United States 172–173, 174, 177–178
chartered vessel
arrest 180
asset of debtor, whether 5, 64, 179–186, 190
Australia 82, 180
bareboat charter hire purchase agreements 8, 117–119, 184–185
bareboat charters 8, 64, 119
breach claims in rem 42, 72
centre of main interest of debtor 168
conflict of laws 64–65
demise charters 5, 179, 180–186, 183n, 190
finance lease and 8, 117, 181–186, 183n
master and crew 64
Model Law 5, 64
owner 64

owner *pro hac vice*
(owner ad hoc) 64, 180–186
personification doctrine 115
sale-and-leaseback 116–117
sham charterparty 117
Singapore 137, 180
stay orders 5, 64, 116, 137, 179, 180, 185–186
third-party beneficial cargo owners 118
time charters 5, 64, 117, 119, 179, 180, 186, 190
United Kingdom 102, 180, 183–184
United States 115, 116–119, 180, 181–182, 183
voyage charters 5, 64, 119, 179, 180, 186, 190

China
lex fori rule 159
Qinzhou Guiqin Shipping Group Co 146
recognition of foreign claims 54

The China 115

choice of law
cross-border insolvencies 16–17
new pragmatism 21–24
territorialism 19
universalism 20–21

claim
maritime *see* maritime claim

Coastal Marine Management LLC v Additional Return LLC 145–146

Cohen, Michael 160

collision damage
maritime liens 41–42, 71, 126, 146

Comandate Marine Corp v Pan Australia Shipping Pty Ltd 71, 81–82, 151

common law countries
insolvency law 9, 12, 66
maritime liens 158–159

company
liquidation *see* liquidation
reorganisation *see* reorganisation
statutory declaration of solvency 85
winding-up *see* winding-up proceedings

company arrangements
administration proceedings and 85–86, 87–88
Australia 68–69, 71
deeds of company arrangement (DOCA) 68–69, 71
purpose 85
schemes of arrangement 86, 87–88
secured creditors and 86
stay orders and 87–88
United Kingdom 85–86, 87–88
voluntary (CVA) 85–86, 87–88

concurrent proceedings
co-operation and co-ordination, principle of 39

conflict of laws
arrest and sale of vessel 3, 40–41, 53–54, 76, 161
Australia 76–80
bankruptcy law and maritime law 1, 3, 4, 5, 58–65, 76–80, 95, 131, 139–141
centre of main interest 62–63
chartered vessels 64–65
conflicting claims 16
declaratory relief 39
foreign main proceedings 8, 160–164
forum arresti 3, 59, 60, 62–63, 149, 158–161, 163–164
in rem claims 8, 61–62, 140–141, 161, 164
lex causae rule 54, 158–159, 161, 162–163
lex fori rule 8, 54, 158–164
maritime claims, generally 16, 39, 53–54, 60, 141, 158–160
maritime lien, availability and scope 6, 53–54, 76–80, 141, 160–164
Model Law and 58–62, 76–80
national variations in insolvency law 1, 6, 9, 12, 12n, 16, 31–32, 140, 141
non-maritime claims 158
personification doctrine 61–62
ranking of claims 6, 53–54, 158, 161, 163–164
relief from automatic stay 60–61
Singapore 131, 138
underlying cause of action of claim 53
United Kingdom 95

corporate-charter contractualism
theory, generally 17n

Cosco Bulk Carrier Co v Armada Shipping SA & Another 92, 93

cost minimisation
discharge of debtor 10

creditor
arrest of vessel by *see* arrest of vessel
collective proceedings 10
common pool of debtor's assets 11, 14, 28, 58–59
company arrangements and 86
company reorganisation and 12–13
conflicting claims 16
cross-border insolvencies 16, 17, 25
distribution of assets *see* distribution of assets
domiciled in multiple states 27
equivalent, equal treatment 1, 11–12, 58

foreign, Model Law principle of access 29
hotchpotch rule 62
in personam actions 55, 61
in rem actions 48–59, 61, 152–156
in rem rights 62
legitimate expectations 18–19
liquidation proceedings and 11, 12
local, protection 17, 25
maritime liens *see* maritime lien
maximisation of asset value for all 10–11
Model Law regime 4–5, 59–62
non-maritime 59
overall interests of all 10
personification doctrine and 59–60, 61–62
protection 25, 40
ranking claims *see* ranking of claims
rehabilitation proceedings 11
relief from automatic stay order 59–61, 106–109
secured 6, 13, 14–15, 40–41, 48–53, 58–61, 62, 92–94, 103, 110, 121, 123, 144, 148, 161
security interest or lien debtor's property 14–15, 40–41, 47–48
ship mortgagee 51–53, 156–158
stay order (moratorium) *see* stay order
territorialism and 18–19
treatment, generally 5
unsecured 6, 14–15, 110, 161

crew
chartered vessels 64
need for 45
offshore-registered ships 46
tortious act by vessel 46
wages, maritime lien 41–42, 71, 126
wages, US stay orders 109

cross-border insolvency
assets, generally 16
Australia 66, 73–83
choice of forum 16–17
choice of law 16–17, 19, 24–25
co-operative territorialism 6, 21, 22–23
COMI *see* centre of main interest of debtor
conflict of laws *see* conflict of laws
corporate-charter contractualism 17n
creditors, generally 16, 17
dependent states 25
distribution of assets 17
dominant states 25
generally 1–3, 16
in rem actions, generally 153–156
inconsistencies in law 58
increasing frequency 3–4
international co-operation 6, 22
jurisdiction, choice of forum 16–17
maritime law, conflict with 58–59
modified universalism 6, 21, 23–24
new pragmatism 21–24
pending or subsequent insolvency proceedings 3, 8, 61, 77, 78, 83, 87, 96, 112–113, 123–124, 132–133, 139, 143, 144–146, 149, 152, 153–158, 161–162, 164
personification doctrine 61–62, 115–116
recognition of foreign judgments 16–17, 109
Singapore 120, 129–135
sovereignty and 17, 24–25
stay orders and 60–61
territorialism *see* territorialism
treatment of creditors 17
United Kingdom 91–100
United States 109–115
universalism *see* universalism

custodial expenses
stay order, following 145–146

Cyprus
lex fori rule 159

D

Daebo International Shipping Co Ltd 116–117, 183
Danny Morris & Another v The Ship 'Kiama' 50, 73, 76
Davies, Martin 118, 158, 188

debt
discharged 10–13
enforcement against vessel 6–7, 40, 55–56
restructuring, memorandum of agreement 156
ship mortgage *see* ship mortgage

debtor
administrator, role 13
aims of insolvency law 9–12
assets *see* assets; distribution *see* distribution of assets
COMI *see* centre of main interest of debtor
company liquidation 12
company reorganisation 12–13
discharged debts 10–13
fresh start, insolvency providing 9–10, 13, 58
habitual residence 5, 8, 33, 63, 165
'home country' 20, 21, 22
'honest but unfortunate' 9–10, 58
in rem actions and 58–59, 61
liabilities, evidence regarding 28, 36

non-exempt assets 10
place of establishment 34
registered office 5, 8, 20, 33, 63, 165, 167–168, 170, 172–176, 189
scope of assets 5, 64–65, 179–190
security for release of vessel *see* security for release of vessel
single court adjudicates all claims against 11–12
debtor-in-possession procedure
recognition under Model Law 32, 32n
deeds of company arrangement (DOCA)
administration proceedings 68–69, 71, 85–86
demise charter *see* chartered vessel
The Dictator 44, 56–57, 81, 150
Dillon LJ 184
discharged debt
company reorganisations 13
generally 10
liquidation proceedings 12
non-waivable right of discharge 10
prohibition from collecting 10
distribution of assets
co-operative territorialism 21, 22–23
collective proceedings 11
cross-border insolvencies 17
debtor's centre of main interest 27
discharge of liabilities following 12
equivalent creditors, equal treatment 1
insolvency, following 12, 58
inverse order rule 146–147
modified universalism 6, 21, 23–24, 148–149
national variations 149
new pragmatism 21–24
ranking claims *see* ranking of claims
sovereignty and 25
stay order, effect 13–14
territorialism 18–19
universalism 6, 20–21, 58
value-preservation 10–11
winding-up proceedings 67, 84

E
Electro Magnetic (S) Ltd (under judicial management) v Development Bank of Singapore Ltd 125
Ephedra Products Liability Litigation 35
equity cushion
US stay orders 107
Eurofood IFSC Ltd 167–168, 172
European Union
Eurofood IFSC Ltd 167–168, 172
Recast EU Regulation 91, 166–172, 177
Regulation (EU) 2015/848 166–167
Evridiki Navigation Inc v Sanko SS Co 111–112, 114, 141

F
Fairfield Sentry Ltd 177
The Fierbinti 135
flag of convenience
debtor's centre of main interest 63, 166, 166n, 175–176
foreign creditor
Model Law principle of access 29
foreign proceedings
access, Model Law principle of 6, 28–29
attachment excluded 32
changes in, informing recognising court 31
co-operation and co-ordination, principle of 6, 28, 38–39
collective nature 32, 33, 36
COMI *see* centre of main interest of debtor
commencement point 152
concurrent 39
conflict of laws *see* conflict of laws
defining characteristics 32, 33
definition 31–33
freezing assets 2, 33, 36
garnishment excluded 32
inbound access 28–29
insolvency proceedings, national variation 6, 31–32
interim relief, recognition under Model Law 32, 36–37
liquidation proceedings 32
main proceedings 2, 5, 8, 20, 23–24, 30–31, 33–39, 59–63, 74–83, 92, 94, 96–100, 104, 109–119, 130, 131–133, 139–140, 153–157, 160–165, 171, 177–178, 188
Model Law *see* Model Law on Cross-Border Insolvency
non-main proceedings 31, 33–34, 36, 37, 39
outbound access 28–29
parallel local proceedings 37
public policy exception 30, 31, 34–35
recognition *see* recognition of foreign proceedings
relief, principle of 28, 36–38
reorganisation proceedings 32
shipowner, by 2, 5
stay, automatic 33

timing of writ of arrest and 152–153
US debtor-in-possession procedure 32
foreign representative
access, Model Law principle of 28–29
entrusting the debtor's assets to 36, 38
interim relief applications 36–37
recognition, Model Law principle of 30
forum arresti
conflict of laws in 3, 59, 60, 62–63, 149, 158–161, 163–164
forum shopping 162
maritime liens 158
Model Law on Cross-Border Insolvency 3, 59, 60, 62–63, 149, 158–164
non-maritime claims 158
ranking of claims 158, 161, 163–164
recognition of foreign main proceedings 5
in rem actions 158, 161
sale of vessel 160
treatment of arrested assets 3
forum shopping
centre of main interest (COMI) rule 63, 165
foreign main proceeding (FMP) court 162
forum arresti 162
lex fori rule 159
Model Law on Cross-Border Insolvency 28, 162
universalism and 21
freight
lien *see* maritime lien
fresh start
insolvency providing 9–10, 13, 58
Fry LJ 143

G
garnishment
foreign proceedings and 32
general average claims
in rem proceedings 42, 72
Gibbs J 81
global financial crisis
shipping industry, generally 3–4
going concern
preservation of value 10
Gold & Honey Ltd 33, 35
grab rule *see* **territorialism**

H
The Halcyon Isle 44, 72, 81–82, 126
Hanjin Shipping bankruptcy 4, 4n, 114, 116, 117–118, 133–134, 137, 140–141, 161n, 163, 179–180, 184–186
Hanjin Shipping Co 112–115, 116, 117–118, 141
Harms Offshore 94–95
The Heinrich Bjorn 143
Hertz Corp v Friend 172
Hewson J 49
Hickley Singapore Trading Pte Ltd v Sogo Department Stores (S) Pte Ltd 124
HIH Casualty and General Insurance 35
Ho, Look Chan 171
hotchpotch rule
personification doctrine 62
The Hull 308 128

I
In the Matter of Hanjin Shipping Co Ltd 100, 102
in personam action
breach of contract 55
in rem actions distinguished 44, 56–57
maritime claims 55, 61
ship mortgages 52
shipowner, against 102, 135
Singapore 138
in rem action
arrest and sale of vessel *see* arrest of vessel
Australia 7, 50, 56–57, 72–73, 77, 78, 81–82, 83, 141, 154
breach of contract claims 42, 55–56, 61
Canada 48, 50–51
cargo damage claims 42
characteristics 48
charterparty breach claims 42, 72
claims giving rise to 42, 48, 49, 55–57, 61–62
conflict of laws 3, 8, 59, 61–62, 140–141, 158, 164
creditors 48–59, 61, 62, 152–156
cross-border insolvencies, generally 153–156
enforcement of debt against vessel 6–7, 40–41, 55–56, 164
extinction 48
forcing appearance of shipowner 44, 48, 56, 57, 58, 81, 101, 150, 155
forum arresti 158, 161–162
general average claims 42, 72
generally 2–3, 6–7, 48, 55–59, 61
hotchpotch rule 62
in personam actions distinguished 44, 56–57
limit on value of judgment 55

maritime lien and 41–42, 43–44, 47–48, 49, 58, 142–143, 143n, 149–151
maritime lien compared 48–49, 141, 154–156
Model Law on Cross-Border Insolvency 1–3, 59, 61–62, 152
necessaries claims 42, 153, 161
non-insolvency actions 58–59
non-maritime creditors 59
pending or subsequent insolvency proceeding 3, 8, 61, 96, 135, 152, 153–156
personal injury claims 42
personification doctrine 43–45, 55–56, 61–62, 81–82, 101–102, 115–116, 135–137, 142, 149–151, 153, 155
pilotage expenses 42, 72, 153
procedural theory 44–45, 47–48, 51, 56–57, 88–89, 101, 152, 153
prospective security interest 49, 127–128, 142
purpose 40, 61–62
quasi in rem actions 56
ranking against other claims 42, 48, 154, 158
relief to proceed 7
Rule B attachment 56
sale of ship to third party 49–50, 58–59, 154
secured status of statutory rights 49–51, 90, 152
security for maritime claims 48
security for release of vessel 48, 55, 64–65, 128, 160, 186–188
ship mortgages 52
shipowner, against 101–102, 135
Singapore 50, 56–57, 126–129, 131–132, 133, 135–137, 138, 141, 154
sister ships 55–56, 57
statutory right as, generally 48–51, 152, 154
stay order (moratorium) *see* stay order
stevedore expenses 42, 153
timing of writ of arrest 152–153
towage, claims in rem 42, 153
true in rem actions 101
United Kingdom 48, 50, 56–57, 88–90, 93–94, 101–102, 103, 141, 154
United States 55–56, 110, 115–116, 152
vessel, against 44, 55, 58–59, 61–62, 81–82, 101–102, 115–116
writ, issue 49–50, 152–153, 154

The Indian Grace (No 2) 44, 45, 57, 71, 81, 101–102, 103, 136, 150–151

insolvency
see also bankruptcy law
aim of insolvency law 9–10, 58
Anglo-common law countries 9, 12, 66
arrest and sale of vessel *see* arrest of vessel
assets *see* assets
Australia 66, 73–74
basic principle 1
chartered vessels *see* chartered vessel
collective proceedings 10
COMI *see* centre of main interest of debtor
creditor *see* creditor
cross-border *see* cross-border insolvency
debtor *see* debtor
development of law 1, 5
distribution *see* distribution of assets
equivalent creditors, equal treatment 1, 11–12, 58
foreign proceedings *see* foreign proceedings
fresh start for debtor, providing 9–10, 13, 58
fundamental aims 9–12, 58
in rem actions and 61
liquidation *see* liquidation
maritime creditors, treatment 5
maximisation of asset value 10–11, 13–14, 18, 20, 58
multiple jurisdictions, proceedings in 2
national variations 1, 6, 9, 12, 12n, 16, 31–32, 140, 141
ranking claims *see* ranking of claims
Recast EU Regulation 91, 166–172, 177
reorganisation *see* reorganisation
scope of debtor's assets 5, 64–65, 179–190
single court adjudicates all claims 11–12
stay order (moratorium) *see* stay order
winding-up *see* winding-up proceedings

interim relief
recognition under Model Law 32, 36–37

International Convention Relating to the Arrest of Sea-Going Ships 51

inverse order rule
maritime liens 146–147

The Ioannis Daskalelis 163

Israel
receivership proceedings in 35

J

Jagot J 79, 80

Japan
Corporate Reorganisation Act 96–97
Law on Recognition of and Assistance in Foreign Insolvency Proceedings 34

public policy exception 34
statutory right of action in rem 96
Jervis, Sir John 41
Jeune J 44
judicial management
Singapore 12n, 121, 122, 123, 124–125, 129, 132–133, 141
Justinian
Rhodian Sea Law 2

K
Kim v Daebo International Shipping Co Ltd 73, 77, 152–153
Korea Line Corporation bankruptcy 4, 4n
Kuo Fen Ching v Dauphin Offshore Engineering & Trading Pte Ltd 50, 128, 135, 136, 151
The Kusu Island 135

L
lease
charterparties 8, 117, 181–186, 183n
ship mortgages and 157–158
true lease 158, 181, 183n, 185–186
legal certainty
Model Law principle of 28, 169, 172
United States 104
letter of undertaking (LOU)
security for release of vessel 8, 64, 187–190, 187n
letterbox company
centre of main interest of debtor 168
***lex causae* rule**
Canada 158, 163
maritime claims 44, 54, 158–159, 161, 162–163
United States 158, 163
***lex fori* rule**
forum shopping 159, 162
maritime claims 8, 44, 54, 72, 81, 158–164
ship mortgages 160
lien
maritime *see* maritime lien
possessory 42
Lim Bock Lai v Selco (Singapore) Pte Ltd 127–128, 135
liquidation
administration proceedings 69
asset collection and realisation 12
company ceasing to exist following 12
discharge of liabilities 12
distribution following *see* distribution of assets
equivalent creditors, equal treatment 1, 11–12, 58
foreign proceedings 32
generally 12, 141
insolvency, generally 12
maritime lien accumulated during 147
purpose 12
reorganisation compared 12
stay orders 13–14
termination of business 12
US automatic stay 110
US Chapter-7 proceedings 12, 12n, 105, 109, 141
winding-up proceedings 12n, 67–68, 74n, 84–85

M
M/V Hanjin Montevideo 113–114
M/V Hanjin New York 137
M/V Hanjin Rome 134
McCormack, Gerard 169
Malaysia
lex fori rule 159
maritime liens 54
Mansfield LJ 2
maritime assets *see* **assets**
maritime claim
admiralty law, generally 2–4, 6, 40
arrest of vessel *see* arrest of vessel
conflict of laws *see* conflict of laws
enforcement, generally 2–4, 55–57
in personam actions 55, 61
in rem actions *see* in rem action
lex causae 44, 54, 158–159, 161, 162–163
lex fori 8, 54, 72, 81, 158–164
maritime liens *see* maritime lien
one-ship companies 46–47, 63, 166, 168
ranking *see* ranking of claims
ship mortgages *see* ship mortgage
shipowner, bankruptcy 40
Singapore, secured status in 125–129
stay order (moratorium) *see* stay order
tortious act by vessel, where 45–46, 55–56
UK, secured status in 88–90
US, generally 114–115
maritime creditor *see* **creditor**
maritime law
arrest *see* arrest of vessel
bankruptcy regime, conflict with 1, 3, 4, 5, 58–65, 76–80, 95, 131, 139–141
conflict of laws *see* conflict of laws
development 1, 2, 5, 40
in rem proceedings *see* in rem action

maritime assets *see* assets
maritime exceptionalism 2
maritime liens *see* maritime lien
Model Law on Cross-Border Insolvency and 2–3

maritime lien
accumulated after stay order 147
Anglo-common law countries 158–160
arrest of vessel 2–3, 40–41, 43, 47, 48–51, 53, 72, 88, 141
attachment to vessel 42–43
Australia 42, 48, 53, 54, 71–72, 73, 77, 78, 79–80, 81–82, 141
availability and scope, conflict of laws 6, 53–54, 76–80, 158–164
breach 44, 47, 142–143, 143n
Canada 42, 54
change of ownership of subject 42–43, 48, 154
characteristics 42–43
China 54
claims giving rise to 41–42
clean title, purchaser given 147–148
collision damage caused by vessel 41–42, 71, 126
collision damage to vessel 146
competing liens, priority 158
contractual 15
creation 41, 43, 43n, 47, 114, 142–143, 143n, 154, 160
creditors, treatment 142–151
definition 41, 88
depreciation in vessel's value 36, 107–108, 146, 147, 149
disbursements, master's 41–42, 71, 126
discharge 42–43
effect 41
enforcement 8, 40–41, 43, 47, 142, 145, 148, 164
extinction 43
forum arresti 158–161
generally 2, 6, 58
in rem proceedings and 41–42, 43–44, 47–48, 49, 58, 142–143, 143n, 149–151
in rem rights compared 48–49, 141, 154–156
inchoate nature 41, 43, 44–45, 47–48, 71, 88, 89, 114, 126–127, 142
indelible encumbrance, as 42–43
insufficient sale proceeds to cover 146–147
international recognition 41
inverse order rule 146–147
lex causae 54, 158–159, 161, 162–163
lex fori 8, 44, 54, 72, 158–164
lost or damaged vessels 107–108, 146, 147
Malaysia 54
Model Law and 148–149
national variations 6, 40, 53–54, 141, 144, 158–164
New Zealand 54
non-consensual nature 43
non-possessory nature 43
operation of law, creation by 15
pending or subsequent insolvency proceeding 8, 61, 77, 78, 83, 87, 96, 112–113, 132–133, 139, 142, 144–146, 149, 161–162, 164
perfection 14, 43, 44n, 47, 49, 71, 88, 106, 143, 143n
personification doctrine 43–47, 115–116, 142, 149–151
privileged claim, as 42
procedural theory 43, 44–45, 47–48, 54, 88–89, 126, 150–151, 159–160
protection of holder 2, 40–41
purpose 40–41
ranking against other claims 6, 42, 53–54, 154, 158, 161
relief from automatic stay 142, 144–149
remedial right, as 43–45, 47–48, 88–89
sale of subject 2–3, 40–41, 42–43, 53, 88, 105, 160
salvage claims 41–42, 46, 71, 126
satisfaction 43
secret lien, as 43
secured creditors 14–15, 40–41, 58, 142–143, 144, 145, 148, 161
secured status 47–48, 71–72, 88–90, 114–115, 142–144
shipowner and 42
Singapore 42, 48, 53, 54, 126–127, 132, 133, 141
South Africa 54
South Korea 118
substantive and proprietary right, as 43–45, 44n, 47, 48, 54, 82, 88, 114, 142–144, 149, 158–160
United Kingdom 42, 48, 53, 54, 88–89, 90, 94, 103, 141, 159–160
United States 42, 44, 53, 54, 96, 104, 105–109, 110–115, 119, 141, 146–147
varying implementation 149
wages of crew or master 41–42, 71, 126
wreck, over 42

master
chartered vessels 64
disbursements, maritime lien 41–42, 71, 126
need for 45
offshore-registered ships 46
wages, maritime lien 41–42, 71, 126
wages, US stay orders 109
Millennium Global Emerging Credit 178
The Miss Donna 50
Model Law on Cross-Border Insolvency
access, principle of 6, 28–29
additional relief 36, 38, 78–79
admiralty in rem proceedings and 1–3
adoptive states 27
Australia, adoption by 6, 7, 66, 73–75, 83, 140
automatic relief 36, 37–38
automatic stay order 2, 5, 14, 33, 59–61, 64, 77–79, 94, 139–140, 165, 179, 185–186, 187
chartered vessels 5, 64, 179
co-operation and co-ordination, principle of 6, 28, 38–39, 59, 62, 83
COMI *see* centre of main interest of debtor
conflict of laws *see* conflict of laws
conflicts with maritime practice 58–62
creditors, treatment 5
creditors domiciled in multiple states 27
discretionary relief 31, 36, 38
divergence in implementation and interpretation 28
foreign creditors 29
foreign main proceedings 2, 5, 8, 30–31, 33–34, 36, 37–38, 39, 59–63, 74–83, 92, 94, 96–100, 104, 109–119, 130, 131–133, 139, 153–154, 156–157, 160–164, 165, 171, 177–178, 188
foreign non-main proceedings 30, 31, 33–34, 36, 37, 39
forum arresti 3, 59, 60, 62–63, 149, 158–160, 163–164
forum shopping, potential for 28, 162
foundational principles 28
generally 1
hotchpotch rule 62
in rem rights 1–3, 59, 61–62, 152
interim relief, recognition 32, 36–37
mandatory relief 36, 37–38
maritime creditors, treatment 4–5, 59–62
maritime liens and 148–149
modified universalism approach 6, 27, 148–149
non-binding nature 27–28, 61
objectives 27, 28, 59
procedural nature 28
public policy exception 30, 31, 34–35
recognition of foreign proceedings 6, 28, 30–36, 77–79
relief, principle of 6, 28, 36–38
Singapore, adoption by 8, 120, 129–135, 138
soft law, as 27–28, 61, 140, 148
stay order 5, 14, 31, 33, 59–61, 77–79
subsequent proceedings and 61
UK, adoption by 7, 84, 91
universalism as goal 1, 6, 28, 30, 58, 59
urgent relief 36–37
US, adoption by 7–8, 104, 109–115
US debtor-in-possession procedure 32, 32n
varying implementation 149
The Monica S 49
Moore v Australian Equity Investors 178
moratorium *see* **stay order**
mortgage *see* **ship mortgage**
multinational company
co-operative territorialism 22–23
COMI *see* centre of main interest of debtor
cross-border insolvency, generally 16–17
'home country' 20, 21, 22
The M/V Sanko Mineral 96–98, 111
Myburgh, Paul 143

N
necessaries assistant 45–46
necessaries claims 42, 153, 162–163
new pragmatism
evolution of theory 24–26
New Zealand
lex fori rule 158
recognition of foreign claims 54
Nortel Networks Corporation 39
Northern Ireland
Cross-Border Insolvency Regulations 2007 91
Northsea Base Investment Ltd 168–169
Nugee J 100

O
offshore registration
chartered vessels 184
COMI, determination 63, 166, 168–169, 175, 189
one-ship companies 46, 63, 166, 168

one-ship company
centre of main interest of debtor 63, 166
corporate veil 46–47
meaning 46
open registry
centre of main interest of debtor 63, 166, 166n, 175–176
The Oriental Baltic 128–129
Orlando Coals Inc 108

P

passenger
tortious act by vessel 46
Perpetual Trustee Company Ltd v Lehman Bros Special Financing Inc 39
personal injury claims
in rem proceedings 42
United States 105
personification doctrine
Australia 79, 81–82
chartered vessels 115
The China 115
conflict of laws 61–62
creditors and 59–60, 61–62
equitable principle, as 115–116
hotchpotch rule 62
in rem claims 43–45, 55–56, 61–62, 81–82, 101–102, 115–116, 135–137, 142, 149–151, 153, 155
maritime cross-border insolvency 116
maritime liens and 43–47, 115–116, 142, 149–151
one-ship companies 46–47
rationale 44–47, 62, 150
Rule B attachment 56
sale of vessel 115
secured creditors 62
ship mortgages and 157
shipowner and 46, 135
Singapore 135–137
sister ships 55–56
Tucker v Alexandrof 115
United Kingdom 44, 101–102
United States 44, 55–56, 62, 115–116, 150
vessels, generally 43–44, 55–56, 59–60, 61–62, 81–82
pilotage expenses
claims in rem 42, 72, 153
Pittman 108–109
Precious Shipping Public Co Ltd v OW Bunker Far East Pte Ltd 136, 151
***pro hac vice* owner (owner ad hoc)**
chartered vessels 64, 180–186
Probulk Inc 189
procedural theory
Australia 56–57, 71, 81–82
forcing appearance of shipowner 44, 48, 56, 57, 101, 150, 155
in rem rights 44–45, 47–48, 51, 56–57, 88–89, 101–102, 152, 153, 162
lex fori rule 159
maritime liens 43, 44–45, 47–48, 54, 88–89, 126, 150–151, 159–160
personal liability of owner 56–57
shipowners 56–57
Singapore 56–57
sister ships 57
United Kingdom 44–45, 56–57, 88–89, 103, 150–151
Protection and Indemnity Association (P&I)
club letters of undertaking (LOUs) 8, 64, 187–190, 187n

Q

Qinzhou Guiqin Shipping Group Co 146
quasi in rem action
United States 56

R

ranking of claims
conflict of laws 53–54, 158, 161
forum arresti 158, 161, 163–164
in rem actions 42, 48, 154, 158
insolvency law, generally 58
maritime liens 6, 42, 53–54, 154, 158, 161
national variations 1, 6, 9, 12, 12n
possessory liens 42
secured creditors 15
ship mortgages 48, 52, 96
Rares J 73, 77
Re Taisoo Suk 133–135, 137
Recast EU Regulation 91
receivership
Australia 74
recognition of foreign claims
lex causae rule 44, 54, 158–159, 161, 162–163
lex fori rule 8, 54, 72, 81, 158–164
recognition of foreign proceedings
application for 30, 37, 77–78
Australia 74–76, 77–79, 83

foreign main proceedings 2, 5, 8, 20, 23–24, 30–31, 33–39, 59–63, 74–83, 92, 94, 96–100, 104, 109–119, 130, 131–133, 139–140, 153–157, 160–165, 171, 177–178, 188
generally 16–17
Japan 34
Model Law principle of 6, 28, 30–36, 77–79
public policy exception 30, 31, 34–35
relief 6, 36
requirements for 30–31
Singapore 129–135
timing of writ of arrest 152–153
United Kingdom 91, 92, 93–94, 96, 103
United States 35, 109–115, 119
Yu v STX Pan Ocean Co Ltd 77–79, 140, 151

recognition of foreign representative
Model Law principle of 30

rehabilitation proceedings
administration procedure 85
equivalent creditors, equal treatment 1, 11, 134
South Korea 12n, 77–80, 98–100, 112–116, 133–134, 140, 185–186

relief, Model Law principle of
additional relief 36, 38, 78–79
application for relief 58, 78–79
automatic relief 36, 37–38
automatic stay, relief from 7, 58, 59, 60–61, 98–100, 106–110, 139, 140, 142, 144–149, 154
collective proceedings 36
declaratory relief 39
discretionary relief 31, 33, 36, 37, 38
foreign main proceedings 31, 33, 36, 37–38, 59–61
foreign non-main proceedings 31, 33, 36, 37–38
generally 6, 28, 36–38
in rem action, relief to proceed 7, 80
interim relief 32, 36–37
interpleader relief 136
local additional reliefs 38
local exceptions or limitations 38–39
mandatory relief 36, 37–38
post-recognition relief 38
provisional nature 36–37, 38
recognition of foreign proceedings 6, 30–31, 36–38
secured creditors 58
termination 37
territorialism and 19
urgent relief 36–37

reorganisation
additional relief to achieve 78
approval of plan by creditors 13
assets of debtor 12
court confirmation of plan 13
debtor's administrator 13
differing terms for 12n
discharge of debts 13
foreign proceedings 32
generally 3, 12–13
insolvency, generally 12
liquidation compared 12
maritime lien accumulated during 147
The M/V Sanko Mineral 96–98
payment of creditors 12, 13
proposed plan of 13
purpose 12–13
stay orders 13–14
universalist approach in cross-border cases 20
US automatic stay 110
US Chapter-11 reorganisation 12, 12n, 105, 106–109, 141

repairs
claims in rem 42, 153
necessaries assistant, need for 45–46
necessaries claims 42, 153, 162–163

Rhodian Sea Law 2

risk allocation
discharge of debtor 10

Ritz-Carlton of DC Inc 107

Rôles of Oléron 2

Ronelp Marine 98–100

Rule B attachment
United States 56, 95, 111, 116–117, 141

S

salvage claims
maritime lien 41–42, 46, 71, 126

Sanko Steamship bankruptcy 4, 4n

Sanko Steamship bankruptcy 4, 4n

scheme of arrangement
Australia 66, 69–70, 71, 75
Singapore 121, 122–123, 125, 127, 129
United Kingdom 86, 87–88

Scotland
Bankruptcy Act 1985 92
foreign insolvency proceedings, recognition and assistance 91

security interest in property of debtor
arrest *see* arrest of vessel
charterparties 117–119
contractual 15
maritime liens *see* maritime lien
national variations 15
operation of law, created by 15
secured creditors 6, 13, 14–15, 40–41, 47–53, 58–61, 62, 92–94, 103, 110, 121, 123, 144, 148, 161
ship mortgage *see* ship mortgage
strong arm powers 52–53
unperfected 52–53
security for release of vessel
amount of security 186
asset of debtor, whether 5, 65, 187–190
automatic stay order 187
bank guarantees 8, 64, 128, 186–189
debtor-shipowner, provision by 64–65, 186–190
in rem actions 48, 55, 64–65, 128, 160, 186–188
maritime liens 142, 144
P&I club letters of undertaking (LOUs) 8, 64, 187–190, 187n
prevention of arrest 186–189
surety bonds 5, 64–65, 186–187
third party, provision by 64–65, 186–189
ship *see* **vessel**
ship mortgage
Australia 157
creditors 51–53, 156–158
enforcement 52, 157–158, 164
finance lease and 157–158
generally 6
in personam actions 52
in rem actions 52, 101–102
lex fori rule 160
meaning 51
pending or subsequent insolvency proceeding 8, 156–158, 164
perfection 62–63, 157
personification doctrine and 157
ranking against other claims 48, 52, 96
registration 157
restructuring via memorandum of agreement 156
security interest, as 51–53, 96, 157
Singapore 132, 157
United Kingdom 51–52, 103, 157
United States 52–53, 105–106, 157
unregistered ships 52–53
The Ship Sam Hawk v Reiter Petroleum Inc 72, 81
shipowner
arrest of vessel *see* arrest of vessel
assets *see* assets
change of, maritime liens 42–43, 48, 154
change of, in rem actions 49–50, 58–59, 154
chartered vessels 64, 179–190
cross-border transactions 2–3
forcing appearance of 44, 48, 56, 57, 58, 101, 150, 155
in personam action against 102, 135
in rem action against 40–41, 48, 57, 58, 135
insolvency 2–4, 40, 58
maritime lien and 2, 42, 58
one-ship companies 46–47, 63, 166
personal liability 56–57
personification doctrine and 46, 135
pro hac vice (owner ad hoc) 64, 180–186
procedural theory and 56–57
security for release of vessel *see* security for release of vessel
shipping industry
global financial crisis 3–4, 111
surplus capacity 3–4
Singapore
arrest of vessel 128, 134–135, 136, 137
Beluga Chartering GmbH v Beluga Projects Pte Ltd 133, 153
centre of main interest of debtor 173–174, 177–178
chartered vessels 137, 180
common law 123, 133–134, 144
Companies (Amendment) Act 2017 120, 121, 122, 123–125, 128–129, 130
conflict of laws 131, 138
corporate rescue regime 121, 122–123
cross-border insolvency 120, 129–135
cross-class cram-down mechanism 123
Electro Magnetic (S) Ltd (under judicial management) v Development Bank of Singapore Ltd 125
The Fierbinti 135
foreign main proceedings 130, 131–133
Hickley Singapore Trading Pte Ltd v Sogo Department Stores (S) Pte Ltd 124
High Court (Admiralty Jurisdiction) Act 127, 134
The Hull 308 128
in rem actions 50, 56–57, 126–129, 131–132, 133, 135–137, 138, 141, 154
insolvency regime, generally 121

judicial management 12n, 121, 122, 123, 124–125, 129, 132–133, 141
jurisdiction over insolvency cases 121
Kuo Fen Ching v Dauphin Offshore Engineering & Trading Pte Ltd 50, 128, 135, 136, 151
The Kusu Island 135
lex fori rule 158
Lim Bock Lai v Selco (Singapore) Pte Ltd 127–128, 135
M/V Hanjin New York 137
M/V Hanjin Rome 134
maritime liens 42, 48, 53, 126–127, 132, 133, 141
Model Law, adoption 8, 120, 129–135, 138
modified universalism 120, 138
moratorium 123–125, 126–127, 129, 130–138, 144, 154
The Oriental Baltic 128–129
in personam actions 138
personification doctrine 135–137
Precious Shipping Public Co Ltd v OW Bunker Far East Pte Ltd 136, 151
procedural theory 56–57
Re Taisoo Suk 133–135, 137
recognition of foreign claims 54
recognition of foreign proceedings 129–135
restructuring proceedings 120, 121
schemes of arrangement 121, 122–123, 125, 127, 129
secured creditors 15, 121, 123, 124, 126, 127, 133, 144
secured status of maritime claims 125–129
ship mortgages 132, 157
winding-up proceedings 12n, 120, 121–122, 123, 124, 126, 128–129, 132, 141
Zetta Jet Pte Ltd 173, 177

solvency
statutory declaration of 85

South Africa
lex fori rule 158
recognition of foreign claims 91

South Korea
bareboat charter hire purchase agreements 8, 117–119, 184–185
maritime lien holders 118
rehabilitation proceedings 12n, 77–80, 98–100, 112–116, 133–134, 140, 185–186
Tai-Soo Suk v Hanjin Shipping Co Ltd 79–80, 140

sovereignty
co-operative territorialism 22
cross-border insolvency and 17
distribution of assets and 25
modified universalism 23
territorialism 18–19

Stanford International Bank Ltd 33, 172, 177

statutory rights of action in rem *see* in rem action

stay order (moratorium)
additional appropriate relief, under 38
administration proceedings and 7, 87–88, 90
application of, generally 14, 31
application for relief 58
Australia 66, 70–83, 144, 154
automatic, generally 2, 5, 7, 14, 31, 33–34, 35, 59–61, 64, 139–140, 141, 144–149, 154, 165, 179, 185–186, 187
automatic relief 36, 37–38
chartered vessels 5, 64, 116, 137, 179, 180, 185–186
company arrangements and 87–88
company reorganisations 13
custodial expenses following 145–146
effect 5, 13–14, 132, 139
enforcement of pre-petition judgments 14
foreign main proceedings 2, 5, 31, 33, 36, 60–61, 74–83, 92–93, 97–100, 130, 139–140, 165
freight revenue following 146
interim relief 36–37
local exceptions or limitations 38–39
maritime liens 142
maritime liens accumulated after 147
maximisation of asset value 13–14, 58
Model Law 5, 14, 31, 33, 59–61, 77–79, 139–140, 149, 165, 179
national variations 14, 144
non-automatic 14
parallel local proceedings 37
personification doctrine and 58
protection of creditors 14
relief from 5, 7, 58, 59–61, 98–100, 106–110, 139, 142, 144–149, 154
secured creditors 13, 14, 58, 59, 60–61, 75–76, 144
security for release of debtor 187
Singapore 123–125, 126–127, 129, 130–138, 144, 154
United Kingdom 14, 86–88, 89, 90, 92–93, 94, 97–100, 102, 103, 144, 154

United States 14, 15, 35, 104, 105–119, 144
unsecured creditors 14
vessel removed or hidden during 145, 146
winding-up proceedings and 14, 70–71, 72, 78, 86–87, 123, 126–127
Stena Bulk AB v Copley 102
stevedore expenses
claims in rem 42, 153
need for 46
Steyn LJ 57
strong arm powers
United States 52–53
STX Pan Ocean bankruptcy 4, 4n
surety bond for release of vessel
property of debtor, whether 5, 65

T
Tai-Soo Suk v Hanjin Shipping Co Ltd 79–80, 82, 83
territorialism
areas for international co-operation 22
co-operative territorialism 6, 21, 22–23, 24–26
creditors and 18–19
distribution of assets 18–19
domestic insolvency laws and 18, 20
evolution of theory 24–26
legitimate expectation and 18–19
new pragmatism 21–24, 25–26
piecemeal nature 19
predictability and 19, 22
sovereignty and 18–19
theory, generally 6, 17–19, 21, 129
weaknesses of rule 19
time charter *see* **chartered vessel**
towage
claims in rem 42, 153
need for 46
Tucker v Alexandrof 115

U
United Kingdom
administration proceedings 12n, 85, 87–88, 90, 94–95, 98–100, 103, 141
arbitration, dispute settlement by 93, 100
Aro Co Ltd 50, 89, 90, 127, 128
arrest of vessel 88, 89, 90, 94, 100
Atlantic Computer Systems 124
automatic stay order 86–88, 90, 92–93, 94, 97–100, 102, 103, 154
Belmont Park Investments Pty Ltd v BNY Corporate Trustee Services Ltd 189
The Bold Buccleugh 41, 71–72, 88
The Bolivia 90
The Cella 49
centre of main interest of debtor 171–172, 173, 174, 177
chartered vessel 102, 180, 183–184
common law 7, 91, 144
Companies Act 1948 121
Companies Act 2006 86
company arrangements 85–86, 87–88
compulsory winding-up proceedings 14, 84, 85, 87, 90
conflict of laws 95
Cosco Bulk Carrier Co v Armada Shipping SA & Another 92, 93
Cross-Border Insolvency Regulations 2006 91–100, 130
The Dictator 44, 56–57, 81, 150
Enterprise Act 2002 85
foreign main proceedings 92, 94, 96–100
The Halcyon Isle 44, 72, 81–82, 126
Harms Offshore 94–95
The Heinrich Bjorn 143
HIH Casualty and General Insurance 35
In the Matter of Hanjin Shipping Co Ltd 100, 102
The Indian Grace (No 2) 44, 45, 57, 71, 81, 101–102, 103, 136, 150–151
in personam actions 102, 103
in rem actions 44, 48, 50, 56–57, 88–90, 93–94, 101–102, 103, 141, 154
Insolvency Act 1986 84–88, 90, 91, 92–93, 94, 98, 100, 121
lex fori rule 158–160
maritime liens 42, 48, 53, 88–89, 90, 94, 103, 141, 158–160
Model Law, adoption 7, 84, 91, 140
The Monica S 49
The M/V Sanko Mineral 96–98, 111
Northsea Base Investment Ltd 168–169
P&I club letters of undertaking (LOUs) 189
personification doctrine 44, 101–102
procedural theory 44–45, 56–57, 88–89, 103, 150–151
Recast EU Regulation 91
recognition of foreign claims 54
recognition of foreign proceedings 91, 92, 93–94, 96, 103
Ronelp Marine 98–100
schemes of arrangement 86, 87–88
secured claims 88–90, 103

secured creditors 15, 87, 92–93, 94–95, 97–98, 103, 144
ship mortgages 51–52, 103, 157
Stanford International Bank Ltd 33, 172, 177
stay orders 14, 86–88, 89, 90, 92–93, 94, 97–100, 102, 103, 144, 154
Stena Bulk AB v Copley 102
voluntary winding-up proceedings 14, 84–85, 86
Welsh Development Agency v The Export Finance Company Ltd 184
winding-up proceedings 12n, 14, 84–85, 86–87, 89, 90, 103, 141, 184
The Zafiro 49

United Nations Commission on International Trade Law (UNCITRAL)
Model Law *see* Model Law on Cross-Border Insolvency

United States
adequate protection of interest, lack of 106, 107–109
arrest or attachment of vessel 110, 111–115, 117, 119
automatic stay order 14, 15, 35, 104, 105–119, 144
Bankruptcy Code 8, 104–115, 119, 173
Bear Stearns 173
centre of main interest of debtor 172–173, 174, 177–178
Chapter-7 liquidation 12, 12n, 105, 109, 141
Chapter-11 reorganisation 12, 12n, 105, 106–109, 123, 141
Chapter 15 Bankruptcy Code 8, 104, 109–115, 119, 173
chartered vessels 115, 116–119, 180, 181–182, 183
The China 115
Coastal Marine Management LLC v Additional Return LLC 145–146
cross-border insolvency 109–115
Daebo International Shipping Co Ltd 116–117, 183
debtor-in-possession procedure, recognition under Model Law 32, 32n
Ephedra Products Liability Litigation 35
equity cushion 107
Evridiki Navigation Inc v Sanko SS Co 111–112, 114, 141
Fairfield Sentry Ltd 177
Federal Maritime Lien Act 113
foreign main proceedings 104, 109–119
Gold & Honey Ltd 33, 35
Hanjin Shipping Co 112–115, 116, 117–118, 141
Hertz Corp v Friend 172
inverse order rule 146–147
in rem actions 55–56, 110, 115–116, 140, 152
The Ioannis Daskalelis 163
jurisdiction over bankruptcy cases 105
lex causae rule 158, 163
maritime claims, generally 114–115
maritime liens 42, 44, 53, 96, 104, 105–109, 110–115, 119, 141, 146–147
Millennium Global Emerging Credit 178
Model Law, adoption 7–8, 104, 109–115, 140
necessaries suppliers 105, 113
Orlando Coals Inc 108
over-secured creditors 108
P&I club letters of undertaking (LOUs) 189
personal injury claims 105
personification doctrine 44, 55–56, 62, 115–116, 150
Pittman 108–109
Probulk Inc 189
property not necessary for reorganization, lack of equity in 106–107
public policy exception 35
quasi in rem action 56
recognition of foreign claims 54
recognition of foreign proceedings 35, 109–115, 119
relief from automatic stay 106–109
Ritz-Carlton of DC Inc 107
Rule B attachment 56, 95, 111, 116–117, 141
secured creditors 15, 110
secured property, loss or depreciation 107–108, 146, 147
ship mortgages 52–53, 105–106, 157
strong arm powers 52–53
Tucker v Alexandrof 115
universalist approach 8, 104, 113, 119
unsecured creditors 110
Wasserman 108
Westchase I Associates LP 108
wrongful death claims 105

universalism
choice of law 20–21
cross-border insolvencies, generally 17, 20–21, 58
distribution of assets 20–21, 58
domestic insolvency laws and 20
dominant and dependent states 25

forum shopping and 21
'home country' of debtor 20, 21, 22
main proceeding 20, 23–24
maritime law, generally 40, 58
maximisation of asset value 20
Model Law on Cross-Border Insolvency 1, 28, 30, 58, 59
modified universalism 6, 21, 23–24, 25–26, 120, 138, 148–149
new pragmatism 21–24, 25–26
one law, one court principle 20
predictability and 20–21
reorganisation more likely where 20
Singapore 120, 138
theory, generally 6, 24–26
trend towards 6, 18
United States 8, 104, 113, 119

V

vessel
arrest and sale *see* arrest of vessel
asset, as *see* assets
depreciation in value 36, 107–108, 146, 147, 149
enforcement of debt against 6–7, 40, 55–56
in rem actions against 44, 55, 58–59, 61–62, 81–82, 101–102, 115–116
lien *see* maritime lien
management and ownership, separation 63, 166, 174–176
meaning 42
mortgage *see* ship mortgage
one-ship companies 46–47, 63, 166, 168
owner *see* shipowner
personification doctrine *see* personification doctrine
procedural theory and 56–57, 101–102
repair, claims in rem 42, 153
security for release *see* security for release of vessel
sister ships 55–56, 57
tortious act against, by another vessel 46
tortious act by 46, 55–56, 61–62, 115
wreck 42
voyage charter *see* **chartered vessel**

W

wages of crew and master
maritime liens 41–42, 71, 126
offshore companies 46
US stay orders 109
Wasserman 108
Welsh Development Agency v The Export Finance Company Ltd 184
Westbrook, Jay Lawrence 175
Westchase I Associates LP 108
winding-up proceedings
Australia 12n, 66–68, 72, 73, 78–79, 83, 141
chartered vessels 184
compulsory 14, 67, 68, 70, 84, 85, 87, 90, 121–122, 128
creditors' voluntary liquidation 85
creditors' voluntary winding up 67, 70
distribution of assets 67, 84
liquidator 67, 68
members' voluntary liquidation 85
members' voluntary winding up 67, 74
purpose 84
realisation of assets 67, 84
Singapore 12n, 120, 121–122, 123, 124, 126–127, 128–129, 132, 141
statutory declaration of solvency 85
stay provisions and 14, 70–71, 78, 86–87, 126–127
United Kingdom 12n, 14, 84–85, 86–87, 90, 103, 141, 184
voluntary 14, 67, 84–85, 86, 121
voluntary administration, during 67, 70–71
witness, examination
assets or liabilities of debtor 36, 38
wreck
maritime lien over 42
wrongful death claims
United States 105

Y

Yakushiji v Daiichi Chuo Kisen Kaisha 73
Yu v STX Pan Ocean Co Ltd 72, 77–79, 82, 140, 151

Z

The Zafiro 49
Zetta Jet Pte Ltd 173, 177

www.ingramcontent.com/pod-product-compliance
Ingram Content Group UK Ltd.
Pitfield, Milton Keynes, MK11 3LW, UK
UKHW020808290926
15470UKWH00003B/1023

9 781509 935994